HOW THE DEST...

Each destination in [...]
practical informatic [...]
split into 4 different categories.

- Highlights
- Accommodation
- Eating out
- What to do

You can view the location of every point of interest and save it by adding it to your Favourites. In the 'Around Me' section you can view all the points of interest within 5km.

HOW THE EBOOKS WORK

The eBooks are provided in EPUB file format. Please note that you will need an eBook reader installed on your device to open the file. Many devices come with this as standard, but you may still need to install one manually from Google Play.

The eBook content is identical to the content in the printed guide.

HOW TO DOWNLOAD THE WALKING EYE APP

1. Download the Walking Eye App from the App Store or Google Play.
2. Open the app and select the scanning function from the main menu.
3. Scan the QR code on this page – you will then be asked a security question to verify ownership of the book.
4. Once this has been verified, you will see your eBook and destination content in the purchased ebook and destination sections, where you will be able to download them.

Other destination apps and eBooks are available for purchase separately or are free with the purchase of the Insight Guide book.

Contents

THE BEST OF CHILE: TOP ATTRACTIONS

From the world's driest desert and virgin ice fields to the mysterious ancient statues of Easter Island, here is a rundown of Chile's most spectacular attractions.

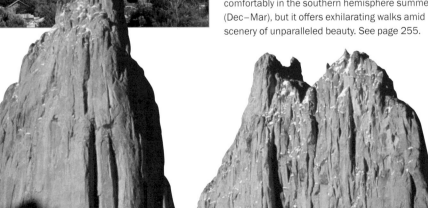

△ **Atacama Desert.** It may be the driest place on earth, but the Atacama Desert is rich in natural and geological treats as well as indigenous history. Don't miss the El Tatio geysers and their stunning display of geothermal energy as they thrust columns of steam into the cold morning air. See page 175.

◁ **Volcán Villarrica.** Look down into the molten lava, listen to its tectonic rumblings and sniff the sulfur; the crater of the conical snow-capped volcano is a relatively easy one-day hike from Pucón, and a sight few will ever forget. See page 208.

▽ **Torres del Paine.** The undisputed queen of Chile's national parks lies at the southern tip of the Andes mountain chain. It can only be visited comfortably in the southern hemisphere summer (Dec–Mar), but it offers exhilarating walks amid scenery of unparalleled beauty. See page 255.

△ **Chile's southern fjords.** With their inlets, islands, glaciers, and dense forests, the fjords are a transport engineer's nightmare, but the boats that ply the channels are a nature lover's dream. See page 293.

△ **The churches of Chiloé.** Notable for their unusual wooden architecture, these churches often stand alone by the sea where they were built by Jesuit missionaries during the colonial period. Some of them have been listed as World Heritage sites. See page 228.

◁ **Valparaíso's** *ascensores.* These funiculars may look rickety but are, in fact, quite safe and afford spectacular views of the bay. One of the most curious is the *Ascensor Polanco*, which rises vertically through the heart of the hill up to a suspended walkway. See page 159.

▷ **The Colchagua Wine Valley.** Although badly damaged by the 2010 earthquake, this prestigious wine-growing area retains its old rural traditions, alongside state-of-the-art wineries and boutique hotels. During the *vendimia*, or grape harvest, which takes place between early March and mid-April, there are numerous festivals. See page 93.

◁ **Tierra del Fuego.** There are few places where it is possible to be so alone as on this windswept island at the tip of South America. You're more likely to see guanacos and, in the woods, beavers than other people. See page 261.

▽ **Palacio de la Moneda.** Santiago's presidential palace is still the seat of government, although no longer the president's home. This is the building that Chilean Air Force fighter planes bombed during the 1973 military coup; its courtyards are open to the public. See page 129.

▷ **Easter Island.** Famous for its mysterious stone statues, this Polynesian island is 2,000km (1,240 miles) away from the nearest inhabited land, farther than any other island in the world. See page 270.

THE BEST OF CHILE: EDITOR'S CHOICE

Vast national parks, world-class rafting, and thermal springs are all waiting to be experienced in Chile, as well as great wines and exotic fruits. Here, at a glance, are the editor's top tips for making the most of your visit.

Parque Nacional Lauca.

BEST NATIONAL PARKS

Lauca. At the heart of this national park on the border with Bolivia, the Chungará Lake lies at 4,500 meters (14,760ft) above sea level against a backdrop of snow-capped volcanoes and teeming with birdlife, including flamingos. See page 180.
Nevado Tres Cruces. Overshadowed by Ojos del Salado, the world's highest volcano, this national park is off the beaten track but includes several Andean lakes and part of the spectacular Salar de Maricunga salt flat. See page 171.
Vicente Pérez Rosales. Founded in 1926, this vast national park, at the eastern end of Lago Llanquihue, has some of the most beautiful countryside in the Lake District and is dominated by the Volcán Osorno. See page 215.

BEST ADVENTURE SPORTS

White-water rafting. From the Maipo River near Santiago to the Futaleufú River in the far south, Chile's fast-flowing mountain rivers are prized by rafters, both for their scenery and their range of difficulty. See page 110.
Surfing. The pick of Chile's surfing beaches is Punta de Lobos in Central Chile, but there are also plenty of good beaches in the north. The coastline around Antofagasta is also popular with kite-surfers. See page 112.
Mountain biking. The Carretera Austral in Aisén is the ultimate goal of mountain bikers in Chile, but the Lake District offers many less challenging, but equally beautiful, routes. See page 112.
Sea kayaking. A kayak is a great way to explore the Patagonian fjords, and the inlets and remote islands of Chiloé. See page 110.
Mountaineering. Climbers from around the world visit Chile, attracted by peaks like Aconcagua, the Ojos del Salado volcano, and the "towers" of Torres del Paine. See page 108.
Paragliding. Although paragliding is practiced at many places along the coast of central Chile, Iquique in the north is by far the most popular center. See page 112.

Kayaking on Lago Grey.

BEST FOOD AND WINE

Fruit. Chilean restaurants only too rarely serve the fresh fruit that is one of the country's joys, whether peaches, apricots, and figs in summer, grapes in fall, or custard apples (*chirimoyas*) in spring. See page 86.

Seafood. Kingclip (*congrio*) and sea bass (*corvina*) from Chile's cold coastal waters, tuna fish from Easter Island, lobster from the Juan Fernández islands, and king crab (*centolla*) from Punta Arenas are just some of the seafood not to be missed in Chile. See page 85.

Carménère. Unique to Chile, this is the country's signature wine, the equivalent of Argentina's Malbec. Lighter than Cabernet Sauvignon, it is suitable for drinking on its own as well as with a meal. See page 93.

White wines. Although Chile is better known for its red wines, it also produces some excellent Sauvignon Blanc and Chardonnay wines. Look out for those from the Casablanca Valley. See page 94.

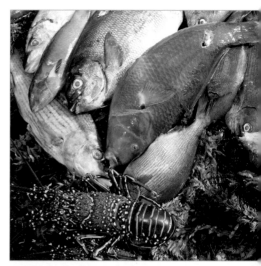

Fresh fish caught off Easter Island.

BEST HOT SPRINGS

Puritama. At these springs, northeast of San Pedro de Atacama, you can wallow in steaming pools or take a natural shower under one of the waterfalls, while looking out over the Atacama Desert. See page 178.

Baños de Colina. There are no facilities at these hot springs in the Andes above Santiago, but the smooth, natural pools on terraces carved into the mountainside are a wonderful place from which to contemplate the moonscape scenery. See page 148.

Cauquenes. In the foothills of the Andes, 28km (17 miles) east of Rancagua, these waters have been venerated since pre-Hispanic times. The cathedral-like building with its individual stone baths is open to visitors as well as guests at the excellent hotel. See page 192.

Puyehue. Both the mud baths at the luxury Termas de Puyehue Hotel and the nearby Aguas Calientes hot springs are renowned for their curative powers. See page 215.

BEST HISTORICAL SITES

Pukará de Quitor. Three kilometers (2 miles) from San Pedro de Atacama, this 12th-century fortress is where the native peoples made their last stand against Pedro de Valdivia and the invading Spaniards. See page 178.

Pablo Neruda's houses. The Nobel poet's three houses in Isla Negra, Santiago and Valparaíso are all open to the public and are much as they were during his lifetime. See page 158.

Cerro Alegre and Cerro Concepción. These two hills in Valparaíso, overlooking the bay, are where English and German immigrants made their home during the port's economic heyday. See page 159.

Chiflón del Diablo mine, Lota. Former miners describe the grueling life at the coalface as they guide visitors down this old mine under the sea. See page 200.

Tulor ruins, Atacama Desert.

The Baños de Colina.

Residents of South American
grasslands are known as gauchos.

Driving to Torres del Paine
National Park.

BIENVENIDOS

Over the past half century, it is mainly politics that have kept Chile in the international headlines, but it is, above all, the country's spectacular scenery that appeals to visitors.

Chiloé islanders.

Squeezed between the Andes and the Pacific, this spaghetti-like strip of land was affectionately tagged "the thin country" by Nobel Prize-winning Chilean poet Pablo Neruda. It is never more than 355km (221 miles) wide, and its coastline extends over 4,300km (2,700 miles). Within its borders are the world's driest desert, lush expanses of forest, and a spectacular array of glaciers and fjords. And, stretched directly along the Pacific "ring of fire," Chile has over 2,000 volcanoes, of which around 60 have erupted in the last 500 years.

Chileans are predominantly mestizos – the descendants of mainly Spanish immigrants and indigenous peoples – although there are pockets of pure-blooded Mapuches, as well as direct descendants of British, German, Swiss, and other immigrants. The traditional hospitality of Chileans, noted by travelers since the 18th century, is even more evident today. They have welcomed the influx of foreigners who come to enjoy the country's invigorating Andean atmosphere as a sign of the international integration that has been key in driving its rapid economic development.

Santiago, a modern city with gleaming office tower blocks and high-speed freeways, is the center of activity and the country's transportation hub. But, after a few days visiting its main sights and enjoying its pavement cafés and excellent restaurants, most travelers head either north into the Atacama Desert and the oasis town of San Pedro de Atacama, or south to the tranquil Lake Region

Mano de Desierto, by the sculptor Mario Irarrázabal.

or the spectacle of the Torres del Paine National Park, or across the Pacific Ocean to Easter Island, also part of Chile, with its mysterious *moai*. And, in all these places, Chile's vast open and uncrowded spaces offer plenty of opportunities for outdoor activities that range from trekking and horseback riding to diving and rafting.

A guanaco in Patagonia.

EARTH, FIRE, AND ICE

From searing desert heat to sub-Antarctic chills, with volcanoes, lakes, and geysers along the way, the natural world makes its presence strongly felt in Chile.

Chile must be a top candidate for the world's strangest geographical layout. In spite of the country's relatively small landmass (756,000 sq km/292,000 sq miles), its 4,300km (2,700-mile) coastline makes it seem enormous. Though the country is never more than 355km (221 miles) wide, a trip from Arica in the north to the port of Punta Arenas in the far south covers the same distance as New York to Los Angeles or Paris to Tehran. Parts of Chile are so narrow that in some areas the Andean peaks of its eastern border can be seen from the Pacific beaches.

The Pan-American Highway, also known as Ruta 5, which runs down the country's spine, connects every imaginable climatic zone: it crosses vast expanses of total desert, an agricultural valley the size of California's, and a province of mountain lakes and volcanoes. Farther south, car ferries and the Carretera Austral highway – actually a dirt road – connect Chiloé, the continent's second-largest island, to hundreds of kilometers of scarcely inhabited fjords and islands. A spectacular glacier field then divides these from the sheep farms of Chilean Patagonia, which is only accessible by road from Argentina.

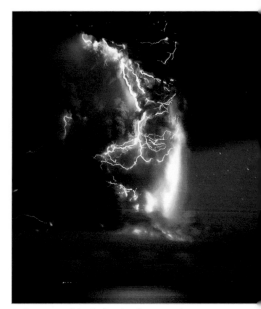

Calbuco erupted for the first time in 42 years in 2015.

> "Such a country should be called an island," wrote the 20th-century Chilean geographer Benjamín Subercaseaux, referring to Chile's unique geographical position, "even though its borders do not strictly fit the definition."

Geographically, Chile has a sense of separateness and forbidding boundaries. Its northern desert, the Atacama, is one of the driest places on earth. The Andes, which form the 4,000km (2,500-mile) frontier with Argentina, rise in sharp grades on the Chilean side, from sea level to as high as 7,000 meters (23,000ft) in little more than 100km (60 miles).

Chile's far southern tip points towards the polar ice of Antarctica. The country's western coastline faces the Pacific, the broadest ocean in the world and one of Chile's south-sea possessions, Easter Island, is the most isolated bit of inhabited land on earth, a thousand kilometers away from any other inhabited island.

From lush valleys to dry desert

In the semi-arid Norte Chico (Little North), irrigation has extended Chile's agricultural heartland north to the dusty valley town of Copiapó. Here, the many mountain rivers maintain a year-round flow, fed by seasonal rains and Andean snows. Despite the blistering sun, there is considerable humidity and minimal temperature change, making the region excellent for irrigated farming. Tropical fruit, especially papaya and *chirimoya* (custard apples), is commercially grown. The region's ideal atmospheric conditions for astronomical work have led to the construction of important observatories in the hills near La Serena.

The vegetation ends where the Norte Grande (Great North) begins. This is the part of Chile that was annexed from vanquished Peru and Bolivia after the 19th-century War of the Pacific (see page 41). Among the brown, barren hillsides and parched Atacama Desert are places where no rain has ever been recorded. But for the visitor, this barren region is fertile in geological spectacle and the fascinating remains of lost civilizations.

Chile's capital city, Santiago, is located at the country's latitudinal mid-point, next to the steep Andean foothills. The city, with a population of more than 6 million (over 7 million in the metropolitan area), is surrounded with a lovely but unfortunately placed set of smaller hills that trap its heavy air pollution. In this central region and

The Valley of the Moon in northern Chile.

RICH MINERAL VEIN

The tangible wealth of Chile's north lies beneath the Atacama Desert; its apparently barren surface conceals rich mineral deposits. Nitrates for fertilizer were once the basis of Chile's economy and two ghost towns still stand testimony to the industry's former glory (see page 181). Today, it is copper that drives the Chilean economy and the Escondida mine, controlled by BHP Billiton, is the copper mine with the largest production in the world. Silver and gold are also present in commercial quantities, while salt is exported for human consumption and industrial use, and attention is increasingly turning to the potential of the desert's lithium reserves.

along the coast, rains come sporadically from May to October, while the summer months of January to March are almost uniformly cloudless and hot.

The Central Valley has abundant agriculture with ample rivers, fed by the melting Andean snows. The famous wine grapes and other fruit such as peaches, nectarines, apples, pears, kiwis, and cherries, flourish in the intense, dry heat.

Towards the chilly south

Farther south in the Lake District, year-round precipitation keeps the landscape green, but limits farming to the cultivation of more traditional grains and the rearing of animals. An active volcano belt provides picturesque landscapes (most of Chile's active volcanoes are in this area), but can also disrupt the lives of villagers with dangerous clouds of toxic particles. Twelve great lakes, including the continent's fourth-largest, Lago Llanquihue, give the area its dominant characteristic – even the high Andean plateaux in this region are strewn with large lakes.

Where the lakes meet the Pacific Ocean, the coastal mountain range becomes a 1,000-island archipelago with the Isla Grande de Chiloé at its head. Rainfall of over 4,000mm (157in) annually is registered in Chiloé and its satellite islands, giving Chile both precipitation extremes, with the Atacama Desert at the other end of the scale.

trademark mountain peaks. Punta Arenas, with just over 123,000 inhabitants, is the southernmost city of its size in the world. Temperatures rarely rise above 10°C (50°F) in this gusty port, which is almost perpetually shrouded in cloud.

Farther south lies Tierra del Fuego, which Chile shares with Argentina and is the largest island in South America. (Chile nearly went to war with Argentina here in the late 1970s, until the Vatican sponsored peace negotiations.) Beyond Tierra del Fuego lies the considerably harsher territory of Antarctica, a large part of which Chile claims.

Parque Nacional Lauca.

The Carretera Austral, an unpaved road from Puerto Montt, allows access to one of the most remote zones on the continent. Foreign trout fishermen fly to the provincial capital of Coyhaique to fish in the pure streams and lakes of the region. The road sweeps past beautiful Lago General Carrera and basks in the microclimate around Chile Chico, ending in the 600-inhabitant frontier town of Villa O'Higgins.

The furthest tip of Chile is accessible only by boat, plane, or via a long detour overland through Argentina. This inaccessibility seems to make Magallanes all the more exciting for many visitors, who come to explore the vast wilderness of Parque Nacional Torres del Paine, with its relatively tame wildlife, accessible glaciers, and

RING OF FIRE

Its position on the so-called Pacific "ring of fire" is the reason why Chile has such spectacular volcanoes. The largest earthquake ever recorded in the world – 9.5 on the Richter scale – occurred in Chile in 1960 and was so strong that it changed the map of large parts of the area's coastline. In 2010 , an earthquake reaching 8.8 occurred in the Central Valley. In 2015 the northern region of Coquimbo was struck by an earthquake reaching 8.4 which killed 15 people and destroyed over 2,400 homes. Chile's long experience of earthquakes has, however, honed its anti-seismic building standards and these are among the highest in the world.

Mapicape family.

DECISIVE DATES

Copper Moche mask.

Prehistoric Times

13,000–10,000 BC

A group of mastodon hunters settle in the area now known as Monte Verde, near modern Puerto Montt.

Pre-Columbian Cultures

c.1450

The Incas, led by Tupac Yupanqui, make their way

Tupac Yupanqui.

down from Peru and conquer northern Chile, but fail to subdue the Mapuches in the south.

European Conquest and Settlement

1520

The Portuguese explorer Ferdinand Magellan becomes the first European to glimpse Chile as he sails through the straits that are later named after him.

1533

Inca rule ends when they are defeated by Spanish conquistador Francisco Pizarro.

1536

Pizarro's comrade Diego de Almagro travels from Cuzco to Copiapó and then on to the Aconcagua Valley in search of gold.

1541

Pedro de Valdivia sets off to conquer Chile and founds Santiago.

1550–1

Valdivia establishes the settlements of Concepción, Valdivia, Villarrica, and several other cities.

1553

Valdivia is killed by the native Mapuches, led by Lautaro, near Concepción.

1557–61

A new governor, called García Hurtado de Mendoza, re-establishes Spanish rule in Concepción and founds Osorno and Cañete.

1599

A major uprising by indigenous tribes wipes out all Spanish settlements south of the Biobío river in the Central Valley region.

17th Century

Ranching becomes Chile's primary export trade, with large estates (*haciendas* or *latifundas*) employing bonded *mestizo* peasants to replace *encomiendas* as European diseases reduce the native population.

18th Century

Around 20,000 Spaniards emigrate to the new colony.

1740

Chile loosens its bonds with the Viceroyalty of Peru, seat of the Spanish American Empire, as direct trade is permitted

with Spain and other colonies in the New World.

1750
Chile is permitted to mint its own coins.

Independence from Spain

1808
The French emperor Napoleon invades Spain, dethroning King Ferdinand VII.

1810
Leading Chilean citizens force the Spanish governor in Chile to resign and, following the example of Spanish cities, select a ruling junta in the name of King Ferdinand.

1811
The first Chilean National Congress gathers, swearing loyalty to the Spanish king.

1812
Following a coup d'état, the Carrera government proposes that the Spanish king should recognize Chile's constitution and sovereignty and establishes democratic rule.

1813
Spain invades Chile.

Workers in a silver mine.

1814
Chilean nationalists are beaten at Rancagua, and their leaders flee to Argentina.

1817
The nationalists, led by Bernardo O'Higgins, defeat the Spanish forces with the help of Argentine hero General José de San Martín. O'Higgins is appointed Supreme Dictator.

1818
Chilean independence is declared. The nationalists win a decisive victory over the royalist forces at the Battle of Maipú.

Growth and Stability

1823
Slavery is abolished.

1829–30
A lengthy period of "Conservative Republic" is

ushered in under Diego Portales.

1839
The first Chilean banknotes go into circulation.

1840s
Prosperity grows as more silver is found in the north, Chilean farmers supply Californian gold-diggers, and Magallanes is founded to take advantage of European trade routes.

1843
The University of Chile is founded in Santiago.

From 1848
German settlement is encouraged, as immigrants flee the revolutions in Europe, bringing European political and revolutionary ideas to Chile. Work begins on Chile's first railroad, from Copiapó to Caldera.

1850s
Guano is discovered, putting the area north of Coquimbo into dispute with both Peru and Bolivia.

1860
Free primary education is introduced.

1876–8
Flooding in the south and drought in the north lead to famine. Agricultural problems combined with a fall in the demand for silver lead to an economic crisis.

1879
Chile declares war on Bolivia and Peru.

1881
Last uprising of Chile's indigenous peoples. The

The Battle of Maipú, 1818.

Mining nitrate in the desert.

rebellion is quashed by the army and the territory of the Mapuches is declared state property.

1883
Peru cedes Tarapacá, Tacna, and Arica to Chile.

1884
Bolivia cedes Antofagasta to Chile.

1891
Civil war breaks out over the issue of presidential powers. After defeat, President José Manuel Balmaceda commits suicide.

The 20th Century

1907
The massacre of striking mine workers at Santa María de Iquique ends a period of intense union activity.

1912
The Chilean Socialist Workers' Party is founded.

1918
The invention of synthetic nitrates makes Chile's "desert gold" obsolete.

1925
A new constitution separates church and state.

1926
Economic and political crises bring army officer Carlos Ibáñez to power. He creates a powerful state system.

1929
The Wall Street Crash and world depression lead to political instability.

1931
Ibáñez resigns and goes into exile.

1932
Arturo Alessandri returns to power, ushering in a period of economic recovery and political stability.

1945
Chilean poet Gabriela Mistral is awarded the Nobel Prize for literature.

1949
Women win the right to vote.

1952
Carlos Ibáñez is elected president and returns to power.

1964
Eduardo Frei leads the Christian Democrat Party to power with US support.

1970
The leftwing coalition Popular Unity, led by Salvador Allende, scrapes to victory as Chile's first Socialist government.

1971
The Allende government nationalizes the copper mines as part of a sweeping reform program. Chilean poet Pablo Neruda wins the Nobel Prize for literature.

1973
The Allende government is overthrown in a violent military coup, ending in the suicide of Allende in Santiago's Moneda Palace, which brings General Augusto Pinochet to power. Thousands are tortured and murdered during his regime.

1980
A new Constitution stipulates a referendum on continued military rule to be held in 1988.

1982–3
Chile's economy nosedives, sparking off strikes and protests.

1986
An attempt to assassinate Pinochet fails.

Anti-Pinochet graffiti during the 1988 referendum.

1988
Fifty-four percent of voters reject Pinochet's regime in a referendum.

1989
Christian Democrat Patricio Aylwin is elected President as the country returns to democracy. General Pinochet stays on as Army commander-in-chief.

1990s
Prosperity increases rapidly, although income distribution remains extremely unequal.

1991
The National Commission on Truth and Reconciliation establishes military guilt in violating human rights, but few of the perpetrators are punished.

1994
Christian Democrat Eduardo Frei, son of 1960s President Frei, is elected to head the Concertación, the center-left government coalition.

1998
Pinochet retires as army commander-in-chief. Later that year, he is detained during a visit to London on human rights charges filed by a Spanish judge and is held under house arrest until March 2000 when he is released on grounds of ill-health.

2000
Ricardo Lagos, a Socialist, is elected to head the Concertación's third term.

2002
Pinochet is declared mentally unfit to stand trial in Chile and retires from public life until his death in December 2006.

2006
Concertación candidate Michelle Bachelet, a Socialist, is elected as Chile's first woman president. Secondary schoolchildren, demanding improvements in the quality of state education, mount the largest protests since the restoration of democracy.

2007
The launch of the new Transantiago public transport system in February plunges Chile's capital into chaos, badly denting the popularity of President Bachelet and her government.

2009
GDP contracts by 1 percent in response to the international financial crisis but counter-cyclical fiscal measures help to take President Bachelet's popularity to record levels.

2010
Sebastián Piñera, a former businessman, becomes Chile's first elected right-wing president since Jorge Alessandri (1958–64). In February, a severe earthquake, followed by a tsunami, causes great damage in the Central Valley, particularly to coastal towns and villages. In October the world breathes a sigh of relief as 33 miners, trapped for over two months in the collapsed San José gold and copper mine in northern Chile, are successfully rescued.

2011
Student protests in Santiago call for a radical reform of the public schools. The police use water cannons and tear gas to break up the demonstrations.

2012
Congress passes an anti-discrimination law following the brutal murder of a gay man. Chile formally establishes the Pacific Alliance with Mexico, Colombia and Peru. Students take to the streets again demanding an end to public financing for private universities.

News of General Pinochet's death.

2013
A smoking ban in enclosed public spaces is introduced. 100,000 students demand free education in Santiago.

2014
Michelle Bachelet assumes presidency for another term, promising to tackle inequality. The International Court of Justice highest court defines a new maritime border between Chile and Peru ending a long-term dispute.

2015
Thousands are evacuated following the eruption of the Villarrica volcano in southern Chile. President Bachelet reshuffles her cabinet after a series of scandals. A devastating earthquake in northern Chile leaves 15 people dead and hundreds injured.

2016
Gonzalo Delaveau, the head of the Chilean branch of the anti-corruption watchdog Transparency International, resigns after his name appears in the notorious Panama Papers, a massive leak of secret offshore financial dealings.

THE WILD FRONTIER

Pre-Hispanic Chilean society was as diverse as the latitudes it covered, which helped the southern tribes to repel invasions by the Incas as well as the Spanish.

Chile was never a top priority for South America's explorers or colonizers. The Incas made their way down from Peru in the mid-15th century, less than 100 years before the Europeans arrived, when Tupac Yupanqui defeated the northern tribes and established Inca rule as far south as present-day Santiago.

The native Atacameño and Diaguita cultures, which had thrived in the northern deserts for centuries, were fairly organized societies compared with the Araucanians farther south. Both of the northern groups were farmers. They grew beans, maize, potatoes, and coca, using irrigation techniques that suggest they had a central authority strong enough to impose rules on their small societies. They kept llamas, wove cloth and baskets, made and decorated pots, and traded with each other and with the peoples in Peru. The Atacameños mummified their dead while the Diaguitas took their wives to the grave with them. Little more is known about their civilizations, though their numbers were estimated to be about 80,000.

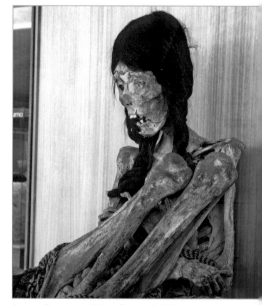

Atacameño mummy, Museo Gustavo Le Paige.

Unconquered tribes of the south

Beyond present-day Santiago, the Incas ran into serious opposition. The Araucanian tribes, who numbered around 1 million in total, lived from the River Aconcagua down to Chiloé. There were three main groups, all speaking the same language, but with significant cultural differences.

The Picunches (men of the north) lived in the fertile Central Valley between the Aconcagua and Biobío rivers. They grew most of the same crops as the Diaguitas and Atacameños to the north, but with much less effort required in their temperate climate and well-watered soil. The Picunches lived in small, generally peaceful, self-sufficient family groups, and were no match for the Incas when they arrived.

It was the less submissive Mapuches (men of the land), the Huilliches (men of the south) and, to a lesser extent, the nomadic Pehuenches, Puelches, and Tehuelches, whom the Incas called "the rebel peoples." The Mapuches lived precariously in the area between the Itata and Toltén rivers, farming temporary clearings in the dense forests and moving on once the land was exhausted. The Huilliches lived in the same way between the Toltén and the island of Chiloé. The Incas gave up on these loosely grouped nomads, who did not recognize a central authority or understand any form of tribute. They set their frontier at the River Cachapoal, near Rancagua, and left the rest of the Araucanians to themselves.

The Incas interfered little with the customs and practices of the peoples that they colonized, as long as they paid tribute, in gold, and provided labor. Inca rule lasted less than 40 years. An internal power struggle developed, and the Inca garrisons were withdrawn from Chile back to Cuzco in present-day Peru. The quarrel ended with their defeat at the hands of the Spanish conquistador Francisco Pizarro and the demise of their empire.

A solitary captain and 80 men were sent down to the Magellan Straits, but they returned, having got no further than the River Itata, with terrifying tales of ferocious natives. Spirits sank, and Almagro's men resisted his proposal to stay and colonize the new territory. Returning empty-handed to Peru in 1537, Almagro tried to take on Francisco Pizarro for control of the Andes. He lost the civil war that ensued and paid for the uprising with his life.

The reward for one of Pizarro's backers was Chile. Pedro de Valdivia set off to subdue the southern territory. He was to take for himself

One of the last Inca strongholds in Chile.

The Spaniards' conquest begins

The first European to see Chile was the Portuguese explorer Ferdinand Magellan, who sailed through the straits which took his name on November 1, 1520. He only glanced at the new territory as he sailed up its coast. Next to arrive was Pizarro's comrade Diego de Almagro, who made his way over the cordillera from Cuzco in 1536 with a couple of hundred men and high hopes of treasure. They reached Copiapó, where the native people received them peacefully enough, and then traveled on to the Aconcagua Valley. All the time the Spaniards scouted about in vain for the fabulous gold mines of which the Incas had spoken.

and his followers any land he found. But Almagro's unfruitful trip had discouraged fortune-seekers, and Valdivia had a hard time finding recruits. Eventually he set off with only a dozen others, and his faithful mistress, Inés de Suárez.

As Valdivia had hoped, many other marauder-explorers joined him on the way. There were 150 in the motley band when they reached the River Mapocho in the Central Valley, and decided to make their first settlement. This was Santiago, founded on February 12, 1541.

Press-ganged into service, the local Mapuches waited for a few months and then rebelled. On September 11 a local chief, Michimalongo, attacked the settlement while Valdivia was away. Inés de Suárez, in a chainmail jacket, fought alongside the men in a day-long battle. By the end of it, the Spaniards stood, triumphant, on the burned-out site, but all of their belongings – food, seeds, even clothes – were destroyed.

Inés de Suárez, born in Spain in 1507, is reported to have met Pedro de Valdivia in Cuzco in 1538 where she had traveled in search of her soldier husband. Her life is the subject of a book by Isabel Allende, 'Inés del Alma Mía.'

Despite living in hunger and scarcity, Valdivia fell in love with the new land, and he wrote to the king with great enthusiasm: "This land is such that life here cannot be equaled. It has only four months of winter... and the summer is so temperate and has such delicious breezes that men can walk all day in the sun and not suffer for it. It is abundant in grass, and can support any kind of cattle or livestock and plants that you can imagine; there is plenty of beautiful wood for building houses, great quantities of wood for fuel for heating and working the rich mines. Wherever you might dream of finding them, there is soil to sow, materials for building and water and grass for the animals, so that it seems as if God had created everything so that it would be at hand."

Death by gold

Gradually the Central Valley Mapuches were subdued. Valdivia handed out parcels of land to his followers, along with groups of Mapuches bonded to labor in *encomiendas*. Theoretically, that made the Spaniards trustees charged with the care and conversion of the local population. In fact they became feudal estates, with the native people simply enslaved labor to work the land or pan for gold.

In 1550 Valdivia founded Concepción, and a year later, Imperial, Valdivia, Villarrica, and Angol. In each settlement, Valdivia left 50 or 60 men to build the "city" with the help of the subdued Mapuches. But his troops were stretched thin. At the end of 1553 he left Concepción with only 50 men. The fort at Tucapel, when they reached it on Christmas Day, was a smoking ruin. As they surveyed the wreckage, the Mapuches attacked. Valdivia and his men fought back, but by dusk most of

them were dead, including Valdivia. He was tied to a tree, legend has it, and forced to swallow molten gold.

The victor was Lautaro, who had worked for the Spaniards before going off to fight against them. He was said to be the first Mapuche to realize that the Spaniard and his horse, which was a creature completely unknown to the native Chileans, were two separate animals. Lautaro advanced on Santiago, but was knifed by a traitor on the night before the planned attack. Morale fell, and smallpox decimated his men. Santiago was saved. With Valdivia's death,

Inés de Suárez defends Spanish battlements.

THE INCA TRAIL

The lasting contribution of the Incas' short-lived rule in Chile was the "Inca Trail," a series of paths which reached as far south as Talca. There were three routes, one along the coast, one through the desert, and one over the altiplano (high plain) and along the Andes. They were later used by Spanish explorers to access their base in Peru and some stretches have now been incorporated into the Sendero de Chile trail (see page 113). One of the most spectacular routes starts at the Chilean-Peruvian-Bolivian border and runs 14km (8 miles) to the tiny Andean town of Visiri.

three rivals fought to succeed him as governor, until in 1557, Peru sent a new governor, García Hurtado de Mendoza. He re-established Spanish rule in the area around Concepción, restored the city and subdued the Mapuches in the region. Two new cities, Osorno and Cañete, were founded. His period as governor, up to 1561, marks the end of the period of conquest.

But the war with the native people of Araucania was far from over, and the Spaniards, fighting as a part-time citizens' army, were ill-equipped to win it. At the end of the 16th century, another governor, Martín García Óñez de

Pedro de Valdivia.

Loyola, lost his life in a major native uprising. The settlements south of the Biobío were wiped out, and the northern bank of the river became the frontier of the Spaniards' territory. By then, the colony numbered about 5,000 Europeans.

Life on the wild frontier

War with the Araucanians was a background noise for the whole of the next century, and most of the one that followed. There were periodic uprisings and massacres, and the governor of the territory was based permanently down on the frontier in Concepción. By this time the colonizers had recognized that there were no rivers of gold or fabled silver cities in Chile, and that wealth needed to be tilled from the land or

dug from the mines. Native people, or mixed-race mestizos were put to work, and before long the new territory was exporting wheat, copper, leather, and wine.

But the Spanish authorities sent from Madrid could not impose law and order. A sinister and unscrupulous figure, Doña Catalina de los Ríos y Lisperguer, known as *la Quintrala*, reflected the worst aspects of the colony in the 16th century. An upper-class lady, she is credited with poisoning her father, cutting off the ear of one of her lovers, arranging a tryst with another and then having him murdered while she watched. "Lower" beings such as servants were killed or mutilated according to her whims.

> *Fights over gambling debts between clergymen became such a problem in 16th-century Chile that the bishop banned them from entering public gambling houses, or from having packs of cards in their own homes.*

Many members of the Church set no better example. Chroniclers recorded open fights between members of the Augustinian and the Franciscan orders. Gambling was a passion in the new colony, and the main entertainment for men. Clothes were of prime importance for society women, and for some men too – the richer and more ostentatiously embroidered, the better.

Cultural influences

By the late 17th century Chile was becoming more civilized. The influence of the French Bourbons (now rulers of Spain) brought French culture and manners to the distant colony. Governor Cano de Aponte arrived in his new domain in 1720 with "twenty-three boxes of furniture and dishes, a clavichord, four violins, a harp and various Andalusian tambourines, as well as fifteen mules loaded with fine clothes."

The Jesuits brought over architects, engineers, pharmacists, weavers, painters, and sculptors. They also collected the best library in the colony – 20,000 volumes by the mid-18th century. Chile was already on the way to becoming the prosperous and highly Europeanized country that would later be seen as an example to the more turbulent emerging nations of Latin America.

INDEPENDENCE AND PROSPERITY

Once independence had been won from Spain, there was
no stopping the new republic, and Chile soon became
one of the strongest economies in the Americas.

Spain tried to keep its colonies free of foreign influences. It banned the entry of
books printed outside Spain and prohibited printing presses within the colonies. But
colonials still traveled to Europe, picking up
"subversive" books, and new ideas.

The French Revolution and the revolt of
the British colonies in North America in the
late 18th century set conflicting examples. The
excesses of the French rebels could be held up
as an awful warning. But the sober, enterpris-
ing North Americans were rather an encourage-
ment to their southern neighbors.

As it turned out, it was the ambitions of
Napoleon that led to the independence of the
Spanish colonies. When the French emperor
invaded Spain, he forced the abdication of
the king, Ferdinand VII, and placed his own
brother, Joseph Bonaparte, on the Spanish
throne. In Spain itself, there was immediate

Foot soldier in Chile's revolutionary army.

> In the first 13 years following independence
> from Spain, Chile tried five different
> constitutional formulas and went through 11
> changes of government.

resistance. In each city the leading citizens set
up a junta to govern in the name of the deposed
king. Soon, the local bodies delegated power to
a central junta in Seville.

A new Congress

According to the Spanish governor in the
American colonies, the junta in Seville represented authority while the true king was absent.
But many colonials felt they shared the same
status as the Spanish cities, and that they should

have the right to elect their own authority, subject only to the king.

In Chile that was what they did. The inept
Spanish governor was persuaded to resign
in favor of a native Chilean, Don Mateo de
Toro y Zambrano. The next step was to form
a ruling junta, as the Argentines had done. In
Chile the governor called a *cabildo abierto*, a
formal meeting of the leading citizens. They
gathered on September 18, 1810 and chose
a junta, which swore undying loyalty to the
Spanish king.

Their first act was to secure the defense of
their new nation. An infantry battalion was
formed, along with two cavalry squadrons and
more artillery. Envoys were sent to buy arms in

England and Argentina. The junta also decreed free trade with all nations, hoping to boost the state's income from customs duties.

Finally, it convoked a National Congress, which was to be representative and also to guarantee that there were no abuses of power – two radical new notions that had infiltrated from Europe and the United States. The voters were people who "by their fortune, work, talent, or qualities enjoy consideration in the parts where they reside, being older than 25 years." They elected deputies who "for their patriotic virtues, talents, and acknowledged

September 4, 1811, Juan José and José Miguel stormed the Congress at the head of a mob and presented a list of "the people's demands." It was a coup d'état. A cowed Congress agreed to sack some of its most conservative members and set up an executive junta. After that, the reforms came faster, but still not fast enough for the Carreras. José Miguel forced Congress to set up a new junta, with himself at the head, and in December 1811, dissolved the Congress.

The Carreras had their sights set on Chile's independence, but they were in a minority. One of their first acts was to acquire a printing

Bernardo O'Higgins, who led Chile to independence.

prudence may have merited the esteem of their fellow citizens."

The selection of the deputies went ahead in early 1811. The first National Congress gathered on July 4 and, once again, its members swore loyalty to the Spanish king. A majority of its members were conservative landowners, who wanted only a minimum of reforms. But an energetic elite wanted radical change.

A radical coup d'état

The first to make a bid for the leadership of the nation were the Carreras. Three brothers – José Miguel, Juan José, and Luis – and one sister, Javiera, came from a wealthy Santiago family. But their ideas were extreme for the day. On

press and put a radical priest called Fray Camilo Henríquez in charge of it. He began publishing revolutionary ideas about popular sovereignty in a weekly paper, *La Aurora de Chile*.

In 1812, the government promulgated a new Constitution. Formally, this still recognized the Spanish monarch, but it proposed that the king should in turn recognize Chile's own Constitution and sovereignty. The new Constitution also established the rights of the individual, and set limits on the powers of the government, which was now to be elected by the people. This was a drastic change from being ruled by a monarch.

Most of José Miguel Carrera's compatriots, especially among the aristocracy, were not ready for such revolutionary gestures, and did not like either the man or his ideas. But before they could get together to do anything about him, the Spaniards took a hand.

The wars of independence

On March 26, 1813, Spain invaded the Chilean Central Valley, using officers from Peru and 2,000 men recruited among royalists in Valdivia and Chiloé. They took Talcahuano and Concepción, and started to move north. Carrera took command of the army and organized the defense of the capital, together with another military leader, Bernardo O'Higgins.

Avenida Libertador General Bernardo O'Higgins, the main east–west road through Santiago, is named after Chile's independence hero and his name crops up in streets, squares, and statues around the country.

O'Higgins was another product of the ruling elite. He was the illegitimate son of a former governor, Ambrosio O'Higgins, an Irishman who had emigrated via Spain and Peru to Chile, where he became one of the most effective governors. An affair with a lady of Chillán, Doña Isabel Riquelme, produced Bernardo, who was sent to Lima and then England for education.

Back in Chile, O'Higgins was elected a deputy to the Congress. He then distinguished himself as a military leader, and took over command of the army in 1813 from the more impetuous José Miguel Carrera. But by the end of the year the war was going badly. A truce was negotiated. Both sides were exhausted.

In March 1814, the Treaty of Lircay was signed. But the Carrera brothers and their troops rebelled and took the government again. O'Higgins set off to overthrow the new regime, but before he and the Carreras clashed the news came that a new royalist army had disembarked at Talcahuano. Divided and unprepared, the patriots met them at Rancagua on October 1, and were soundly beaten. O'Higgins and the Carreras all fled together to Argentina.

Spain back in charge

Ironically, it was the Spanish reconquest which finally convinced the Chileans that independence was their only option. The Spaniards tried to turn the clock back to 1810. Every reform the

patriot governments had made, from allowing free trade to abolishing slavery, was annulled by the royalists.

There was direct persecution of patriots. Many were sent into internal exile – one group was banished to a cave on the Juan Fernández Islands. Nationalists in the public prison in Santiago were shot. The rest of the citizenry had to prove their loyalty to the Crown. Patriot public servants lost their jobs, others, their property. Heavy fines were exacted from all wealthy citizens. Chileans were not allowed to travel without permission, or carry arms. Public festivals

Clergymen, early 19th century.

were banned, a very unpopular move, and the gaming houses were closed.

Meanwhile, the remains of the patriot army, led by O'Higgins, had joined forces with the Argentine General José de San Martín and spent the next two years in Mendoza preparing to invade. A spy network kept the patriots in touch with sympathizers in Chile. Its leader was Manuel Rodríguez, a young lawyer who helped form guerrilla bands to harass the Spaniards. Rodríguez became a national folk hero; the tales of his clever disguises and narrow escapes from the Spaniards passed into legend. On one occasion he took refuge in a Franciscan monastery and, disguised in a monk's robes, showed his pursuers around the convent to prove he was not there. Another time he dressed as a beggar and politely helped the Spanish governor to alight from his carriage. Even if they were not all true, the stories helped to keep up people's spirits.

Triumph for the nationalists

By 1817, O'Higgins and San Martín were ready, and their 3,600-strong "army of the Andes" crossed the mountains. On February 12, they defeated royalist troops at Chacabuco, then entered Santiago in triumph, welcomed by vast crowds of Chileans.

patrolled the coasts of Peru, disrupting the enemy's supplies. At the end of the year, the navy took Valdivia, which was one of the few remaining royalist strongholds in Chile.

On August 20 1820, the army of the Andes, now mainly composed of Chileans but led by the Argentine San Martín, set off for Peru. With the fall of Lima and the final defeat of the Spanish, Chile's independence was assured.

Tribulations of the new republic

Once independence was secure, the Chileans had to work out how to replace two and a

Valparaíso, one of the world's busiest ports by the late 19th century.

The first job was to set up a new government. O'Higgins was named *director supremo*. On January 1, 1818, the new regime declared the independence of Chile. But there was still fighting to be done. The royalists counter-attacked with a new force from Peru, and took Talca. The patriots soon recovered and inflicted a final defeat on the Spaniards at the Battle of Maipú on April 5, 1818. That settled Chile's future.

But O'Higgins continued to fight for the independence of the rest of South America, not least because Chile would never be secure while the royalists held Peru. A navy was formed under Lord Cochrane, a Scot, with ships begged and borrowed from all parts, and mostly foreign officers and sailors. In 1819, the new force

half centuries' rule by an absolute monarch with a republic. Most of the trial Constitutions and reforms introduced were received quite peacefully but were not always popular. In 1823, O'Higgins ran into determined opposition from the landowning aristocracy. He was forced to resign and went back to Peru, where he lived the rest of his days dreaming of return. He eventually died in 1842, but his body was not brought back to Chile until 1869.

The other revolutionaries fared worse. Two of the Carrera brothers were shot by the Argentines in 1818; then José Miguel, too, was shot, in Mendoza three years later. A secret society, known as the *Logia Lautarina*, formed originally by O'Higgins and San Martín in

1815, was said to have given the orders for their executions. Only Javiera Carrera survived and returned to Chile after the downfall of O'Higgins.

Manuel Rodríguez, who had been closer to the Carreras than to O'Higgins, presented a problem for the new government. He was a headstrong, popular leader. O'Higgins tried to send him into gilded exile in the United States as a diplomat. Rodríguez refused, and ended up first in prison and then, in 1818, shot – "while trying to escape," said the official report.

But most of the decade was taken up with the struggle between conservative landowners and the Church against the Chilean liberals, who were strong in the towns, and among the intellectual elite. The liberals hung on to the government until 1829, when they lost control of Santiago and the administration.

Finally, in 1833, the conservatives were able to impose an authoritarian model of government that lasted until the next century. On paper, the president was all-powerful and Congress was a mere sideshow. It sat for only four months of the year, while the president could veto laws, and had personal representatives in each province. The president could

> Diego Portales argued that Latin America was not ready for democracy: "When morality has been established, then comes a true liberal government, free and full of ideals, in which all citizens can take part."

also veto electors, giving him enormous influence over the election of congressmen and of his successor.

Conservative values

The real leader of the conservative movement, though he never ran for president and preferred to rule from behind the throne, was Diego Portales, best-known until then as a businessman.

Like other leaders of the independence movement, he was committed to liberal ideas in the abstract but argued that, in practice, Latin America was "not ready" for democracy. It was never made clear when the transition would take place or under what circumstances what came to be called the "enlightened despotism" would end.

While the Congress was writing the new Constitution, Portales was busy imposing the authority of the central government. He himself was minister for the interior, foreign affairs, the army, and the navy. He purged the army of its rebel leaders and reorganized the military academy: officers were to return to the professional, non-political status they held before independence. To encourage this, Portales reinstated a system of local militias, directly loyal to the government.

A successful campaign stamped out banditry in the countryside. Economic and financial

Southern market town in the 1860s.

reforms reduced the size of the army and the civil service and brought in better bookkeeping and fiscal controls. Such was Portales's influence in these years that in 1833 the British consul wrote home that "Every measure of the government originates with him (Portales) and no state body dares carry out any order without his express approval..."

Portales was murdered by political opponents in 1838. The organizational model he had established, however, lasted for nearly a century. By and large, the deeply conservative Chilean bureaucracy was better-organized and less corrupt than others in the region – on the other hand, Portales's expressed desire to extend democracy to Chilean society as a whole would only be fulfilled much later and in the wake of major social conflicts.

Stability and prosperity

Chile developed through the 1800s in largely stable conditions, though violence and social unrest erupted in the 1850s as the undemocratic manner of selecting presidents came into dispute. Reforms of the electoral system in the early 1870s temporarily resolved the issue.

Throughout most of the 19th century, a strong state oversaw an economic growth concentrated in overseas trade and copper and silver exports. Like its neighbor Argentina, Chile encouraged European immigration; in the south, for example, German immigrants came to control some of the larger and most profitable estates, while European dominance of trade ensured that the British and French occupied key positions elsewhere in the economy. The British led the shipping business. In 1825, 90 British ships called at Valparaíso compared with 70 from the US. Fifteen years later, the number of British vessels had doubled, while the number from the US continued to fall. By 1875, Britain took 70 percent of Chile's exports and sold it 40 percent of its imports.

Market forces

Much of Chile's growth came from copper exports. In 1826, 60 tons were shipped out of the country; by 1831, that was up to 2,000 tons, and by 1835, it was 12,700. By 1860, copper represented 55 percent of all Chile's exports. However, copper sales taught Chile about the dangers as well as the benefits of joining the world economy. The industrial revolution in Britain had boosted demand for copper in the 1830s. But industrial slumps in Europe in the 1850s and 1870s hit Chile hard. From then on, the daily price of copper on the London Metal Exchange became a national obsession.

Another problem that Chile faced in this period was the cost of being so far from its markets. In the 1840s, Chile found a profitable new market for its wheat and flour in California, at the height of the gold rush. Its exports leapt more than 70-fold in three years. But by 1854 the North American farmers were back on top, and Chile's sales slumped. When the gold rush started in Australia a little later, Chilean farmers could not compete in price with their Californian rivals. For the rest of the century there was a steady flow of migrants from the countryside and its decreasingly profitable farms, to the towns and the mining centers of the north.

Arturo Prat, a national hero.

CHILEAN DIARY

In 1822, an English woman, Maria Graham, decided to stay in Chile after her husband, the captain of HMS *Doris*, died during the voyage to South America and was buried in Valparaíso. She traveled extensively in central Chile and became friends with many of the country's leading figures, including Bernardo O'Higgins and Lord Cochrane. Her journal, *Diario de Mi Residencia en Chile* and drawings are a fascinating insight into life and customs in Chile at the time, and include a detailed account of one of Chile's worst ever earthquakes. She subsequently went on to travel to Brazil with Lord Cochrane where she also wrote a journal.

Rail, cables, and banknotes

Transportation was a problem internally. The first railroad track was planned in 1845, from Copiapó to the little port of Caldera. An energetic North American, William Wheelwright, organized the finances from the private sector and by 1851 the first 81km (50 miles) were inaugurated. Another track from Valparaíso to Santiago was finished in 1863. A telegraph line linked the main port with the capital in 1852; by 1876 there were 48 national lines, and one each to Argentina and Peru. In 1853, Chile introduced postage stamps, just 13 years after Britain.

Getting a banking system organized was a major task. There was a physical shortage of coins and paper money – the first banknotes began to circulate in 1839. In the mining sector the owner-entrepreneurs started to use their own trade bills as a form of exchange, and to coin lead tokens to pay their workforce. Their

the population was literate, but 60 years later the figure had risen to a creditable 50 percent.

War with the neighbors

In the first half of the 19th century, the northern desert area close to the Peruvian and Bolivian borders had attracted little attention. But from the 1850s onwards, deposits of natural fertilizers (guano and nitrates) were discovered there. Guano became a major source of income for Peru, and Chile and Bolivia disputed deposits along the coast north of Coquimbo. By 1874 Peru and Chile had

Mineworkers became the backbone of Chile's union movement.

logical next step was to set up a bank. By 1850, there were 60 operating, including the Banco de Chile. The government regulated their currency issues, but did not produce its own.

Already by the 1840s, contemporary chroniclers were writing about the effects of a period of stability and prosperity. There were fine new houses in Santiago, such as the Palacio Cousiño, as well as two theaters, a school of painting, and several literary magazines.

In 1843, the University of Chile was founded for research and debate. The Instituto Nacional was the only higher-education center, but there were schools for music and art. In 1860, primary education was made free and a state responsibility. At this date only 17 percent of

agreed for both to exploit the guano, but the labor was mostly Chilean.

In 1878, new disputes broke out, this time over nitrate deposits. In 1879, Chile occupied Antofagasta, which until then was Bolivian territory. When it discovered that Peru and Bolivia had a secret defense pact, Chile declared war on both its neighbors. The ensuing War of the Pacific resulted in Chile gaining a future source of wealth, nitrates, and its best-loved national hero, Captain Arturo Prat. Today, his statue graces the plaza of even the smallest village, and the day of his death, May 21, is a national holiday.

The Chilean army marched to the Peruvian capital, Lima. Peru had to sue for peace; the Treaty of Ancón, signed in 1883, gave Chile

Tarapacá and the towns of Arica and Tacna for a 10-year period. Bolivia ceded Antofagasta in 1884, thereby losing its only exit to the sea. Since then, successive Bolivian governments have pressed the Chileans to give them even just a strip of coast for a port. Peru eventually resigned its claim to Arica in exchange for Tacna in 1927.

Nitrate boom and bust

One result of the war with Peru was that Chile now controlled the nitrates deposits of the north. Taxes from the new nitrates mines were

Santiago shopping arcade, late 19th century.

the primary source of income for the Chilean state for many years thereafter.

The man who made the most money out of nitrates, however, was not a Chilean but an Englishman, John Thomas North. During the War of the Pacific, he bought up cheap title deeds to some of the best nitrates deposits. Then, back in England, he raised money on the stock market to work the mines. "Chile saltpeter" caught the British public's imagination. The shares sold like hot cakes, and North became a famous figure. "He's the most important man in England at the moment," wrote one of his competitors, "with the possible exception of [Prime Minister] Gladstone."

However, by the 1890s the nitrate bubble had burst. There was overproduction and, as a result, prices plummeted. Then, early in the 20th century, a cheaper substitute was invented. Attempts to cut production failed, the price went on falling, and the industry declined, until by the 1930s only a handful of offices were still producing. Once-bustling camps and villages such as Humberstone still stand today, now deserted and ghostly witnesses to Chile's past (see page 181).

Power struggle and civil war

The power struggle between president and Congress had been muted during the 1860s and 1870s by a series of mild-mannered presidents and minor reforms. However, the key issue remained – the president's power to elect the Congress that he wanted.

Congress was not much more than a debating society, although it could block effective government. Presidents played off party factions against each other to buy support. By the end of the century the factions, now more like organized parties, were becoming harder to pacify with crumbs of power.

Under President José Manuel Balmaceda, the issue came to a head. Balmaceda faced a factious Congress, made some politically inept appointments, and reacted to criticism by trying to assert his presidential powers. He finally lost his majority in Congress. When he tried to rule without it, and refused to convoke a special session to approve the military budget, the navy rebelled. Congress and the rebels organized an army and defeated government troops at the battles of Placilla and Concón, seizing Santiago. Balmaceda took refuge in the Argentine embassy, where he committed suicide.

DEATH OF A HERO

The story of Arturo Prat's death is in the best naval tradition of heroic defeats. His ship, the *Esmeralda*, was trapped in the Bay of Iquique by the largest battleships in the Peruvian fleet, the *Huascar* and the *Independencia*. Prat's ship resisted enemy fire for two hours, until the *Huascar* rammed it. Sword in hand, Prat leapt into the *Huascar* with a handful of men, and was cut down. The Peruvian commander, Admiral Grau, was gentlemanly enough to send back the captain's sword and a letter he had written to his wife. It earned him equally generous treatment when the Chileans captured the *Huascar* later that year.

The navy rebellion at Valparaíso in 1891.

LA REVOLUTION AU CHILI
(L'attaque de Valparaiso)

An armed guard watches prisoners after the 1973 coup d'etat, which toppled President Salvador Allende.

A CENTURY OF UPHEAVALS

From democracy to military rule and back to democracy – the 20th century saw extraordinary reversals in Chile's political, social, and economic arenas.

The civil war of the 1890s tilted the balance of power in favor of the Congress and against the presidents, who were reduced to refereeing the fights for cabinet posts among the parties. But by this time there were new actors on the political scene. The railroads had made travel easier and the towns were growing, and with them a new cultural and social life. A new middle class was organizing in the recently founded Radical Party. A strong force within it were the freemasons, whose lodges were political debating centers.

A new working class was forming, too. Industry had grown up in the early and mid-century in specific centers – everything from biscuit and pasta factories in Valparaíso that supplied passing ships, to breweries started by German settlers in the south. The new railroads needed workshops, and the growing towns needed textiles, shoes, soap, and furniture. Business boomed, as did the numbers of urban artisans.

It was getting ever harder to scratch a living in the countryside, so many peasants were drawn to the nitrate mines of the north. Once there, they were often trapped, earning low wages paid in tokens that could only be exchanged for goods in the company store. Schools, a police force, and courts were practically non-existent. Alcohol was easier to come by than water in the northern mining camps of the pampas (lowlands).

Demonstration against the military rule of General Augusto Pinochet.

Birth of the trade unions

It was in these harsh conditions that the modern Chilean trade union movement was born, evolving out of the early mutual aid societies. The miners formed the basis for Chile's early political movements, anarchist at first and later socialist. One figure stands out in that early history of working-class organization. Luis Emilio Recabarren, a former print worker, traveled the country as a union organizer. He got an audience among the miners for his political message by publishing newspapers which carried news from other parts of the country. They helped the immigrants isolated in the pampas to keep in touch with their homes, and also provided a means of communication between groups of workers in the cities, the mines, and the countryside, who until then had been isolated from one another. In 1912, Recabarren founded the Chilean Socialist Workers' Party. After the Russian Revolution in 1917, it was the basis of the Chilean Communist Party.

In 1969, the musician Luis Advis composed a famous oratorio based on the tragedy at Santa María de Iquique which he performed and recorded with his folk music group, Quilapayún (see page 78).

Recabarren traveled to Russia, and met Lenin and Trotsky, as well as trade union and political leaders from across the world. He was elected to the Chilean parliament twice during this period, though he was never

what he had to say. Four-and-a-half thousand of them were crammed into the local school, and 1,500 more were in Plaza Manuel Montt. An eyewitness gave a chilling account of what happened as squads of soldiers began to appear in the plaza.

"On the central balcony... stood 30 or so men in the prime of life, quite calm, beneath a great Chilean flag, and surrounded by the flags of other nations. They were the strike committee... All eyes were fixed on them just as all the guns were directed at them. Standing, they received the shots. As though struck by light-

Nitrate workers, Antofagasta.

allowed to take his seat. Although he was a key figure in the early history of the Chilean left, Recabarren's relationship with the Communist Party was always difficult. Political difficulties may well have been the cause of his suicide in 1928.

Desert slaughter

The massacre at Santa María de Iquique, a remote mining town in northern Chile, has come to symbolize the struggle of Chile's mineworkers in the early 1900s. In 1907, the miners went on strike for better pay and conditions. When an envoy was sent from central government to speak with them, the miners and their families gathered in the town center to hear

ning they fell, and the great flag fluttered down over their bodies."

Most thought that was the end of the incident. But, said the witness, "There was a moment of silence as the machine guns were lowered to aim at the schoolyard and the hall, occupied by a compact mass of people who spilled over into the main square... There was a sound like thunder as they fired. Then the gunfire ceased and the foot soldiers went into the school, firing, as men and women fled in all directions."

The army general later reported that there had been 140 victims. The eyewitness quoted talked to doctors and others involved, and estimated the figure at 195 dead and 390 wounded. Others reported many more.

Social inequalities

Experiences like these, combined with the organizing work of Recabarren, laid the foundations of Chile's strong trade union tradition. At one stage, before and during World War I, sections of the ruling classes gave some consideration to the implementation of basic social welfare legislation – the nitrates industry, after all, was booming as a result of the war. But the discovery of artificial nitrates had a powerful impact on Chile, putting a swift end to the boom, and all such proposals were shelved.

Agriculture was stagnant, dominated by huge landed estates whose owners lived either in town or in Europe, and had little interest in raising productivity or modernizing. Import figures for 1907 show the ruling class's priorities: 3.7 million pesos were spent on importing agricultural and industrial machinery, while 6.8 million went on the purchase of French champagne, jewels, silk, and the latest perfume from Paris. As tax revenues from nitrates declined and the foreign debt grew, increasing numbers of ordinary Chileans found themselves without work or the possibility of it, and facing poverty and collapsing living standards.

Power struggles

In conditions of growing social conflict, there often emerge leaders who claim to bridge the conflicting interests of all social classes. In Chile, that "figure above society" was Arturo Alessandri, the son of an Italian immigrant.

Typically, his rhetoric was nationalistic and deliberately vague, enabling him to appeal to different sections of Chilean society at the same time. His election to the presidency in the early 1920s did not give him the power over Congress he aspired to, and in deepening conditions of crisis he turned to the younger and more restless sections of the army.

The result was a military coup in 1928, which gave military caudillo Colonel Carlos Ibáñez del Campo dictatorial powers. His models were Mussolini and Spain's José Primo de Rivera, and he was a fierce critic of the traditional political structures, especially the parties, some of whose leaders he "invited" to leave the country. But he was even more fiercely anti-Communist, and had Communists and union leaders arrested and deported. It was a return to authoritarianism such as Chile had not seen since the years of Diego Portales.

In a sense, the coup brought an end to a system of power which had observed the democratic rules but within a limited framework, in which power was simply exchanged between sections of the ruling classes. Chile has a reputation for a long democratic tradition; yet this was pushed aside in the 1920s, as it would be again in the 1970s, with considerable ease.

Ibáñez set about creating a powerful state sector of the economy, establishing the national airline and a daily government newspaper *La Nación*. This was an attempt to shift resources into new areas of the economy, placing them

Arturo Alessandri, who had two shots at leadership.

under national control and overcoming the resistance of the traditional ruling classes, using the state as an instrument of economic control.

Recession and social unrest

This was a bad time to be increasing state expenditure. With the Wall Street Crash in 1929 and the world recession that followed, the Chilean economy went into a crisis. Nitrate sales had long been declining, and now the expanding copper industry was also hit as the Great Depression squeezed its markets. There was widespread unemployment and social unrest. The government set up an emergency employment program, and printed money to pay for it. Inflation rose, and so did the protests.

Ibáñez was forced to resign. He left for exile in July 1931, but his elected successor was promptly overthrown by a military-civilian junta. In June 1932, a "Socialist Republic" was installed by Colonel Marmaduque Grove. Grove belonged to a group of radical young officers whose aim was to bring about a redistribution of wealth, particularly through land reform, that would set the economy to work again. The new republic lasted only 100 days, however, before Grove was exiled to Easter Island and Arturo Alessandri returned with a draconian program in October 1932. He purged

Salvador Allende.

the army of dissident elements, clamped down on trade unions, banned strikes, and closed down the opposition press.

Although Grove's social experiment had achieved very little, some proposals had reached the statute book: 40 years later, President Salvador Allende would begin to implement some of the changes that Grove had envisaged.

Recovery and reform

A new Chilean government, elected in 1938, offered a program of mild economic and social reform. Headed by a Radical, Pedro Aguirre Cerda, it enjoyed the support of both the Communist and the Socialist parties, but disputes later broke the alliance. Aguirre

> *During World War II, and later in the Korean War, the US government bought copper from US-owned copper companies in Chile at a special low price, which meant a substantial loss of tax revenues for the Chilean state.*

Cerda's elected successor, another radical, quickly outlawed the Communists.

The radicals boosted the state sector of the economy substantially, with a steel industry and a nationwide electrification program. But in the countryside, government intervention had a negative effect. Strict price controls on farm produce meant that the landowners had little incentive to invest and produce more. Public opinion was beginning to sense that farming would simply never take off under ruling-class ownership and that the only hope was to take away the land and give it to those who could produce.

The other conflict that began to loom was the ownership of the copper mines. The main deposits had always been owned and worked by US corporations. Control of such a major source of national wealth was bound to become an issue.

The caudillo returns

By the late 1940s, party infighting and petty corruption had again paved the way for a "strong man." Carlos Ibáñez was returned to power by the electorate in 1952, demanding "a fundamental change of direction," and brandishing a symbolic broom with which he would sweep away politicking and corruption. He had the support of a redoubtable figure, María de la Cruz and her Feminine Party of Chile – women got the vote, finally, in 1949 and promptly strengthened the conservative forces.

Ibáñez had the personal charisma to get himself elected, but no organized support. He tried to get the Constitution reformed to give more power to the presidency, failed, and sat out the rest of his term in political impotence. In 1958, Arturo Alessandri's son, Jorge, succeeded the old general, elected almost entirely on the strength of his father's name. He was Chile's last elected president from the political right for over 50 years.

The Christian Democrats

The center and the left were now grouped in two easily definable camps. In one were the

Socialist and the Communist parties – full-blooded Marxist-Leninists who talked of armed struggle to overthrow "the bourgeois state," but who were actually engaged in building up their electoral strength to win it by peaceful means.

Their rival, proposing very similar reforms in, for example, land ownership and nationalization of the copper mines, was the Christian Democrat Party. It developed in the 1930s out of a movement started by a group of young Catholics from the Conservative Party, initially with vaguely Fascist leanings, who called themselves the Falange Nacional. By the end of the 1950s their ideas had been modified to Christian socialism and they were growing rapidly among both the middle and working classes. They had strong links to the Catholic Church and a comparably strong anti-Communist message. There was not a vast difference between the programs of the two camps.

In the early 1960s when the influence of the Cuban revolution was sweeping through Latin America, the Christian Democrats throughout the region appeared to many people to be the best answer to the Marxist threat. The Chilean Christian Democrat Party was the first of its kind in Latin America to get into government, in 1964, with a good deal of North American financial support. The following year they won a solid majority in Congress, with party leader Eduardo Frei Montalva becoming the first president in Chilean history to have at least theoretical control over both the executive and the legislature.

Success went to their heads, and they boasted that Christian Democrats would govern for the next 30 years (like their Italian counterparts). However, the Frei government made two powerful enemies: the old landowning class, who opposed its attempt at land reform, and the military, who felt underpaid and unappreciated. An army general, Roberto Viaux, led an uprising in 1969 to protest against their conditions.

The old political right, which had helped vote Frei into office, now withdrew to reform itself into a new party, the Nationals. Tensions within Frei's own party led to a split in 1969, and his left-wingers, who felt that the reforms had not gone far enough, went off to join the Marxists.

The Allende years

In 1970 a left-wing coalition known as Popular Unity put forward as their candidate a middle-class doctor turned socialist senator, Salvador Allende. Allende won his fourth attempt at the presidency by a paper-thin margin (36.3 percent). One of the first electoral promises he honored was to give every poor child in Chile a pair of shoes, and to provide free milk in schools.

But the new government faced formidable enemies in the United States. President Nixon's government pumped in approximately US$8 million in covert financing over the next three years to boost the opposition and to help, for example, to keep the anti-Allende publishing group *El Mercurio* in business.

General Augusto Pinochet.

At home the government had some early successes. In 1971, it got all-party support in Congress for the nationalization of the copper mines. But Allende's decision not to pay compensation to the North American owners sparked an official US boycott of non-military aid and credits for Chile. The US government also tried to ban Chilean copper from world markets.

Social discontent

The political tension grew. When Fidel Castro visited Chile in November 1971, upper- and middle-class women held the first "march of the empty saucepans" to demonstrate against food and other shortages. A year later, the shortages were even worse and truck owners went

> *US Secretary of State Henry Kissinger condemned Allende's reform program, saying that he did not see why the US should stand idly by "and let a country go Communist due to the irresponsibility of its own people."*

on strike following a government proposal to create a state transportation system.

Doctors, shopkeepers, and bus owners joined in, and industrialists staged lockouts. Workers in small factories reacted by taking over their

The bombing of the presidential palace, during the 1973 coup.

workplaces. Neighborhood committees set up their own retail networks, bringing goods direct from the factories. By this time the opposition had convinced itself that Allende was out to install a full-blooded Marxist state. The far left of Allende's own Socialist Party encouraged this view – ironically, the Communists were moderators in the unruly coalition, committed to a "peaceful road to socialism."

The tanks roll in

In March 1973, despite the growing chaos, the government won an increased majority (44 percent) in the parliamentary elections. The opposition decided that it could not wait until the next presidential elections, which were scheduled

for 1976. In late August, Congress declared the government unconstitutional. Days later, on the morning of September 11, tanks rolled into the streets of Santiago, and the military took over the radio stations and announced a curfew, calling on President Allende to resign.

Besieged in the presidential palace with only a few advisers, Allende refused to resign. Photographs from the palace show him in a helmet and armed with a machine gun given to him by Fidel Castro, and the popular image remains of Allende fighting to the end. In his final broadcast to the nation, he ordered his supporters not to resist, yet he himself refused an offer of a safe conduct to the airport and exile. Allende's doctor testified that he died by his own hand, alone, in the ruined palace which the air force had bombed.

Pinochet's rise to power

The Chilean coup sent shock waves around the world. For some, the 1970 elections had proved the possibility that social change could occur peacefully, gradually, and via the ballot box. That hope now lay in ruins. Chile's reputation as a haven of democracy in a subcontinent given to resolving its political problems by violent means had now lost its legitimacy – in fact, military intervention had been a feature of 20th-century political life in the country.

Though the coup was led by a junta of the heads of all the armed forces, it was Augusto Pinochet who would emerge over the following two years as its undisputed head. And it was he who was largely responsible for the violence that followed the coup. The military took power quickly, pursuing and detaining all those who had led the trade unions, popular organizations, student groups, and cultural movements most identified with the Allende regime.

The descent into brutality

The particularly brutal murder of the singer Víctor Jara (see page 78) came to symbolize thousands of other, equally violent deaths, as the foreign journalists who were herded into the National Stadium together with Jara and other suspected left-wingers to suffer beatings and torture, would later testify. Thousands of people were murdered, many more were tortured, and hundreds of thousands went into exile to escape persecution.

All opposition activity was banned. The last demonstration in Chile for some 10 years was the funeral of Chile's great poet Pablo Neruda, who died just two weeks after the coup. The 3,000 mourners who marched between ranks of soldiers through the streets of Santiago shouted slogans against the military and carried placards bearing the names of Neruda and Allende. Thereafter there would be no more public expressions of hostility to Pinochet until the 1980s.

Initially, churches provided refuge for those who could not find asylum in foreign embassies. From its formation in 1976, the Vicariate of Solidarity, organized by the Catholic Church, helped the victims of repression to find legal aid and became a focus for protests against the human rights abuses that continued in the years following the coup.

Free-market economics

By 1977 it was clear that Pinochet's regime had its own economic as well as political agenda. The crude anti-Communism of the earlier years now combined with a new economic philosophy of neo-liberalism, or complete openness to the world market – ideas advocated by Milton Friedman and a group of his Chilean acolytes known as the "Chicago boys". Their recipe was free-market policies and the "trickle-down effect" – the theory that wealth created by the private sector would flow down and benefit the workers. These policies were imposed by a military dictatorship in a country without a Congress, without a free press, and with restricted labor organizations – ideal, if abnormal, conditions for such an experiment.

But the regime's economists made some bad mistakes, even on their own terms. In the late 1970s, the Finance Ministry fixed Chile's exchange rate for more than two years, and lifted controls on bank lending. When the peso finally had to be devalued, there was a near-fatal bank crash. As a result, the state had to bail out most of the private banks, but many companies went bankrupt, mortgage repossessions soared, and an economic recession followed, lasting until mid-1980s. The high unemployment and economic hardship of this period were key factors in mounting discontent with the dictatorship.

> The Italian film 'Il Postino' was based on the novel 'Ardiente Paciencia', by Chilean novelist Antonio Skármeta, which depicted the weeks following the 1973 Pinochet coup.

Crisis and disintegration

In 1983 trade unions again began to call strikes, and there was widespread protest as gross domestic product (GDP) collapsed. All political organizations remained illegal, and most of the left-wing groups had been destroyed after the coup. In this new climate of protest, however, they began to reorganize.

The Communist Party had taken a moderate line under Allende, and had argued after 1973 that the coup happened because things had gone too far too fast in the Allende years. The party now turned in a radical direction as

Demonstrators mourn the missing on the day of Pinochet's funeral, 2006.

a new generation of young people joined its ranks. By 1985, the creation of the Manuel Rodríguez Patriotic Front marked a commitment to armed struggle, which culminated in the failed attempt to assassinate Pinochet in 1986.

Thereafter the old enemies came together in a series of agreements to build a joint campaign for a "No" vote in Pinochet's 1988 plebiscite, which was designed to confirm him in power for another eight years at least. In the event, and to the dictator's evident surprise, 54 percent of the Chilean people voted "No."

Elections followed in 1989, amid intense negotiations at a number of levels. The pace and direction of the return to democracy had to be agreed on by businessmen and trade unionists, Christian Democrats, and Communists who supported the "No" campaign – people whose purposes were very different. The hopes for a peaceful transition led the campaign into a series of talks with Pinochet. While he yielded the presidency, and formal authority, it could hardly be said that he relinquished power.

The end of the party for Pinochet

A new constitution written by the dictatorship in 1980 remained largely in force; the judiciary was dominated by Pinochet's appointees; some sena-

A young Socialist Party supporter at a rally in Santiago.

tors would continue to be nominated directly by the armed forces, giving them a controlling voice in parliament; the financial gains Pinochet had made as president would remain untouched. Pinochet stayed on until 1998 as head of the army and, while a commission of investigation would seek the truth about the "disappeared" and the human rights abuses that had occurred under his rule, there would be neither revenge nor restitution.

The memories of the 1973 coup and its aftermath were sufficiently fearsome for the suggestion of renewed military intervention to silence any complaints. Thus it was that Pinochet could display such absolute confidence and certainty when, in March 1998, he retired as commander-in-chief of the army, at the age of 82. He had

already been named *senador vitalicio* – a senator for life – and in this capacity was given effective immunity from prosecution for crimes against human rights committed in Chile during his regime, for which there were some 200 cases pending in the Chilean courts.

It was with the same confidence that he left for Britain in September 1998 for medical treatment. Pinochet's period in power had largely coincided with the governments of Margaret Thatcher in Britain, and her relationship with him had always been cordial and admiring – as had US President Ronald Reagan's with them both.

In the meantime, a series of cases had been brought before courts elsewhere on behalf of the families of Pinochet's non-Chilean victims. Among the cases pending was one brought before a Spanish court by a team of lawyers including Joan Garcés, ex-adviser to Allende. While Pinochet was in London, the Spanish Justice Ministry initiated extradition proceedings with Britain, and he was placed under house arrest. An extraordinary chain of events was set in motion, as the House of Lords in London confirmed by a majority that he had a case to answer under international law, and later overturned their own ruling when it was revealed that one of the Law Lords had links with the human rights group Amnesty International. Meanwhile, journalists and commentators began to revisit the experience of Chile in 1973, while those Chileans still in their countries of exile even after 1990 emerged in demonstrations.

In March 2000, the British Home Secretary agreed to the release of Pinochet on the grounds of ill health, opening the way for his return to Chile. The local courts later removed his immunity from prosecution, but then declared that the former dictator was unfit to stand trial.

Forced to resign his Senate seat and, subsequently, further discredited by the revelation of secret multimillion-dollar bank accounts held abroad in his name and those of family members, the former dictator gradually disappeared from public life and died in December 2006.

An economic example

By the late 1980s, the Chilean economy was well on the way to recovering from the 1982–3 crisis. Exports were growing rapidly, with the development of the forestry, fruit farming and wine industries that were later to play a key role in driving the country's economic growth. There was also a lot of interest from foreign investors and the dictatorship's creation of a private pension (AFP) system to replace the former state pay-as-you-go system had laid the foundations of an active capital market.

Income distribution, however, remained extremely unequal and one of the first challenges of the center-left Concertación coalition, which took office in March 1990 under Christian Democrat Patricio Aylwin (1990–4), was to attempt to narrow the huge gap between the very rich and the very poor, without upsetting Chile's healthy balance of payments and finances. The coalition accepted the main tenets of the macro-

At the same time, Chile began to recover the international integration denied it under Pinochet because of repudiation of his dictatorship's human rights violations. The free trade agreements subsequently signed with the country's main markets, including the United States, the European Union, Japan, and China, played a key role in the sustained growth of its exports.

Road to development

Aylwin was succeeded in 1994 by President Eduardo Frei, a son of the 1960s Christian Democrat president, heading a government of

Pinochet supporters gather outside Santiago Military hospital following his death.

economic policies of the "Chicago boys" and even the Socialist Party admitted that "the market has the main role in assigning resources".

With the grudging assent of the right-wing political parties, the Aylwin government raised corporate and income taxes to finance improvements in health and education. The new government also battled some fairly timid labor reforms through Congress to help improve wages and working conditions, and give the unions more strength to defend their members. These were much more controversial than the tax increases. The business community insisted that low wages for miners, forestry, and industrial workers were crucial if Chile's exports were to remain competitive in world markets.

the same center-left coalition, the Concertación. As well as launching major school and criminal justice reforms, President Frei, a civil engineer by profession, concentrated on projects like improving roads and airports (usually through private concessions), and on privatizing ports and water companies. These reforms vastly improved infrastructure – laying the foundations for the international-standard highways seen in Chile today – and increased productivity as the key to the international competitiveness of the small Chilean economy.

President Ricardo Lagos (2000–6) headed the Concertación's third government. A moderate socialist, he sought to combine economic growth with greater social justice and to extend the benefits of increased prosperity not only to the urban poor, but also to provincial Chile. Despite slower economic growth from 1999 through 2003, owing mainly to the weakness of international export markets, his government introduced unemployment insurance and embarked on a major reform of public and private health services in a bid to increase their efficiency and achieve greater equality of access to care, guaranteeing timely and low-cost attention for a growing number of important illnesses.

A national census, carried out in 2002, revealed a radical improvement in material welfare since the previous census a decade earlier. Ninety-six percent of Chile's homes had access to electricity, up by a fifth on 1992, and 91 percent had drinking water, representing an increase of more than a quarter. Similarly, 82 percent had a refrigerator, as compared with 55 percent in 1992, while 79 percent had a washing machine, as compared with 48 percent a decade earlier.

Impatience for change

By 2006, the poverty rate had, moreover, dropped to less than 14 percent, down from 40 percent in 1990 and per capita income had

Street celebrations in Santiago following news of Pinochet's death.

REGIONAL RELATIONS

Globalization has served Chile's small economy well, not only opening up new export markets for products, but also bringing in the foreign investment that has helped to finance economic growth.

Chafing at their small market, many Chilean companies have expanded to surrounding Latin American countries. This is particularly true of the retail sector but, as land in Chile has become more expensive, its two main forestry companies have also acquired plantations in Argentina, Uruguay and Brazil.

Despite something of a rocky road in the past, Chile's relationship with Argentina today is strong, bound by economic ties and cooperation.

Relations with its northern neighbors are, however, more fragile for reasons that date back to Chile's victory in the 19th century War of the Pacific. Bolivia still views the loss of coast in the war as limiting its economic development and, although a growing number of Chileans consider that it should be returned, general public opinion is still overwhelmingly against such an initiative. Peru, meanwhile, has taken a long-standing dispute about its sea border to the International Court of Justice. Its ruling, which was finally announced in 2014, established a new maritime border between two countries, which granted a large swath of water to Peru in the process.

reached US$8,900, up from just US$2,400 in 1990 (by 2014, it was running at almost US$11,000). However, despite the impact on living standards, the unequal distribution, combined with improvements in education, only fueled social demands. According to a government survey in 2009, the richest tenth of the population received 40.2 percent of national income while, at the same time, seven out of ten university students were the first in their family to go on to higher education.

These pent-up demands came to the fore under President Michelle Bachelet (2006–10), a socialist who headed the Concertación's fourth term and was the country's first woman president. Only a matter of months after she took office, marches and sit-ins organized by secondary schoolchildren in support of better state education mushroomed into the largest show of civil defiance since the Pinochet days. The movement was another symptom of the maturing of Chilean democracy – with no memory of the Pinochet dictatorship, the schoolchildren lacked their parents' fears for its potential fragility.

After initially floundering in face of the protests, Bachelet went on to focus on "social protection" as the theme of her government. The first major overhaul of the private pension (AFP) system left in place by the Pinochet dictatorship increased the role of state in supporting low-income senior citizens and, as it comes into gradual effect, is significantly increasing their (albeit still meager) pensions. Her government's creation of new state childcare centers for poor families also laid the foundations for an increase in women's participation in the labor force which had been very low, even by Latin American standards. In addition, she continued to reduce the housing deficit, with a greater emphasis on the standards of the social housing built by private companies with state support and their future owners' participation in the process.

However, despite these spending increases, her government also maintained the fiscal and macroeconomic discipline that had characterized Chile since 1990. In a key step, it established two offshore sovereign wealth funds into which part of fiscal revenues are paid when the price of copper – a key source of government income – is high. This was one of the complaints of the protesting schoolchildren

who accused the government of "tightfistedness" but it stood Chile in good stead in 2009 when its small, open economy was hit by the international crisis and GDP contracted by 1.7 percent. Mitigating the impact of the crisis, the government used part of these savings to finance a fiscal stimulus plan worth US$4 billion that, relative to GDP, was one of the largest such plans in the world.

The right returns

Bachelet ended her term with record popularity ratings – 84 percent! However, after 20

Michelle Bachelet, Chile's first female leader.

Fees at Chile's top private schools, at around US$700 per month, are over ten times the per-pupil subvention received by state schools in Chile.

years in office, the Concertación was tired, had lost much of its original mystique and was widely perceived as having become complacent in power. The result was the election of President Sebastián Piñera who took office in March 2010 at the head of center-right Alianza por Chile coalition. This was the first time that Chile had elected a president from the right since the 1950s.

A former businessman and billionaire, Piñera comes from the National Renewal Party, the smaller, more centrist party in the government coalition where its partner is the Independent Democratic Union, many of whose older members served under the Pinochet dictatorship. His position, close to the center of the political spectrum, and his family ties with the Christian Democrat Party and his opposition to the dictatorship in its latter days were important factors in his triumph.

The government's first months in power were devoted to grappling with the conse-

Right-wing president Sebastián Piñera.

quences of the February 2010 earthquake and its promised greater efficiency in government was apparent in these early days, particularly in getting public infrastructure back into working order, although it has been less successful in the longer-haul task of rebuilding housing and, according to critics, has failed to take into account the views of the affected families.

Piñera's popularity surged later in 2010 during the two-month operation to rescue 33 miners trapped underground in the San José gold and copper mine near Copiapó in northern Chile. He personally received the miners as, one-by-one, they were hauled to the surface. The success of the operation was certainly a triumph of perseverance against the odds and

of Chilean engineering (although international mining companies operating in Chile also made an important contribution) and was facilitated by Piñera's ability to take quick decisions and lack of aversion to risk.

In 2011, however, his approval ratings sunk to the lowest level of any president since 1990, despite strong economic growth and virtually full employment. Like President Bachelet, he faced protests about the quality of state education, led this time by university students, rather than schoolchildren. As well as standards, their demands extended to the cost of education – monthly university tuition fees start at around a third of the country's average wage – and in response, the government agreed to increase the number of state grants and reduce their cost.

The most important achievements of Piñera's government include creation of 1 million jobs, robust economic growth exceeding 5 percent and the signing of the Alianza del Pacífico (Pacific Alliance) regional integration agreement with Mexico, Colombia and Peru. Towards the end of his term in 2013, Piñera was supported by 50 percent of Chileans. His successor turned out to be again Michelle Bachelet who led the New Majority coalition in the presidential elections. She became the first Chilean politician to be re-elected for the presidential post since 1932. Bachelet assumed power in March 2014, promising to draft the new constitution, introduce free higher education and overhaul tax system. However, despite pushing through the much needed tax and education reforms, her approval ratings sharply dropped to a record 22 percent late in 2015 as a series of corruption scandals, one involving her son and daughter-in-law, marred her government. In an unprecedented move, the president asked all her ministers to resign and then reshuffled the cabinet.

Constitutional reform

On many indicators, Chile is close to becoming a developed country. In the UN Development Programme's 2014 Human Development Index, for example, it ranked in 42nd place, only two places below Argentina. Its progress was also recognized in 2010 when it became the first country in South America to join the Organisation for Economic Co-operation and Development (OECD).

However, in its last mile to development, it still faces a number of important challenge, including not only the inequality of income distribution but also Chileans' mounting demand for a greater say in decisions that affect their lives. This has become more acute because the return of the right to power has heightened the perception that the country is closely controlled by a small political-business elite which is, moreover, supported by its main media.

Complaints focus partly on the 1980 constitution drafted by Pinochet. A reform in 2005 repealed some of its least democratic provisions, including the existence of nine non-elected senators who previously sat alongside the 38 elected senators (four appointed by the armed forces, three by the Supreme Court and two by the president). Increased participation in elections has also been facilitated by a reform, which came into force in early 2012, under which voter regulation became automatic for all those aged 18 and over. In a reversal of the country's previous tradition under which registry had been compulsory, the 1980 constitution made it voluntary and, moreover, requiring a personal visit to an election service office with only limited opening hours in the weeks prior to an election. Partly as a result, only 8.3 million people were registered to vote in the 2009 presidential and congressional elections (out of an estimated population of 16.9 million) as compared to the 7.6 million voters registered for the 1989 elections when the population reached 13.2 million.

The key barrier to increasing the representativeness of democracy is, however, the binominal electoral system, also introduced by the 1980 constitution. Under this system, unique to Chile, each constituency returns two representatives to each house of Congress, with the party or coalition that comes second only needing a third of the vote to take one of the two seats. Designed to force political parties into two broad coalitions and ensure

that neither has a large majority, it guarantees that, in most constituencies, the government and opposition coalitions will each take one of the two seats.

This not only means that the political parties, in practice, "designate" their representatives in Congress, it also makes it very difficult for minority parties outside the two main coalitions to obtain representation. Several attempts to reform the system have been made since 1990 but all failed in the face of the vested interest of incumbent members of Congress in maintaining the existing system. President Piñera him-

Student leader Camilla Vallejo.

self was in favor of reform – like, according to polls, some 77 percent of the population – on the grounds that the system, although useful in providing stability during Chile's transition to democracy, has now served its purpose. However, his proposal to present a reform bill to Congress during 2012 met with a storm of protest from the Independent Democratic Union and is unlikely to prosper. President Bachelet is determined to succeed where her predecessor failed. The first stage of drafting the new constitution (the process might take several years), the so called 'civic education' period, has already begun. It will be followed by public consultations and, eventually, a referendum on the proposed projects.

> Since Argentina ceased to export natural gas, Chile has faced a tight energy supply that has been compounded by public opposition to new coal plants and hydroelectric dams. Electricity prices are among the highest in Latin America.

Chess players in Santiago's main square.

THE CHILEANS

In a land where the "melting pot" has well and truly melted, social hierarchies are, however, still firmly in place. But there are fascinating contradictions as rapid change takes place.

For centuries lonely travelers have made brief visits to Chile that have stretched into lifetimes. Maybe that's because the Chileans are among the most contradictory and intriguing of Latin America's peoples. They are inherently careful and cautious – quite unlike their more effusive and spontaneous Argentine neighbors. Yet it was Chile that, in 1970, elected the socialist government of Salvador Allende, beguiled by its promise of radical economic and social change, an experiment that ended in the tragedy of the 1973 military coup.

> 88 percent of the Chilean population lives in cities and 40 percent of the total population is to be found in Greater Santiago.

And the contradictions have continued. Chile is – as Isabel Allende points out in her nostalgic autobiographical book *Mi País Inventado* (My Invented Country) – the end of the line and, in terms of geographic distance, about as far away as you can get from the world's main consumer markets. Yet, over the last 20 years, it has used international trade and integration to build one of Latin America's most successful economies.

Chileans take great pride in this achievement and in their modern economy, yet – another contradiction – the country remains in some ways an island of social conservatism. Until 2004, it was the only country in the western hemisphere not to have a divorce law and a bill submitted by President Bachelet in 2015 to decriminalize abortion in cases where the mother's life is at risk, where the fetus will not survive pregnancy, or in the case of rape, has yet to be approved by the Senate.

Street art.

For most of its history, Chile was cut off from the rest of the world by the Andes mountains in the east, the Atacama Desert in the north, the Pacific Ocean on the west, and the Strait of Magellan and Antarctica in the south. Even during its period as a Spanish colony, Chile was on the periphery, an isolated outpost that looked towards the empire's center of operations in Peru.

Isabel Allende, in fact, describes her home country as an island. And that is key to understanding many aspects of the national character, including a fierce pride in all things Chilean. She advises foreign visitors "not to question the wonders they will hear about the country, its wine, and its women, because the foreigner is not allowed to criticize; for that, there are 17 million Chileans, who do it all the time."

Chile's roots

Chileans are primarily mestizo, the product of unions between the country's original peoples, especially the Mapuches of the south, and the Spanish colonizers. Chileans' great admiration for patriotic symbols, like the Spanish conquistadors and the great Mapuche guerilla fighters, is the source of another striking contradiction. They idolize both the conquerors and the natives who resisted them.

In the wealthy areas of Santiago and luxury vacation spots in southern Chile, shopping centers and resorts often have names of native origin. However, the native peoples themselves mostly live in poverty, whether it be in traditional rural communities or in the cities to which many have migrated. In addition, urban Chileans know surprisingly little about the country's indigenous cultures. In fact, they are likely to tell you they were "poor", especially by comparison with the Inca and Aztec cultures, and not really worthy of interest.

Many families have two or three children.

INSIDE INFORMATION

Perhaps the best source of behind-the-polite-smile information about Chileans are Chilean writers. Chile may be a small country, but when it comes to literature it's a giant. Two Nobel prize-winning poets, Gabriela Mistral and Pablo Neruda, have plumbed Chileans' contradictions and aspirations through their work, which is widely available in English translation. Chilean novelists have participated in the "boom" in Latin American literature. José Donoso, Jorge Edwards and, more recently, Ariel Dorfman, Isabel Allende and Roberto Bolaño have written books with universal appeal, enhanced in many cases by prolonged experience abroad.

Physical beauty in Chile, as in many other Latin American countries, is also associated with being tall, thin, and fair. By contrast, the Mapuches are brown-skinned with strikingly black hair, and tend to be short and stocky. Skin color in Chile is, in fact, synonymous with class – the whiter your skin, the higher your class.

There are still many Aymara and other native communities high up in the northern Andes or on the border with Bolivia, while many Mapuches (see page 71) continue to live around the southern city of Temuco. Reduced to small patches of land, generally of poor quality, they suffer from many of the ills of native peoples throughout the Americas. Those who haven't moved to the cities usually live in large extended families, cultivating wheat, corn, potatoes, and other vegetables.

Others combine farming with traditional handicrafts: woven ponchos, woodcarvings, handmade ceramic pots, and baskets can make a significant contribution to family economies, along, increasingly, with rural tourism projects.

New arrivals

A mixed bag of surnames bears testimony to the variety of settlers who followed the Spanish to Chile and eventually formed small foreign enclaves within the larger population. Ethnic

cakes, and pastries. Many small farmhouses offer *küchen* to passers-by.

British immigrants were also important in the nitrates industry and the construction of railroads, as well as in shipping and banking, particularly in the port of Valparaíso. Chileans have a great admiration for the British and like to call themselves the "English of South America" in reference to their phlegmatic temperament and lack of "tropical" excitability.

Although immigrants from France were smaller in number, French culture had a profound influence on the development of the

Market traders.

groups include the British, Germans, immigrants from the former Yugoslavia, and, more recently, the Spanish (exiled during the Civil War), the Arabs, the Italians, and the Jews.

The German "colony" played an important role, particularly in southern Chile (see page 218). In 1853, German settlers founded the city of Puerto Montt on the shores of the Gulf of Reloncaví and, by 1860, more than 3,000 immigrants had built homes along Lago Llanquihue, and in Osorno, Río Bueno, La Unión, and as far north as Valdivia. By 1900, 30,000 German colonists had cleared the native forests, planted crops and created small towns. Today, German surnames are still common, as is the language, and the area is famous for its sausages,

newly-independent Chilean republic in the 19th century. Both the government and wealthy families hired French architects whose work is still ubiquitous in Santiago.

A small country

When one lives in Chile, one quickly realizes that in spite of the huge distances from north to south, it's a small country as far as the people are concerned. The same surnames crop up again and again in Chilean history – even today, a person's surname can help or hinder a career.

Chilean politics are rife with influential families wielding power publicly or behind the scenes, generation after generation. Even the democratic Congress, which was elected in

December 1989 after 16 years of military rule, was full of the brothers, sisters, sons, and daughters of past and present leaders.

And although Santiago has a population of over 6 million, it's common to bump into friends and acquaintances, even if you haven't been there very long. That is partly because the people you'll meet tend to frequent just a few areas of the city, mainly in the Las Condes and Providencia districts.

Newspapers also reinforce the small-town feeling. *El Mercurio*, the grande dame of the Chilean press, has a large section of social pages – at weekends, they take up more space than international news – in which the same faces appear time and time again in events that range from the opening of art exhibitions to embassy cocktail parties.

That is also a reflection of the closely knit nature of the Chilean political, business, and intellectual elite. Most of its members went to the same private schools and to the same universities, live in the same neighborhoods, and even take holidays in the same places.

If you're in Santiago long enough, you'll soon realize that the city is unusually segre-

Recreation time.

FREE TRADE AGREEMENTS

Chile is regarded as one of South America's most open economies. The 22 Free Trade Agreements (FTAs) that it has signed with a total of 59 countries, including the USA, Canada, the European Union, China, Japan and South Korea, have not only helped to diversify the country's export markets but have also – particularly in the case of its FTA with China which came into force in 2006 – facilitated the access of the new middle class to consumer goods, ranging from electronics to clothing. The OECD, for example, estimates that the price of clothing fell by 40 percent between 2009 and 2013, thanks mainly to the FTA with China.

gated. There are virtually no areas in which different classes live side by side, and a person's home address is an almost fail-safe guide to social extraction. The moneyed elite, who have gradually moved out towards the mountains, now tend to live in La Dehesa or Vitacura, while Las Condes and Providencia are upper-middle-class territory, and nearby La Reina and Ñuñoa are popular with less conventional but successful professionals. The west of the city and the densely populated southern outskirts are where most of the working class lives.

Over the last 20 years, increasing prosperity has gone a long way to reduce poverty, although it has made little dent on the country's extremely unequal income distribution. In

According to the World Health Organization, life expectancy in Chile reaches 80.1 years as compared to 75.4 years in Mexico, 76.3 years in Argentina, and 75.2 years in Brazil.

2013, the poverty rate was running at 14.4 percent, down from 38.6 percent in 1990. Shantytowns, once common on the periphery of large towns and cities, have gradually been eradicated and replaced by state-subsidized housing, often taking the form of the large and bleak apart-

estimates that, by 2015, the middle-class households in Chile accounted for 47 percent of the total population. In Santiago, the new middle class lives in suburbs like La Florida in the south of the city and, for a slightly lower income level, Maipú in the southwest. All these areas have modern shopping malls and the same supermarkets as in the *barrio alto*, although the range of goods they carry is different.

This new middle class not only attaches great importance to the material trappings of prosperity but also makes important economic sacrifices for its children's education. This helps to

Family life is important in Chilean society.

ment blocks that you'll see alongside any of the main roads into the city. These are cramped affairs but do, at least, have all the basic services.

A new middle class

Over the past two decades, per capita income in Chile more than trebled in purchasing-power-parity terms, according to the International Monetary Fund (IMF), and this is reflected in the emergence of a new middle class. A phenomenon also common to other Latin American countries, this trend has been boosted by increasing access to consumer finance, provided by banks or, more usually in lower-income segments by department stores.

The AIM (Asociación de Investigadores de Mercado), a Chilean market research organization,

explain why the cost of higher education and student loans were an important rallying call for the student protests of 2011 (see page 55).

Women and family

Another factor in the development of this new middle class has been the increasing incorporation of women into the labor force. Helped by the example of President Michelle Bachelet, the country's first woman president, and, more practically, by her government's creation of free childcare centers for low-income families, more women have started to go out to work, providing the second income that, for poor families, is the fastest leg up. According to the National Statistics Institute (INE), women's participation in the workforce reached 48.3 percent at the end of 2014, up from 38.8 percent eight years earlier.

Few women, however, reach positions of power, either in politics or business. For example, only some 14 percent of members of the Chilean Congress are women as compared to 38 percent in Argentina and 22 percent in Peru. Moreover, women who work in the private sector earn an estimated fifth less than men.

With live-in domestic service now increasingly scarce, men tend to share more in childcare and housework. Indeed, under a recent extension of paid maternity leave, they can take part of the six months (although few do for fear of their employer's disapproval). However, as working women often complain, men still tend to see participation in household tasks as "help" for their wife or partner, rather than a natural part of their responsibilities, and, below the politically-correct surface, there is still plenty of ingrained *machismo* among women as well as men.

The standard nuclear family that predominated in Chile until ten or 15 years ago has diversified. The average marriage age has increased significantly and couples often live together, something that was unheard of and would have

Couples tend to marry later in modern Chile.

MEATY GATHERINGS

One of the most cherished social events among all age groups is the *asado* – a huge steak or roast cooked over hot coals, not to be compared with the rather squalid (at least to Chileans' eyes) hamburgers and hot dogs that you might find at North American or Australian barbecues. This ceremony usually occurs either in someone's backyard or in a park. While the men compare recipes and worry about how the meat is shaping up, the women prepare huge tomato, potato, and other salads. Everyone drinks abundant quantities of red wine, and the meal ends with sweet desserts or whatever fruit is in season (or both).

been considered shameful as recently as the 1990s. For different reasons, including choice as well as separation, many households are also single-parent, usually with a woman as head of the household.

A bill passed in 2015 recognizing civil unions for same-sex couples provides gay couples with the same legal protection as heterosexual married couples, with the exception of adoption rights and the title of marriage.

The Catholic Church

According to a poll conducted in 2015 by the Pontifical Catholic University of Chile and Adimark, 59 percent of Chileans identify themselves as Roman Catholics but a much smaller number attend Mass regularly and the influence of the exceptionally conservative Church has been greatly undermined in recent years by a number of sexual abuse scandals and, more importantly, evidence of a deliberate cover-up by the Church hierarchy and failure to prevent known offenders' access to children and young people.

However, the Opus Dei and the Legionaries of Christ, two bastions of conservatism within the Catholic Church, remain strong and active in Chile. They control private schools and universities and have a great deal of influence in the business community. The legacy of the

In 2013, the average age for marrying in Chile reached 35 years for men and 32 years for women, up from the 27.7 years for men and 24.6 years for women in 2002.

Work ethic

Chile has worked hard for its economic success, and expatriate businesspeople posted to Chile are often surprised by the long hours put in by their Chilean staff. Schools start at eight in the morning, so many parents, after dropping their

Aymara goatherd.

Church's influence is also apparent in the fact that abortion remains illegal, although opinion polls indicate that a majority of Chileans favor its legalization when a mother's life is in danger and in cases of rape. Individual politicians from across the political spectrum have advocated a change in the law but, so far, no political party has been willing to spearhead reform.

The evangelical churches that have also experienced rapid growth in other Latin American countries, particularly Brazil, have become strong in Chile, particularly among lower-income segments of the population. Although providing an important support network for problems such as alcoholism, they also, however, tend to advocate very conservative social attitudes.

children off, are in the office by half past eight and usually stay there until at least seven. Nor do Chileans indulge in long lunches – unless business is being discussed, an hour is the norm.

Overseas executives frequently complain that they find it embarrassingly difficult to head for home at half past five, or whatever is their usual time. Long hours also help to explain why few women reach positions of power in the private sector.

Chileans are often very late if invited to dinner at someone else's house, but for business meetings, they are rarely more than 10 minutes behind schedule. And, in one of the keys to Chile's success in attracting foreign investment, they are reliable. Their word is their bond, and corruption, although it certainly exists, is scarce by Latin American and even international standards. In many neighboring countries, taxi drivers will happily tell you the amount of the bribe expected for different traffic offenses; in Chile, an attempt to bribe a policeman is more likely to get you arrested.

Chile's economic growth has attracted immigrants from neighboring countries. Argentines tend to be found mostly in office jobs while Peruvians, although many have successfully set up their own restaurants, tend to have lower-paid jobs in the construction industry in the case of men or, in the case of women, as live-in maids. Many live

Artisan, Puerto Varas.

in very poor conditions in order to save as much as possible to send to families back home.

Folk traditions

Scratch any older Chilean, no matter how urban or sophisticated in appearance, and you'll find someone superstitious and sentimental about the country's folklore. September is the best month for observing Chile's folk traditions, as Chileans dust off their ponchos and handkerchiefs and get ready to celebrate Independence Day on September 18.

For children, the traditional pastime is kite flying; for adults, it's lots of *chicha* (fermented grape juice) and *empanadas* (savory turnovers); and for just about everybody it means at least one visit to the *fondas*, eucalyptus-roofed shelters that

suddenly crowd empty lots, turning them into improvised dance halls.

The *cueca* is Chile's official national dance, and September is also the best time to catch a glimpse of everyone from the national president down, strutting their stuff and doing some serious flirting as men, women, and children stomp the floor in the traditional one-two rhythm, twirl their handkerchiefs, and generally go after each other in what is supposed to be a stylized imitation of mating chickens. You'll also see *cumbias, corridas,* rock, and jive, since cultural influences from more northerly countries are also strong.

Each of Chile's various regions has its own version of the *cueca,* and there's also a kind of class division between the *cueca patronal* (boss's *cueca*), characterized by the women's elegant dresses and men's colorful ponchos and shiny black boots with silver spurs, and the *cueca campesina* (peasant's cueca), whose performers are far more simply dressed and go barefoot. The dance's formal gestures and rather strict stereotyping between the aggressive, strutting male and the shy, fluttery female have changed over the years, and young people's versions of the dance often challenge more traditional versions. Chile's folk traditions are more than skin deep. They include a wide variety of folk music, which varies from the Andean music of the *altiplano* (high plain) prevalent in the north, to the music of Chiloé towards the south, and various ethnic songs and dances, particularly of Yugoslavian origin, around Punta Arenas.

Payadores are grassroots poets and musicians, who engage each other in witty, passionate poetic duels whenever andwherever they meet.

Folk traditions include stories about each region's original inhabitants, be they human, ghostly, godly, mythical, or immortal. Popular beliefs have blended with grassroots medical knowledge to create different kinds of faith healers. In rural areas, *mal de ojo* (evil eye) is still considered a common cause of stomach and other health problems, and the person most equipped to cure it is still the *curandera*, whose knowledge of herbal – and magical – medicine works more frequently than skeptics might care to believe.

Maybe it's not surprising that in a country of such intense geological activity, earthquakes are central to Chileans' mentality. Popular wisdom has it that every (democratic) government in Chile gets welcomed into office by an earthquake – an act of God which was conspicuously absent after the 1973 military coup.

THE MAPUCHES

They were unconquered until the late 19th century. But now the native people of the Araucanía struggle to maintain their culture in cities as well as in their homelands.

In a survey carried out by the Chilean government in 2009, 1,188,340 people, equivalent to 6.9 percent of the country's population, indicated that they belonged to one of the country's nine surviving indigenous peoples. Of these, by far the largest are the Mapuches. According to the 2002 National Census, they numbered just over 600,000 but estimates by NGOs suggest a number closer to 800,000.

Music always accompanies Mapuche rituals, particularly percussion instruments like the kultrun, a ceremonial drum, and wind instruments like the trutruca, which is made of type of bamboo.

Most Mapuches still live in the Araucanía Region of southern Chile, which accounts for a quarter of the country's total indigenous population, but many have migrated to the cities, particularly Santiago, where they often form tight-knit communities, notably in the La Pintana district of southern Santiago.

Although much progress has been achieved in recent years in providing the Mapuche communities of the south with basic services and, for example, access to health care, poverty remains rife. Indeed, the Araucanía Region – where 30 percent of the population is indigenous – is still the poorest in Chile, with a poverty rate of 27.9 percent in 2013 as compared to a national average of 14.4 percent.

Mapuche communities try to keep their traditional customs alive and, in some areas, the national health service offers Mapuche remedies. However, it appears that knowledge of the Mapuche language is declining, with

Mapuche women.

77.3 percent of Chile's indigenous inhabitants unable to speak or understand their language, according to the 2009 survey.

Mapuche cosmology

Before the arrival of the Spanish conquistadors, the Mapuches, or "people of the earth," were used to living from the earth's fruits and from hunting. They lived in scattered settlements from the Aconcagua Valley in the north to as far south as Chiloé. They also inhabited most of what is now Argentine Patagonia.

In their myriad mythologies, they believe in a perfect balance between the positive and negative forces present in every act. Ngenechen, the positive god, represents the forces of life, creation, and love. His counterpart is Wekufu, god of death and destruction. It is in these terms that the Mapuches understand the meeting of European and American cultures 500 years ago.

From their point of view, the arrival of the Spaniards meant the destruction of the delicate balance of forces which had until then sustained their culture, their way of life, their language, their habitat, and their religion. Wekufu's spirit threw its mantle over the world's boundaries, leaving Ngenechen unable to keep up his end of the balance.

Mapuche chiefs at a meeting in Lumaco, Araucania.

The Spanish passion for gold overwhelmed the "love of God" or "loyalty to the Crown" that they used as excuses to commit abuses against indigenous peoples. The Mapuches, living in the continent's extreme south, were not exempt from this treatment. But their reaction was a long and often successful resistance to the theft of their lands and the violation of their traditions.

Freedom-lovers

During the first 100 years of war between the Mapuches and the Spanish, the northern limit of their territories was reduced to the River Biobío, a border that remained for more than 300 years. The cross and the sword could not defeat the lances of the naked-chested Mapuches, and the

> *When the Conquest started, the Mapuches believed the Spanish attacker and his horse were one creature, unbeatable, a god which had come to conquer them.*

Spanish Crown was finally forced to negotiate. It recognized borders and established trade and transport agreements between the territories.

Many historians who defend the Spanish cause speak of the Mapuches as belonging to a "military race" or being a "fierce people." Nevertheless, the testimony of friars who accompanied the Conquest indicates that the Mapuches were peaceful and friendly. It became convenient for pro-Spanish historians to paint the Mapuches as "ferocious warriors" in order to justify their side's defeat. The reasons for the long struggle are to be found not so much in their "warrior virtues" as in a profound dignity and immense love for their land and their freedom.

Their devotion to their own cultural values led the Mapuches to acts of great heroism and impassioned resistance. They quickly learned about their enemy and its weapons, and developed the tactics necessary to defend themselves.

Perhaps the most striking reason for the Spaniards' inability to conquer the Mapuches was that, unlike the Incas and Aztecs, they had no central authority. Their political and economic organization was based on the family. The family head was the polygamous *cacique* (pronounced "ka-see-kay"), or *lonko*. He could have as many as 10 wives, forming an extended family group of up to 500 members.

The *lonko* developed his prestige through the accumulation of wealth and the wise advice that he gave to youths inclined to fight among themselves. Faced with a warlike situation, the Mapuches chose a *toqui* as their leader, and their peacetime authority was the *ulmen*. Both were chosen for their gifts for public speaking and their decision-making abilities.

Alliances between *caciques* were established to develop economic activities like the gathering in of breeding stock, hunting, and fruit collection, and the benefits were shared among the participating members.

This loose organization meant that the Spanish could not seize control through capture of a single political leader. The Mapuches didn't have villages to harass and destroy. While they weren't nomads in the strict sense of the term, they lived in *rucas* or huts, which they moved from place to place according to need.

Lautaro the liberator

When the Spanish began their advance they were fast and efficient, but when the Mapuches realized that these horseback attackers were only human they began to develop unique military strategies to defend their land. Lautaro, a Mapuche who was barely 20 years old, escaped from the Spanish camps where his intelligence had caused him to be trained as the page of the conquistador Pedro

infantry" where each rider also carried along a foot soldier holding onto the horse's tail. This allowed rapid movement of large parties of fighters. The second and more devastating tactic was the constant replacement of squadrons: each group fought ferociously for 15 to 20 minutes before being replaced. The Spanish soldiers labored under their heavy armor, and finally yielded to the waves of native fighters who, fresh and rested, gave them no respite.

These tactics led to enormous victories for Lautaro, who not only killed Pedro de Valdivia himself, but also secured for his people all the

Playing a traditional wooden whistle.

When the Spanish arrived in Chile, the Mapuches did not have a writing system and controversy still exists today as to the alphabet for mapudungun, their language.

de Valdivia. He was chosen as *toqui*, leader of the *caciques*, to lead the war against the invaders.

Lautaro – who now knew the language, weapons, tactics, and weaknesses of the enemy – taught his warriors to ride. They became better horsemen than the Spaniards. He also developed two combat tactics which today are recognized as the beginning of guerrilla warfare in this continent. The first was "mounted

southern territories, burning and destroying the Spanish forts until, after four years of victorious campaigns, he reached the gates of Santiago.

During Lautaro's northward push, many Yanaconas, another indigenous people who had until then formed part of the Spanish troops, joined Lautaro's forces. One of these betrayed Lautaro, killing him while he rested in his tent the night before the great assault on the capital. This was a terrible blow to the Mapuches, who decided to retreat southward, where they continued to defend "their" border for 300 years.

The last uprising

The last general uprising of Chile's indigenous peoples took place in 1881. This time it was

> *Lorenzo Colimán, a 19th-century Mapuche lonko, lamented his people's loss of freedom: "What we've achieved with the civilization they say they have given us is to live squeezed together like wheat in a sack."*

directed against what was now the Chilean Republic, which was doing everything possible to take over the southern lands. Mapuche *huerquenes*, messengers specially educated for eloquence and good memories, began to travel

Mapuche boy helps out on a farm near Temuco.

through mountains and valleys, bearing knotted red cords around their wrists. Every day they undid one knot. When these were all gone, the *caciques* simultaneously attacked the forts, towns, and missions of the Chileans – an impossible attempt given the superiority of the army's weaponry, but another example of the Mapuches' dedication to their independence and freedom. The army, fresh from its victories in a war against Peru and Bolivia, suffocated the bloody rebellion.

Integration and adaptation

Throughout the 1880s, the indigenous territories shrank. A decree made Araucanía (the Mapuche territory) property of the state, and a colonization process began in which the native people

received very little for their land. Along with this, a process of cultural transformation began. It was a time of fear, disease, hunger, and loss of identity, as the Mapuches became an ethnic minority within Chilean society.

Efforts to integrate the Mapuches into Chilean society were encouraged by missionaries. Education and evangelization would, according to this view, "absorb" the Mapuche culture. Many, however, rejected integration and, instead, sought to recover their stolen lands and culture. The first attempts in the 1920s were led by Manuel Aburto Manquilef, a descendant of *caciques*, who mobilized huge numbers of Mapuches in search of their own identity. This movement insisted that the central problem was the seizure of the Mapuche lands. Its activists revived the rites and traditions of the *malones* (meetings to listen to dreams and predict the future) and *machitunes* (collective prayers to the gods). It organized many congresses and made the native voice heard in Santiago.

One of the great merits of this group was its ability to find allies within other social movements of the period. Its leaders had the vision to recognize that the problem wasn't simply between Mapuches and *huincas* (the name that the Mapuches gave to the Spanish invader), but rather between the wealthy and the poor. This led to the Mapuches' own struggle being more generally recognized as one of the social problems of the 1930s. In this period, the Workers' Federation of Chile (FOCH) became the Mapuches' mouthpiece in Santiago, helping them to participate in mainstream politics through the Democratic Party and eventually through elected representatives in the House of Deputies.

> *According to the latest national census in 2002, the Aymaras of northern Chile are the country's second largest indigenous people, followed by the Atacameños.*

Recent history

The 1973–90 Pinochet dictatorship was another period of fear for the Mapuches. Their organizations were heavily repressed, and many native people were arrested and "disappeared." Moreover, the dictatorship introduced an Indian Law that allowed the Mapuches to split their collectively held land into small farms with individual titles. With no access to credit or technology, many were forced to sell their land to wealthy landowners.

A new Indian Peoples Law was passed in 1993 by the recently restored democratic government, but failed to live up to the expectations of the Mapuches who, in the 1990s, found a new enemy – the expanding forestry industry. As well as occupying land claimed by Mapuche communities, the industry has deprived them of access to the woods that are their traditional source of fuel, medicinal plants, and food.

Another focus of protest in the 1990s was the construction of the vast Ralco hydroelectric

for planting trees for which they lack capital and would, in any case, have to wait at least 20 years to generate income by harvesting the trees.

The resulting frustration is reflected in the violence that flares up sporadically in the Araucanía, directed principally against forestry companies and their installations but also against neighboring farms owned by *huincas*. In turn, the Mapuches complain of undue use of police force in raids on their communities.

Moreover, the intensely proud Mapuches – who consider themselves the "true Chileans" – resent their lack of political status. Chile is the only

Mapuche demonstration in Santiago.

dam on the upper reaches of the River Biobío. The reservoir, which began to be filled in mid-2004, flooded land belonging to some of the last remaining communities of Pehuenches, a branch of the Mapuches.

The border lands today

For the last 20 years, the Chilean government has gradually been returning land to Mapuche communities but, for some, it will never be enough. More extreme radical organizations want to recover all the Mapuches' ancestral homeland south of the Biobío river and, even for those communities that have received land, the outcome has often been disappointing. Some of the land is, for example, suitable only

Latin American country that does not afford its indigenous minorities constitutional recognition, and no Mapuches – or, indeed, members of other ethnic groups – sit in Congress. Their lack of say, even at local government level, in decisions that affect their lives also means that too many well-intentioned government initiatives fail to achieve their objective. Greater consultation would certainly help but, just as the Spanish invaders found to their cost, modern Chilean governments complain that the Mapuches' multiplicity of leaders and organizations makes this difficult. In recent years, the so-called Mapuche conflict has intensified with hunger strikes in prisons, and land occupations and the burning down of private property in Araucanía.

A CULTURAL RENAISSANCE

After contributing to the downfall of the
Pinochet dictatorship, the arts in Chile have
blossomed and diversified under democracy.

Chileans will often tell you that their country's arts scene is not a patch on neighboring Argentina and there is some truth in that – movies, for instance, tend to arrive later in Santiago than in Buenos Aires. Outside Santiago, live performances are rare except in summer when, for example, the little town of Frutillar on Lago Llanquihue in the Lake District holds its famous classical music festival. But Chile's capital city is bursting with theater and music of all types and regularly receives visits from major international artists, although ticket prices can be very high.

Parra family

One of Chile's most emblematic artists is Violeta Parra whose life was portrayed in the internationally successful movie, *Violeta Se Fue a Los Cielos* (Violeta Went to Heaven), by local director Andrés Wood. The moving simplicity of her voice, accompanied by a lone guitar, echoes through the movie, bearing testimony to the inspiration of a woman who sang to life, but succumbed to death. Her song *Gracias a la Vida* (Thanks to Life) – composed, ironically, after one of her suicide attempts – is one of Latin America's best-loved songs.

Violeta was born in Chillán in the south of Chile in 1917. Her family was poor, but artistically prolific. It produced not only Violeta, but also her brother Nicanor (Chile's "anti-poet" and a many-time Nobel candidate) and Roberto, the creator of a new style of *cueca* (Chile's national dance) and the author of *La Negra Ester* (Black Esther), the play seen by the largest number of people ever in Chile's history.

Francisca Gavilán as Violeta Parra in 'Violeta Went to Heaven'.

A tragic star

Violeta received little recognition during her lifetime. Her work was characterized both by the incomprehension with which it was met, and by the irrepressible creativity seen both in her music and her tapestries, which have been exhibited in the Louvre in Paris. The appreciation of her work outside Chile led Violeta to settle in France for two years, a period during which she toured Europe. But, in 1965, she returned to Chile where, apparently overwhelmed by frustration, isolation, and an ill-fated love affair, she committed suicide in 1967.

But her legacy and quest to rediscover Chile's musical roots, which she revitalized with lyrics protesting against social injustice, lived on. She was followed by a generation of singer-composers, led by Víctor Jara, who continued her work and whose influence is still very present in the music of Chile today.

Amid the social upheaval of the 1960s, Jara and other artists, including Ángel and Isabel Parra (children of Violeta), Patricio Manns, and the Inti-Illimani and Quilapayún groups, gave birth to a new type of music: *La Nueva Canción Chilena* (Chilean New Song).

Their rebellious songs were in stark contrast to the romantic melodies of the radio singers who then dominated popular music in Chile, imitating the ballads of their American contemporaries. This harsher music was not only a perfect soundtrack for the changes taking place in Chile in the early 1970s, but also became the official music of President Salvador Allende's Popular Unity government. So much was this the case that one of Víctor Jara's songs was used each day to start the transmissions of the state television channel.

The 1970s saw the emergence of a new strand of the New Song movement when a younger generation took the elements and instruments

A guitarist pays tribute to Víctor Jara on the anniversary of the military coup.

GRACIAS A LA VIDA

Gracias a la vida, que me ha dado tanto
Me dio dos luceros, que cuando los abro
Perfecto distingo, lo negro del blanco
Y en el alto cielo, su fondo estrellado
Y en las multitudes, la mujer que amo.
(English Translation)
Thanks to life, which has given me so much
It has given me two eyes, which, when I
open them
I can clearly distinguish black from white
And in the infinite sky, its starry depths
And in the crowds of people, the woman I love.
by Violeta Parra

of Latin American folklore and merged them with rock music. The result was revolutionary, and *Todos Juntos* (Together), sung by Los Jaivas, became a symbol to an entire generation. Together with Los Blops and Congreso, they formed a generation whose careers in Chile were cut short by the military coup of September 11, 1973.

After the 1973 coup

The seizure of power by the armed forces meant the death or exile of the icons of the New Song movement. Inti-Illimani and Quilapayún were performing in Europe at the time of the coup, but Víctor Jara was immediately arrested, brutally tortured, and shot in the Estadio Chile (Chile Stadium), now known as Estadio Víctor Jara. Ángel Parra also suffered at the hands of the dictatorship, first as a prisoner in the National Stadium and then in the Chacabuco concentration camp. Los Jaivas emigrated to Argentina and, later, France, where they were joined by Quilapayún and Illapu, a group that had become famous thanks to their song *Candombe para José* (Candombe for José).

This exile had unanticipated consequences for Chilean music. Awakening the sympathy of the countries where they were granted asylum, these groups sang songs of protest against General Augusto Pinochet to an international audience. As a result Inti-Illimani, for example, sold more than a million records in Italy alone. But while their music was acclaimed abroad, cultural repression reigned in Chile as the military attempted to stamp out any hint of ideological opposition. Records made during the Popular Unity government were banned.

However, the growing discontent felt by many Chileans found an echo in the work of exiled artists, which was smuggled into the country, and the New Song movement was kept alive as a vehicle for expressing – between the lines – opposition to the dictatorship. Groups such as Schwenke y Nilo, Huara, and Sol y Lluvia peppered their songs with contemporary references that escaped the military's grasp.

In the 1980s, in France, Los Jaivas launched *Las Alturas de Machu Picchu* (The Heights of Machu Picchu), a conceptual album that set to music the words of Chilean poet Pablo Neruda. The acclaim with which this album was received was such that the group was allowed to return to Chile to perform at massively attended concerts.

It was at this time that Los Prisioneros, from San Miguel, a working-class district of Santiago, made its appearance. Mixing punk, rock, and techno music with the angry lyrics of its vocalist, Jorge González, the trio was a phenomenon in its own right. Despite the efforts of the dictatorship, the band became a reference point for an entire generation as cassettes were passed from hand to hand. Los Prisioneros also opened the way for many new bands, which took their place in the late 1980s, when Los Prisioneros broke up.

The end of the most brutal period of the dictatorship gradually permitted the return of exiled musicians, who became influential in the protest movement that, in 1988, culminated in the "No" vote against General Pinochet (see page 51).

Into a new era

The return of democracy brought with it a new generation of musicians. Los Tres, a band from Concepción in southern Chile, led by Álvaro Henríquez and including a grandson of Violeta, was in the forefront of this generation. Mixing

Víctor Jara.

the rockabilly of Chuck Berry with the lyrics of Roberto Parra, Los Tres gave new popularity to the *cueca*, freeing it from the stigma it had acquired when harnessed to the dictatorship's efforts to foster patriotic support. The band broke up in 2000 but staged a return in early 2007, with a series of mass concerts and a new album, and still continues to play.

By dint of combining pop with Anglo-Saxon aesthetics, another Chilean band, La Ley, successfully launched an international career. However, after receiving the highest accolades ever achieved by a Chilean band, the group, led by Beto Cuevas, split up in 2005.

Funk also became an established taste with Chancho en Piedra, which remains one of

Chile's most popular bands, while pop was revitalized by the appearance of Lucybell, a band whose dark lyrics and aesthetics combined with meticulous sound production carried it to success not only in Chile, but also in Mexico.

However, since 2000, Chilean music has again returned to its roots. The appearance of groups like Los Bunkers, a young rock quartet from Concepción influenced both by 1960s British rock and protest songs, and the return of Los Tres have led a revival of traditional folkloric music, while pre-dictatorship music has also become popular among young people. Up-and-coming bands venerate and pay homage to "old" musicians, with covers of songs by Violeta Parra and Víctor Jara frequently included in new albums and recitals, while their pictures – the image of pure and rebellious talent – are a common sight at concerts and demonstrations. Two of the most influential modern artists representing this musical trend are Manuel García and Nano Stern. Another recent phenomenon is a hugely popular genre known as New Chilean Cumbia, with Chico Trujillo being one of the leading bands.

Ballet performance at the Teatro Municipal.

TE RECUERDO AMANDA

Te recuerdo Amanda, la calle mojada
corriendo a la fábrica, donde trabajaba Manuel
La sonrisa ancha, la lluvia en el pelo
no importaba nada, ibas a encontrarte con el
con el, con el, con el...
(English Translation)
I think of you Amanda, in the wet street
running toward the factory, where Manuel
worked
With a broad smile, the rain in your hair
Nothing mattered, you were meeting up with him,
with him, with him, with him...
by Víctor Jara

Classical music

Santiago's historic Teatro Municipal is home to the city's Philharmonic Orchestra which gives regular concerts from April to December, often under leading international conductors or with invited soloists. Similarly, although the Teatro has its own ballet company, this often incorporates guest soloists and it is also part of the international opera circuit, attracting leading international singers. In 2012, for example, it put on *Il Postino*, an opera about Pablo Neruda, first performed in Los Angeles, California, with Plácido Domingo in the role of the Nobel poet.

The city's other main orchestra, the Symphonic Orchestra, performs mainly in the

Teatro Universidad de Chile on Plaza Italia, which is also home to the country's National Ballet Company. Smaller orchestras often give free concerts in the city's churches, which are advertised in the newspapers and are well worth attending.

Outside Santiago, the main classical musical event of the year is the festival held each year in February in the picturesque town of Frutillar in the Lake District. Held mostly in the new Teatro del Lago, built on a pier stretching out into Lago Llanquihue, this includes local as well as international per-

of private banks during the 1982–3 economic crisis. The supposed work of old masters like Pedro Lira, Juan Francisco González and Onofre Jarpa, sometimes appears in auctions but requires authentification.

Santiago's main art galleries, located principally in the Vitacura district (see page 141), regularly show the work of living Chilean painters and sculptors, including both those living abroad and at home. Other exhibitions, such as those put on by the main university art schools and the studios to be found in the city's Bellavista district, are also worth a visit.

Lollapalooza Festival of alternative music, Santiago.

formers (but tends to sell out well ahead of time).

Chilean visual arts

Chileans love painting and, as prosperity has increased, a buoyant market has emerged for the work of living artists, both established – such as Gonzalo Cienfuegos, Samy Benmayor and Bororo – and emerging. Their work, acquired partly as an investment, is a frequent feature of the homes of well-off Chileans, particularly in Santiago.

The country's old masters are on show at the Museo Nacional de Bellas Artes (see page 138) in Santiago but much of their work is in private collections such as that of the Central Bank, acquired largely in payment of the debts

A moving image of Chile

Filmmaking in Chile dates back to the early 20th century, when Salvador Giambastiani and his wife, Gabriela von Bussenius, made the 1919 documentary *Recuerdos del Mineral de El Teniente* (Memories of the El Teniente Mine), and, in 1926, Pedro Sienna, an actor, producer, and director, made the movie *El Húsar de la Muerte* (The Hussar of Death), about the life of Manuel Rodríguez, one of the heroes of Chile's independence from Spain (see page 37). Other movies made in this early period include *Sueño de Amor* (Dream of Love), in which Chilean pianist Claudio Arrau played the role of Franz Liszt.

In the 1940s, local film production received state support and a number of memorable

> "A country without documentary films is like a family without a photo album."
> Patricio Guzmán, director of The Battle of Chile, the prize-winning documentary about the Allende years.

movies were made, including *La Dama sin Camelias* (The Lady without Camellias) by José Bohr while, in the 1960s, it received a new injection of life when the University of Chile set up its Department of Experimental

Production at Santiago's annual Teatro a Mil festival.

Cinema, again with state support. *Ayúdeme Usted Compadre* (Help Me, Mate), a movie by Germán Becker that was seen by a then record 370,000 people, and Raúl Ruiz's *Tres Tristes Tigres* (Three Sad Tigers) correspond to this period.

In 1970, Miguel Littín directed one of Chile's most famous films, *El Chacal de Nahueltoro* (The Jackal of Nahueltoro). This recounts the true story of a man who, while under the influence of alcohol, murdered his partner and children. The incident caused considerable public commotion at the time, not only because of the brutal nature of the crime, but also because of the murderer's fate. A man of virtually no education, he changed

dramatically while in prison, acquiring schooling and reformed attitudes. However, despite this, the courts showed no mercy and he was executed by a firing squad.

During the Popular Unity government, only nine movies were produced, despite state incentives. It was in this period that Raúl Ruiz made *Palomita Blanca* (White Dove) – although it was not screened until 1993 – and Patricio Guzmán, a documentary-maker who has recorded much of Chile's recent history, made *El Primer Año* (The First Year).

After the military coup, many filmmakers were forced into exile. Nonetheless, seven full-length movies were shot in Chile between 1973 and 1985. These include *Julio Comienza en Julio* (Julio Begins in July) by Silvio Caiozzi, the story of an adolescent boy from an aristocratic Chilean family at the beginning of the twentieth century.

A fertile time

Since the return of democracy, film production has boomed. Initially, movies tended to focus on political issues, such as the classic *La Frontera* (The Frontier) by Ricardo Larraín, about the relegation to remote areas of the country used by the dictatorship to punish its opponents. However, movies have increasingly sought to depict the everyday life of Chileans.

Examples of this type of movie include *Historias de Fútbol* (Football Tales) by Andrés Wood. More recently, they have also begun to mirror changing attitudes toward sex. The success of *El Chacotero Sentimental* (The Sentimental Teaser), based on a radio phone-in in which young listeners talked about their sex life, and *En La Cama* (In Bed) by Matías Bize, one of Chile's most successful new directors, which takes place entirely in a motel room in Santiago, are a clear sign that Chileans are avid to see themselves portrayed on the screen with their behavior stripped naked.

However, one of the most important movies of the past decade was *Machuca* (2004). Directed by Andrés Wood, this tells the story of the friendship of two 11-year-old boys, one from a prosperous neighborhood of Santiago and the other from a nearby shantytown, who meet towards the end of the Popular Unity government as a result of a Catholic school's social integration program. The two boys and their homes – divided by the city's river – are a reflection of a yawning social divide that their friendship attempts to bridge, and of how the 1973 military coup took advantage of this gulf and prized it further open.

Pablo Larraín's *No* (2012) won critical acclaim when it became the first Chilean movie to be nominated for an Academy Award in the Best Foreign Language Film category.

Chile on stage

The theater in Chile has survived in the face of constant difficulties. Its inventiveness

> One of the few Chilean playwrights to have triumphed abroad is Ariel Dorfman, whose La Muerte y la Doncella (Death and the Maiden) was made into a movie in 1994 by Roman Polanski, starring Sigourney Weaver.

in 2002. A director, playwright, dancer, and choreographer, he studied for six years at the Théâtre du Soleil in France before returning to Chile to found the Gran Circo Teatro, which mounted many memorable produc-

Scene from 'Machuca'.

allowed it to survive the dictatorship and even to serve as a channel for veiled criticism, particularly by the Ictus group. But, since the return of democracy, it has taken on a new lease of life, thanks to initiatives like the Santiago a Mil International Theater Festival, which takes place in January in Santiago and other major cities.

Local playwrights, such as Ramón Griffero, Marco Antonio de la Parra, Egon Wolff, Juan Radrigán, and Benjamín Galemiri, regularly have plays on show and, as audiences become better acquainted with the theater, are expanding the range that is on offer.

Perhaps the most venerated figure of Chilean theater is Andrés Pérez, who died of Aids

tions. He is most remembered as the director of *La Negra Ester*.

Over the past few years, theater companies have also branched out into more commercial productions, often starring soap-opera television actors. Such plays tend to be put on in new and more comfortable theaters (some of which are to be found in shopping malls).

If proof of the Chileans' avid interest in the arts were required, this was abundantly provided when France's Royal De Luxe street theater company took its *Little Giant* to Santiago in 2007. The performance lasted three days and its final procession was followed by 300,000 people – an all-time record for an event of this type.

A TASTE OF CHILE

Chile, the home of the potato and the strawberry, used to be known for its bland fare. That has changed as the country has rediscovered the indigenous origins of its cuisine.

Pablo Neruda's *Oda al Caldillo de Congrio* (Ode to Conger Eel Soup) is a recipe in verse that lingeringly savors each step in making this rich and fragrant soup from the "giant eel with snow-white flesh." Flavored with potatoes, onion, and garlic, this is one of Chile's most traditional and best-loved dishes. The poet was mistaken on one count: *congrio* isn't – despite the common belief in Chile – an eel at all, but a fish known internationally as kingclip. But Neruda's ode – as do the many others he wrote about the simple joys of Chilean food – makes no mistake about the satisfying pleasure of a steaming bowl of *caldillo*, especially on a cold winter day.

Congrio, with its springy white flesh, is also popular *frito* (fried), when it is traditionally served with *ensalada chilena* (a salad of sliced tomato and blanched onions). "If you visit Chile without trying *congrio frito*, you haven't really been there," warns Chilean chef Carlo von Mühlenbrock.

In Santiago, the Mercado Central, the city's old fruit and vegetable market by the River Mapocho, is a good place to try *congrio*. The main restaurant, Donde Augusto, has become over-priced but, at the smaller restaurants around the edge of the market, you'll find excellent *caldillo* and *congrio frito* at modest prices, as well as *corvina* (sea bass) and a variety of the shellfish that flourish in the cold Antarctic waters that are carried up the Chilean coast by the famous Humboldt Current.

Another of the treats not to be missed in Chile is the *cordero* (lamb) that is raised in the far south of Chile around the Magellan Strait. It has a special taste attributed to the sea winds that feather the grass with salt, and to the fact that, in this area's virtually virgin pastures, the land is free of herbicides and insecticides. Unfortunately,

Traditional Mapuche cooking.

though, lamb is not very popular in Chile (most of the Magellan lamb goes straight for export) and, except in Patagonia, it tends only to be served in more expensive restaurants.

Chile is also famous for its farmed salmon which, over the past 20 years, has developed into a major export industry. Salmon is rarely absent from a restaurant menu in Chile and is widely considered to have a more pleasant, less strong taste than that of Norwegian or Scottish salmon. It was the target of international criticism for the industry's heavy use of antibiotics and its poor environmental practices but, in recent years, following a devastating outbreak of a salmon virus, important improvements have been made on both fronts.

Fresh fruit

Chile's fresh fruit is also not to be missed if you visit in spring or summer. Too infrequently served in restaurants – on the grounds that fruit is not a "real" dessert – it is a delight. If you visit the Sernatur tourist office on Santiago's Providencia Avenue, you'll find an excellent fruit and vegetable market just around the back of the building.

In summer, the roads are lined with stalls offering the pick of the season: plums, strawberries, peaches, apricots, figs, cherries, melons, watermelons and kiwis, and, as autumn

Indigenous roots

Some scientists believe that the potato originated in Chile, probably in the Chiloé archipelago 13,000 years ago – although Peru disputes this – before spreading to the Andean altiplano where the Spanish conquistadors found it in the mid-16th century. Even today, the potato forms a staple part of the Chilotes' diet as, for example, in *milkao*, a traditional flat bread made with grated potatoes and fried in lard or steamed on top of a *curanto* (a Chilote stew cooked over red-hot stones in a hole in the ground). And, on the smaller islands of

Raspberries – one of Chile's most profitable food exports.

approaches, the famous Chilean grape, sweet and luscious. And, during a spring visit, don't neglect to try the *chirimoyas* (custard apples), a sweet and fragrant fruit grown mostly around La Serena, and best eaten just with a dressing of freshly squeezed orange juice. Prickly pears, or *tunas*, are as common as apples in Chile, where they droop like large, green teardrops on cactus arms. They are particularly popular crushed and blended into refreshing juices, with the pips filtered out.

In Chile, it is hard not to miss the *paltas* (avocados) that have also become an important export. They are excellent and will turn up in nearly all your salads, on most hamburgers and, in mashed form, on *completos* (hot dogs).

the archipelago, many varieties have survived, some with graphic names like the long thin black potato that is known as *mojón de gato* (cat's dung).

It is, therefore, all the more surprising that only one standard variety of potato is generally sold in Chilean supermarkets or served in the country's restaurants. But that is changing; eyeing a new market, small farmers have begun to rescue and produce varieties that did not previously reach consumers.

Carlo von Mühlenbrock is one of a generation of Chilean chefs who rebelled against the international, and frequently undistinguished, fare that used to be standard in most Chilean restaurants. "Restaurant owners used to think that local dishes weren't chic; they scorned them as rustic and not sophisticated enough," he recalls. But that has also changed. Until a few years ago, most Chileans had never heard of *merkén*, a Mapuche seasoning. However, thanks to research by von Mühlenbrock and other like-minded chefs, it is now a common feature of restaurant menus. A red spicy paste that the Mapuches spread on bread or use to liven up stews, it is made from red chili peppers – traditionally smoked by being hung above the cooking fire in Mapuche homes – which are then ground to a powder with cilantro (coriander) seeds, garlic, and salt, and mixed with water when needed.

Another popular addition to restaurant menus are *piñones*, the fruit of the monkey puzzle tree, and the staple diet of the Pehuenches, the branch of the Mapuches who live in the Andes mountains. The Pehuenches use *piñones* to make bread, or simply eat them boiled, much like chestnuts, which they resemble in taste, although not in their long, thin shape. Today, you may find *piñones* served as a garnish alongside a piece of meat.

Beans and sweetcorn

The Chilean word for beans – *porotos* – is believed to originate from the language of the Quechua people of the Andes, but beans were also an important part of the Mapuche diet.

Beans are popularly eaten in Chile as a rich summer soup known as *porotos granados*. This is made from shelled haricot beans, pumpkin, onion, and sweetcorn, seasoned with basil, and is usually eaten with chopped tomatoes and chili pepper but, in the countryside, sometimes comes with a beefsteak *(bifstek)* on top. *Porotos con riendas* – literally, beans with reins – is a bean stew with spaghetti added, a typically rural dish that is rather despised by urban Chileans. But there is wisdom in the hearty mixture; recent research has shown that it is an ideal mix of readily-digested proteins.

Sweetcorn, which is known as *choclo* (the Quechua name for corn) is also used in many other Chilean dishes, but the most famous are *humitas* and *pastel de choclo*. *Humitas* are the Chilean equivalent of the tamales found in many other Latin American countries, with the difference that they contain only mashed corn – no meat, as is often the case in other countries – and are always wrapped

in corn leaves and not, for example, banana leaves. *Humitas* are usually served with *ensalada chilena* and finely chopped chili pepper, although some Chileans prefer to eat them with sugar.

Pastel de choclo has a minced-meat base that includes quarters of hard-boiled egg, olives, and sometimes a piece of chicken, and is covered with a mashed corn layer. It is, in fact, much like a cottage pie, with corn replacing the potato. Raisins are often added to the meat base, and sugar is sometimes sprinkled over the corn top before it is put in the oven to brown.

Choclo (sweetcorn).

VEGETARIAN RESTAURANTS

Vegetarians used to have a hard time in Chile, but that is changing. Chileans are ever more health-conscious and, partly as a result, almost all larger restaurants now carry vegetarian dishes on their menu, whether a main-meal salad, a bean-based dish, or a vegetable lasagna, for example. In Santiago, there are also a number of specifically vegetarian restaurants such as El Huerto in the Providencia district and La Chakra organic café in Las Condes, which also cater for vegans, and the same is true of most other cities and large towns, particularly those popular with tourists, such as Pucón.

The popular *empanada* – a savory pastry turnover – is found in most Latin American countries, although the name varies, and has a definite Spanish origin. In fact, it traces its roots back to the hollowed-out loaf of bread in which European farmworkers used to carry their midday meal to the fields.

In Chile, it is most commonly filled with *pino* – the same mixture of minced meat, onions, hard-boiled egg, olives, and raisins that is used in *pastel de choclo*. In this version, it is baked in the oven, but there is also a tasty fried version, with a flakier pastry, that is filled with cheese.

> The 19th-century traveler Edward Revel Smith described the cazuela as "the best dish that can be had in Chile, and one which, I believe, can be had nowhere else."

known as *parrilladas* and at the *asados* (barbecues) with which Chileans love to celebrate everything from birthdays to national holidays. The *parrilladas* cook every type of meat over a charcoal grill – anything from a steak to a sausage or chop. In some of the *campesino* (farm-

Traditional asado.

On the coast, *empanadas de mariscos* – filled with shellfish and, typically, the rosy-fleshed *macha* razor clam – are a popular alternative.

Another Chilean favorite, *cazuela*, is a winter dish. It starts with a meat *(carne)* broth in which potato, pumpkin, corn, and peppers are cooked. The dish arrives at the table as a sea of steaming soup, with large vegetable and meat islands, under which a bed of rice is discovered. As well as beef, this is often made with chicken or turkey and, in the latter case, is sprinkled with *chuchoca* (milled corn that is similar to Italy's polenta). This is a very hearty meal and is usually cheap.

While not considered as fine as Argentine meat, Chilean cattle produce very creditable steaks, which are served up in restaurants

ing) areas, you can find great cheap *parrilladas*, usually with a big fire in the middle of a rustic, checked table-clothed room, complete with a guitar-playing *huaso* (cowboy). This is a good place to try a *prieta*, a Chilean blood sausage. If you simply order a *parrillada*, you'll get meat grilled (possibly at the table). It is also quite common to order pure entrails if you like them.

Post-Conquest influences

Chileans consider – with some justification – that their cuisine is a poor relation to Peruvian and Mexican cuisines, undeniably the most varied and interesting in Latin America. The difference, says Carlo von Mühlenbrock, is explained largely by the lack of post-Conquest influences in Chile. The lack of the African influence that is so clear in Peru reflects the fact that few black slaves were taken to Chile, and those that were did not, except in the far north, survive its harsher climate. And the Chinese and Japanese immigrations that, in Peru, merged with the local cuisine, to produce the *chifa* and *nikkei* cuisine, were virtually absent in Chile.

In addition, argues von Mühlenbrock, Chilean society was less permeable to outside influence, perhaps partly because of its difficulty in establishing control over Mapuche lands. That also explains, he says, why there are so

Pickled fruits and preserves.

the 19th century. This may explain the importance that cabbage now has in the Mapuche diet, and it is certainly reflected in the widespread use of the word *küchen* to describe any sort of fruit tart.

Küchen is, in fact, one of the few traditional sweet pastries in Chile. However, in the sweet line, *manjar* is very popular. Similar to Argentina's *dulce de leche* (which literally translated means milk jam), *manjar* is traditionally made by slowly boiling up a mixture of milk and sugar, flavored with a vanilla pod, until it thickens and turns a light caramel brown. It turns up

Postre (dessert).

few regional variations in Chilean food. "An empanada is an empanada from Arica to Punta Arenas because that's the way Chileans wanted it to be," he notes.

In fact, only two post-Conquest influences have played a significant role in the development of Chilean food – Italian and German cuisine. Italian immigration into Chile was small, but pasta is a common main course in restaurants and homes, a custom probably learned through Argentina, where Italian immigration was far more important and pervasive than in Chile.

The German influence is seen most strongly in the Lake District of the south, which is where most settlers from Germany arrived in

> The Emporio Nacional with branches at Bellavista 0360 and in the Galería Drugstore on Providencia, is one of the best places to buy Chilean gourmet specialties, including some of the best of the country's cheeses.

in *alfajores* (two biscuits sandwiched together with *manjar*) and, for example, in *dulces de La Ligua*, cakes of sponge or meringue filled with *manjar*. La Ligua is just off the PanAmerican Highway traveling north around an hour and a half out of Santiago, and the *dulces* are well worth the detour, although they can also be acquired in bakeries in Santiago.

Globalized tastes

In recent years, as prosperity has increased with economic growth, more and more Chileans have had the opportunity to travel abroad and, much as occurred in Britain in the 1960s and 1970s, this has been reflected in the incorporation of new ingredients on supermarket shelves, the appearance of new ways of using traditional Chilean ingredients and, above all, a greater variety of restaurants.

Today, most supermarkets, at least in prosperous areas of Santiago, have a section devoted to the materials for preparing Japanese and Thai dishes include *palta* (avocado). The number of Indian restaurants, although still small, has also increased.

Putting a new spin on Chilean fish, many restaurants now also serve *ceviche*, a Peruvian specialty of raw fish cooked in lemon juice. With immigration from Peru, Peruvian restaurants have also become ubiquitous. In the downtown area, they cluster in the streets alongside the cathedral and are an excellent option for a cheap and very tasty lunch.

In fast-food restaurants too, the influence of globalization is clear – you'll be just as likely to find tacos and burritos as hamburgers and

Carpaccio of beef.

A German café in the Lake District.

as well as Peruvian and Mexican food. Whether it is wasabi, rice vinegar, or lemon grass that you want, the chances are you will be able to find it.

Chinese restaurants and takeaways, long common in Chile, have been joined by ubiquitous sushi bars, some more authentic than others. Chilean salmon is the staple ingredient of rolls that – to the surprise of foreigners – often also

> Chile has recently begun producing olive oil and has won a number of international prizes. The flavor varies from fruity and mild to very strong. At some restaurants, oil seasoned with merkén (a Mapuche seasoning) is served.

chips and, in line with a growing concern about obesity, salads. But Chile also has its own version of fast food in the meal-sized sandwiches served in restaurants like those of the Dominó chain (not be confused with Domino's Pizza). As well as *completos*, they serve *churrascos* (with thinly sliced beef) and *lomitos* (with pork), with the option of a vast array of other fillings. An *italiano*, for example, includes mashed avocado, diced tomatoes and mayonnaise.

A day of dining

Breakfast is *desayuno*. In most *residenciales* this will simply be bread with jam and butter (*mermelada y mantequilla*) and coffee or tea. Coffee will almost certainly be instant. *Café con leche* (with milk) is milky coffee; if you want just a little milk, ask for *un café cortado*. Tea-lovers should prepare themselves for a challenging time in Chile. Asking for a cup of tea usually gets you a tea bag in a cup of hot, but not necessarily boil-

> The names for Chilean fish can be confusing. Corvina is sea bass and, unlike bacaloa de profundidad (Patagonian tooth fish), a type of cod often referred to as sea bass abroad, is not in danger of extinction.

stew) or *pollo con arroz* (chicken with rice), and then there may be a little *postre* (dessert). Tea or coffee, or a soft drink, is usually part of the deal.

In Chile, late afternoon, between 5 and 7pm, is somewhat confusingly the time for *onces* (elevenses). These usually include tea, coffee, sandwiches, and cakes. The name is said to come from the British custom of having "elevenses," a late-morning snack. An alternative theory is that this used to be the time when the man of the house would sneak off for a peaceful drink of *aguardiente*, the local firewater, the name of which contains 11 letters.

Catching up over a pitcher of cerveza.

ing, water. Beware, also, of asking for milk with your tea. This will almost certainly be warm and often in a larger quantity than you anticipated.

A fuller breakfast can be ordered anywhere that serves *desayuno*. Eggs and toast (*huevos con tostadas*) should be no problem. Fried eggs are *huevos fritos*, scrambled are *revueltos*, poached are *pasados*, hard-boiled are *huevos duros*, and soft-boiled are *a la copa*.

Lunch (*almuerzo*) is served after 1.30pm and can run until around 4pm. Set lunches (*colación* or *menú del día*) are usually very good value, and give you the opportunity of trying something typical without having to know what to order. As a starter, you'll be served a little salad, before a main dish of perhaps *porotos granados* (bean

As in most Latin American countries, dinner (*cena*) isn't served until after 8.30pm, and usually runs on until late. If you don't drink coffee after dinner, try an *aguita*, a fresh herb tea found everywhere.

Drinking water, even in small towns and villages, is of excellent standard. However, because of the Andes Mountains, it can contain a high level of mineral salts that sometimes upsets visitors. Bottled water is, however, readily available even in the smallest restaurants. Alternatively, try the fruit juices. In both the cartons sold in supermarkets and in restaurants, these come in two types – freshly squeezed and reconstituted from pre-prepared pulp – of which the latter may be too sweet for some tastes.

FRUIT OF THE VINE

Immensely popular internationally, Chilean wines
may be from the "New World" but they are made
from grapes with an ancient European pedigree.

Chileans have been making fine wines for more than a century, and have probably boasted about them for almost as long. Their great selling point, as every Chilean schoolchild knows, is that the best wine is produced from vines that can trace their ancestry straight back to cuttings brought over in the middle of the 19th century from France by some enlightened Chilean vineyard owners.

Before that era, the Spanish conquistadors had grown vines, legend has it, by planting the pips of the raisins they had brought over with them from Spain. This was the origin of what is known as *país*, or "native" wine, the equivalent of California's "mission" wine. Winemaking was also an essential part of the activities of the Jesuit missionaries, who settled in the country throughout the 18th century.

French roots

A century later, an affluent landowner, Don Silvester Ochagavía, decided to improve the quality of his vines and went to France. It was a timely visit, as Ochagavía brought back cuttings not long before a plague of the dreaded phylloxera beetle began to chew away at the roots of the parent stock in Europe, and nearly destroyed the wine industries in France, Italy, and Germany.

The European growers saved their vines by eventually grafting tougher, beetle-resistant American stock onto them. But while the European vineyards were being replanted, several out-of-work French enologists went to Chile, together with their vines, to give technical advice on planting and wine-making.

The phylloxera blight never reached Chile, cut off as it is from the rest of the world by natural barriers – the Pacific Ocean, the Atacama Desert, and the Andes. So Chilean vineyard

Chile has been making fine wines since the 19th century.

owners boast that their vines grow naturally, ungrafted, from original European stock. Wine buffs argue about whether this makes any difference to the wine's taste. It certainly does make a difference to the economics of the industry, because ungrafted vines can go on producing for three or four times longer than the grafted stock that now dominates in Europe.

Señor Ochagavía brought cuttings of Cabernet Sauvignon vines, which is now the most common type used for red wine (*vino tinto*). It is usually produced as a 100 percent unblended wine, though it is sometimes blended with other varieties such as Merlot or Syrah. At around the same time, someone – it is not known who – also brought cuttings of Carménère from its

Bordeaux homeland. The plant and its wine are similar to Merlot, but with subtle differences – so subtle, in fact, that until the late 1990s, when a sharp-eyed (or nosed) Frenchman spotted it, it was marketed as Merlot. DNA testing proved that it was Carménère, and it has become a Chilean signature because of its rarity value. White wine comes mainly from Chardonnay grapes and from Sauvignon Blanc. Señor Ochagavía brought his cuttings of the Sauvignon Blanc vine from Bordeaux rather than the Loire Valley, and the flavor is softer and less pungent than the Loire Valley variety.

wine consumption is well below that of European wine-producing countries and much less than neighboring Argentina.

Modernizing for export

In the 1980s, the future looked bleak for wine producers. However, some of the bigger enterprises decided to test their reputations by trying to sell in a big way to the outside world. That meant changing the heavy, full-bodied wines – with the strong tannin taste that Chileans were used to – and going for the lighter and fruitier unblended wines (*varietales*) that are popular in the United

Filling wine barrels at Viña Veramonte.

Changing tastes

By the 19th century, Chilean wine growers already had the best vines and an excellent place to grow them – the long Central Valley, with its ideal temperate climate, hot sunny days and cool nights, and the right type of soil for the vines to flourish. But it is only since the late 1980s that they have really begun to make consistent top-quality wines that sell successfully in Europe, the United States, and Asia, and are now making important inroads into the giant Chinese market.

Local consumption of wine, however, has been dropping steadily since the 1970s, although there is a strong wine-drinking culture among the middle and wealthy classes. Even so, beer and fizzy drinks have become far more popular, and

States and Europe. That called for investment in new equipment. For example, red wine was traditionally matured in big, old casks of *raulí*, the native oak, which masks the taste of fruit. The vineyards that decided to go for export markets had to import very expensive small casks, made from French oak, each of which lasts for only three or four years before it has to be replaced.

The investment for making good white wine was even larger, since white wine needs more careful handling. The grapes have to be picked in the cool hours of the morning, not in the heat of a summer afternoon. It is also important to pick them when they are not too ripe, or the wine will lack acidity, at least for non-Chilean tastes.

Vineyards have installed computerized

pneumatic grape presses, which don't crush pips, and, for white wines, stainless-steel tanks, in which the temperature of the fermenting juice can be rigidly controlled.

More recently, in a bid to broaden their range of exports, wine producers have begun to experiment with new varieties. They now produce some Malbec – the flagship wine of Argentina's Mendoza province just across the Andes – and have had considerable success with Pinot Noir, a light red wine, in the cooler valleys where most of Chile's white wines are grown and, more incipiently, are experimenting with Carignan. New white wines, such

Wine growing in the Casablanca Valley only started a little over 20 years ago. Its "discovery" is generally attributed to pioneer Pablo Morandé, who was looking for a cooler place for white grapes.

in the Limarí Valley but most of the vines there are for table grapes, with the exception of the *pisco*, a pink Muscatel-like variety which is distilled to make the spirit of the same name.

The Valle del Elqui, near the pretty northern

Viña Mar, in the Casablanca Valley.

as Viognier, Riesling, and Gewürztraminer, have also begun to appear, although the main change in white wines has been the production of Sauvignon Blanc in valleys close to the sea, which gives them a different bouquet and flavor.

Wine producers

By far the largest producer-exporter is Conchay Toro with its subsidiary, Santa Emiliana, while other key players include Santa Rita, which also owns Viña Carmen, and San Pedro, which owns Tarapacá. However, Chile has some 150 wineries, all of which produce mainly for export.

Most of the winemaking areas are located in the Central Valley to the south of Santiago. To the north, some wine is produced, for example,

city of La Serena, is the most famous *pisco* area. Three main brands are distributed nationally, but if visiting the valley or La Serena it is worth tasting and shopping around for local brands, which have the finest taste and smell of ripe grapes.

Visiting vineyards

The *vendimia*, or grape harvest, takes place between early March and mid-April – the farther south the vineyard, the later the picking starts. By far, the largest festival takes place in Santa Cruz, in the Colchagua Valley, 178km (110 miles) south of Santiago. It includes a craft fair and concerts as well as wine-tastings. There are also other festivals in the nearby towns of Curicó and San Fernando, and, in the north, in the Limarí valley, the last area where wine is produced before the Atacama Desert begins.

The Colchagua Valley also offers organized tours of its vineyards. Starting in Santa Cruz, they range from a half-day tour to a two-day package that includes an overnight stay in the Santiago. Tastings are usually included in the tour, and most wineries have added elegant sales rooms and, in some cases, restaurants.

The closest to Santiago – indeed, now almost swallowed up by the city – is **Cousiño Macul** winery (tel: 02-351 4100; www.cousinomacul.com), one of the oldest in Chile. Grapes have been grown there since vines were planted by its first owner, Juan Jufré, one of the conquistadors who came with Pedro de Valdivia. The winery has been in the Cousiño Macul family since 1856, and the person most responsible for its development was the daughter-in-law of the first Cousiño, Doña Isi-

Wine-tasting at Colchagua Valley vineyard.

Hacienda Los Lingues in the Colchagua Valley.

Santa Cruz Hotel (tel: 072-209 600). Bookings for the wine tour can be made through the hotel or directly with the Ruta del Vino (Wine Route) office in Santa Cruz (tel: 072-823 199). Santa Cruz can easily be reached by taking the train to San Fernando and a *colectivo* from the station. Visitors can also ride the "Tren Sabores del Valle" (www.rutadelvino.cl), hauled by a refurbished 19th-century steam engine through the Colchagua Valley, stopping off to visit state-of-the-art wineries and taste their wares.

Public visits to most vineyards in the off-season are usually limited to the bottling plant and the original cellars. This kind of tour takes only about an hour, so you might plan a visit as part of a day out in the countryside around

dora Goyenechea, who had the cellars built and brought over an enologist from Bordeaux to produce quality wine. A leafy oasis on the outskirts of Santiago, it is well worth a visit.

Concha y Toro (tel: 02-476 5000; www.conchaytoro.com) has its estate house in the direction of the Cajón del Maipo, about an hour's drive southeast of Santiago or a short taxi ride from the Puente Alto subway station. A tour of the plant and old family estate might be included in a weekend trip to the mountains, but requires a booking.

Santa Rita (tel: 02-362 2594; www.santarita.com), near Paine just off the Pan-American Highway south of Santiago, has a lovely little Precolombian Museum and, with its excellent restaurant, makes a pleasant day trip from Santiago. Booking is advised, particularly for the restaurant. **Viña Undurraga** (tel: 02-372 2900; www.undurraga.cl) is near Melipilla, about an hour's drive toward San Antonio, and could be combined with a visit to the resorts of Algarrobo or Las Cruces, or the port of San Antonio. Tours run daily starting at 10.15am. Again, booking is advisable.

Another happy hunting ground for wine lovers is the Casablanca Valley, between Santiago and Valparaíso. This is where Chile's best white wines are produced and visits or an overnight stay can be organized through the **Casablanca Valley Wine Producers Association** (tel: 032-274 3755; http://rutadelvinodecasablanca.cl/). Some of the vineyards also have excellent restaurants, making the valley a favorite excursion for *santiaguinos* on a sunny Sunday.

The **Casas del Bosque** (tel: 02-480 6940; www.casasdelbosque.cl), just outside the town of Casablanca, offers tours all year round but, during the *vendimia*, also allows visitors to participate in the harvest, cutting grapes and learning more about the process that follows. Lunch is available at its Tanino restaurant (May–Oct; closed Mon).

Viña Morandé (tel: 032-275 4701; closed Mon; www.morande.cl)**.** This vineyard's House of Morandé restaurant, conveniently on the Santiago–Valparaíso side of Highway 68, just past the Zapata toll booths, is renowned for its excellent food and has a lovely little park for a stroll after lunch.

Viña Indómita (tel: 032-215 3902; www.indomita.cl). The restaurant of this vineyard, a striking white building on a hill overlooking the highway, offers an excellent menu and also offers tours. The only drawback is that it's on the Valparaíso–Santiago side of the road and, if coming from Santiago, involves a detour to the Algarrobo-San Antonio turn-off and returning towards Santiago by a side road.

Viña Matetic (tel: 09-8920 2066; http://matetic.com/), on the western edge of the Casablanca Valley, not only produces some very interesting wines, it also has a stunningly designed restaurant that is widely acclaimed for the quality and creativity of its food, as well as a guest house.

Trying and buying

Wine buffs might enjoy a visit to the **Restaurant Camino Real**, on Santiago's pleasant wooded Cerro San Cristóbal, where you can sample a range of wines at about US$2 a glass. The restaurant is open Tue–Fri 8pm–1am and Sat 6pm–3am.

> At the beginning of the 1970s, the average Chilean drank 50 liters (106 pints) of wine a year; by 2000, this had dropped to 15 liters (32 pints), in favor of beer and soft drinks, but has since risen to around 18 liters (38 pints).

If you arrive unannounced, there will be no expert on hand to comment on or recommend wines. But if you want to take sampling more seriously, you can make an appointment and arrange for a private tasting session (tel: 02-232 1758).

Wine tours usually include an opportunity to sample the produce.

If you want to take some Chilean wine home, try one of the big supermarket chains, such as Jumbo or Líder, in upmarket areas of Santiago such as Providencia, Las Condes, Vitacura, or Avenida Kennedy. These stores offer large wine selections at good prices. But, if you want expert advice, you'd be better off in one of the specialized wine shops in the El Golf area. El Mundo del Vino (www.elmundodelvino.cl), on Isidora Goyenechea, is one of the best, and the staff are generally well informed. El Mundo del Vino also sells some cheap and very useful inflatable plastic sheaths for wine bottles that allow them to be safely carried in bags that go in the hold of a plane, now that they are not allowed in hand baggage.

The elusive puma.

WILD CHILE

Chile's wide range of climatic zones gives it an
unusually diverse flora and fauna in vast and
often virtually pristine countryside.

With the world's driest desert in the
north and the continent of Antarctica
in the south, it is not surprising that
Chile's climate is divided into extremely different zones and that its wildlife varies tremen-
dously. Add to this the country's huge extension
of ocean (the 320km/200-mile territorial limit
is almost the width of Chile at its widest point)
on the west and the lofty Andes on the east, and
you have a world of differences packed into one
long strand of a country.

Chile's wilderness areas hold few dangers
for the intrepid camper or hiker. There are no
bears in the mountains, no poisonous snakes,
and only two kinds of poisonous spider (the
corn spider or *araña del trigo*, with a red
splash on a black body, and the brown corner spider, *araña del rincón*, found in houses),
which you're unlikely to run into. Way up in
the mountains there are wildcats and pumas,
but they usually avoid people. Unfortunately,
while Chileans are generally proud of the
numerous species endemic to their country, some are in danger of, or vulnerable to,
extinction. These include the world's smallest deer, the *pudú*, and the *huemul*, the large,
royal-looking deer which appears on the
Chilean coat of arms as well as two species
of chinchilla (on the critical list) and a number of species of frog, including the famous
pointed-nose Darwin's frog (also on the critical list). On Chile's island territories (Easter
Island and the Juan Fernández Archipelago)
are species that, developing in isolation, have
formed their own unique gene pools. Juan
Fernández, in particular, is rich in endemic
plant species, including its characteristic towering ferns, while an endemic hummingbird,
the Juan Fernández firecrown, lives only on

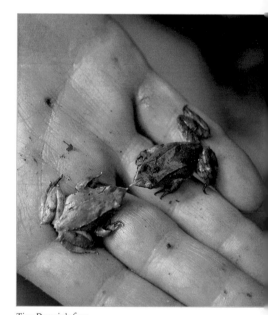

Tiny Darwin's frogs.

one of the archipelago's three islands. In the
mid-20th century, the Juan Fernández fur seal
was thought to be extinct but, after a few were
discovered, was protected and has recovered
quickly.

The far north

The soils of Chile's northernmost desert
regions are dry, and the climate is harsh, but
the coastal areas teem with seals and all kinds
of birds: seagulls, pelicans, petrels, penguins,
and *jotes* (vultures). High up in the Andes, disguised among the low shrubs and rocks, is the
occasional herd of *huemules* deer, hard to find
but protected in the national parks. Parque
Nacional Lauca (see page 180) is the only

area in Chile where the *huemul* is easily spotted at dawn or dusk, maybe hiding amongst the *queñoa* trees.

Chilean flamingos can be seen picking bugs out of the mud around altiplano lakes. The Andean flamingo and the James flamingo are also often seen in the salt marshes south of Parque Nacional Lauca. Conservation groups are working to protect flocks from collectors who gather the eggs to sell as food.

At least 150 other bird species have been noted in the park, one of the most obvious being the giant coot, a turkey-sized bird that builds huge nests up to 2.4 meters (8ft) wide, floating or resting on piles of stones in water.

Mountain cats, wild ducks, *ñandúes* (rheas), owls, eagles, and condors also add life to the dry landscape of Chile's far north, at 3–4,000 meters (9,800–13,000ft) above sea level. The *vizcacha* or Andean rabbit is endemic to the Andes. Its fluffy tail, tufted ears and long whiskers give it a rabbit-like appearance, but this rodent is actually a relative of the chinchilla and guinea pig. *Vizcachas* are quite easy to spot as they run around, popping out from behind rocks during the day.

Guanaco family in Torres del Paine National Park.

PERILOUS PENGUINS

Chile has nine species of penguin, the largest of which is appropriately called the emperor. These penguins can grow as tall as 1.2 meters (4ft), and are characterized by a yellowish-orange patch on both sides of their chests. They live in colonies of up to 5,000.

The most common species is the Magellanic penguin, which nests in sandy burrows in colonies of up to several thousand birds. If frightened, it hastens back to its burrow making a braying call like a donkey. Though seemingly tame, these penguins have been known to bite. Be warned if you see one pointing its beak towards you and hissing.

High in the altiplano (over 4,500 meters/ 14,800ft) is one of the world's last reserves of wild chinchilla. Claudio Gay, a French botanist who visited Chile extensively in the early 19th century, described the chinchilla as "one of Chile's most beautiful animals" and said they were easily tamed. They live in extensive caves dug under the ground, and come out only at night, so their eyes are extremely sensitive to the light. According to Chile's Committee for Defense of Flora and Fauna (CODEFF), these wild chinchillas are particularly important because most existing animals have been born and bred in captivity, with the resulting damage to gene pools which results from excessive in-breeding. These last, wild chinchilla are key to the renewal of breeding animals and have been studied by professors at the University of Chile.

In the broad plains formed between the coastal and Andean mountain ranges can be found the occasional hollow covered with the only sparse grasses capable of resisting the extreme saltiness of the soil. Climbing slightly higher into the mountains, around 2,200 meters (7,200ft) above sea level, cacti appear, accompanied by birds, some insects and lizards – the main life forms capable of surviving in the area.

of their neck… Their only form of defense is spitting at people who try to come near them: at the slightest provocation they lay their ears back and fling saliva mixed with other matter which doesn't cause the least damage."

Toward the Norte Chico

South of Parque Nacional Pan de Azúcar (see page 171) there is enough humidity to permit the growth of a large variety of cacti, many of which are valued abroad. Over the years ruthless hunting has reduced the herds of guanacos and the number of *vizcachas* and

Pelicans are found along Chile's northern coastline.

Magellanic penguins.

The camelids

All over the northern territories, as well as in many parts of the south, are herds of the animals most closely identified with (and arguably best adapted to) the extreme conditions of the altiplano: llamas, vicuñas, guanacos, and alpacas. All relatives of the camel, these four species are hard to tell apart, though the llama and alpaca are long-haired (and valued for their wool).

The botanist Claudio Gay described guanacos as "animals with gentle, timid and very curious personalities… They're very sociable and live in herds of many females with one male… They're hunted for their edible flesh and because exceptionally strong lassos can be made from the skin

CAMELID SPOTTING

Visitors to Chile will almost certainly spot a few camelids on their travels, but few will be able to say with certainty whether the wooly creatures are llamas, guanacos, vicuñas, or alpacas. Here's how to tell them apart and impress your travel companions. The guanaco and llama are the largest of the camelids. The guanaco has rust-colored fur with a dark head and tail, while the vicuña has creamier-colored fur. Alpaca and llama may be a combination of black, grey, white, rust, or cream, the alpaca being slightly smaller and with a fatter, often shorter neck. Alpacas have short, straight ears, while llamas have longer, curved ears.

chinchillas as well. Colorful beetles of all kinds are noteworthy throughout this region.

Thorns, shrubs, and small trees, along with wild flowers like the Cordilleran violet and chamomile, give way to the forests of the Talinay Hills, with the Fray Jorge National Park, full of trees more commonly found further south (particularly the *canelo* and *olivillo*). The vegetation hums with abundant insects, including dragonflies, butterflies, and beetles, which in turn sustain a sizeable population of lizards and non-poisonous snakes. Wild donkeys live in the Andean foothills.

From this region down toward Santiago, the climate, while still dry, is considerably more generous toward plants and animals. The average temperature for the area is around 14°C (57°F) all year round, and mists blown off the ocean condense on the coastal mountains, ensuring sufficient moisture to support a wide variety of flowers, trees, and other vegetation necessary to maintaining animal life. However, the landscape pays dearly for those years when the moisture is not sufficient: huge dunes have formed and have begun to creep steadily into formerly

Great Spotted Woodpecker, Lake District.

PUMAS - LIONS OF THE MOUNTAINS

Chileans who live in the mountains frequently see pumas (*felis concolor*, but popularly known as *leones* – lions), particularly in winter. Pumas rarely attack people, however, unless they are cornered. The presence of guanaco may indicate that pumas are nearby, as these animals are a key part of their diet. Guanaco skeletons found in remote areas often have dislocated necks, which is a sign of the work of this powerful mountain lion. Pumas also feed on hares, *vizcachas*, and *huemules*, attacking domestic animals only occasionally.

Despite this, hunting has seriously reduced their numbers. In 1980 the government banned the hunting of pumas; in response, many sheep farmers have since switched to raising cattle as their sheep were being increasingly ravaged by pumas.

A solitary animal, the puma reaches maturity at two or three years of age, and usually has two kittens per litter. Pumas and their relatives are found throughout Chile, particularly in the mountainous areas of the Lake District and Tierra del Fuego. Indeed, they are among the few animal species found throughout the Americas, all the way from Canada right down to the Strait of Magellan. This elusive creature grows up to 1.5 meters (5ft) in length and stands 63cm (2ft) at the shoulder. It has a light-brown coat with a white muzzle, and is hard to see, but sightings of footprints are fairly common.

fertile areas, turning them into semi-deserts, which may be virtually impossible to recover.

In these more temperate regions, sea swallows and cormorants join the bird species more common farther north, and farther inland there are thrushes, turtledoves, and partridges along with the other species named above. Wasps, scorpions (although their sting is painful, it is not dangerous), *tábanos* (horseflies), and both black and large hairy spiders form part of the anthropod population, while frogs and toads join the lizard and snake community.

The central region

From the early days of the Spanish Conquest, Chile's fertile Central Valley region, where Santiago is located, became the principal area of settlement and agriculture. As a result, the main animals of the area are people.

As you travel farther south, the landscape changes and with it the animals which inhabit it. In the lush forests which cover a large part of the southern region are rabbits, hares, *coipo* and mice, wildcats, and other small animals. The *coipo*, a sort of Chilean beaver, is hard to see in the wild because it usually only comes out at night. Many of the animals which formerly populated the coast have been virtually wiped out by indiscriminate hunting, particularly the different species of seal which once thrived in the area.

Birds with names such as *huairavo, piquero, pollito de mar, pinguera, chucao, run-run*, and *becacinas* populate the forests, and the lizards are joined by four-eyed toads, the cowboy toad and different kinds of frogs. This is where Darwin's frog can be found. It lays eggs, which are then swallowed and tended by the male, who, upon their maturation, "gives birth" through the mouth to the young tadpoles.

The insect community includes a fascinating beetle, the *madre de la culebra* (snake's mother), which is a couple of centimeters or more in length, with long claws. Praying mantis, colorful "stink bugs" of a bright metallic blue, and different kinds of butterflies also thrive under the trees – although they, like all species, have been affected by the wholesale cutting and burning of Chile's native forests and have not adapted well to foreign species like the radiata pine planted by forestry companies.

Long-tailed snakes (which look very similar to North American garter snakes) and short-tailed snakes feed on mice, toads, and small birds. They're about 8cm (3in) long at birth and can grow to 2 meters (7ft). They are not poisonous.

Condors inhabit the high peaks of the cordillera, and Chile's mountain forests also provide homes for wild ducks, mountain partridges and tricahue parrots. *Felis colocolo* (mountain cats), which are peculiar to Chile, are an altogether unnerving sight – their physical appearance is exactly that of

The culpeo, or Chilean fox.

the marmalade domestic cat, but they live in the wild, surviving on partridge, hare, rabbit, mice, and birds.

The Lake District

Between Lago Vichuquén and the coastal village of Llico is the Reserva Nacional Laguna Torca, where graceful black-necked swans crowd the lake, feeding on aquatic plants and laying their eggs on floating nests. Upon hatching, the white offspring climb onto their parents' backs. Along the coast, colonies of penguins and swamp cormorants can be seen.

Farther south, the climate becomes increasingly damp and rainy, and the species change somewhat as a result. However, considerable deforestation in the area has severely cut back on what would otherwise be a numerous population of wild animals. There are still some foxes, *pudús*, wildcats, and pumas, but they tend to concentrate as far from human inhabitants as they can get, and are very difficult to spot.

The *pudú*, a tiny reddish deer which is endemic to Chile, lives in thickets in the densely forested areas between Chillán and Chiloé, and is almost impossible to spot in the wild. Also found in this region is the *llaca*, the only marsupial left in the southern Andes. It spends its life in the trees and feeds on fruit and insects. In winter it goes into a state of semi-hibernation, just lazing around in the trees.

Chile's smallest and rarest fox is the Darwin's or Chilote fox. The destruction of its natural habitat has put it in critical danger of extinction. It has, however, been sighted on the Isla Grande de Chiloé and in the forests north of Osorno.

The Lake District is home to one of the world's largest beetles, the stag beetle, which

Llamas inhabit the altiplano.

RESOURCEFUL REPTILES

Chile's varied landscapes are home to 76 species of lizard and six species of snake. Unlike most Chilean wildlife, reptiles are common throughout the country – except in the Magallanes region in the south. Many of these species are endemic to Chile. The history of their development has been extremely difficult to trace, but the sparse evidence available indicates that lizards go back about 70 million years in Chile.

Chilean lizards live in the desert, on the coast, in tropical forests, in the heights of the Andes, and on the Patagonian and southern steppes. Some lizards have been found at altitudes of up to 4,900 meters (16,000ft). These species live in underground burrows and have evolved special adaptations for keeping warm by absorbing more radiation from the sun.

Some lizards reproduce by laying eggs, while others give birth to live young. Sizes range from 10cm (4in) from nose tip to tail, and up to half a meter (1.5ft) long, as is the case with the Chilean iguana.

Lizards play a key role in the ecology, living on flies, crickets, locusts, and other insects, thus controlling the insect population. Many birds and several species of Chile's snakes in turn live on the lizards. None of the species found in Chile are dangerous: lizards generally prefer to get away if approached by humans and will only bite when there is no alternative.

grows as long as 9cm (3.5in) and lives in the oak and *coigüe* forests of this southern region. Woodpeckers and hummingbirds are common in the forests of the region, especially near wild fuchsia (bleeding hearts). Dolphins appear in the coastal areas, where whales were once hunted virtually into extinction.

Magallanes and Tierra del Fuego

High up in the most isolated southern parts of the Andes are small herds of *huemules*. In Chile's southernmost region, sea lions can also be sighted along with seals and dolphins. Beavers (which are introduced from abroad), muskrat and *coipo* are also common here, along with petrels, albatrosses, cormorants, and other seabirds. Foxes, guanacos, pumas, and skunks roam the pampas of Tierra del Fuego.

Magellanic penguins can be seen in colonies on the Otway Sound, situated 60km (37 miles) north of Punta Arenas, and on the island nature reserve of Monumento Natural Los Pingüinos, near Punta Arenas. Magellanic penguin skins were once heavily sought after by indigenous people in the area for clothing, and penguin eggs provided an important source of food.

Other birds scouring the beaches and fishing the coastal-shelf waters include blue-eyed cormorants, pintado petrels, wandering albatross, brown skuas, pink-footed shearwaters, chinstrap penguins, gulls, oystercatchers, and steamer ducks.

Within the chilly Antarctic waters, the delicate food chain depends first on marine zooplankton (arrow worms, microscopic crustaceans and shrimp-like krill). These zooplankton thrive in the nutrient-rich Antarctic water and feed the ecosystems of the continental shelf. Small marine species in the area depend on marine zooplankton for survival. There are hundreds of endemic mollusks, starfish, sea urchins, sponges, jellyfish, and other marine species that have adapted to the extreme temperatures and harsh conditions.

A little higher in the food chain are an estimated 25 species of octopus and squid, along with five fish families. Toward the top of the food chain are seals (Weddell, elephant, Ross, and leopard), fur seals, and sea lions, which, with their thick blubber and fur, are all well adapted to the cold Antarctic water. Unfortunately, hunting in the 20th century has significantly reduced their overall number; however, an international treaty has now been put in place to protect them.

The Weddell seal is the deepest diver, reaching depths of 600 meters (1,968ft), with the ability to hold its breath for over an hour. Fish, shellfish, and squid make up the bulk of the seal's diet, but the leopard seal will also feed on penguins and other seals.

The blue whale, measuring a massive 20–30 meters (66–98ft) in length and weigh-

Lesser Chilean flamingo.

Avoid contact with field mice or their droppings if camping or staying in rural cabins as some mice carry hantavirus. Cases are few and far between but the virus, which causes a form of pneumonia, can be fatal.

ing over 100 tons, consumes about 40,000kg (88,000lbs) of zooplankton each day. Orcas (killer whales) also inhabit the waters of southern Chile. They are particularly fond of eating sea lions, tossing them into the air with their tail fins to stun them before moving in for the kill.

Climbers in an ice cave on Grey
Glacier, Torres del Paine
National Park.

ADVENTURE ACTIVITIES

Chile's great outdoors is unusually tempting,
and there are many ways to enjoy it, whether
on skis, on a surfboard, in a boat, or on foot.

With over one third of the nation's population living in the capital Santiago, it is easy to find somewhere in Chile to get away from it all. But Chile offers more than remote and pristine wilderness. Its dramatic, untamed, and highly varied landscape makes it a land of adventure.

The options are as varied as the country's many geographical zones. In the north, the vast empty desert can only be crossed in a four-wheel drive. The heart of the Andes must be reached either on foot or on horseback. There are volcanoes to be climbed and rivers to be rafted, while the glacier-riddled islands of the southern archipelago can often only be visited on organized boat trips.

The season for adventure tourism is summer: November to March. This is when the weather stabilizes, save on the Andean high plain at the northeastern border with Bolivia, where electric storms are common. Do not expect rain in the Atacama Desert, even in the foothills – some parts only see rain every 30 to 50 years. From there to Santiago, rain rarely falls between October and March.

The spectacular Alpine and coastal wilderness of southern Chile attracts visitors from October through April. The town of Pucón is a good base from which to organize hikes, climbs, river rafting, mountain biking, and horseback riding into the nearby national parks of Huerquehue and Villarrica.

Chile's many volcanoes offer treats for hikers, while thrill-seekers scale the sheer rock faces of Patagonia, whose main attraction is Parque Nacional Torres del Paine. Here are great opportunities to hike or go horseback riding past towering granite spires and azure lakes, amid roaming guanaco and *ñandú* (rheas).

Chile has some of the world's best ski runs.

Hiking in Torres del Paine

Several companies offer trekking excursions in the most beautiful national park in the country, Parque Nacional Torres del Paine, created in 1959 and declared a Biosphere Reserve by Unesco in 1978.

The park itself is centered around the amazing "towers" and "horns" of rock, sculpted by glaciers, which point heavenward like daggers ripping at the sky's fluffy white belly. Here, the visitor will not only see some of the most incredible and beautiful Chilean landscapes, but will also experience everything that comes under the title "weather" – from cloudless skies to deafening thunderstorms, often in a lapse of only 24 hours.

Along the trails, there are log-cabin refuges belonging to two Puerto Natales-based companies, Fantástico Sur and Vértice Patagonia, but they get very full and, for the summer

Hiking in Monumento Natural El Morado.

season, need to be booked several months ahead. The distances between them are also sometimes a hike of as many as seven to eight hours and, for those visitors wishing to hike alone, a tent is a necessary precaution, as weather conditions can slow the hiker down, and rivers can swell, making it necessary to postpone a crossing. Garbage must be taken with you – abandoned garbage is often the only sign that one is not the first explorer to set foot in this unblemished, primeval territory and, although this is the far south, the pampa gets very dry in summer so extreme care is required with fires.

The rolling hills of Easter Island are another lovely and less strenuous place for trekking

(although beware of the sun). The pick of the hikes is along the northern coast where there are fewer *moai* sites than in the south but the scenery, with the white-flecked Pacific Ocean glistening beneath the cliffs, is spectacular.

Climbing a volcano

Chile has over 500 geologically active volcanoes of which around 60 have erupted in the past 500 years. Many are in the Lake District of southern Chile where Volcán Villarrica, near the resort town of Pucón, erupted in 2007, and again in 2015, causing substantial damage and triggering the evacuation of thousands of people. East of Puerto Montt lies Volcán Calbuco which also erupted in 2015. Copahue, a stratovolcano on the edge of the Bío-Bío region has erupted ten times in the last century, most recently in 2012–14.

If you care to take on one of these roaring giants, agencies in Pucón organize hiking tours right up to the very crater of Villarrica (2,840 meters/9,320ft). Walking up the conical mountain takes you through one of the centers of the Pacific "Ring of Fire," surrounded by volcanic peaks. Here and there are emerald and sapphire lakes. Sometimes you hear some of the dark, hidden underground groans of Mother Earth, and feel a few tremors and shakes. To stare down the 100-meter (330ft) drop into the crater of hellishly boiling molten lava is a sight few will forget. Here, the subterranean noises reach a roar and the stench of sulfur can be almost overpowering.

The ascent of the western face of Volcán Villarrica takes around four hours, thanks to a ski-lift that cuts the climbing distance. The descent of the volcano takes about three hours. The climb is strenuous, but anyone who is in reasonable health and physically fit should be able to make it.

It is also possible to ascend other volcanoes such as Llaima, with access from Parque Nacional Conguillío, and Osorno, near Lago Llanquihue. The ascent of the latter, however, is quite a bit more difficult, requires climbing gear and should not be undertaken without a guide.

In northern Chile, it is possible to climb Ojos del Salado, the world's highest active volcano, in the heart of the Atacama Desert, surrounded by green lagoons that are home to colonies of flamingos. Although a period of acclimatization is needed, the ascent is not difficult, and there are two mountain shelters on the route.

Horseback riding

Horseback riding is a popular way of exploring almost any part of Chile from the Atacama Desert to Torres del Paine and also Easter Island, and there are many places hiring horses or organizing treks. In central Chile, the best time of year is spring or fall when the days are long but the temperatures not as high as in summer.

Exploring the many nooks and crannies of the high Andes from the back of a horse and even crossing the mountains into Argentina is not as difficult as you might think, either in Santiago or the south. Riding skills are not required either, as, given the terrain, most of the trip is a walking tour. The guides for these trips are often *arrieros*, men who run cattle herds over the Andes or take them up to pasture after the spring snows melt. Many have learned the trails from their fathers and grandfathers before them. Their tales, related around the campfires as the beef sizzles on the spit, are worth learning Spanish to understand, and there is usually a musician to liven up the evenings.

Camping

Most of the national parks, managed by the National Forestry Service (CONAF), have camping facilities, ranging from very basic – leveled ground and a wooden picnic table – to those that include hot showers and, in some cases, a small shop. In summer, forest fires are a serious risk throughout Chile and it is essential to light fires and cook only in the permitted areas or, if camping outside a national park, to watch the wind carefully.

> There are an ever increasing number of cruises to Antarctica, most of which include opportunities to land on the Antarctic Peninsula. With its albatrosses, petrels, and penguin colonies, this is a birdwatchers' paradise.

The most popular national parks for camping are Pan de Azúcar in the Norte Chico and Conguillío and Vicente Pérez Rosales in the Lake District as well as Torres del Paine. Other less visited parks such as Tolhuaca in the northern

Lake District, however, offer great opportunities for trekking in almost virgin countryside.

For those who wish to camp on the banks of the fjords in Aisén or in Chiloé, beware of the large differences between low and high tide in the area. Grass-covered islands in the rivers, which are common at the inland extremes of fjords, can gradually disappear at high tide, particularly around the time of the full moon. More than one camper in the Cahuelmó fjord has had to keep warm in the thermal tubs carved into the hillside after he and all his gear were soaked at 2am, when the full moon's

Horseback riding through the Andes.

tide came in. Short, yellow, wild flowers with bunches of tiny concave petals mark the highest tide level.

When camping in dense forest it is worth bringing a machete to clear the site. Ferns and the gigantic leaves of the *nalca* vie with the native bamboo *quila* and towering trees for ground space. Hanging, flowering vines twist up trunks bearded by thousands of varieties of multicolored lichens. Where the forest canopy allows sufficient light, one finds native blue *calafate* and red *murtilla* berries growing.

Sailing the southern channels

A number of boats visit the archipelagos of southern Chile. In many cases, small short-distance vessels are rather lacking in safety measures and have a tendency toward dangerous overcrowding during the peak season. The calmest parts of the day for naviga-

> Easter Island is a diver's paradise and, although the coast of the Chilean mainland, washed by the cold Humboldt Current, is not usually thought of as diving territory, it is an increasingly popular activity, particularly in the Norte Chico.

Camping out in the Chilean Andes.

tion tend to be early morning and sunset. On these journeys, it is a good idea to take your own life jacket and water, and a sleeping bag to put over the bare mattresses or reclining chairs on the freighters. Other recommended items include woolen pants, socks, and a heavy sweater or fleece jacket. Rubber boots are best for going ashore. Stops are often made in pristine, uninhabited environments and where the clear, unforested land tends to be marshy at the water's edge. Here, birds which have no fear (or knowledge) of humans will sometimes hop onto your shoes, to pull at the laces, presumably mistaking them for hefty worms.

The most luxurious cruise boats are those of Skorpios (see page 293) for trips from Puerto

Montt to Laguna San Rafael by way of the Northern Ice Fields, or from Puerto Natales to the glaciers of the Southern Ice Fields. Navimag (see page 293) runs regular scheduled freighters on rather spartan voyages between Puerto Montt and Puerto Chacabuco, or through the windswept Golfo de Penas to Puerto Natales.

Cruceros Australis operates the comfortable *Stella Australis* and *Via Australis* ships that navigate the Patagonian Channels from Punta Arenas to Ushuaia in Argentina, passing through the Strait of Magellan and the Beagle Channel and its glaciers at the very southern tip of Chile. On the way back, it visits Isla Magdalena, which is inhabited by thousands of breeding pairs of Magellanic penguins and their chicks from October through March.

Sea kayaking

The fjords and majestic mountains of northern Patagonia make a spectacular backdrop for sea kayaking. The Canal de Dalcahue (Dalcahue Channel) is a good area for beginners to practice before heading out to the other islands off Isla de Chiloé. Altué Active Travel organizes sea kayaking trips that last from one to nine days. Around the Golfo de Ancud (Gulf of Ancud), in northern Patagonia, particularly Hornopirén and the fjords of Comau, Quintupeu, and Cahuelmó off the Pumalín Park are glacial valleys, thermal hot springs, and temperate rainforests, with dolphins, sea lions, and penguins. It is also possible to kayak in Laguna San Rafael among the blue and lavender icebergs that calve off its gigantic glacier.

> The River Biobío in central Chile used to be one of the most exciting rivers in all the Andes. However, following the construction of the vast Ralco hydroelectric dam, only the rapids on its very upper reaches remain.

White-water rafting

The River Futaleufú, southeast of Chaitén, in Aisén, is Chile's white-water paradise. Depending on the water level, the river's rapids are rated grade 4+ on the international scale of 1 to 6, while upstream, the Inferno Canyon and Terminator sections can reach grade 5+, and this is not a trip to be attempted by anyone but expert kayakers with guides. Shorter excursions on other rivers, such as the Palena in Aisén or the Petrohué in the Lake District, are not quite as wild as the Futaleufú, but every bit as exciting, and can be easily arranged. Relaxing day trips floating down stretches of the River Trancura can be organized in Pucón; the upper reaches of the river are stunning, with a backdrop of high volcanoes, while in the lower part, it becomes calmer, but "bouncy."

Near Santiago, rafting on the River Maipo is also popular and can be included as part of a day trip into the Cajón del Maipo. This can be arranged through travel agencies in the city or the Cascada de Las Animas cabin-and-restaurant center in the Cajón.

Skiing and snowboarding

Chile has some of the best long ski runs in the world. Most runs are at altitudes of around 3,000 meters (9,843ft), and there is an abundance of natural snow, particularly "champagne" snow blown in from the Antarctic storms. Resorts stretch from just north of Santiago all the way to Patagonia. Portillo, in central Chile near the border with Argentina, is one of the most famous ski resorts in South

Rafting on the Maipo river.

NORTHERN JEEP EXCURSIONS

The Chilean Norte Grande offers a wide selection of geological phenomena and archeological sites, from ancient civilizations to the remains of early 20th century nitrate-mining "ghost towns" (see page 181). However, vast distances between sites and roads that are often barely distinguishable tracks make traveling difficult. Some sites are very hard to find so a good option is to pay for a driver or an organized excursion in a four-wheel drive vehicle. Tours can be arranged in Arica Iquique, Calama, and San Pedro de Atacama.

The main rule of thumb in the desert is never to leave the road unless you know exactly where you are going. It can take hours of pushing and shoving in the blazing sun to free a vehicle stuck in the sand. It is also important to take a large supply of fresh water along. Even up in the mountains where it is possible to find streams, a high mineral content often makes the water brackishly saline and generally undrinkable.

The desert can be very cold after the sun goes down so take warm clothing even if it seems a ludicrous prospect in the cloying heat of the desert. Prepare also for the effects of altitude if you are embarking on a trip to the El Tatio geysers or the high altiplano.

America. Frequented by skiers from around the world, it is often used by northern hemisphere national teams for training during their summer. Valle Nevado, near Santiago, is the seat of snowboarding world cups. Heli-skiing, paragliding, and parascending are also available here. The best time to visit is June to October (see page 151).

Termas de Chillán, situated in the Central Valley, 80km (50 miles) east of Chillán on the slopes of Volcán Chillán (3,122 meters/10,243ft) is famous for its thermal springs. There are plenty of groomed runs, but

Mountain biking through the Salar de Atacama.

if you want to get away from the crowd, it is easy to find virgin powder runs.

To reach the extreme runs, you can either hike up the mountain or go for the easy (and pricey) option and take a helicopter. A special park has been set up for snowboarders to show off their freestyle moves. Other attractions at the resort are snowmobile and helicopter tours. After a long, hard day on the snow, you can relax in the thermal baths. The season runs from June to September.

Mountain biking

There are endless places to go biking, particularly in southern Chile, and this is also one way to explore Easter Island, but it's probably best to bring your own bike if you want to go any distance in Chile. If you go biking in the desert north, where trails pass through the salt flats, national parks, and indigenous villages, it's essential to carry water supplies. The Carretera Austral often attracts cyclists along its unpaved road. Group expeditions are organized by Pared Sur.

Fishing

Wild rainbow and brown trout and six species of Pacific salmon may be the reward for a fishing expedition anywhere in the south of Chile. Two- to 3.5kg (4-8lb) trout are a rule rather than an exception. Some say that the trout are so abundant you have to use a stick to prevent smaller fish from jumping into your boat – which may or may not be another fisherman's tale. In the Lake District, Aisén and on Tierra del Fuego, upmarket lodges cater for the flyfishing market; otherwise contact local hotels or travel agencies for organized excursions.

Surfing

Many spots along the coast of Chile have acquired a worldwide reputation as surfing centers, with good conditions virtually all year round. In the north, the most popular center is Iquique but, Arica also has good and less crowded beaches. Farther south, the water becomes colder and a 3x2 wetsuit will be needed.

From the Santiago region the coastal shelf is more abrupt, and swell conditions pretty consistent. Punta de Lobos near Pichilemu, a popular beach resort just south of Santiago, is internationally renowned. Adventure travel agencies in Santiago such as Chile Extremo offer all-inclusive trips from Santiago, accompanied by an instructor.

Paragliding

With its mountains and long coastline, Chile offers many opportunities for paragliding (*parapente*). It is most popular in the north, particularly Iquique, and at seaside resorts along the coast near Santiago. There are paragliding schools in many of these resorts and the Civil Aviation Board (www.dgac.gob.cl) maintains a list of clubs, many of which offer classes. Some adventure tourism agencies, including Chile Extremo, offer all-inclusive tours with an instructor.

The Chilean Trail

The creation of the Sendero de Chile has opened up a network of hiking trails through some of Chile's most spectacular scenery.

One of Chile's main attractions is its variety of landscapes – from the vast, windswept expanses of the *altiplano* (high plain) to the huge salt flats of the north to the lush virgin forests of the south. The only catch is that much of the most beautiful scenery is far off the beaten track and not easily accessible, but, for those visitors who like walking, biking, or horseback riding, there is a solution – the Sendero de Chile (Chilean Trail).

The trail, on which work started in 2003, currently comprises segments in different parts of the country – selected as particularly representative of some of Chile's most unique scenery – that will eventually connect. When it is complete, the trail will cover over 8,500km (5,300 miles) of paths, making it the longest hiking trail in the world.

Joining the trail

A convenient place to join the Sendero de Chile is the Mahuida Park in the La Reina district of eastern Santiago. From there, it is possible to walk or cycle 8km (5 miles) along the foothills of the Andes with a magnificent view of the city spread out below. Just south of Santiago, another segment starts from the Termas de Cauquenes (see page 192) and climbs steadily 26km (16 miles) alongside a small river to the Portezuelo de las Nieves Hill (1,850 meters/ 6,070ft).

Longer segments of the trail are to be found in the north of the country and the far south. In the north, to the east of the port of Iquique, two separate stretches, both of some 100km (62 miles), run through salt flats as they weave their way beneath snow-capped volcanoes, following a route once used by the Incas. The first starts in Colchane, a town with a bus service from Iquique, while the other can be joined at the Coposa salt flat, close to the road from Iquique to the Collahuasi copper mine.

In the far south, a segment of a similar length stretches from Palena, near the border with Argentina, south to the beautiful Lago Verde (Green Lake), passing through dense forests and rolling grasslands against a backdrop of mountains and glaciers. This part of the trail, which crosses several rivers with abundant fish, can only be covered on horseback and in summer (November to March).

In a token to Chile's numerous island territories, small segments of the trail also exist on Easter Island and Robinson Crusoe Island. There is an 8km (5-mile) stretch of the trail on Easter Island that is suitable for both trekking and horseback riding.

Trails all over Chile will join up to create the Sendero de Chile.

Use of the trail is free, except when it passes through a national park (where the normal entrance fee is charged). In national parks, camping facilities are normally available, and, because the project has been developed in close collaboration with the communities along its path, some of these offer basic accommodations as well as an opportunity to pick up provisions. However, elsewhere, visitors are literally on their own – except for the company of the wildlife and the unparalleled scenery.

The Chilean trail is being developed further by the Ministry for the Environment and the Sendero de Chile Foundation. Further information can be found at www.senderodechile.cl.

THE SKILLS AND THRILLS OF THE RODEO

The horse is the star of Chile's national sport, demonstrating skills of patience and agility, with the help of its close companion, the *huaso*.

The stocky Chilean horse, or *corralero*, is the inseparable companion of the horseman, or *huaso*. This working pair still dominates in the movement of stock in the Chilean countryside. The *huaso* and his horse are also the protagonists in one of Chile's national sports – the rodeo.

Most rodeos are held between September and May. The most famous is the Chilean Championship, held at the end of March or in early April in Rancagua, in the Central Valley. In a semicircular arena, or *medialuna*, a pair of riders and their mounts attempt to chase and maneuver a steer to a padded section of wall. Here it must be stopped and held by direct horse-to-steer body contact. The curved shape of the corral means the horse must learn to gallop sideways, an extremely difficult task. The *huasos* must work in close, fast coordination, one chasing the steer, the other hemming it close to the wall. This exercise produces spectacular shows of horsemanship, with horses spinning about on their back legs, changing direction, rearing, and galloping as they track the steer about the ring. Riders earn *puntos buenos* (good points) or *puntos malos* (bad points) depending on where they hit the steer, if brute force is used (the rougher, the more bad points), and their appearance.

Unlike Australian and American rodeos, in Chile there is no roping or riding of wild beasts, although the animal still gets knocked about somewhat.

A huaso's Cuban-heeled boots sport large spoked spurs, ensuring a melodic jangle when he walks. He also wears finely plaited, tasselled leather leggings.

Rodeo beauty queen, Valparaíso.

Dancing the cueca at a rodeo.

DANCING WITH THE DEVIL

After the excitement of a rodeo, a hearty meal of beef and beans is knocked back with red wine. Then out from the pockets come the handkerchiefs for the *cueca*, Chile's national dance. The *cueca* is an integral part of the event, and a *huaso* is not roundly accomplished if his Cuban-heeled boots don't do a coordinated stomp.

To begin the *cueca* (pronounced like "quaker"), the man first advances toward his female partner in a courting fashion. She, keeping her distance, establishes the pattern of pursuer and pursued. Folklore has it that the dance is inspired by a rooster stalking a hen. As the courting continues, both partners hold their handkerchiefs aloft and flick them about as they step in a smooth, shuffling manner. The dance must be accompanied by festive music and a crowd of clapping onlookers, spurring the man on in his hot pursuit.

The *cueca* produces such a high-spirited response that Chileans believe even the devil himself can't help but uncrumple his scarf and join in with a young *señorita*.

Tense spectators at a rodeo near Valparaíso.

A well-stocked talabartería, or saddlery, will offer an impressive selection of hand-made leather tack and carved wooden stirrups.

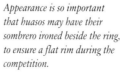

Appearance is so important that huasos may have their sombrero ironed beside the ring, to ensure a flat rim during the competition.

Quad biker in the desert, near Copiapó.

INTRODUCTION

A detailed guide to the entire country, with
principal sites clearly cross-referenced
to specially drawn maps.

Easter Island.

Despite its elongated shape, Chile is one of the easiest countries in South America to travel around. Domestic flights connect the country's major cities; modern passenger buses run to almost every minor town (and depart punctually every time), and passenger boats link remote locations in the far south.

Almost all travelers flying into Chile arrive in the bustling capital of Santiago. At the country's midway point, Santiago is the logical base for exploring. Just a 90-minute drive away is the capital's colorful port city, Valparaíso, while neighboring Viña del Mar is one of Chile's most popular beach resorts. Irregular flights from Santiago also reach the Juan Fernández Islands, famous as the temporary home of the Scottish sailor whose experiences inspired the novel *Robinson Crusoe*.

The landscape north of Santiago becomes progressively drier as it extends toward the hauntingly beautiful Atacama Desert. Many travelers fly directly to Calama, support town for the spectacular Chuquicamata copper mine, before heading for the oasis village of San Pedro de Atacama. In the vicinity are ancient pre-Columbian ruins, thermal springs, salt flats, and dramatic geyser fields.

Most of Chile's vineyards are located south of Santiago in the lush Central Valley. Farther south, beyond the River Biobío, lies one of Chile's most famous attractions, the Lake District, with its spectacular rivers, volcanoes, forests, and lakes. The fishing port of Puerto Montt marks the end of the Lake District. South of this point, the landscape becomes wilder and travel more unpredictable, although boat cruises through the southern archipelago are popular. Aisén is a vast area of woods and glaciers opened up over the past 30 years by the Carretera Austral road. Then come the sheep plains of Magallanes and Parque Nacional Torres del Paine. At the southernmost tip of Chile is the windswept island of Tierra del Fuego, shared with Argentina.

Osorno volcano, National Park Vicente Perez Rosales.

Chile's most remote outpost is Easter Island, 3,800km (2,360 miles) west of the mainland. This mysterious speck of land covered with ancient statues continues to attract and intrigue visitors from all over the world.

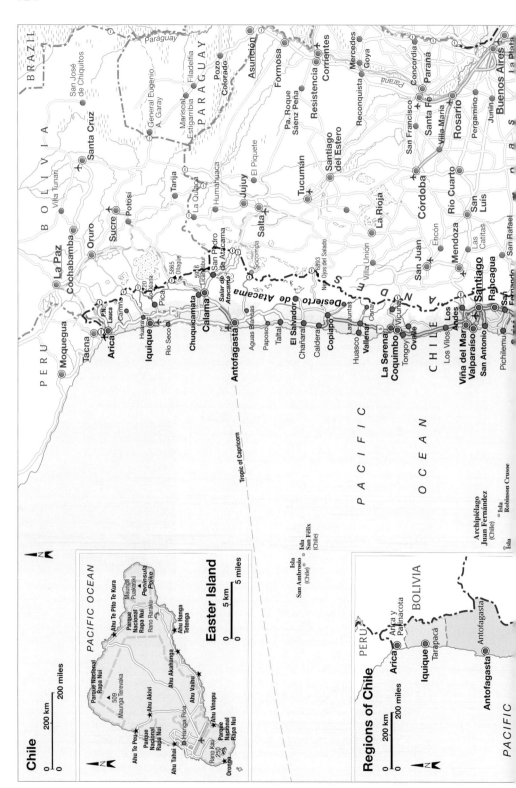

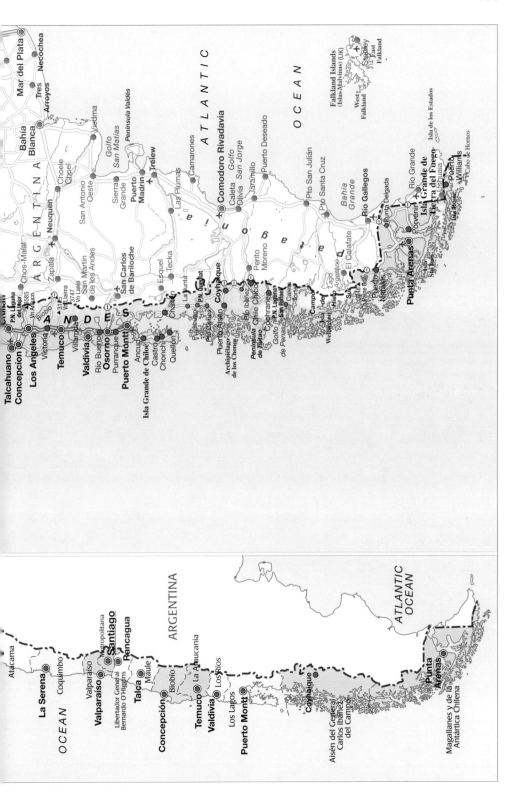

Santiago at night.

SANTIAGO

Most of Santiago's main sights cluster in the downtown area but, beyond that, there are parks and markets to explore and, in El Golf and El Bosque districts, smart sidewalk cafés and some of the capital's best restaurants.

When Chilean children draw or paint, in the background there is almost always a stylized line of snow-capped mountains. In Santiago, it is easy to see why. Rising immediately alongside the city, the Andes are a constant presence, engraving themselves on the minds and subconscious of *santiaguinos* from birth. For the visitor, they not only impress with their beauty (above all when bathed in the rose-colored light of a clear sunset), but also serve a very practical purpose: it is hard to lose your bearings in Santiago.

So long, that is, as the smog does not cloud your vision. Air pollution is a serious problem in Santiago, especially during the winter when it is worsened by the city's almost windless location between the Andes and nearby hills, making one wish fervently that the Spanish conquistador Pedro de Valdivia had been forewarned about the internal combustion engine before siting Santiago here in 1541. But this is the only real drawback to a gently attractive and unpretentious city, whose people, though less effusive than others in Latin America, are friendly and always ready to welcome foreigners. Endowed with an ideal Mediterranean, or Californian, climate it is a pleasant place to visit at any time of year.

Santiago is also one of the most manageable capitals in Latin America

for the first-time visitor. It is a big city but, standing in the compact few blocks and narrow streets of its center, it's hard to believe you are at the heart of a conurbation of over 6,1 million people. The city's sprawling extension gives it a feeling of spaciousness, despite the mountains; only in the center is there much of the sense of pressure and density characteristic of most cities of this size. Most of the rest is residential suburbs: leafy avenues and sophisticated shopping malls in the plush *barrio alto* (high

Main Attractions

Palacio de la Moneda
Plaza de Armas
Museo Chileno de Arte Precolombino
Mercado Central
Museo Nacional de Bellas Artes
Cerro San Cristóbal
Barrio Bellavista
Parque Quinta Normal
Museo de la Memoria y de los Derechos Humanos

Taking in the view.

Central Santiago

0 — 200 m
0 — 200 yds

neighborhood), and vast swathes of well-tended middle-class neighborhoods and poor working-class areas – labyrinthine networks of tiny adobe and wooden dwellings, and bleak state-subsidized apartment blocks.

Avenida Bernardo O'Higgins

Many visitors are struck by the European feel of Santiago, with its tidy grass verges and elegantly fading French-style buildings, but after three decades of free-market economics, the North American influence is more apparent in more recently developed areas of the city. The old buildings of the city center were built by European architects, inspired by Paris and Rome, but the glass and marble of the *barrio alto* offices transport the visitor to Chicago or Houston rather than a European capital.

Getting around Santiago is easy. A brief glance at a map will reveal just how straightforward the city is. You're almost bound to enter the city along **Avenida Libertador General Bernardo O'Higgins**. This broad avenue, named after the Chilean-Irish independence hero and father of the republic, has been the city's main thoroughfare since a fork of the River Mapocho was filled in before independence to create it. It is known universally as the "Alameda" (a word of Arab origin meaning an avenue with trees and spaces for recreation).

If you enter Santiago on the old road from the airport, rather than taking the ring road or the Costanera Norte highway, your first main point of reference will be the imposing wrought iron of the **Estación Central**, the city's only remaining functioning railway station.

Palacio de la Moneda

The ugly concrete telecommunications tower run by the company Entel announces the beginning of the city center proper. A block farther on, the Alameda broadens, and the low form of the presidential palace, **La Moneda Ⓐ**, rises to the left. La Moneda, so called because it was originally designed by the Italian architect Joaquín Toesca as the country's mint, was built between 1788 and 1805.

The Entel telecommunications tower – one of the city's less attractive landmarks, but the center of a great firework display on New Year's Eve.

Palacio de la Moneda.

Negotiating your way around Santiago is pretty straightforward as much of the city is built on a grid system. Free street maps are available at Sernatur tourist offices.

Between 1846 and 1958, Chile's presidents lived there, sharing the premises with the mint until 1929. Squat by comparison with the high ministerial buildings around it (Toesca designed it low to resist earthquakes), many consider La Moneda one of the finest examples of colonial public buildings in the subcontinent.

The building's tragic international fame came with the military coup led by General Augusto Pinochet on September 11, 1973, when much of its interior was destroyed by bombing from Air Force Hawker Hunters, and its image – smoke and flames belching from its northern side – leaped onto the world's front pages and TV screens. It was here that the overthrown president, the socialist Dr Salvador Allende, committed suicide during the onslaught.

The restored palace was re-inaugurated in 1981 as the seat of government. The free guided tours (Mon–Fri 9.30am, 11am, 3pm, 4.30pm) of some of the beautifully restored rooms, with their prime collection of Chilean painting, can be arranged by appointment at http://visitasguiadas.presidencia.cl or visitas@presidencia.cl; www.gob.cl)).

Around La Moneda

In front of the palace's main entrance, in the **Plaza de la Constitución**, former presidents Jorge Alessandri and Eduardo Frei, the father of President Frei who was elected in 1993, and Salvador Allende stare at each other from their pedestals on opposite sides of the square. The plaza was remodeled by General Pinochet, who built underneath it a complex network of meeting rooms, offices, an emergency war room, and a television studio for making broadcasts to the nation, all known popularly as *el bunker* – the entrances are visible on three sides of the square. On the west side of the plaza is what was once the **Hotel Carrera** and is now the Ministry of Foreign Affairs. It was from the upper stories of the Carrera that the bombing of La Moneda during the 1973 coup was filmed.

On the south side of the palace is the **Plaza de la Ciudadanía**, inaugurated in 2006, and one of a number of projects implemented to celebrate the

Watching the world go by in Bellavista.

Over the last 50 years, Santiago has grown from a compact city of 2 million inhabitants to one that, with a population of over 6 million, has spread east up the Andes foothills, creating the prosperous residential districts of La Dehesa and Lo Barnechea. To the north, housing estates with large gardens, favored by middle-class families with young children, have also sprung up on what was once agricultural land. The working-class districts of southern Santiago have expanded all the way up to Puente Alto, a former country town that has become a major dormitory with its own subway link to the city center. New business centers have also appeared and, although many banks still have their headquarters in downtown Santiago, other businesses have moved to the more fashionable El Bosque and El Golf districts.

bicentenary of Chile's independence in 2010. Underneath the esplanade, with its glistening expanses of water, lies the **Centro Cultural Palacio de La Moneda**, a beautifully designed arts center. As well as exhibition rooms, it houses a collection of Chilean films, which are shown regularly in its movie theaters, and an excellent craft shop run by the Artesanías de Chile Foundation which ensures its suppliers fair prices (www.ccplm. cl; daily 9am–9pm; exhibitions daily 9am–7.30pm; free until noon).

Across the Alameda is the Plaza O'Higgins, flanked by the headquarters of the armed forces and the Carabinero police. Every other day at 10am (Mon–Fri) or 11am (Sat–Sun), a green-uniformed, jackbooted detail of the Carabinero palace guard, a special unit whose members are selected for their height, marches from the Carabinero HQ to La Moneda in an impressive changing-of-the-guard ceremony.

Along the Alameda

Continuing along the Alameda, past the **Banco del Estado** on the left is the

Club de la Unión (www.clubdelaunion. cl), Latin America's oldest gentleman's club. The building, inaugurated in 1925, is lavishly decorated inside in Louis XIV and XV, Gothic, and other European styles. All the club's tableware was specially imported from France, Spain, and England, and it has an excellent collection of Chilean art.

Opposite, on the southern side of the Alameda is the yellow-washed central campus building of the **Universidad de Chile ⑧**. The building, begun in 1863, was designed by Lucien Henault, one of the contracted French architects who founded the neoclassical style which dominated Chilean public architecture of the time and hence much of the profile of Santiago's city center. Outside is a statue of the university's founder, the Venezuelan exile Andrés Bello, one of the continent's great intellectual figures of the 19th century.

Back on the north side of the Alameda, beyond Calle Bandera, is the **Paseo Ahumada**, a busy pedestrian walkway that bisects the city center from north to south. On the other side

Santiago's efficient Metro system provides a cheap and easy way to get around the city.

Underground art at Centro Cultural Palacio La Moneda.

of the Alameda is one of Santiago's best-known landmarks: the red-washed colonial church of **San Francisco**  (daily), the oldest in the capital. Franciscan friars built the first church on this site in 1572 to house the "Virgen del Socorro" (the Helpful Virgin), which Pedro de Valdivia himself brought to South America, firmly attached to his saddle. The original adobe church was destroyed by an earthquake in 1583 and replaced by a stone church, the nave of which survives, that was completed in 1612. The church's distinctive tower was added in 1860. The "Virgen del Socorro," of Italian or Spanish origin, was declared the patron of Santiago by the conquistadors after she was said to have saved them during the first major Mapuche attack in the Mapocho Valley by appearing before them and throwing dirt into the attackers' eyes. Much-venerated, she can still be seen above the church's main altar.

Inside the church, note the wooden ceiling, built in the first half of the 17th century. The attractive cedarwood choir stalls are the oldest in Chile. The museum in the adjacent Franciscan monastery (Mon–Fri 9.30am–1.30pm, 3–6pm, Sat–Sun 10am–2pm; http://museosanfrancisco.com) has a fine collection of Chilean and Peruvian colonial art, including 54 large-scale paintings of the life of San Francisco.

Behind the square outside the church is the quaint **Barrio París-Londres**, two short streets named after these European capitals, whose houses, designed as a whole by a group of architects in the 1920s, jumble together imitations of styles ranging from neoclassical to Mudéjar and Gothic. The next structure of note is the **Biblioteca Nacional** , which occupies the main part of a block on the northern side of the Alameda. The imposing building, in late 19th-century French style, opened in 1924 and houses one of Latin America's largest national libraries and archives, with a reading room open to the public and free concerts, talks, and film shows (tel: 02-360 5400; Mon–Sat, closed Sat pm; free guided tours can be arranged by appointment; www.bibliotecanacional.cl).

Cerro Santa Lucía

Beyond the Biblioteca is one of Santiago's most curious and historically significant sites, the **Cerro Santa Lucía**  (Tue–Sun 9am–8pm; free). It was here, on what was then a rocky outcrop known by the indigenous people as Huelén (Pain), that Pedro de Valdivia and his 150 men first encamped, and Valdivia decided to found the city. He renamed the *cerro* (hill) after the saint of the date on which he reached it, December 13, 1540. In August 1834, Charles Darwin stayed for a week in Santiago and climbed the "little hillock of rock," noting the striking view. A plaque on the hill commemorates his visit. In 1872, the great historian and governor of Santiago, Benjamín Vicuña Mackenna, began to transform the hill into the baroque maze of pathways, gardens, fountains, and squares which it is now.

Together with the **Parque Forestal** (see page 138) by the River Mapocho, the Cerro is one of the city's best-loved

The former National Congress building.

venues for lovers and strollers. There is a lift on the west side, on Calle Santa Lucía.

At the foot of the Cerro, on the Alameda, is a fine mural in homage to Gabriela Mistral, representing the poet herself and the main themes of her work. A few yards farther on, a smooth rock is set in the skirt of the hill, engraved with an extract of a letter sent by Pedro de Valdivia to Emperor Charles V in 1545, extolling Chile's climatic virtues.

The Cerro marks the end of the city center as such, and the start of the last stretch of the Alameda. On its north side is the former Diego Portales building, erected in record speed and constructivist style in 1972. After part of it was destroyed by a fire in 2006, it was given a face lift and transformed into the **Centro Cultural Gabriela Mistral** ❻ – or, as it is more commonly known, GAM (www.gam.cl) – an arts center with, among other facilities, lovely wood-paneled concert rooms, a library, cafés, restaurants and an antiques market (Tue–Sun 11am–8pm).

Just across the road stands the Carabineros' church, the small neo-Gothic **Iglesia de San Francisco de Borja**, and in front of it a monument to members of the police force who were killed in the line of duty. Immediately afterwards is the Crowne Plaza Hotel (www.ihg.com), located opposite one of the city's best art-house movie theaters, the Centro Arte Alameda (www.centroartealameda.cl).

A few meters farther on, the Alameda ends at the junction with Avenida Vicuña Mackenna and the Plaza Italia (also referred to as Plaza Baquedano), centered on the equestrian statue of General Manuel Baquedano, commander of the Chilean army during the War of the Pacific against Peru and Bolivia. This spot – the city's traditional gathering point for everything from the celebration of football victories to protest demonstrations – marks the end of central Santiago and the beginning of Providencia and the *barrio alto*.

Shopping and business

If the Alameda is the center's main thoroughfare for motor traffic,

FACT

Gabriela Mistral (1889–1957) was the first person in Latin America to be awarded the Nobel Prize for Literature, in 1945. See page 171.

Picturesque Cerro Santa Lucía.

Ahumada is the pedestrian hub. At its southern entrance is the Universidad de Chile subway station, decorated with giant murals by Chilean painter Mario Toral.

Everyone – shoppers, businesspeople, and street artists – seems to converge in Ahumada. Business gossip is exchanged in cafés like the Haiti (www.cafehaiti.cl), where mini-skirted young women serve *expresos* and *cortados* (black and white coffee) with glasses of mineral water. Crowds press past the Paseo's many and varied shops, banks, department stores, and well-stocked newspaper kiosks.

To the left of Ahumada is the *barrio cívico*, a few blocks built in the 1930s around La Moneda in rigorously utilitarian style. This area holds the **Intendencia** (corner of Moneda and Morandé), the **Stock Exchange** (Calle La Bolsa, just behind the Club de la Unión), the **Banco del Estado**, the **Central Bank**, and most government ministries.

Uptown from Ahumada, three blocks along Calle Agustinas, is the recently restored 17th-century church of **San Agustín**, site of an interesting wooden crucifix above the northern altar carved in Peru in 1613 (daily, closed Sun pm). Beyond the church is the **Teatro Municipal** Ⓖ (www.municipal.cl; guided tours available in English). Designed and restored by French architects – its original plans were approved by Charles Garnier, the architect of the Paris Opera – the theater opened in 1857. Housing the city's symphony orchestra and ballet and opera companies, the theater has played host to artists from Sarah Bernhardt to Plácido Domingo, who appeared there in 1990. Opposite the theater is perhaps the city's finest example of the influence of late 19th-century French architecture: a house built by the millionaire wine-producing family of French origin, the Subercaseaux, now occupied by the Air Force Officers' Club (www.clubfach.cl).

Plaza de Armas and the Cathedral

Ahumada ends in **Plaza de Armas** Ⓗ, the city's historic center. Originally

Changing of the guard at the Presidential Palace.

traced out by Pedro de Valdivia in 1541, it takes its name from the weapons held in the fort built in the square to shelter the first settlers at night. Thereafter, the plaza was used for all public activities from troop parades and religious processions to hangings. It is always a hive of activity: shoe shiners, portrait painters, and Pentecostal preachers ply their trades while chess players gather on the bandstand on its eastern side.

The **Catedral** ❶ (www.iglesiadesantiago.cl; daily 9.30am–8pm), on the west side of the plaza, is the fifth on the site. Earthquakes destroyed its predecessors in 1552, 1647, and 1730, while the first was burned down in an attack by native people shortly after Pedro de Valdivia built it. Work on the present building began in 1747, but the final design was by Joaquín Toesca, who was brought from Italy for this task, moving on later to La Moneda (see page 129) – though the twin towers were not added until 1899 by another Italian, Ignacio Cremonesi. The cathedral's interior bears the somewhat heavy imprint of the Bavarian Jesuits who created much of it, although some of their work, and important local handicraft adornments, were destroyed by clumsy restoration carried out by Cremonesi. Those buried in the cathedral include the three Carrera brothers and their sister, partners and rivals with O'Higgins in the country's liberation from Spain (see page 36), and Diego Portales (see page 39), considered by many as the founder of Chile's 19th-century conservative state. After the Conquest, the land along the northern face of the plaza was owned by Pedro de Valdivia, who lived in a house on the site now occupied by the **Correo Central** (central post office). In 1541, however, the house was burned down in an attack by native people; later, Valdivia sold the land to the Royal Treasury in order to finance further expeditions south. Two centuries later, the post office site saw the city's first, and reputedly magnificent, theater. Chile's first stamps, printed in England, were sold here in 1857 and the present building was finished in 1902. Following damage caused by the 2010 earthquake, the church underwent a

The city's historic Cathedral on the Plaza de Armas.

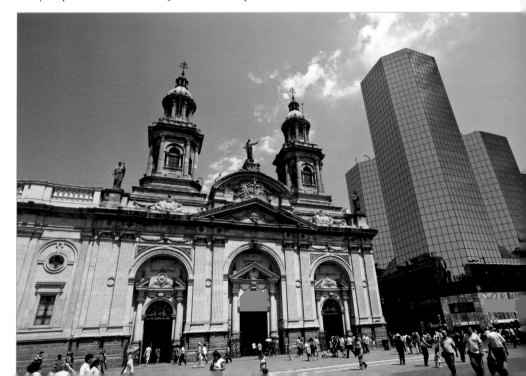

TIP

Chile celebrates its
National Heritage Day
on the last Sunday of
May, when historic
buildings that are not
usually open to the
public can be visited.

complete renovation, with steel and carbon fiber reinforcements added to protect its structure.

Museo Histórico Nacional

Next door to the Correo Central is the Palacio de la Real Audiencia, now the **Museo Histórico Nacional** (Tue–Sun 10am–6pm; free; www.museohistorico nacional.cl), which was inaugurated in 1808 to house the sessions at which the Spanish Crown's representatives heard local reports and dispensed justice. This purpose was short-lived, however, and two years later the building was used for the swearing-in of the first revolutionary government junta. The first Congress met here, and the palace was the seat of government until President Bulnes moved to La Moneda in 1846. The museum, which traces Chilean history from the pre-Conquest to the 20th century, moved there in 1982 and is well worth a visit.

The last building along the plaza's northern edge is the **Municipalidad** or Town Hall (not open to the public). Formerly the Palacio Consistorial, it was designed by Toesca for the colonial

Statue of Pedro de Valdivia, in front of the Museo Historico Nacional, Santiago.

cabildo and opened in 1790. The facade was replaced in the 1890s by the present neoclassical design, and restored again after the 1985 earthquake. High on the facade, and in the wrought ironwork above the entrance, you can see the red lion coat of arms granted to the city by the Spanish Crown after the first *cabildo* met. In front is an equestrian statue of Pedro de Valdivia donated by Chile's Spanish community in 1986.

On Calle Merced, at the southeast corner of the square, is the striking red-washed **Casa Colorada**. Built in 1769, this is the best-preserved colonial house in the city. It was the residence of the president of the first revolutionary junta, Mateo de Toro y Zambrano and, for a time, of Lord Thomas Cochrane, the maverick Scottish admiral hired by O'Higgins to command naval operations against Spain. It now houses a tourist office. Plaza de Armas has two sidewalk cafés, but, behind the Casa Colorada, there is a small plaza, sheltered from the city noise, with a restaurant, Ambrosia (www.ambrosia.cl), that is a good place for a coffee or light lunch.

Museo Chileno de Arte Precolombino

Two blocks westward, the excellent **Museo Chileno de Arte Precolombino** ❶ (Bandera 361; www.precolombino.cl; Tue–Sun 10am–6pm; free first Sun of the month) occupies what used to be the Real Aduana (Customs House). This museum is widely recognized as the best and most important in Santiago following a major renovation completed in 2014. Immediately west are the Law Courts, and across Calle Compañía is the neoclassical grandeur of what was the pre-1973 Congress Building. Previously, this was the site of the Jesuit headquarters (hence the name of the street, after the Compañía de Jesús), until they were expelled from the country in 1766, and later of a church which burned down in 1863, at the cost of 2,000 lives. Also close by is the curious but sadly run down **Palacio de la Alhambra** (Compañía 1340; closed for renovation), begun in the 1860s and later transformed into a miniature copy of the famous Mudéjar palace of the same name in Granada, Spain, complete with mock-Arab furniture made in Paris.

Mercado Central

If you're feeling hungry and like seafood, you can do no better than walk north from Plaza de Armas along Calle Puente (the continuation of the Paseo Ahumada) to the **Mercado Central** ❷ (daily until 5pm; www.mercadocentral. cl). This, together with **La Vega** (www.lavegacentral.com), on the other side of the River Mapocho, is the city's central market. Bustling with the character of such markets around the world, both the interior and the exterior of this elegant structure are worthy of attention. Designed in Chile but built in England, the market was inaugurated in 1872 by Vicuña Mackenna as the site of a national exhibition to celebrate the thrusting and confident economy of the time. It is full of cheap eating places, and above all *marisquerías* where abundant portions of Chile's remarkable seafood are served, considered by many the best in the world.

Here, too, is the fine, copper-roofed shell of what used to be Santiago's

Mid-morning coffee.

Inside the huge wrought-iron Mercado Central.

second train station, the **Estación Mapocho** (www.estacionmapocho.cl). Opened in 1912, and designed by another of Chile's leading French architects, Emile Jécquier, this once served as the terminus for trains arriving from the coast, but it is now an arts and convention center.

Parque Forestal

The Parque Forestal, which is generally referred to by Chileans as their Bois de Boulogne, was laid out by the French landscaper Georges Dubois in the late 19th century. The idea was to make use of the wasteland left over after the canalization of the Mapocho in its now characteristic stone course. Looking at the generally narrow flow of the Mapocho (a name which in Mapuche means "river which loses itself in the land," in reference to its partially subterranean course west of Santiago), it is hard to believe that it is capable of swelling suddenly with torrents of melting snow or rain from the Andes. In the past, flooding caused several disasters and was dealt with first by wide stone

embankments, or *tajamares*, built by the Italian architect Toesca, then by the present channel.

Planted with varieties of native and imported trees, the park contains several small squares and monuments to figures such as Columbus, Bach, the god Pan, and the seminal Nicaraguan modernist poet, Rubén Dario (opposite Merced 230), who wrote his most important work, *Azul*, while exiled in Chile in the 1890s.

Museo Nacional de Bellas Artes

Halfway along the park, close to the northern tip of the Cerro Santa Lucía, is the **Museo Nacional de Bellas Artes** ❶ (www.mnba.cl; Tue–Sun 10am–6.45pm; free), the country's principal art gallery. Designed by Jéquier as an approximate copy of the Petit Palais in Paris, it owns a rich collection of contemporary and past Chilean art, although sadly little is on permanent display, as well as hosting visiting exhibitions. The University of Chile's collection of Chilean art from the first half of the 20th century is

The water fountains in the Plaza de la Aviación, near the Salvador metro station in Providencia.

The colorful Universidad de Chile metro station.

housed in the **Museo de Arte Contemporáneo** in renovated premises in the back part of the building (www.mac.uchile.cl; Tue–Sat 11am–7pm, Sun 11am–6pm; free). In front of the building is a bronze sculpture of a horse by the Colombian artist Fernando Botero.

Farther east still is the extraordinary **Palacio Bruna**, another turn-of-the-20th-century mansion designed in part by one of Chile's leading poets, Pedro Prado, who studied architecture without ever graduating. It is now occupied by the National Chamber of Commerce.

Shortly before you reach the *palacio*, a few steps backtracking along Calle Merced takes you to Calle José Victorino Lastarria and the pleasant **Plaza Mulato Gil de Castro Ⓜ**. The **Museo de Artes Visuales** (www.mavi.cl; Tue–Sun 11am–7pm; free on Sun) in the plaza holds a small but choice private collection of Chilean painting and sculpture from the 1960s onwards. The adjoining **Museo Arqueológico de Santiago** is also worth a visit (www.mavi.cl/mas; Tue–Sun 11am–7pm; free on Sun). Nearby is the **Biógrafo** art cinema (www.elbiografo.cl). The Parque ends with the extravagantly symbolic **Fuente Alemana**, representing Chile and its wealth of natural resources. This monument was presented by the country's German community in 1910 for the first centenary of Independence, and its fountains serve as an impromptu bathing pool for schoolchildren. Note, too, the strange Art Deco house, complete with mythological beast, at Merced 84.

Cerro San Cristóbal

Just ahead is **Plaza Italia**, shadowed on the left by the looming shape of the **Cerro San Cristóbal**, which was named after St Christopher, the patron saint of travelers, by the Spanish because of the landmark it offered to travelers. To reach the Cerro, cross the river by the **Pío Nono bridge** and proceed past the 1930s pile of the University of Chile's Law School up Calle Pío Nono. At the far end is the entrance to the **Parque Metropolitano**, the park containing the Cerro's attractions. You can tour the Cerro completely by car,

The Museo Nacional de Bellas Artes.

TIP

The government tourist service, Sernatur, (www. sernatur.cl) has its main office in the old Providencia fruit and vegetable market (Providencia 1550).

a minibus service, or on foot. But a more picturesque route is to ascend by the 60-year-old funicular (daily 10am–7.45pm, until 6.45pm in winter, closed Mon am), following in the footsteps of Pope John Paul II, who rose to bless the city during his 1987 visit in his bulletproof "pope-mobile."

Perched halfway up the hill is the **Zoo** (www.parquemet.cl; Tue–Sun 10am–5pm, until 6pm in summer), and at the top there are lookout points and the **Santuario de la Inmaculada Concepción** (Shrine of the Virgin Mary). In front of the nearby chapel is a tree from the Basque town of Guernica, planted by Chile's Basque community. The 46ft (14-meter) -high statue of the Virgin, dating from 1908, is frequently the focus of religious ceremonies.

Other attractions in the park include cafés, restaurants, Chilean and Japanese gardens, a wine-sampling center and exhibition (Camino Real), and two open-air swimming pools.

From Plaza Italia, you can also take the metro (Line 5, southbound) to visit the **Museo Interactivo Mirador**

The Shrine of the Virgin Mary.

(Sebastopol 90, La Granja), an interactive science museum that children enjoy enormously (www.mim.cl; Sept–Apr Tue–Sun 9.30am–6.30pm). From the Mirador metro station, *colectivos* (communal taxis) run to the door of the museum. The visit is also an opportunity to get a glimpse of one of Santiago's working-class suburbs.

Bellavista

The area between the Cerro and the Mapocho is called **Bellavista**, which is the closest Santiago gets to a bohemian barrio. This is a mixed residential and artistic neighborhood with lots of charm and interest. Nobel poet Pablo Neruda had one of his houses, **La Chascona**, here (see page 158). This house is open to the public (Fernando Márquez de la Plata 0192; www. fundacionneruda.org; Jan–Feb Tue–Sun 10am–7pm, Mar–Dec 10am–6pm). One of the most popular places is the **Patio Bellavista** (www.patiobella vista.cl; daily 10am–2am, until 4am at weekends), a lively restaurant, arts and crafts center located in the heart of the Bellavista neighborhood filling almost

THE BIGGER THE BETTER?

Coming into Santiago from the airport, it is impossible not to notice a building so tall that it towers above even the Cerro San Cristóbal. The Gran Torre Santiago was designed by Argentine-American architect César Pelli, whose creations include some of the world's tallest buildings, most famously the Petronas Twin Towers in Kuala Lumpur. Located on the banks of the Mapocho River on the western edge of the El Bosque business district, this 70-story skyscraper is the highest in Latin America and has a spectacular observation deck on the 61st and 62nd floors, the **Costanera Sky** (www.sky costanera.cl; daily 10am–10pm). While for some the building is a sign of Chile's prosperity and modernity, for others it is an eyesore out of proportion with its surroundings.

a whole block from Pío Nono to Constitución and from Calle Bellavista to Dardignac. The food options range from a French bistro to Peruvian food and an Irish pub. The center holds many cultural events.

Bellavista's main streets, apart from Pío Nono, are Purísima, running parallel, and Antonia López de Bello, cutting across laterally. A great variety of restaurants are scattered through the barrio. There are also, artists' studios and several theaters, and at night there is considerable street life, with musicians, and handicrafts sold from the sidewalk. Calle Bellavista itself has a string of more tourist-oriented shops specializing in Chile's national stone, lapiz lazuli.

Bellavista is skirted along the Mapocho by Avenida Santa María and, in a tunnel, the Costanera Norte highway, the fast route uptown to the wealthy neighborhoods of **Las Condes**, **Vitacura**, **La Dehesa**, and **Lo Curro**.

Providencia

Across the river from Bellavista, Avenida Providencia runs uptown from the Plaza Baquedano (also known as Plaza Italia). Several squares cluster around the point at which the Alameda becomes Providencia, with monuments to historical figures, including the Cuban independence leader José Martí and the hero of Chile's Independence War, Manuel Rodríguez. Between Providencia and the river is the long Parque Balmaceda, with children's amusements and the Café Literario (http://biblioteca.providencia.cl), a bookstore and coffee shop.

Avenida Providencia continues on through the shopping and residential area into Avenida Apoquindo, its continuation under another name, now the site of some of the city's most modern office blocks. This is also a good place from which to walk towards Avenida Isidora Goyenechea, the heart of the El Golf neighborhood where, on Sundays, there is a small antiques market in Plaza Perú.

Parque Quinta Normal

Quinta Normal, a shady 35-hectare (87-acre) park in western Santiago is home to five museums while two more are only just across the road. During the week, it is quiet but, on Sundays, families from the surrounding lower-middle class neighborhoods flock there to boat on the artificial lake, kick a ball around or simply relax under a tree. Visited by some 800,000 people a year, this is, along with the Parque O'Higgins in southern Santiago and the Cerro San Cristóbal, one of the city's most popular parks.

It dates back to 1841 when it was opened under the government of President Manual Bulnes on what was then the city's western limit as a center for agricultural training and experimentation. Some of the trees were reportedly planted by Claudio Gay, a French botanist who traveled extensively In Chile in the 1830s and early 1840s.

The park takes its name from the word *quinta* – used to refer to farms that paid a fifth (*quinta*) of their income to the government – and, in honor of its educational purpose, the

Waiting tables in a Bellavista café.

View towards Gran Torre Santiago, looking out over the Providencia and Las Condes districts.

École Normale Supérieure in Paris. Between 1882 and 1925, Santiago's zoo was located here before being moved to the Cerro San Cristóbal. In 1928, the park was transferred to the University of Chile and, until 1971, housed its Faculty of Agricultural and Veterinary Sciences.

Quinta Normal museums

The Quinta Normal metro station – only four stops from Plaza de Armas on Line 5 – is at the entrance to the park on Avenida Matucana. Just across from the metro station, the **Museo de la Memoria y los Derechos Humanos** (Matucana 501; www.museodelamemoria.cl; Tue–Sun Mar–Dec 10am–6pm, Jan–Feb 10am–8pm), which commemorates the victims of the military dictatorship, recalling the somber atmosphere of the Pinochet era through interactive and multimedia displays.

Within the park itself lies the **Museo Nacional de Historia Natural** (www.mnhn.cl; Tue–Sat 10am–5.30pm, Sun from 11am; free) in a building designed in the 1870s by French

Museo Nacional de Historia Natural.

architect Paul Lathoud, but since then much repaired, including after the 2010 earthquake in which it suffered severe damage. The Copper and Civilization Room, showing the use of copper across the ages, is interesting as is the Easter Island Room, and children like the skeleton of a blue whale in the central hall, put there in 1895.

Just opposite is a branch of the University of Chile's **Museo de Arte Contemporáneo** (www.mac.uchile.cl; Tue–Sat 11am–7pm, Sun 11am–6pm; free). Housed in a French-style building, originally commissioned by the National Agricultural Society, it puts on mainly temporary exhibitions largely of experimental work. The main museum is in Parque Forestal (see page 138).

Straight on from the entrance past the lake is the **Museo de Ciencia y Tecnología**, a small interactive museum that also has interesting collections of old phonographs, calculators, computers and mobile phones (www.mucytec.cl; Jan–Feb Tue–Fri 10am–6.15pm, Sat–Sun 11am–6.15pm; Mar–Nov Tue–Fri 10am–5.15pm, Sat–Sun 11am–5.15pm).

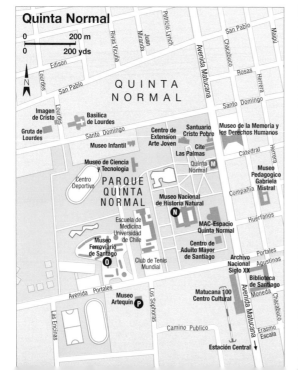

On the western edge of the park is the **Museo Ferroviario de Santiago** ⏺ (www.corpdicyt.cl/mferroviario; Tue–Fri 10am–5.50pm, Sat–Sun 11am–5.50pm, until 6.50pm in summer), one of the largest of its type in South America. It has more than a dozen steam locomotives and three passenger trains, some of which can be boarded. One of the stars is an old locomotive that used to haul trains across the Andes until the early 1970s.

The **Museo Artequín** ⏺ (www.artequin.cl; Mar–Jan Tue–Fri 9am–5pm, Sat–Sun 11am–6pm), just across Avenida Portales from the Museo Ferroviario, is housed in the lovely and colorful Pabellón París, built for Chile's participation in the 1889 Paris International Exhibition and subsequently dismantled and shipped back to Chile. This is a children's museum and a very good one, with didactic areas explaining different aspects of art and techniques as well as reproductions of famous artworks.

Along Avenida Portales south from Quinta Normal towards the Alameda is the **Matucana 100** arts center (www.m100.cl) in the converted former warehouse of the government procurement service. As well as plays, films and concerts, it holds regular art exhibitions mostly of contemporary work.

Estación Central

Estación Central, on the other side of the Alameda at the junction with Avenida Matucana, is now the city's only functioning railway station, with trains running to the south as far as Chillán and providing commuter services for towns near the capital. Although a station has existed there since 1857, the current building was inaugurated in 1897 and its wrought-iron structure was designed and built by a French company, Schneider & Cie. de Le Creusot. It was declared a National Monument in 1983.

The area around Estación Central is the place *santiaguinos* go for cheap shopping and it is always a hive of activity, with street vendors as well as established shops. It is fun but a place to keep a tight hold of your belongings.

Bohemian Bellavista.

Relaxing in the Baños de Colina.

SANTIAGO EXCURSIONS

The countryside around Santiago is perfect for day trips, with numerous outdoor activities possible, from wallowing in hot mud to wine tasting, and skiing to sunbathing – and all amid gorgeous surroundings.

Santiago

On an average day the jagged peaks of the Andes loom mistily over the eastern end of Santiago, a distant yet overbearing presence. In fact, you can travel within a day, by car or bus, far up into the mountains beside the winding course of the **Río Maipo**. This rushing torrent sweeps the loose earth of the mountains downstream toward the rich agricultural plains of Chile's central valley region, pouring itself finally into the Pacific, 4km (2.5 miles) south of San Antonio. The Maipo Valley, or **Cajón del Maipo**, is a popular weekend venue for *santiaguinos* anxious to escape the relentless pace of the city streets for a few hours of fresh air and relaxation.

For the sedentary, the canyon offers an easy but visually seductive drive toward the mountains' heart; and for the more active, depending on the season, there are plenty of opportunities to swim (in open-air pools), ride horses, picnic, hike, camp, or cabin overnight. The river is too rough for regular canoeing or kayaking, but agencies like Cascada Expediciones (www.cascada.travel) offer raft rides all year round. You must be over 10 years old (or more, depending on the time of year and river conditions) and know how to swim.

There's also a surprising variety of wonderful country restaurants, with varied menus that include traditional Chilean foods, espresso coffee, and *küchen*

Roadside fruit vendor.

that would be a credit to any German pastry chef. The delicious home cooking draws heavily on the canyon's almond, walnut, and cherry orchards. The canyon's economic base depends largely on tourism, but prices tend to be reasonable and the Chilean flavor of the area remains distinct.

Exploring the lower Andes

Strung out along the road are stopping points affording spectacular views of the canyon itself, as well as small towns and villages, campgrounds, parks, and

Main Attractions

San José de Maipo
Monumento Natural El Morado
Baños de Colina
Pirque
Pomaire
Isla Negra
Farellones

The town of Pomaire is known for its clay pottery.

an obelisk marking the site where, in 1986, the Manuel Rodríguez Patriotic Front (a Marxist guerrilla group) staged a daring ambush of General Augusto Pinochet's cavalcade, which almost put an end to his dictatorial rule.

As you pass through **La Obra** you will be able to see craftspeople working at the roadside with the pale-pink stone that characterizes the area and is popular for terraces and other building projects. Just past La Obra is **Las Vertientes**, one of the local small towns with campgrounds, hotels, gorgeous swimming pools surrounded by grass and flowers (see www.cajondelmaipo.com/piscinas.php for more information), where you can spend the day swimming and sunbathing.

San José de Maipo

San José de Maipo ❶, around 25km (16 miles) from Santiago, is the canyon's main town, founded in 1792 after silver deposits were discovered in the surrounding area. The town's buildings are constructed in the adobe and straw common to the region. This is a pleasant place to stretch your legs, enjoy the fresh air, and absorb some of the tranquility of a traditional Andean town. On the outskirts of San José, a narrow gravel road sheers off from the main highway and begins climbing up to **Lagunillas ❷**, a ski resort (www.skilagunillas.cl) perched on a mountain peak, overlooking an immense bowl formed by part of the cordillera. Good nerves and a head for heights are required for this trip, but it is worth it, especially during the ski season.

San Alfonso and Cascada de las Animas

If you prefer to continue along the canyon, you will pass through the towns of **El Toyo** and **El Melocotón** before reaching **San Alfonso ❸**. The Proyecto Ave Fenix in El Melocotón is an initiative aimed at restoring the old mining railroad between Puente Alto and El Volcán. It can be visited at weekends and there are occasional train rides. San Alfonso sits in a generous hollow, which was carved through the Andes by the river itself. The people who live around the village are a curious mixture of old country-dwellers and New Agers attracted by the

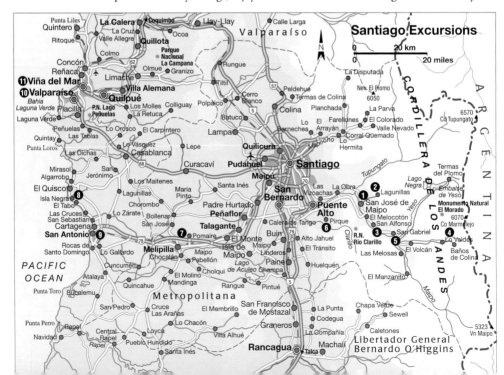

area's spectacular natural setting, the peace, and the proximity to Santiago.

Cascada de las Animas (Waterfall of Souls), a camping and picnic ground, captures this peculiar mix. It has a circular swimming pool and handmade cabins built with local materials, and belongs to a family who once owned most of the land on which the town now sits. The sons and daughters of the original *latifundista* have established a community based on New Age ideals and sensitivity to the natural environment. The result is that the park and campgrounds are maintained extraordinarily well, and the trail rides (usually over weekends and for week-long periods) provide an excellent opportunity to explore some of the remoter areas of the Andes. Other activities offered by the community include guided walks and rafting on the river. For more information or to reserve a cabin, visit www.cascada.net.

For the less adventurous or for those with less time, the Hostería Los Ciervos serves meals in a garden lined with lush, well-kept plants and, if the weather is cold, has a cozy dining room with the purple abundance of a bougainvillea visible through a window.

San Alfonso is a good stopping and turning point for a leisurely day. However, it's also possible to start early in the morning from Santiago and head straight up the canyon 70km/44 miles to **Lo Valdés ❹**, although the last 14km/9 miles on a gravel road may be difficult in winter. The road passes the rather run-down hot springs of **Baños Morales** (http://banosmorales.cl) and continues up past a checkpoint (the Chile–Argentine border is near) to the **Refugio Lo Valdés**, (www.refugiolovaldes.com), a comfortable inn with a good restaurant, a spectacular view of snowy peaks, and a deep natural pool, surrounded by fossils from the period when the Andes were under the sea. Baños Morales is also the entry point to the **Monumento Natural El Morado**, where a three-hour hike through majestic scenery will take you to the San Francisco glacier. The park is administered by CONAF (www.conaf.cl), the national park service, and basic camping facilities are available.

Zip-lining in the Maipo Valley.

Goats in El Morado National Park.

TIP

The Reserva Nacional Río Clarillo (www.conaf.cl), one of the closest to Santiago, is 23km (14 miles) southeast of Pirque on a tributary of the Maipo River. Buses leave from the Bellavista de La Florida metro station.

Baños de Colina

A further 11km (7 miles) on are the **Baños de Colina**, hot springs which are open to the public from September to April, where the water reaches temperatures as high as 60°C (140°F). The drive (feasible only in summer) takes you through a spectacular moonscape, completely different from the rest of the canyon, and the baths themselves are arranged in smooth, natural pools on terraces carved into the mountainside. At the source, hot water steams out of natural caves into the hottest bath, which in turn jets into pools farther and farther down. The farther away from the source the pool is, the more bearable the temperature. In the second pool, you can rest your elbows on the edge and gaze down the valley at the mountains' extraordinary shades of gray, green, and subtle pinks, as your body soaks in warm, sulfurous luxury.

Another alternative is to turn left at **San Gabriel ❺** (before El Volcán) and follow the **Río Yeso** to the Yeso dam, high up in the Andean cliffs. You'll have to stop at a control on the way and leave your identification at the checkpoint, because this is a pass to Argentina. The round trip from Santiago is 170km (106 miles), 65km (40 miles) of it on a dirt road, so it's a good idea to carry a picnic lunch.

Pirque

To return it's possible to retrace your steps as far as El Toyo and then cross the River Maipo and follow the other side of the canyon back down to the Las Vertientes bridge. Here you can cross the river again and retrace your path to Santiago, or carry on through **Pirque ❻**, a picturesque country town with a public sales and tasting room of Concha y Toro, Chile's largest wine producer. You can tour the huge vats where wines are stored and matured and peer through the gloom and dust into the "devil's locker room" where one of the company's top wines, *Casillero del Diablo*, is aged. The original country estate and family mansion can be seen from the road, surrounded by the smaller cottages of the vineyards' workers. The main house, which appears on some of the labels, was built around 1875, at roughly the same time that the French

Vineyards at Pirque.

HOMEMADE PRODUCE

As you drive up Cajón del Maipo, especially on weekends, you'll see white flags and small tables by the roadside, piled with round breads of more than 30cm (1ft) in diameter, known as *tortillas de rescoldo*. The white flags mean someone is selling something they've prepared in their kitchen: bread cooked in ashes, often in the traditional ovens of baked mud; jams made with local walnuts, almonds, and berries; fresh honey; or the ubiquitous empanadas, as common in Chile as the hamburger is in the United States. The sight of the sellers' bread with *chicharrones* (fried pork skin) evokes nostalgic enthusiasm from most Chileans, especially those who have spent part of their childhood in the country.

landscape designer Gustavo Renner was designing the surrounding park.

A car gives the most flexibility for traveling up and down the canyon, allowing plenty of time for visiting anything that catches your fancy. However, buses run regularly from Santiago up the canyon, some of their routes ending in San José de Maipo or San Alfonso. Take Line 5 of the metro to the Bellavista de la Florida station and, from there, catch the frequent Metrobus 72 (one-way fare approximately US$1.60) or a *colectivo* (collective taxi) for around US$3.50. During January and February there is also a daily bus up to Baños Morales (weekends only in winter). To visit Pirque, take Line 4 of the metro to Puente Alto and a *colectivo*.

Pomaire

It is easy to catch a bus from Santiago that will drop you off at the crossroads to **Pomaire** ❼, a town where clay pottery is the sustaining activity for almost the entire population. The road to the town, about a half-hour's walk from the highway, stretches between an avenue of trees and green fields.

In 1985, an earthquake razed the original adobe homes, and they have mostly been replaced by simple wood houses. The reddish clay once common in the town is now virtually exhausted, and the raw material for the pottery is mostly imported from other parts of the country, but this small village is still attractive.

Designs are primarily traditional, including *miniaturas* – small figures inspired by country stories and religious beliefs – decorative work, and, perhaps most beautiful, the utilitarian ovenproof clay pots of all shapes and sizes, ideal for many Spanish and Chilean dishes. A shapely, sensual parade of vessels are displayed for sale, with names like *pailas*, *fuentes*, *tinajas*, *maceteros*; all are considerably more enticing than the one English word that sums them up: pot.

You can easily spend an enjoyable morning or afternoon wandering up and down Pomaire's two main streets, trying in vain to resist the temptation of taking at least a *chanchito* (a peculiarly Chilean pig pot) or an old worn-out clay shoe, back to your homeland to hold plants or trinkets. Tucked in between the potteries are small plant stores and

In the villages around Santiago you can find all sorts of handmade souvenirs, from pottery to pencils.

Cazuela pots in Pomaire.

TIP

For a contrast to the busy port of San Antonio, take the short trip south to Las Rocas de Santo Domingo. The beach is notoriously windy but that hasn't stopped it being a favorite town for the summer homes of wealthy Chileans, who take great pride in their lovely gardens.

greenhouses, along with restaurants offering traditional Chilean fare such as *empanadas* and *cazuela*, a stew made with a variety of vegetables and containing a piece of meat, traditionally, turkey.

Isla Negra

If you're traveling by bus, the round trip to and from Pomaire is probably enough for a good, full day. If you're using a car and you don't mind driving back to Santiago after dark, you have the option of carrying on to **Isla Negra** ❽ on the coast. Returning from Pomaire to the tolled Autopista del Sol (Highway of the Sun), continue along this stretch until just before San Antonio, where you turn north to head toward the popular seaside resorts of **Cartagena**, **Las Cruces**, and **El Tabo**. (Be careful to take the old coast road, rather than the tolled highway.) Cartagena became popular in the early 19th century, with the arrival of the railroad from Santiago.

Isla Negra, a little farther up the coast, has a special quality. It is unclear whether this is because Pablo Neruda (see page 158), one of Chile's most influential poets, chose to live there, or

Isla Negra, home to the Nobel Prize-winning poet, Pablo Neruda.

whether he chose to live there because it is so special. Neruda's favorite house overlooks a particularly rough stretch of Isla Negra's beach, where the waves crash against humped rocks rising abruptly out of the white sand like children's castles. You can easily lose an hour or two, gazing out over the restless, changing landscape that cast its spell on so much of Neruda's work.

From here it's a short trip back down the coast to **San Antonio** ❾, a working port with the grime of hard labor in evidence and fishing boats moored in the harbor. There are a few good restaurants in San Antonio, but the *picadas*, as the Chileans call them, are right on the harbor itself: these are where the fishing people themselves like to eat. Here you'll get huge platefuls of your favorite dishes, with a fresh Chilean salad, rice, or French fries, at very reasonable prices.

If you're looking for slightly more comfortable surroundings, then try the Juanita (Antofagasta 261), which serves all of Chile's most traditional fish dishes at affordable prices. The drive back to Santiago takes about an hour and a half, all on the Autopista del Sol.

Andean Ski Resorts

The ski season in Chile runs from June to October, drawing winter sports enthusiasts from all over the world to its top-class resorts.

There are five ski centers near Santiago: Portillo, Valle Nevado, El Colorado, La Parva, and Lagunillas. All of them are located in the same area about 50km (31 miles) from Santiago except Portillo (www.skiportillo.com), which is 164km (102 miles) away, close to the border with Argentina.

Farellones

The road to Farellones, the village at the base of the El Colorado, La Parva, and Valle Nevado slopes, winds narrow and steep through the cordillera, following most of the Mapocho River Canyon deep into the Andes. This is an excellent day trip whatever the season, but snow chains are required in winter (they're available for rental where the road begins) and the road gets very crowded. Careful driving is essential at any time of year. Access to the road is controlled by the police in winter, and on weekends and public holidays. Drivers are allowed to head up until 2pm, but it's best to start the journey early in the morning. Cars can begin the return descent only after 4pm. Warm clothes are essential, whatever the temperature in Santiago when you leave. Snow usually begins in June and lasts until September.

Even if you're not a skier, it's well worth making the trip to Farellones. The view from the road as you ascend higher and higher, the pure sky, the clear air, and the chance to enjoy the Andes from the inside out all make the drive worthwhile.

El Colorado and La Parva

The center closest to Farellones, this provides excellent conditions, and equipment rental and classes can be arranged there. It has 19 lifts and 74 runs for beginners through to experts. Both group and private classes are available. See www.elcolorado.cl for more details.

Also near Farellones is the hamlet of La Parva, situated at 2,816 meters (9,239ft), with a spectacular view down the valley toward Santiago. La Parva usually enjoys snowy conditions until well into October and you can ski as high as 3,630 meters (11,910ft). See www.laparva.cl for further information.

Valle Nevado

The turn-off to Valle Nevado, 2km (about 1 mile) before Farellones, takes you 10km (6 miles) deep into the mountains. This modern ski center first opened in 1988 and today attracts both families and daredevil heli-skiers. The resort contains three luxury hotels and four luxury apartment buildings, providing services as varied as movies, a discotheque, a French restaurant, a gymnasium, a pool room, a sauna, a whirlpool bath, and a snack bar (see www.vallenevado.cl). Stores sell and rent ski equipment and clothing, and there is a day-care center and a medical center equipped for any emergency. The highest point you can ski at is 3,670 meters (12,040ft) above sea level.

Lagunillas

Lagunillas is located 80km (50 miles) southeast of Santiago in the Cajón de Maipo. This small resort offers skiing and snowboarding. For more information, visit www.skilagunillas.cl (in Spanish).

Skiing in Chile is an expensive activity; prices of equipment and accommodations are similar to those in European ski resorts. More information on all of the ski resorts around Santiago can be obtained from the Sernatur Tourist Office in Santiago (tel: 600-7376 2887). Alternatively, visit www.sernatur.cl.

The ski resorts around Santiago offer some fantastic high-altitude pistes.

Brightly colored houses on Cerro Alegre.

VALPARAISO AND VINA DEL MAR

The port and its neighboring beach resort are steeped in history, but it's the unusual ascensores *scaling Valparaíso's hills that will leave a lasting impression.*

Valparaíso and Viña del Mar may sit side by side on Chile's Pacific coast, but when it comes to urban character, they are worlds apart. One of the first Chilean cities founded by the Spanish in 1541, Valparaíso was Santiago's thriving port for centuries. It is spread along some spectacularly steep hills, with stairways and streets winding up past splendid aging buildings, many built by the British in the 19th century, when the port was virtually run from the City of London.

Viña, on the other hand, is a tourist city of steel, glass, and neon. Traditionally the reserve of the well-off, it is now middle-class territory and a pleasant enough place to relax, but Valparaíso holds the attractions of its wild and varied history. And, although the poverty that followed the opening of the Panama Canal is still apparent, Valparaíso is now gradually being smartened up again, particularly since Unesco declared its historic center a World Heritage Site in 2003.

Arriving in Valparaíso

Three bus companies run a shuttle service to Valparaíso and Viña from the Pajaritos metro station in Santiago, and this is by far the easiest – and cheapest – way to visit them. A car is more of a liability than a help on Valparaíso's steep hills, and

there are regular bus and train services between the port and Viña. The 90-minute bus journey from Santiago will take you through the vine-draped Casablanca Valley, where sea breezes help to produce some of Chile's best white wines.

From Santiago you enter **Valparaíso ⑩** along Avenida Argentina. On Wednesdays and Saturdays, this avenue's central walkway becomes a city market, groaning with vegetables and fruit, fresh fish and shellfish, dry goods, and spices. On

Main Attractions
Museo a Cielo Abierto
La Sebastiana
Cerro Alegre
Cerro Concepción
Ascensor Polanco

A cobbled street in Valparaíso.

Sundays, it is home to a vast flea market, or *feria persa*.

As you reach Avenida Pedro Montt, a former horserace track, the Congress building rises up imperiously. For some, this is the symbol of Chile's restored democracy but, for most, the exile of Congress to Valparaíso, dictated by the outgoing military government, is just one more reminder of this painful period.

Foundation of a great port

The sea has shaped Valparaíso's history since its foundation, four and a half centuries ago. Before the Spanish arrived, the region was inhabited by the Chango people, who fished the bay and called it Quintil. In 1536, Juan de Saavedra sailed down from Callao in Peru to meet a supply ship for Diego de Almagro's earlier foot expedition to Chile. The bay's beauty flooded him with such nostalgia for his distant homeland that he named it Valparaíso (Paradise Valley) after his hometown in Spain.

In 1547, Pedro de Valdivia, the founder of Santiago and governor of Chile, would find himself here, isolated, impoverished by wars, and discouraged by the lack of news and support from the Crown. With characteristic (and very Chilean) ingenuity, he called on colonists wishing to return to the more developed northern colonies to load their fortunes (built through the exploitation of gold reserves using native slaves) and themselves onto his ships. About 20 families boarded. On the last night before setting out, under the pretext of a final goodbye banquet in the port, Valdivia set them all ashore where they cheerfully set to consuming wine and meats in huge quantities. But as the feasting reached its height, Don Pedro weighed anchor and set out with the gold, leaving a beach full of furious victims.

Valparaíso went on to become the main port for the growing city of Santiago. This made it a tempting target for pirates, mostly of English or Dutch origin, and the port had to build strong fortifications to repel the attacks, which continued through most of the 16th and 17th centuries. Its defensive towers and forts not only

discouraged potential attackers but also acted as a strong stimulus to trade and the warehousing of merchandise. Soon the English stopped raiding and became the largest trading partner of the newly independent Chile, buying up large parts of Valparaíso.

Revolutions and riots

Occasionally laid waste by earthquakes and tidal waves, Valparaíso also became notorious for political disturbances. Two of the city's governors died tragically within 20 years of each other. The first was the powerful "kingmaker" Diego Portales, who was shot to death on his way to Quillota in 1837, during a brief military uprising. The other was an army general, killed on September 18, 1859, during a civil uprising at the doors of the La Matriz church, during a religious ceremony giving thanks for Chile's independence.

But, by the early 20th century, the old port had begun to assume its present look. Builders battled the sea for a few extra meters of earth for the *costanera* (coast road) and the railway line. European-style buildings marked the skyline, and the old street of trade became the financial and banking center for all the maritime and port activity. The growing population began to spill out of the city's basic *plan* – as the lower part of the city is called – and the incredible feat of building on the *cerros* (hills) began. Each individual builder found his or her own techniques for fighting gravity and resisting earthquakes, creating a unique city of winding streets, stairways, walks, and lookout points, which began to string together the different hills, each one separated by the abrupt ravines that characterize the area.

To conquer the hilltops, the *ascensores* (funiculars or cable-cars) were introduced, and remain an important means of transportation up the city's hills (although an increasing number have fallen into disuse). No visit to Valparaíso is complete without a trip in an *ascensor* – appearances aside, they've proven a secure means for traveling up the hills, while affording spectacular views of the bay.

Cerro Artillería is dotted with charming restaurants and cafés, some which have fantastic views over the bay.

Colorful facades in Valparaíso.

An interesting feature of Valparaíso is the numerous murals that decorate the streets of Cerro Alegre.

Political mural, Cerro Alegre.

Exploring the city

The best way to see Valparaíso is on foot, and the best place to start is by the Cathedral on **Plaza Victoria Ⓐ**. General Augusto Pinochet was born in Valparaíso and must have known this square well because he spent his childhood in a nearby (unmarked) house. Nothing suggested the prominent role that Pinochet, a mediocre student at the old Sacred Heart School, would play in Chilean history. In the center of the plaza sits the lovely **Neptune Fountain**, a war trophy that was stolen from the Peruvians in 1879.

A block along Calle Condell is the neoclassical **Palacio Lyon Ⓑ**, once the mansion of a wealthy family, which now houses the city's natural history museum and municipal art gallery, the **Museo de Historia Natural** (www.mhnv.cl; Tue–Sat 10am–6pm, Sun 10am–2pm; free). At the bottom of Calle Huito, which runs alongside the Palacio, the Ascensor Espíritu Santo (the Holy Spirit Lift), one of the city's funiculars, will carry you up to **Cerro Bellavista Ⓒ** and its

Museo a Cielo Abierto (Open-Sky Museum; www.museoacieloabierto.ucv. cl), a collection of murals painted on the sides of houses, some of them by leading Chilean artists. Along Calle Ricardo Ferrari, you will reach **La Sebastiana** (www.fundacionneruda.org; Jan–Feb Tue–Sun 10.30am–6.50pm, Mar–Dec 10.10am–6pm), one of the homes of Chilean poet Pablo Neruda. Although Neruda actually used this house relatively little, many visitors find it the most attractive of his four homes, partly because they are allowed to wander through it without taking a guided tour, but also because of the spectacular view over the Bay of Valparaíso that Neruda could enjoy from his bed.

Alternatively, from the Palacio Lyon continue along the narrow, curving Calle Condell – on which buses race at great speed, contributing to the air pollution of this lower part of the city – to Plaza Aníbal Pinto, with one of the landmarks of the city's gastronomic history: the old **Bar Cinzano** (www.barcinzano.cl), a traditional spot frequented by locals where tango and

Chilean music are played live. From there, Calle Esmeralda leads to the **Reloj Turri** , Valparaíso's equivalent of Big Ben. This is where Avenida Prat, the city's financial heart, begins. The British influences are so obvious here that it's hard to believe you're in a Latin American city. At Cochrane 851 is the **Bar Inglés** (English Bar), a wood-paneled reminder of the city's past.

Plaza Sotomayor

At the end of Esmeralda you'll find yourself in the open expanse of **Plaza Sotomayor** Ⓔ, overlooked by the gray-washed Naval Headquarters. The plaza is dominated by the Monument to the Heroes of Iquique, who died in a key naval battle in the 19th-century War of the Pacific (see page 41). In a crypt under the monument, naval hero Arturo Prat and his crew are buried. The handicraft stalls on the nearby pier, Muelle Prat, are tawdry, but this is the departure point for boat trips out into the bay, with a magnificent view of the port's amphitheater of hills. On New Year's Eve, you can enjoy Valparaíso's unique fireworks show on

the water: all the ships anchored in the harbor sound their horns together to welcome the New Year.

From Plaza Wheelwright, six blocks north of Plaza Sotomayor, take the Ascensor Artillería to the Paseo 21 de Mayo where there are some of the best views of the bay and over to Viña del Mar. Here you'll also find the neoclassical mansion that once housed the country's naval school and is now the **Museo Marítimo Nacional** Ⓕ (www.mmn.cl; Tue–Sun 10am–5.30pm) with exhibits about the port and its history.

This is part of **Cerro Playa Ancha**, one of the city's largest hills in both size and population. Residents proudly call this the "People's Independent Republic of Playa Ancha." A walk around Playa Ancha is a reminder of the port's better days of fine but unostentatious buildings that populated the hill, little by little.

In Caleta El Membrillo, a restaurant run by the Fishermen's Co-operative (www.caletaelmembrillo.cl), serves up a variety of local specialties, in particular, fantastic shellfish and fish which,

The port.

Memories of Pablo Neruda

Chile's most revered poet was an avid collector of books, paintings, shells, wines – and houses, three of which are now open to the public.

A winding street leads to a modest bungalow with a rough stone face that sets it apart from its showy neighbors. But where the inside should begin there's a leafy patio of ladders and stairs leading to rooms of glass scattered among gardens, terraces, and mosaics. This is La Chascona – meaning "woman with tousled hair" – on Cerro San Cristóbal in Santiago. Built between 1953 and 1958, it was the home of Chile's most famous poet, Pablo Neruda, who won the Nobel Prize in 1971 and died shortly after the military coup in 1973. He built the house for his lover Matilde Urrutia while he was still married to his second wife, the painter Delia del Carril. Neruda named La Chascona for his lover's rebellious hair. Neruda and Matilde later married.

By the time of his death Neruda had four houses: La Chascona, Isla Negra (see page 150), La

Pablo Neruda in the 1940s.

Sebastiana in Valparaíso (see page 156), and La Quinta Michoacán in Santiago.

Friends called Neruda a spontaneous architect: his houses just grew. "In Isla Negra everything flowers," Neruda wrote. "The sea flowers all year round. Its rose is white. Its petals are salt stars." This is the place where Neruda and Urrutia are now buried, after being moved there in 1992 from Santiago's General Cemetery.

Poetry and politics

Neruda's thirst for life and his love for poetry were tempered by his sensitivity to the poverty around him. He joined the Communist Party in 1943 and was elected senator for Antofagasta and Tarapacá, but was later forced into hiding and then into exile in Argentina and Europe as a result of his opposition to center-right president Gabriel González Videla.

While alive, Neruda dedicated his work to the daily struggles of Chileans. In death, he left his wealth to them. "Neruda didn't collect things in order to hoard them, but rather to share them," said Juan Agustín Figueroa, head of the Neruda Foundation. "He always imagined that his things would become the heritage of the people of Chile."

Upon the deaths of Neruda, Delia del Carril, and Matilde Urrutia, the four houses were to be donated to the Communist Party, for use as cultural centers. But after the 1973 coup, the military confiscated their goods. Military patrols repeatedly sacked La Chascona and La Sebastiana.

This didn't stop Matilde from holding Neruda's wake there, and his funeral became the first march against the military regime. From then until her death in 1985, she and a small group of lawyers, writers, and artists waged silent war against the military's bureaucracy. Matilde spent her last years in La Chascona, repairing the house and organizing Neruda's library, papers, and writings. After her death, the Neruda Foundation published her memoirs and made La Chascona its headquarters. The military confiscated the house in Isla Negra, but Matilde never gave up possession. After a lengthy struggle, the government eventually recognized the Foundation.

Today, visitors can follow a guided tour of La Chascona or stroll around La Sebastiana at their leisure. The Isla Negra house has been turned into a permanent museum by the government. Guided tours can be arranged in advance through the Fundación Pablo Neruda in Santiago (tel: 02-777 8741; www.fundacionneruda.org).

eaten with a glass of wine, give the sensation of a perfect world. However, this is definitely a place to keep a close eye on your possessions.

Museo de Bellas Artes

From Plaza Sotomayor, you can also take the Ascensor El Peral (opposite the law courts) to **Cerro Alegre**, which, along with neighboring **Cerro Concepción** ⓖ, is part of an area declared a World Heritage Site. At the top of Ascensor El Peral is Paseo Yugoslavo, one of a number of similar short promenades that look out over the bay, with the **Museo de Bellas Artes** (Fine Arts Museum; www.museobaburizza.cl; Tue–Sun 10.30am–5.30pm), and its excellent collection of Chilean paintings, housed in Palacio Baburizza.

From the Paseo Yugoslavo, it's a short walk down and up again to Cerro Concepción, also accessible by the Ascensor Concepción (close to the Turri Clock). This was the residential area preferred by the British in the late 1800s, and it is still a haven of attractive buildings, broad avenues, and sea views, principally from Paseo Atkinson and Paseo Gervasoni. From there, it's a short walk back down to Plaza Aníbal Pinto.

Both of these hills have become fashionable places for a weekend home, and, as well as tasteful renovation, this has brought a sharp increase in property prices. However, they are full of small, moderately priced restaurants, especially along Almirante Montt, and tiny art galleries of varying quality.

Ascensor Polanco

As a general principle, the hills of Valparaíso become poorer the higher you climb. And some are, indeed, very poor. However, during daylight, they are perfectly safe: their people are generally warm and welcoming – much more so than in Santiago – and they will be only too happy to share their love of their city, and its many attractions, with you. And, although the streets twist and turn, it's not easy to get lost, as the sea is always there as the ultimate landmark.

It's worth going up the **Ascensor Polanco** (http://ascensoresvalparaiso.org),

FACT

In 1834, Charles Darwin climbed Cerro La Campana, east of Valparaíso, which is now a national park. The adjoining Parque Nacional Ocoa is one of the last reserves of the native Chilean palm.

Viña del Mar seafront.

A mural on Cerro Artillería.

The steep hills of Valparaíso.

on the eastern side of Avenida Argentina. This ingenious *ascensor*, built in 1915 and now a National Monument, is a feat of engineering. Reached by a walk through a long, narrow, but well-lit tunnel, it rises vertically through the heart of the hill, before emerging into daylight at the top of a tower that is connected to the hilltop by a suspended walkway. The poverty here is apparent, and the contrast with the monumental Congress, although now muted by new blocks of high-rise apartment buildings, gives some idea of why, when it was built in the late 1980s, the ostentatious Congress building seemed so out of keeping with its surroundings.

From here, you can walk north toward **Cerro Barón**, so called because a European baron once built his castle there, and then on to **Cerro Los Placeres**, literally "the hill of pleasures." This hill is virtuously protected by the imposing Castle of Don Federico Santa María, today a university which bears his name.

Valparaíso is a good base for day-trips by car to **Parque Nacional La Campana** (www.conaf.cl) and the region's interior cities. Quilpué, Limache, Quillota, and San Felipe are all small towns whose buildings recall colonial times. Plazas and squares full of palm trees, the peaceful, slow pace, and a climate especially kind to the elderly, make these towns particularly agreeable for relaxing.

Viña del Mar

Just northeast of Valparaíso is the adjacent resort haven of **Viña del Mar** ⑪. Viña is an affluent city, with elegant hotels, a casino, and many restaurants, all set in wide palm-lined avenues. It was born as Valparaíso's seaside resort in the mid-19th century, when the two were connected by railroad. In spite of some industrial development (principally textiles, mining, and metal), its major source of income is still tourism. The Cerro Castillo palace, on a hill overlooking the city, is the summer home of Chile's presidents.

If Valparaíso is the city where Augusto Pinochet grew up, Viña is the city that sheltered the remains of Salvador Allende, the Chilean president who committed suicide amid the relentless bombing of the Air Force's Hawker Hunters during the 1973 military coup. His tomb in the Santa Inés cemetery remained unmarked until 1989, but was always covered with fresh flowers placed by admirers. On September 4, 1990, exactly 20 years to the day after he was elected president of Chile, Dr Allende's remains were finally moved to his permanent resting place, in a mausoleum in Santiago's General Cemetery.

Fall is the best time to see Viña, when summer tourists have abandoned it and only its inhabitants remain. Avenida Perú is the perfect place to stroll along the shore, enjoying the sunset. Take time to visit the **Quinta Vergara** (daily 7am–6pm; free). This is where the city's annual song festival takes place but it is also a

glorious park and home to the **Palacio Vergara**, built in the Venetian style by an Italian architect for a local family after the devastating 1906 earthquake. The Museo Municipal de Bellas Artes here is currently closed for restoration following damaged caused by the 2010 earthquake.

Coastal towns

For those with a car, the northbound coastal road out of Viña is lovely on a clear day, although gradually being built up with (often unsightly) blocks of flats. Reñaca, which now adjoins Viña, is a concrete jungle and unbearably crowded in summer, but drive on farther and, particularly once you've crossed the estuary of the Aconcagua River in Concón, you'll find quieter places. **Maitencillo**, with its two long beaches separated by the rocks that shelter its fishing bay, is a delight, with plenty of relaxed places to eat or have a drink along the main street, Avenida del Mar.

Further north still is Cachagua, 60km (37 miles) from Viña, with a protected island inhabited by Magellan and Humboldt penguins, and Zapallar with its old family houses. The traditional summer retreat of the Chilean aristocracy, Zapallar maintains an exclusive air that some visitors find off-putting, and there is, indeed, a clear upstairs-downstairs divide between the extravagance of the beach houses and, above them, the village of wooden houses where the permanent population lives.

On your way back to Santiago from Viña, climbing Cerro Agua Santa, you will have a clear view of Valparaíso. If you pass this way in the dark, you can enjoy a view from the crest of the hill of the marvelous firmament of lights of both Valparaíso and Viña. By night the two very different cities can barely be distinguished, blending together in a clandestine love affair.

Just off the road to Santiago, 30km (19 miles) from Viña, is Quintay, a lovely little fishing village with a small museum about its whaling past (banned since 1967). The remains of the abandoned whaling factory can also be visited.

TIP

Viña del Mar's annual song festival, the Festival Internacional de la Canción, takes place in February in the Quinta Vergara, one of Chile's most beautiful parks.

Fishermen on Maitencillo Beach.

Outside Copiapo in
the Atacama Desert.

EL NORTE CHICO

Chile's "Little North," the area just north of Santiago, is a dry, mostly flat region of wide Pacific beaches, mining settlements, and spectacularly starry night skies.

Main Attractions

Monumento Arqueológico
  Valle del Encanto
Valle del Elqui
Salar de Maricunga
Parque Nacional Nevado
  Tres Cruces
Laguna Verde

Hop on a northbound bus in Santiago and, in just a few hours, the crush and bustle of the city will be replaced by windswept coastal expanses and, beyond La Serena, the first signs of the Atacama Desert.

Much of the north was annexed by Chile late in the game; in 1884, Chile defeated a confederation of Peru and Bolivia in the War of the Pacific to take control over the flourishing nitrate mines. This "white gold," a key ingredient in the production of fertilizer, provided fabulous wealth for several decades, while copper and silver mining already flourished in the provinces closer to the capital. Later, a vast copper mine was developed at Chuquicamata (see page 176), part of the captured spoils.

The distances from the northern deserts to Santiago and the few transportation options available encouraged the idea of a journey north as a sort of banishment – whether it was self-imposed exile in the pursuit of spiritual or material gain, or literally an attempt by others to get the unlucky subject out of the way. The central male character in Isabel Allende's famous novel *The House of the Spirits*, published in 1985, makes his way north early in life to slog out a miserable living in the nitrate mines. He manages to accumulate capital and returns to lay claim for the hand of his chosen fiancée. But he never goes near the north again for the rest of the book.

The north is unofficially split into two regions: for convenience, the southernmost part is known as El Norte Chico (The Little North), and the northernmost part as El Norte Grande (The Great North). This terminology reflects the awe inspired by the extreme conditions and vast extension of the Atacama Desert, beside which the dry scrublands closer to Santiago seem a pale

Cerro Tololo observatory.

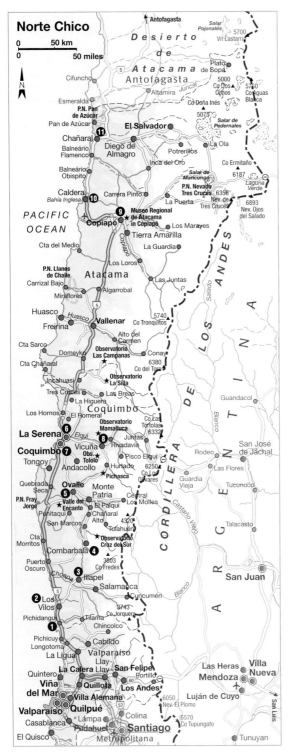

Norte Chico

imitation. But both regions are characterized by expansive Pacific beaches and resort towns, and both bear the scars of Chile's mining enterprises, with the skeletons of old mines open to visitors (see page 181). The two areas also contain petroglyphs and other archeological remains of ancient desert cultures.

Northern Chile's extraordinarily clear night skies, which are so exceptional that the region has a number of major observatories, are on best display in El Norte Chico, where four of these observatories, along with several smaller ones, are located. Pisco, Chile's piquant grape brandy, is produced in this region, which was also the birthplace of the Nobel Prize-winning poet Gabriela Mistral.

The Diaguitas culture moved into the Norte Chico region from across the Andes around AD 900 and flourished until the Inca conquest 500 years later, quickly followed by the arrival of the Spaniards. Ceramic work of this group is considered among the best in the Americas, and the black-and-white geometric designs on a red base are widely copied in Chilean decoration. Both La Serena and Ovalle have anthropological museums with excellent artifacts.

Pichicuy and Pichidangui

Driving north from Santiago, the Central Valley vegetation soon disappears, to be replaced by hardy thorn trees. Signs of inhabitants become fewer and fewer, and lands are no longer enclosed in farm plots or ranches. The highway descends to the coast, where a series of popular beach resorts are located, far enough from the capital to retain their small town dimensions. Long stretches of deserted beach are surrounded by rocky cliffs. Pichicuy and **Pichidangui ❶** ("pichi" means "little" in the Mapuche tongue) have white sand beaches with strong surf. At Pichicuy there is a church built on a promontory over the sea. A bird sanctuary with abundant sea life is located in between at the **Los Molles** rock gardens, where underground caverns produce a thunderous roar. Nearby is the **Governor's Chair**, which, at 695 meters (2,280ft), is the country's highest sea cliff, and visible from Valparaíso in good weather.

From Los Vilos to Combarbalá

Just off the highway is the lively tourist town of **Los Vilos ②**, which is full of rustic seafood restaurants and artisans who carve in *guayacán*, a durable wood once plentiful in the district. The **Bodegón Cultural** (Cultural Warehouse; Elicura 135; www.bodegonlosvilos.cl; Tue–Sat 10am–2pm and 4–7pm, Sun 10am–2pm; charge depending on event), in the restored 19th-century Customs building, holds regular art exhibitions in summer. A sculpture park, created by a local architect on the cliffs, is open to the public and worth a visit.

North of Los Vilos is the Choapa River Valley and the city of **Illapel ③**, its principal urban center. Illapel, like many northern towns, had a mining boom and bust and has since returned to its original agricultural economy. Some 18th-century construction is preserved, both in the town and on the road to Salamanca, giving an idea of how rural estates were built around a central courtyard. A typical mansion has an adobe first floor which blocks the heat and a wooden upper floor with balconies surrounding the inner patio. Sometimes the adobe walls are painted brightly.

The entire zone is arid and mountainous but has some surprisingly green valleys and attractive river beaches with excellent trout fishing. It is good for camping off-season when the sun is not so strong. The old north–south road which followed the Inca route, and which predates the Pan-American Highway, can be taken from Illapel up a severe climb through the narrowest part of Chile, in which the sea is only 80km (50 miles) from the Argentine border. The view from the top just before **Combarbalá ④** is superb, with views of the snow-topped

Rocky coastline near Pichidangui.

TIP

The Cruz del Sur Observatory (http://observatoriocruzdelsur.cl) offers talks about astronomy as well as viewing opportunities.

Andes. The design of the town's central plaza is inspired by the colors and geometrical schemes of the Diaguitas people. *Pirquineros*, artisan miners, are plentiful in the zone, where the soil has a reddish tinge due to its copper content. A whitish, marble-like stone particular to the area, called *combarbalita*, is cut and polished by the artisans to make miniature figures.

Ovalle

The next valley to the north is the **Limarí**, with the city of **Ovalle ❺** at its center. The surrounding area is an agricultural zone traditionally dependent on the city of La Serena to the north, but recently the expansion of irrigation has added new lands for export grapes and a burst of unevenly distributed prosperity. Five kilometers (3 miles) southeast of Ovalle is the **Monumento Arqueológico Valle del Encanto** (Enchanted Valley National Monument; daily approximately 8.30am–8pm, until 6.30pm in winter), which is rich in archeological treasures. There is evidence

of a hunter-gatherer civilization here dating back 4,000 years, though the bulk of the artifacts are from the Molle culture of around AD 700. This idyllic valley contains over 30 petroglyphs – designs carved into rocks – as well as 20 *piedras tacitas*, groups of circular indentations hollowed out of flat rocks in the riverbed. The number of petroglyphs that are visible depends on the angle of the sun and late afternoon is a good time to visit. The Museo del Limarí in Ovalle has an interesting collection of Diaguita pottery (www.museolimari.cl; Tue–Fri 10am–6pm, Sat–Sun 10am–2pm; free).

Around Ovalle

To the north of Ovalle is the **Recoleta Reservoir**, a popular lake resort. En route, the junction of the Grande and the Hurtado rivers can be seen from a high altitude. Farther toward the cordillera along this route is the **Monumento Natural Pichasca**, with gigantic rock formations and petrified wood. Many of the hamlets in this region, lying along the original north–south route through the

San José mine rescue.

MINE RESCUE

On August 5, 2010, the collapse of the San José gold and copper mine near Copiapó trapped 33 miners underground. For 17 days, nothing was known of their fate and then it took almost another two months to drill a new shaft and bring them safely back to the surface. The accident highlighted the poor safety conditions that exist in many small – but not large – mines in Chile. However, their rescue – followed by media from around the world as one by one the miners were hoisted out of the mine in a specially built cage – was seen as a triumph of Chilean engineering, discipline, and perseverance against all the odds. The site of the mine is 45km (28 miles) north of Copiapó but there is little left to see. *The 33* (2015), a movie starring Antonio Banderas, Gabriel Byrne and Juliette Binoche, is based on this events.

mountains, were Inca outposts ruled by a representative of the empire. The town of **Hurtado** is known for its dried fruit, figs, quince jelly, and nuts, as well as its flower farms of dahlias and chrysanthemums. From here, the mountains can be crossed straight north toward Vicuña (see page 169) on an unpaved road which offers a panoramic view of both the Andes and the next valley north, the **Valle del Elqui**.

Just southeast of Ovalle is the giant **La Paloma reservoir**, responsible for much of the new agricultural wealth of the region. Planted with stands of trees, it presents a refreshing spectacle in its dry setting. At the end of the difficult gravel road is the small village of **Las Ramadas**, whose nearby hills contain one of the two known lapis lazuli mines in the world (the other is in Afghanistan). This semi-precious blue stone is worked into a variety of pendants, earrings, and decorations, and sold in artisan markets throughout the country.

Back on the Pan-American Highway is a turn-off for **Parque Nacional Fray Jorge**, a dense green forest, which is surrounded by near-desert. This concentration of plant life is the result of an almost constant ocean fog that hugs the hillside. In nearby **Tongoy** (town names now begin to be Quechua in origin, rather than Mapuche), the beaches are among the finest in Chile, composed of extremely white pulverized conch shells. Tongoy is also one of the best places to try the local scallops, served in the innumerable beachside restaurants.

La Serena

The northern city of **La Serena** ❻ – whose name means "the serene one" – was founded by Pedro de Valdivia in 1544 as part of his plan to secure the region for Spain. From the beginning of the colonial period, it became an important resting place for travelers making the long trek across the desert. Religious orders also built receiving houses for their missionaries, and the city still has 29 churches; the oldest of these have remarkable stone facades. The discovery of silver

A beautiful stained-glass window in a church in Pisco Elqui.

San Francisco Church, La Serena.

FACT

Parque Nacional Fray Jorge (www.conaf.cl) is an unusual example of a small cloud forest in an otherwise dry area. Located 22km (14 miles) off the Pan-American Highway, just north of the turning to Ovalle, the park was declared a World Biosphere Reserve in 1977; the trees and ferns are very similar to those found in the wetter south of Chile.

in 1825 led to an upsurge of prosperity and a construction boom, though most of the original buildings were superseded by an ersatz "Spanish colonial" style imposed in a 1940s urban renewal scheme.

All the landowning families of the Limarí, Elqui, Huasco, Choapa, and Copiapó valleys had their own residence here. On one corner of Plaza de Armas, the main square, is the house of native son Gabriel González Videla, Chile's president from 1946 to 1953. Now a museum (www.museohistoricolaserena.cl; Mon–Fri 10am–6pm, Sat 10am–1pm; free), it houses the city's fine arts collection as well as some of his personal possessions.

The **Iglesia San Francisco**, two blocks away on the corner of Balmaceda and Eduardo de la Barra, probably built between 1585 and 1627, was the only church to survive a fire a 1680 that razed much of the city. From there, a pleasant walk along Avenida Francisco de Aguirre towards the sea and **El Faro** (Lighthouse) monument will take you to

La Silla observatory.

Casa de Las Palmeras, the house on the corner of Francisco de Aguirre and Juan José Latorre that Nobel poet Gabriela Mistral acquired in 1925. The building is part of the Ruta Mistraliana (Gabriela Mistral's Route) commemorating this great Chilean poet.

The **Museo Arqueológico** (www.museoarqueologicolaserena.cl; Tue–Fri 9.30am–5.50pm, Sat 10am–1pm and 4–7pm, Sun 10am–1pm; free) is an excellent insight into the region's history and has an impressive collection of Diaguitas artifacts. The city's cemetery provides an ample view of the river valley from above and, as well as the tombs of Gabriel González Videla and relatives of Gabriela Mistral, contains a monument to local supporters of the Salvador Allende Unidad Popular government who were shot or "disappeared" in the days after the 1973 military coup.

Coquimbo

Today, La Serena virtually joins the neighboring port of **Coquimbo** ❼, forming a metropolis of over

ASTRONOMY HUB

The clear skies of the Norte Chico and the area's lack of light pollution, provide ideal conditions for astronomy. Four major international observatories – Cerro Tololo (tel: 051-2205 200; www.ctio.noao.edu/noao; tours Sat 9am and 1pm, booking essential), Gemini Sur (www.gemini.edu), La Silla (www.eso.org; tours Sept–June Sat 2pm), and Las Campanas (tel: 051-207301; www.lco.cl) – are located within driving distance of La Serena. Tololo and Gemini Sur are in the Elqui Valley, off the road to Vicuña, while La Silla and Las Campanas are off the Pan-American Highway, some 130km (80 miles) north of La Serena. All can be visited free of charge and by appointment only, particularly in summer, it is usually necessary to book several weeks ahead.

400,000 inhabitants, the fourth largest In Chile after Santiago, Valparaíso-Viña de Mar, and Concepción-Talcahuano. Some elaborate woodcarving, the handiwork of foreign carpenters, can still be seen on a few buildings in Coquimbo. These craftsmen arrived as the mining industry grew, since local tradesmen did not know how to build on the scale required. Shipped in from abroad were Oregon pine (neither pine nor from Oregon) and a sturdy species of bamboo from Ecuador, which could be planed to form a solid surface. These materials and techniques were used to build the region's churches, most of which have a high central bell tower and have survived severe earthquakes. The city also has a large mosque, donated by the king of Morocco and built by Moroccan workmen.

Just south of Coquimbo, on the other side of the peninsula is La Herradura (Horseshoe), named for the shape of its sheltered bay, once used mainly for fishing but now an important beach resort.

Valle del Elqui

The sleepy village of **Vicuña** ❽, east of La Serena in the Valle del Elqui, was the birthplace of Gabriela Mistral (see page 171), and houses a museum of the famous poet (www.mgmistral.cl; Jan–Feb Mon–Sat 10am–7pm, Sun 10am–6pm, Mar–Dec Mon–Fri 10am–5.45pm, Sat 10.30am–6pm, Sun 10am–1pm; free). The Mamalluca Municipal Observatory, 9km (5 miles) northeast of Vicuña, was the first observatory in Chile opened specifically for tourists. Two different programs, both including observation – one on basic astronomy and the other on Andean cosmology – are available (tel: 051-670 330; daily from 6.30pm onwards). Prior booking is advisable but not always essential and this is a fun visit for adults and children alike.

From Vicuña, the road continues up to **Monte Grande**, where Gabriela Mistral is buried. This is also Chile's main pisco-producing area, and plants can be visited without appointment. The outlying hills of the Valle del Elqui are the haunt of a variety of esoteric movements and guru-led communities, in part, no doubt, due to the great

FACT

Chile's two species of carnivorous plant, known as fox's ear, grow between La Serena and Copiapó.

Vineyard near Vicuña.

DRINK

To make a pisco sour, mix three parts pisco with one part lemon or lime juice, then add sugar, one egg white, and some crushed ice.

clarity of the night skies and the sensation that, as the title of a book about the zone suggested, *Heaven is Nearer*. North of La Serena, the Pan-American Highway cuts back toward the interior, but a side spur leads to the interesting beaches and fishing villages at **Temblador** and **Chungungo**, the last being the name of a local species of otter.

Bethlehem Steel ran the world's largest iron mine between 1914 and 1954 at **El Tofo**, 10km (6 miles) in from this part of the Chilean coast, and its abandoned remains can still be seen. Also nearby is the Camanchaca Project; here the heavy mist that rolls in from the sea (called *camanchaca*) is captured and condensed on fine netting to provide a water supply. The area just north of La Serena is the transition zone between the transversal valleys, where agriculture is still possible, and the Atacama Desert, where it is frankly inconceivable. The Copiapó is the last river to make its way down from the mountains to the sea. North of here, any mountain flows evaporate into nothing along the way, with the one exception of the River Loa in the Norte

Laguana Verde, also known as the Lake of Chile, Atacama Desert.

Grande. The Andes now divide into two parallel ranges, trapping the melting snows in an interior basin to form enormous salt flats, a phenomenon repeated all the way north into Bolivia. These deposits have great commercial potential for the concentrations of lithium, potassium, and borax as well as being used to produce salt for human consumption. In the central plain, followed by the Pan-American Highway, an occasional wet winter brings the desert into flower the following spring. This rare and short-lived display is an unforgettable sight.

Around Copiapó

Copiapó ❾, the capital of the region, is now a grape-growing zone par excellence, the result of enormous investments in earthmoving and irrigation. As these grapes are the first to ripen and hit US supermarkets around Christmas, they are worth the expense. From Copiapó it is possible to drive eastward through the desert to the salt flats, an extraordinary trip if correct precautions are taken: wear warm clothes; bring food, water, and petrol; and register

your route and the duration of the trip with the local *carabineros* (police).

The **Salar de Maricunga** salt flat is impressive for its setting near the Andes, including the world's highest volcano, Ojos del Salado (6,893 meters/22,615ft), which last erupted in 1956. For a longer stay, the national park service (CONAF) has a very basic guesthouse in **Parque Nacional Nevado Tres Cruces**, a bit farther along the road. Overlooked by the Ojos del Salado Volcano, this National Park, created in 1994, includes the Negro Francisco and Santa Rosa Lagoons, protected by the Ramsar Convention on Wetlands. On their brackish water, there are Andean gulls and three species of flamingo while, on the banks, vicuñas and guanacos graze.

Near the Argentine border, the **Laguna Verde** lake is apparently dead, but flamingos live in the salt flat, contentedly picking bugs out of the oily ooze in the rocks. Explorer/conqueror Diego de Almagro used this crossing from Argentina in his ill-fated 1536 journey: he lost most of his men en route in the frigid passes. Legend has it that half-frozen survivors often pulled off a couple of toes along with their boots.

Bahía Inglesa, near Copiapó, is said to be the most beautiful beach of the north, but there are many bathing spots along the Pan-American Highway, which returns to the shore for a long stretch between **Caldera** ➓ and **Chañaral** ➓. The latter port was severely polluted by wastes from the copper mine at Salvador. Deposits from the copper mine are now diverted to a desert site, ending 60 years of contamination. North of Chañaral is the wildlife refuge **Parque Nacional Pan de Azúcar**. Stretching some 40km (25 miles) along the coast, this has some of Chile's most spectacular coastal scenery as well as a wealth of plant and birdlife. It's the best place to see a climatic phenomenon known as *desierto florido* (flowering desert), when during years of a especially high rainfall in the region, the arid Atacama Desert covers itself with wild flowers from September to November. Just offshore is a small island, with a large colony of Humboldt penguins, to which boat trips are available.

FACT

The Museo Regional de Atacama in Copiapó (www.museodeatacama.cl; Mon–Fri 10am–5.45pm, Sat 10am–12.45pm, 3–5.45pm, Sun 10am–1.30pm; free) offers a good introduction to the local history.

Chilean poet Gabriela Mistral.

GABRIELA MISTRAL

Vicuña is the birthplace of Gabriela Mistral, one of Chile's greatest poets. An austere rather than popular heroine, Mistral is treated in Chile like the precious mineral commodities that are unearthed from the dry, surrounding hills – a resource to be claimed and honored for its undeniable value, but not in itself a source of joy or pleasure. Awarded the national literary prize six years after winning the Nobel Prize, she was mistrusted as an eccentric during her life and was never one of the darlings of Chile's literary elite. A schoolteacher by profession, she spent much of her life abroad, first in Mexico, where she participated in educational reform and, later in life, as Chilean Consul in different countries.

Her first book of poetry, *Desolation*, was published in New York, the city where she died. The themes of her work are displacement, separateness, and the difficulty of romantic love in a world ruled by a punishing God.

Further up the Valle del Elqui from Vicuña is Monte Grande, the village where Mistral spent most of her childhood under the watchful eye of her elder sister, the local school and postmistress. The school is now a small, very pleasant museum. Here too, on a rocky outcrop overlooking the valley, Gabriela Mistral is buried.

Llama, Volcán Isluga National Park.

EL NORTE GRANDE

Chile's far north, or "Great North," is an area of spectacular beauty, with Pacific beaches, deserts, volcanoes, lakes teeming with wildlife, and the remnants of ancient civilizations.

The Atacama Desert is located in the same latitude belt as other deserts in the Southern Hemisphere, whose dominant high-pressure systems prevent storms from moving in. Chile's twin mountain ranges aggravate the situation; no precipitation has been measured in this desert since the Spanish colonization, giving it the title of driest spot on earth. The Altiplanic Inversion occurs around the summer equinox (December 21), when strong evaporation generates sometimes violent rain and hailstorms in the mountains, and the water rushes down the dry gorges. These storms last until March, and serious flooding can make many roads virtually impassable.

The extraordinary dryness is responsible for great archeological treasures, such as the famous Atacama mummies, which predate the Egyptian varieties by several thousand years. All sorts of artifacts are easily preserved, and new finds occur regularly. The Museo Arqueológico Gustavo Le Paige in San Pedro de Atacama, founded by a Belgian Jesuit, Gustavo Le Paige, has 380,000 objects while a 2,800-year-old site called Tulor has been unearthed nearby. Water is obviously a major logistical problem, not only for personal use but also to satisfy the enormous demands of modern mining. Huge investments have been made

in pipelines to bring Andean waters to the coast or to mining outposts. At the Conchi bridge north of Chiu Chiu (near San Pedro), six pipelines come together. The first known industrial use of solar energy in the world was in a water desalinization plant built in 1872 at Carmen Alto near Antofagasta.

Antofagasta

Antofagasta ❶ is the fourth-largest city in Chile and the most populous of the Atacama Desert. It is still an important port for export of minerals.

Main Attractions
Pukará de Quitor
San Pedro de Atacama
Valle de la Luna
El Tatio Geysers
Museo Arqueológico San
  Miguel
Parque Nacional Lauca

Atacama mummy.

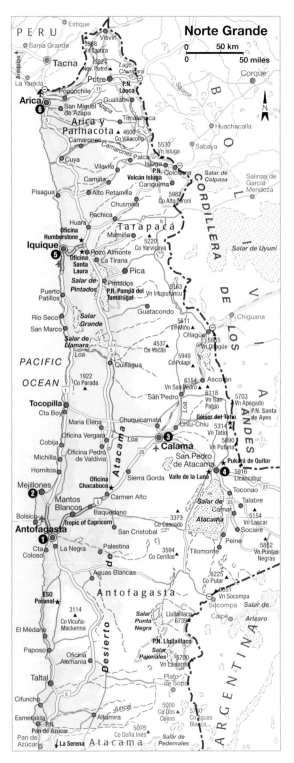

Norte Grande

0   50 km
0   50 miles

However, an alternative port has developed in nearby Mejillones, mostly to relieve road congestion in Antofagasta. Antofagasta's 20km (12-mile) beachfront gives it a fresh, gracious air, despite the unrelieved brown of the hills. A financial dispute and property seizure here in 1879 sparked the War of the Pacific, which ended Bolivian control of the town and lands to the east. This portion of Chile is the widest, measuring 355km (221 miles) from the Andes to the sea.

In Antofagasta, the excellent **Museo Regional** (www.museodeantofagasta.cl; Tue–Fri 9am–5pm, Sat–Sun 11am–2pm; free) relates local history and includes archeological exhibits relating to the area's indigenous peoples, but the city has few other attractions for visitors.

Some 13km (8 miles) north of the city is the famous **La Portada**, a huge rock eroded into an arch by the sea. Across a peninsula to the north is the town of **Mejillones ❷**, which started out as the northern railroads' mechanical shop, producing wagons and locomotives. One of the most sheltered bays in the area, it now houses thermal power plants and other heavy industries, as well as port facilities.

Copper mines

Northeast of Antofagasta were two of the world's largest copper mines: Escondida copper mine, controlled by BHP Billiton, an international mining company, and the state-owned **Chuquicamata** mine, or Chuqui as it used to be fondly known. Together, these two mines produced around a tenth of the world's copper, but in 2008 the Chuqui was eventually closed and all the habitants were relocated to the nearby town of **Calama ❸** that has little to offer besides streets full of cheap bars and strip joints.

Nearby **Chiu Chiu** was the pre-Hispanic crossroads at the fork of two rivers. It fulfills the stereotype of a desert oasis, a green speck in the midst of a hostile brown sea, and has a 1675 church whose construction borrowed elements of the Atacameño indigenous culture.

The road toward San Pedro de Atacama crosses the Plain of Patience, whose name soon begins to make sense: the landscape between two distant ridges appears not to change at all for miles. An advertised alternative route to San Pedro though the **Valle de la Luna** (Valley of the Moon) is not advised for small cars as sand accumulated on the road can trap them.

San Pedro de Atacama

The oasis town of **San Pedro de Atacama ❹** is a popular base for exploring the north's most spectacular sights. A dry salt lake, the **Salar de Atacama**, stretches beyond the town to a distant row of snowcapped volcanoes – including Licancábur which, at 5,916 meters (19,410ft), is one of the highest extinct volcanoes in the Andean chain.

San Pedro is extremely popular with backpackers and, although fun, has become a little touristy and can get crowded. It has a restored adobe house on one side of the plaza that is universally called Pedro de Valdivia's residence but is now thought to be pre-Hispanic in construction. Opposite is a 16th-century church, one of the oldest in Chile.

San Pedro's **Museo Arqueológico Gustavo Le Paige** (Mon–Fri 9am–6pm, Sat–Sun 10am–6pm; guided tour available in English) was founded by the former village priest after whom it is named and has an unusually wide array of pre-Columbian artifacts. However, the museum's most famous exhibits – its collection of ancient mummies of both children and adults, preserved in the dry desert air, with their deliberately deformed skulls – were withdrawn in 2007 at the request of local indigenous communities who protested about this display of their dead ancestors.

Southeast of San Pedro is the village of **Toconao**, past a plantation of *tamarugo* trees which provide a tiny seed for animal pasture. A guide can be hired here to drive to **Lago Chaxa** and observe pink flamingos. The entire

FACT

The clock tower in the middle of Antofagasta's Plaza Colón is a miniature replica of London's Big Ben, down to the chimes. It was erected by British residents in 1910 to celebrate the centenary of Chile's independence.

The Cerro Paranal Very Large Telescope.

DELVING INTO THE UNIVERSE

With its clear skies and lack of light pollution, northern Chile's Atacama Desert is the ideal place for astrology enthusiasts, and new and ever more powerful telescopes are being installed there. One of the most important is the Very Large Telescope (VLT) on the Cerro Paranal, a hill that is 120km (75 miles) south of Antofagasta. Owned by the European Southern Observatory (ESO), a 14-country alliance, the observatory officially became operational in 1998 and comprises an array of four telescopes, each with a mirror of 8.2 meters (26.9ft) in diameter. The four telescopes are named *Antu*, *Kueyen*, *Melipal* and *Yepun*, all of which are names for astronomical objects in Mapuche. ESO has also selected the nearby Armazones Mountain as the site for its European Extremely Large Telescope (E-ELT), which will have a 42-meter (137.8ft) mirror – four times that of the largest telescope currently in operation, anywhere in the world. The E-ELT will be used primarily to search for planets at just the right distance from their sun – in other words, neither too close nor too far, neither too hot nor too cold – to facilitate the possibility of sustained life. Cerro Paranal is open for visits on Saturdays (closed in Decemeber; free of charge). However, prior booking is required. Book at www.eso.org.

Salar de Atacama can be circled in a two-day trip, passing through impressively desolate landscapes and curious desert outposts.

Three kilometers (2 miles) northwest of San Pedro, at **Pukará de Quitor** (daily 8am–8pm), are the ruins of a 700-year-old pre-Columbian fortress. This was where the native peoples made their last stand against the invading Spaniards under Pedro de Valdivia.

The **Tulor** archeological site (daily 8am–8pm), 9 kilometers (5.5 miles) southwest of San Pedro contains the remains of the area's oldest known civilization. Discovered in the mid-20th century by Le Paige, it was home to the Linka Arti people about whom little is known except that they lived in mud huts resembling igloos. Thirty-two kilometers (20 miles) northeast of San Pedro are the hot springs called the **Termas de Puritama** (daily 9.15am–5.30 pm), where you will find a choice of steaming pools to wallow in, as well as a few waterfalls for a natural shower, although the entrance fee is expensive.

Valle de la Luna

The famous **Valle de la Luna** is about 8km (5 miles) from San Pedro. As the name suggests, this is a haunting landscape of colored gypsum, clay, and salt, without a hint of organic life to be found. The valley is at its eeriest at sunset, while under a full moon the beams reflecting off the salt crystals of the region make it a truly spectacular sight.

But perhaps the most interesting excursion from San Pedro is the one that leaves at 4am to visit the daily show of at least 100 geysers at **El Tatio**, which burst forth just before sunrise every morning. As they exit the frozen earth with strange gurgling subterranean sounds, they thrust their columns of steam high into the air. Some are wide, boiling pools, while others resemble mini-volcanoes with cones of bright yellow mineral deposits. Be very careful not to step too close to the edge of the pools; there have been some fatal accidents. The display dies down at about 10am until the next morning. The visitor can bathe in a huge pool of tolerably hot thermal waters before returning.

El Tatio geyser field.

Iquique

Traveling north toward **Iquique** ⑤ takes you past numerous geoglyphs carved into the hillsides. The best collection is in the **Reserva Nacional Pampa del Tamarugal** (www.conaf.cl), 48km (30 miles) south of the turning to Iquique (daily 9.30am–5pm). This is also the zone of nitrate ghost towns. The detour to Iquique is close to **Pozo Almonte**, 47km (30 miles) across a plateau that abruptly ends with a breathtaking view over the city. Between it and the 600-meter (1,968ft) cliffs lies a huge sand dune whose dimensions only become clear from below – this is a popular venue for sand-skiing. Iquique's golden era was the nitrate heyday from 1890 to 1920, when European opera singers appeared in the elegant **Teatro Municipal** (closed for restoration) and adjourned to a replica Mudéjar palace, now the **Centro Español**, across the plaza, for a late meal.

The **Museo Regional** (Baquedano 951; Tue–Fri 9am–5.30pm, Sat 9.30am–6pm; voluntary contribution) is worth visiting, with mummies, archeological artifacts and exhibits from the nitrates era. The nearby **Museo Naval** on Calle Esmeralda is also worth a visit (Tue–Sat 10am–1pm; voluntary contribution) as well as the Museo Corbeta Esmeralda on Paseo Almirante Lynch (www.museoesmeralda.cl; Tue–Sun 10am–1pm and 2–6pm). One of the city's new attractions, a scale reproduction of the Esmeralda, a Chilean boat that played a key role in the 19th-century War of the Pacific (see page 41), is very popular with visitors and booking is recommended. But the main interest is in the range of stately 19th-century mansions that are kept as national monuments; many are clustered around Plaza Arturo Prat, with its clock tower. The whole center has been declared a National Monument.

About 70km (44 miles) east of Iquique is the village La Tirana, the site of the Virgen del Carmen religious festival. This annual event takes place during mid-July and goes on for a week. The festival has dance groups composed of virginal maidens and men disguised as devils. The whole experience is a compromise

DRINK

The town of Pica, southeast of Iquique, is famous for its tiny lemons – *limones de pica* – that are considered the best for making pisco sour.

The Salar de Atacama covers 750,000 acres and contains Chile's largest deposit of salt.

between Catholic rite and indigenous animist influences.

Arica

Arica ❻ was the first port for exporting the fabulous silver wealth of Bolivia's Potosí mine. (In 1611 Potosí was the largest and richest city in the Americas.) Under Peruvian rule until the 1880s, Arica is now the international link to Bolivia and Peru. Its warm-water beaches make it a popular summer resort, particularly for Bolivians. A small church in the town center was built by the French architect Gustave Eiffel, better known for his Paris tower.

The **Museo Arqueológico San Miguel de Azapa** (Mar–Dec daily 10am–6pm, Jan–Feb daily 10am–7pm) is 14km (9 miles) from town and has an impressive collection of sand-preserved mummies older than their Egyptian counterparts. The Azapa Valley in which the museum is located demonstrates the desert's fertility: given an adequate supply of water, brightly colored flowers grown commercially suddenly appear in the distance.

The town of Putre, east of Arica.

From Arica, passing the ancient geoglyphs near **San Miguel de Azapa**, and taking the inland road toward Lago Chungará, you pass through pre-Hispanic and colonial villages with baroque churches and *pukarás*, or stone forts, used by native tribes from unrecorded times to defend themselves from invaders. As you ascend 4,500 meters (14,800ft) into **Parque Nacional Lauca** (www.conaf.cl), the mighty 19,700ft (6,000-meter) -high volcanoes Parinacota and Pomerape – sacred gods to the inhabitants of the high Andean plain – dominate the landscape. During most of the year, only a handful of people live in the town of Parinacota but it fills up for colorful religious festivals such as the Fiesta de la Virgen de Candelaria in early February and the Fiesta de las Cruces in May. Outside the whitewashed church, Aymara women in their brightly colored shawls and bowler hats sell local craftwork.

On **Lago Chungará**, declared a World Biosphere Reserve by Unesco, wildlife teems. The large flightless *tagua-tagua* make their nests on floating reed islands; the chinchilla-like *vizcachas* with their hopping scamper could be mistaken for fleeing gray hares; the sand-colored vicuñas often tag behind llama herds; the black-and-white *piquén* (Andean geese) will show themselves far from their nesting offspring as decoys; but perhaps most famous are the pink flamingos which dwell in the lake's shallows. Covering the rocks at this altitude like a green carpet is the pungent native lichen *llareta*, which grows a centimeter a year and has been used almost to extinction for fuel farther south. Chile's Forestry Service (CONAF) has an office just before the lake.

Andean geese also nest on the **Lagunas Cotacotani**, a string of little lakes 8km (5 miles) east of Parinacota. The bleak moon-like landscape here was formed by successive volcanic eruptions.

Ghost Towns

The north of Chile is dotted with abandoned mining towns, some of which have been preserved and are open to visitors.

The collapse of the nitrate or saltpeter market at the end of World War I was so sudden that the mining towns, which had no other reason to exist, were abruptly abandoned. A German-invented synthetic nitrate had eliminated the need for the raw material rendering Chile's "desert gold" obsolete.

Mining camps were known as *oficinas* (offices), referring to the offices of the purchasing agents, who bought everything mined within a certain radius. Virtually anyone determined and hardworking enough could be a miner, since the earliest production method consisted of simply digging up the readily visible *caliche* (nitrate ore), grinding it, and selling it at the "office." When the best ore, which had a grade of 50 to 60 percent, was exhausted, the office simply moved elsewhere.

More complicated processes which could utilize lower-grade ore led to more permanent settlements. These offices are identifiable by waste piles of gravel built up into cake-like constructions. Many are visible from the highway between Antofagasta and Calama, and south of Iquique. A small roadside marker gives the history of each site.

World Heritage sites

The best-preserved ghost town is Oficina Humberstone on the turn-off from Pozo Almonte to Iquique. Established in the mid-19th century, it had a population of 5,000 and provided an unusually varied existence for its inhabitants. A few *tamarugo* trees remain standing around the plaza, and the town's theater, including its seats, the church, and the market are still intact. The abandoned frames of workshops and homes are spread out over a large area; everything is covered with dust and battered by the steady desert wind. The air of recent habitation is genuinely spooky, as if the inhabitants had suddenly fled without warning.

In mining towns such as Humberstone everything was owned and controlled by the mining company. It built the housing, stocked the town's stores, decided who worked, for how long, at what rates, and what he did with his wages (miners were often paid in *fichas*, tokens only valid for company goods).

Nearby is Oficina Santa Laura, where a processing plant and administrative complex are preserved. In 2005, Unesco placed the two towns on its World Heritage in Danger list, citing wind damage to wooden structures and the effect of wind-borne salt on metal, as well as looting, as the main threats. They are open to visitors 9am–7pm, but guided tours are available only until 2pm (www.museodelsalitre.cl).

Along the Antofagasta–Calama road just past Carmen Alto is the Oficina Chacabuco and the nearby Salinas train station, site of an abandoned 1872 drinking water plant which used solar energy. Chacabuco was one of the Chilean locations used in 2008 to film the James Bond film *Quantum of Solace* but is also notorious for its use by the Pinochet dictatorship as a prison camp for dissidents.

Between Antofagasta and Tocopilla lies the only functioning nitrate center, María Elena. Workers live in María Elena, which has a street plan based on Britain's Union Flag. It's owned by the Chilean Chemical and Mining Company SOQUIMICH, which was returned to private ownership during the military regime.

An abandoned train, Humberstone ghost town.

THE ATACAMA DESERT

This mysterious, barren region of haunting beauty is home to spectacular natural phenomena and the well-preserved remains of ancient civilizations.

Chile's far north is made up of barren desert and scrubland, and the forbidding high plains of the altiplano or Andean Plateau. No wonder most of the population prefer to live along the coast, in towns like Antofagasta and Iquique, famed for their architecture and expansive Pacific beaches. For the visitor, however, the mountain and desert regions present a series of awe-inspiring spectacles. The Atacama Desert is reputed to be the driest in the world, yet every decade or so a rare downpour (usually linked with the El Niño weather system) in the southern part around Copiapó and Vallenar brings dormant seeds into bloom, in a phenomenon known as "The Flowering Desert."

The oasis town of San Pedro de Atacama (see page 177), dominated by the Licancábur volcano, is at the center of a region of immense geological interest, with huge salt lakes, hot springs, and unusual desert formations. East of San Pedro the terrain ascends steeply to the altiplano, where it meets Argentine and Bolivian territory. In this chilly region lie more hot springs, geysers, and mountain lakes of ethereal beauty.

More natural and geological delights lie farther north of the Atacama Desert, toward Peru, where national parks like Lauca and Volcán Isluga, and Reserva Nacional Las Vicuñas are home to a variety of distinctive wildlife.

From Calama, it is possible to drive to Oruro in Bolivia. Rewards of this grueling trip include more altiplano highlights, such as the immense salt basin of Uyuni, and Lagunas Verde, and Colorado.

Some of the flora in the southern Atacama Desert comes into bloom just once every 10–15 years.

Volcán Licancábur (5,916 meters/19,410ft) presides over the ancient village oasis of San Pedro de Atacama, marking the place where the flat desert meets the chilly altiplano.

The largest of the camelids, llamas, thrive in the barren desert conditions of the Atacama region.

Flamingos are a common sight around altiplano lakes. Three species of flamingo breed around Laguna Chaxa, south of Toconao.

Visitors bathe in thermal springs at the El Tatio geysers, 4300 metres (14,100ft).

The smallest and rarest of the camelids, the vicuña, prefers the highest altitudes, mostly in northern Chile.

A CHECKERED HISTORY

Although remote from the main economic centers of central Chile, the Atacama Desert has played an important role in the country's history. Peopled before the Spanish conquest by the Atacameños and, on the coast, the Changos, it was conquered in the mid-15th century by the Incas but their reign was short. By 1557, the Spanish invaders had already established a mission and chapel in San Pedro de Atacama, an oasis town that was later to become an important trading center.

Despite its apparent infertility, the Atacama Desert has, over the past two centuries, provided an important part of Chile's wealth – first, In the form of nitrates for fertilizer and, now, copper, by far the country's largest export. In the future, it also promises to become an important source of lithium, already obtained from the Salar de Atacama but also present in large quantities in other salt flats.

But, looking to the future, the scarcity of water – key in preserving the area's rich archeological remains – poses a huge challenge for the region. Mining companies, with their ever-increasing demands, compete for the resource – and often come into conflict – with local farmers. Desalination of seawater is the only viable solution and is, indeed, already beginning to be used, but is expensive and very heavy on energy consumption.

The adobe church in the oasis town of San Pedro de Atacama dates back to the 16th century. Inside, the ceiling is made from chañar and algarrobo, two native tree species.

Robinson Crusoe Island.

JUAN FERNANDEZ ISLANDS

Famed as the temporary home of the real-life
Robinson Crusoe, the inaccessibility of these
Pacific islands makes them natural biospheres,
replete with abundant endemic wildlife.

Main Attractions
San Juan Bautista
El Mirador de Selkirk
Fuerte Santa Bárbara
Cuevas de los Patriotas

Most people have never heard of the 18th-century Scottish sea dog named Alexander Selkirk or the **Juan Fernández Islands**, 650km (404 miles) off the Chilean mainland. Yet they are part of our popular mythology. Try to imagine being marooned on a desert isle and you will probably see a man dressed in goatskins, flintlock at the ready, scanning the horizon for passing ships. His island – unlike the barren, windswept rocks where most mariners were washed up – has plentiful wood, crystal waters, abundant food, and no wild beasts. The scene is from *Robinson Crusoe*, of course. But although Daniel Defoe set his classic novel in the Caribbean, he based it directly on Alexander Selkirk's real-life adventures on Chile's tiny Pacific possession.

The foul-tempered young Scotsman spent four years and four months on the largest of the three deserted Juan Fernández Islands. Finally rescued by a group of English privateers, Selkirk was clad in goatskins and could barely speak, croaking rather than talking. He had made himself two wooden huts with fur-lined interiors and had become incredibly fit from chasing wild animals around the rocky shores. The marooned sailor became a minor celebrity on his return home and

– with the more debauched side of his character being carefully tidied up – inspired one of the most enduring classics in the English language.

The inhabitants of the Juan Fernández Islands today certainly aren't shy about this unique claim to fame. Selkirk's island was renamed **Isla Robinson Crusoe** in the mid-1970s, while another, which the Scotsman never visited, was renamed **Isla Alejandro Selkirk**. Hotel and street names in the islands' only township refer insistently to the shipwrecked hero.

Hiking on Robinson Crusoe Island.

Due to its remoteness, the archipelago is one of the least visited places in Chile and its tourist infrastructure is only gradually recovering from the tsunami that hit it in February 2010, washing away most of San Juan Bautista, the only town. But, as well as several fascinating excursions relating to Selkirk's adventures there, the real reason for visiting is the archipelago's attraction as a unique wilderness area, declared a Biosphere Reserve by Unesco in 1977.

The real-life Crusoe

While Daniel Defoe's fictional hero was shipwrecked in a tropical storm (and so, in his more meditative moments, saw the Hand of God at work), the real-life mariner Alexander Selkirk could only blame himself for his predicament: Selkirk actually asked to be let off his ship in the middle of nowhere. As sailing master of the *Cinque Ports*, a privateering vessel making a circumnavigation of the globe in 1704, the quarrelsome Selkirk found himself constantly at odds with the ship's captain. Feelings finally

came to a head over some poor repairs that had been made to a leak in the hull: Selkirk snapped that, if the boat were to go down, it would be without him. The captain agreed to land the Scotsman at the nearest island with a few supplies.

Selkirk stubbornly held to his demand until the very last moment. Sitting on the shore of Más a Tierra (as the island was then known), watching his former shipmates row back to their ship, the enormity of his decision struck him. Marooning was considered by pirates to be the ultimate punishment, far worse than walking the plank. A slow death by starvation or dehydration was the usual result. Most were put ashore with only their sea chest and a pistol with one ball; tales abounded of ships' crews finding a lone skeleton with a shattered skull and a rusting pistol clenched in one hand.

Selkirk is said to have plunged into the ocean and chased after the departing rowboat, screaming madly that he had changed his mind. "Well I have not changed mine!" spat the

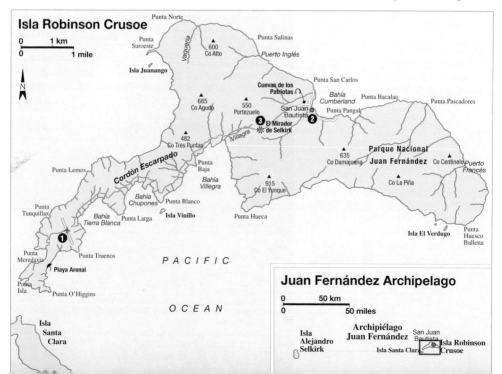

captain. "Stay where you are and may you starve!"

Goats, rats, and feral cats

This indecorous scene was the beginning of 52 months of isolation for Selkirk. He spent most of his time reading the Bible. A journalist who interviewed the Scotsman in a London tavern after his return to England noted that he believed himself "a better Christian while in this solitude than ever he was before, or than, he was afraid, he should ever be again."

Yet in the beginning, Selkirk hardly took his fate philosophically. For several weeks after the marooning, he apparently wandered the coast, wailing and staring at the empty horizon. He simply could not believe that his shipmates would leave him there to rot on the shore. It took him 18 months to accept his fate, tear himself away from the shoreline and explore the rest of his island prison. At least Selkirk was not starved for animal company. Every night he heard the "monsters of the deep" whose cries

were "too terrible to be made for human ears" – which, it turned out, were sea lions that had come up to shore. Eventually Selkirk overcame his fear, and learned how to climb behind these ponderous beasts and crack their skulls with a single blow of his hatchet.

Domestic animals had been introduced during an ill-fated attempt by the Spaniards to colonize the island following its discovery by the navigator Juan Fernández in 1574. Wild goats became the Scotsman's staple food: after his ammunition ran out, he chased them on foot with a knife and became an impressive athlete. He even chased goats for sport, marking their ears as a record. However, this diversion had its dangers: on one occasion Selkirk grabbed a goat just as it was leaping off a precipice. He was able to use the beast's body to cushion his fall, but was knocked unconscious for at least a full day. After this debacle, he decided to raise goats in a compound.

Wild rats were less amusing animal neighbors, invading Selkirk's hut by

FACT

The Juan Fernández native eagle lives only on the small Isla Alejandro Selkirk. It visits the other two islands, but never settles on them; no one knows why.

Fishermen setting off from Isla Alejandro Selkirk.

night to nibble his feet and tear his clothes. The Scotsman tamed feral kittens and laid them around his bed as a defense. Apparently he also taught some of his cats and kids to dance. "Thus best we picture him," intones the early 20th-century poet Walter de la Mare, "praying aloud, singing and dancing with his kids and cats in the flames and the smoke of his allspice wood, and the whole world's moon taunting and enchanting him in her seasons."

Return to civilization

Charming as these bestial balls must have been, Selkirk did not waver in his attempts to escape the island. Every day he climbed up to a lookout to survey the horizon. On two occasions ships actually pulled into the bay and Selkirk thought himself saved – only to discover that they were Spanish barks that would have taken him as a slave to the mines of Peru if they had caught him. (On the second visit, Spanish sailors even fired on the maroon and chased him into the bushes, but were no match

for Selkirk's superhuman speed. The Scotsman hid up a tree until the danger had passed.)

Finally, Selkirk spotted the English *Duke* and *Duchess* lowering anchor on the island with 50 scurvy-ridden sailors. Brought on board, the goat-skin-clad Selkirk cut an extraordinary figure, but disbelievers were soon silenced when William Dampier came forward to recognize the maroon and confirm his story.

Despite romantic reports to the contrary, Selkirk appears to have had few qualms about returning to his old life of privateering and debauchery. Appointed a mate on the voyage, he took part in the pillage of various Spanish ports before returning with the profits to celebrity in London and his hometown of Lower Largo in Fife, Scotland. He was no doubt gratified to learn that the captain and crew of the *Cinque Ports*, after dumping him at Juan Fernández, had spent the last four years in a festering Lima jail, having been captured by the Spanish when the vessel foundered, just as Selkirk had predicted.

Drinking and whoring soon took its toll on Selkirk, sapping his unnatural fitness. He even became sentimental for his island prison, noting to one journalist that "I am worth eight hundred pounds, but shall never be so happy as when I was not worth a farthing." The Scotsman may have gone a little batty: he reportedly dug a cave in his parents' backyard to hide in, ran away to London with a milkmaid, dumped her, then signed on for another privateering expedition. He caught a fever in the tropics and died on board in 1723, at the age of 47. Selkirk never knew that his marooning on Juan Fernández – extended by Defoe to 28 years and with a Man Friday thrown in – would become a legend.

Traveling to the islands

Getting to the Juan Fernández Islands today can seem as complicated as it

Fisherman in Bahía Cumberland.

was for Alexander Selkirk to get off them 300 years ago. Weekly flights are operated by three companies: Lassa, ATA, and Aerocardal, but their. frequency depends on demand, and getting a confirmed departure date requires luck and dedication. Even in summer, flights can be postponed for several days depending on weather conditions.

The flights depart from Santiago's Tobalaba airport early in the morning, leaving the capital behind in a bed of smog. Two hours later, the tiny green specks of Juan Fernández appear, looking as tall as they are wide. For years it was considered impossible to build an airstrip on this rugged terrain, but in the 1970s something looking like a giant ski-jump was blasted through a far corner of the largest island. From the **airstrip ❶**, a jeep heads down a 45-degree angled road to the sea, followed by a 90-minute journey in an open fishing boat to town. On a fine day, the water is clear and blue, with schools of fish zigzagging below and the obese Juan Fernández seals

sunning themselves by the shore. The boatmen often smoke succulent lumps of fresh cod caught on the outward journey and share them around with bread and water.

San Juan Bautista

The town of **San Juan Bautista ❷**, where almost all of the archipelago's 600 inhabitants live, is located roughly where Selkirk spent his enforced leisure time. This is a lobster town and not poor, although prices of goods imported from the mainland are high.

Set beneath forest-covered fists of stone with their peaks continually lost in gray mist, it has only a few unpaved streets, a small museum-library, a handful of restaurants and bars, and a soccer field. With motor vehicles few and far between on the island, the only noise is the never-ending howl of the wind.

Along the path running north from the town is a spot where famous gun shells can be seen embedded in the cliff side. They were fired by the British warships *Glasgow* and *Kent* at the German cruiser *Dresden* when

TIP

The El Palillo beach to the south of San Juan Bautista is the best place for swimming or snorkeling.

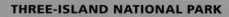

Firecrown hummingbird.

THREE-ISLAND NATIONAL PARK

Except for the town of San Juan Bautista and its surrounding area, all the Juan Fernández archipelago is a vast national park that is carefully controlled by CONAF, Chile's national park service, to protect the endemic flora and fauna that put the islands on Unesco's Biosphere Reserve list. There are three official trails that visitors can take on their own but they must register at the Park administration office and, in some parts of the islands, only guided hikes are permitted. An alternative way to see the park is by boat, also visiting colonies of the native fur seal that was once close to extinction.

Plant life is unusually varied in the archipelago, with 101 endemic varieties, including a range of enormous ferns, many of which look like they belong in a Dr Seuss book, and biologists regularly turn up new finds. Of the endemic animals, the red Juan Fernández hummingbird is most famous for its needle-fine black beak and silken plumage.

CONAF spends most of its time trying to eradicate threats introduced by man: everything from mulberry bushes to the wild goats and feral cats descended from Selkirk's days. Rabbits were a problem, but they have been controlled by the simple solution of paying a trapper to catch and sell 150 a day (the islanders thought this a more humane solution than using the fatal viral disease myxomatosis).

it tried to retire here for repairs in 1915, during World War I. The captain blew up the ship rather than surrender.

El Mirador de Selkirk

The classic hike from town follows Selkirk's path to **El Mirador de Selkirk ❸** – the lookout used by the marooned sailor every day to scan the horizon on both sides of the island. Start early, at about 8am, to arrive before the mists roll in. The path runs through crops of introduced eucalyptus into higher forests of indigenous trees. It passes the remains of the **Fuerte Santa Bárbara**, an old Spanish fort built in the 18th century to ward off pirates, and a turning leading to a rock with carvings on it from 1866 – sailor's graffiti showing a ship and giant fish. The trail becomes a corridor through rainforest before revealing a knife-shaped peak.

The saddle of the mountain is the only place from which to view both sides of the island: the lush green San Juan Bautista side to the east giving way to dry brown swirls and jagged

peaks on the northern side of the mountain. A plaque commemorating Selkirk's ordeal was erected here by the crew of a British warship in the 19th century. It has more recently been joined by a small memorial from one of the mariner's descendants from Largo in Scotland.

On the return journey, call in at the **Cuevas de los Patriotas** (Caves of the Patriots), where 300 pro-Spanish soldiers fled in 1814 after Chile's declaration of independence. Unlike Selkirk, they couldn't stand the wind and rain in their huge but damp caves, so gave themselves up. Back on the shore, a number of other caves vie for the title of Selkirk's home – although for most of the time the mariner lived in his own handmade huts.

Modern-day paradise

One of the real pleasures of any visit to Isla Robinson Crusoe is just taking a seat by the wharf and watching the world go by, sipping on a beer and chatting with the islanders. And, although the archipelago doesn't boast the swaying palms or golden sands of most South Pacific islands, it does have plenty of other elements to make it a contender: beautiful scenery, good weather, plenty of food, no crime, no poverty, no racial tensions, and no pollution.

The people of the Juan Fernández Islands are not a remote group being dragged into the 21st century, with a delicate society about to buckle under the strain. Everyone is descended from Chilean or European immigrants, and has grown up within a Western culture – albeit a detached version. The islanders take what they want from the modern world, such as medicine, music, radios, or television soap operas, and leave the rest. Perhaps that's why the half-familiar world of Juan Fernández is so beguiling: one admires the islanders' good sense but, already being a part of the outside world, can never share it.

View from the Mirador de Selkirk.

CENTRAL VALLEY

Vineyards and fruit flourish in the temperate climate of this lush, fertile region, yet until the late 19th century it marked the border of the wild, unconquered southern lands.

Main Attractions
Sewell Mining Town
Termas de Cauquenes
Santa Cruz
Lago Vichuquén
Mercado de Chillán
Salto del Laja
Lota
Chiflón del Diablo

The cueca, Chile's national dance.

Running parallel between the towering Cordillera de los Andes and the lower coastal mountain range is the Chilean **Central Valley**. The area from Los Andes, just 80km (50 miles) north of Santiago, to some 500km (300 miles) farther south is the richest farmland in the country. Vineyards have been established here since the arrival of the Spanish conquistadors, and, today, wine-making for export is among its most important activities. Similarly, most of the traditional agricultural activities of the old landed aristocracy, such as growing wheat and fodder for domestic animals, have given way to the much more profitable cultivation of fresh produce for export worldwide.

Leaving the main roads, however, is to take a step back in time to a simpler, slower-paced, infinitely more relaxing era. Never is this truer than during the Independence Day celebrations held annually on September 18, which offer an inside view to festivities in rural areas throughout the country. *Fondas* or *ramadas*, outdoor ballrooms with thatched eucalyptus-leaf roofs, are erected all over the countryside. People gather from miles around to watch the competition between *huasos*, the Chilean cowboys (see page 114); to dance the *cueca*, the national dance; to eat empanadas (meat and onion pasties), and to drink *chicha*, fermented grape juice.

Termas de Cauquenes

The busy town of **Rancagua ❶**, 87km (54 miles) south of Santiago, is as much an agricultural center as the home of miners employed in the **El Teniente copper mine**. The mine, and a heritage-listed workers' camp called **Sewell**, is at the end of the Carretera del Cobre (Copper Highway), which runs from Rancagua east and up into the mountains.

Travelers may, however, simply prefer to visit the thermal baths of **Termas de Cauquenes ❷**, 28km

(17 miles) east of Rancagua, in the Andean foothills. Used by native peoples long before the arrival of the Spanish, the first to lay claim to the medicinal waters were Jesuits. The baths were frequented by the Chilean founding father Bernardo O'Higgins during rests from his revolutionary bouts against the colonial authorities.

The construction of what is today a hotel and spa (www.termasdecauquenes. cl) began back in 1885. The huge high-ceilinged bathhouse with stained-glass windows leads up an enormous staircase to the dining and game-room area. Rooms and suites are set around large open gardens or at the back overlooking the Cachapoal River. The surrounding hills are filled with *peumos*, a native tree with bright red edible fruit and shiny green leaves.

In their quest to compete with the smart new boutique hotels springing up all over the country, traditional establishments such as this have used top cuisine to draw visitors. Diners at the hotel's immense restaurant are transported back a century, with its fine old furnishings contrasting deliciously with the modern fare prepared in the kitchen.

Nearby is the **Reserva Nacional Río de Los Cipreses**, an excellent place for hiking and horseback riding with spectacular views of the Andes towering above. Camping facilities are available and the National Forestry Service (CONAF) has an office in the Reserve.

Santa Cruz

Once back on the main highway, the next city south of Rancagua is **San Fernando**, a bustling rural center, which is gradually succumbing to the advances of shopping malls, internet cafés, and smarter urban life. For the tourist, though, it serves simply as a reference for **Santa Cruz ③**, a charming little town 40km (25 miles) toward the coast. At the heart of the Colchagua wine valley, it was – like the other surrounding towns and villages – a sad sight after the February

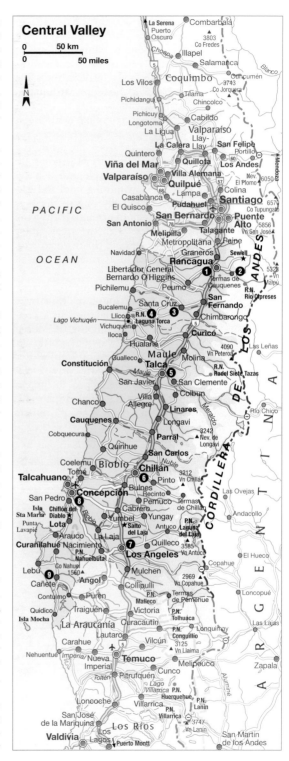

A blue heron in the Reserva Nacional Laguna Torca.

Punta de Lobos beach.

2010 earthquake, but it has made an enormous effort to get back on its feet. The old adobe buildings that are an important part of its charm are, for example, being rebuilt in the same style but with a more earthquake-resistant structure.

No visit is complete without at least a night in the Hotel Santa Cruz (www.hotelsantacruzplaza.cl), a restored colonial building. Its 116 rooms are extremely comfortable and it has a landscaped swimming pool and gardens and arguably one of the best restaurants south of Santiago. Its wine list is replete with the area's finest varietal whites and oak-matured reds, and tours of local vineyards can be arranged at the hotel.

The town is also home to an excellent historical museum. Run by a not-for-profit foundation in a converted 18th-century house, the Museo de Colchagua (www.museocolchagua.cl; daily summer 10am–7pm, winter 10am–6pm) houses the private collection of Carlos Cardoen, the hotel's owner. The Gran Rescate display tells the gripping story of the 33 miners trapped for over two months in 2010 in a collapsed mine in northern Chile (see page 166).

The Museo San José del Carmen de El Huique (www.museoelhuique.cl; Tue 2–6pm, Wed–Fri 10.30am–noon and 2–6pm, Sat 10.30am–noon and 2–5pm) in Palmilla, a 15-minute drive from Santa Cruz, the former home of the wealthy Errázuriz and Echeñique families and Chile's closest equivalent to a stately home, provided a rare glimpse of 19th-century rural elegance but was severely damaged by the earthquake.

A coastal tour from Curicó

While the colonial town of Vichuquén can be reached by bus from **Curicó**, there is so much to see in this interesting coastal area that it's worth hiring a car. The 110km (68-mile) road that follows the northern bank of the Mataquito River from Curicó as far as Hualañé is a route of breathtaking scenic beauty, bordered by vineyards. But the cut-off route from the highway near San Fernando, through Santa Cruz, Lolol, San Pedro de Alcántara, Rarín, and the coastal town of Llico, also has its own charm, revealing rolling hills and hidden, sleepy country towns.

Farther north, at the end of the main road west from Santa Cruz, is **Pichilemu**, Chile's surfing capital. This one-time rural center and fishing village has been transformed into a hip destination for surfers from around the world, most of whom stay in the beachside cabins dotting the road to **Punta de Lobos** and Bucalemu. Diehard surfers should ask around for details on how to reach "secret spots" farther north toward Navidad.

Lago Vichuquén

The town of **Vichuquén** existed before the invasion of the Incas from Peru in the 15th century, who formed a colony there with the native Mapuches. The name of the town comes from the Mapuche language and means "the serpent lake." Time seems to have stopped some 100 years ago along its orange-tree-lined streets, where unhurried locals linger along the covered wooden sidewalks. The town's

museum (Tue–Sun 10am–1pm and 4–8pm), opened in 1991 by the Carlos Cardoen Foundation, tells the town's history and is well worth a visit.

The main attraction here, however, is **Lago Vichuquén**, only 5km (3 miles) toward the coast. Pine forests that grow in record time surround the summerhouses that line the shore. Windsurfers and small sailboats cut silently across the mirror-like surface of the lake to explore the uninhabited Isla del Cerrillo that sits alone in the lake's center. There are two main hotels on the lake, both situated on the southern side. The Hotel Playa Aquelarre has spectacular views of the lake and the myriad species that make the area a birdwatchers' paradise. Binoculars and ornithological guides are provided for guests. At the nearby Hotel Marina Vichuquén (www.marina vichuquen.com), the accent is on aquatic pursuits. There are also several campgrounds and cheaper lodgings around the southern end of the lake.

Just 3km (2 miles) north of the lake is the **Reserva Nacional Laguna Torca** ❹. The lagoon is a nesting ground for

Sewell mining town.

THE CITY OF STAIRWAYS

Located at 2,000 meters (6,600ft) up in the Andes east of Rancagua, the Sewell mining town was built by the Braden Copper Company in 1905 – and named for Barton Sewell, a company executive – to house workers at what was to become the world's largest underground copper mine, El Teniente. At its peak, Sewell had 15,000 inhabitants and facilities that included its own hospital and industrial school. The wooden houses, painted in vivid reds, greens, yellows, and blues, cling to the steep mountainside around a large central staircase that starts at the train station and opens out into other stairways as it climbs, hence Sewell's popular name of "The City of Stairways."

The mine, now operated by Codelco, the state copper company, is still active, but fell into disuse in the 1970s. It was later renovated and declared a Unesco World Heritage Site in 2006 as an example of a company town developed in a remote and difficult natural environment. Independent visits are not allowed on the grounds of nearby mine activity, but guided tours, available on Saturdays and Sundays (in Spanish only), can be booked through four companies (see www.sewell. cl) working with Codelco, including VTS (tel: 072-210 290; www.vts.cl). Private tours, with an English-speaking guide, can be arranged during the week but are significantly more expensive. Tours start in Rancagua or Santiago. Children under 7 years and over-75s are not accepted.

black-necked swans and another 80 or so species of exotic birds. Great blue herons hide in the reed-lined banks. The S-shaped bodies of stark, white herons wade through the shallows, while an enormous variety of ducks and the small, black *tagua* coots keep up a tremendous clatter of quacking.

Returning to Vichuquén, an unpaved road forks off and runs south through a series of beachside towns famed for their seafood *picadas* (cheap restaurants). Locals and visitors alike say Donde Gilberto (www.dondegilberto.cl) in the Duao fishing village, 7km (4 miles) before the town of Iloca, is the pick of the bunch. It also has reasonably priced accommodations offering spectacular sea views.

Talca

Continuing south on the Pan-American Highway, the town of **Talca** ❺ is 60km (37 miles) southwest of Curicó. An important urban center since its founding in 1742, Talca was the traditional residence of the landed elite. The older part of town, as in most Chilean colonial towns, surrounds the **Plaza de Armas** with its jacarandas, palms, magnolia trees, cedars, and other conifers.

The **Museo O'Higginiano** (www.museodetalca.cl; temporarily closed; free), on the corner of Norte 1 and Oriente 2, was the childhood home of the Chilean hero and father of independence, Bernardo O'Higgins. The building was also the home in 1813 of José Miguel Carrera, who presided over the first governmental junta.

Carrera declared Chile a sovereign, autonomous state in the 1812 Constitution, and also – with the help of O'Higgins – organized resistance to invading royalist troops from farther south (see page 36). In one of the house's many salons, Bernardo O'Higgins signed the Act of Independence. The museum also features an important collection of paintings, sculpture, historical manuscripts, and pre-Columbian artifacts.

From Talca, one of Chile's few remaining rural train services runs to Constitución on the coast. Largearge parts of the town were washed away by the tsunami that followed the 2010

The Death to the Invader mural in Chillán, painted by Mexican artists following the 1939 earthquake.

earthquake) and subsequently rebuilt. The train stops at a multitude of tiny farming communities, for many of which it is the sole form of transportation; the 106km (66-mile) journey takes three hours, but offers a unique insight into a way of life that is rapidly disappearing.

Chillán

Farther south on the highway is the town of **Chillán** ❻. Repeatedly destroyed by earthquakes and rebuilt – and, again, badly damaged by the 2010 earthquake and later restored – most of its buildings are not more than 50 years old. In 1939, a nighttime earthquake killed 15,000 people and destroyed 90 percent of the town. Mexico donated a school to the city as part of the reconstruction. The Mexican muralists David Alfaro Siqueiros and Xavier Guerrero painted representative scenes of Chilean and Mexican history there in 1941.

The Escuela México (corner of Av. Bernardo O'Higgins and Vega de Saldías) still operates as a school, but staff welcome visitors who want to see the heritage-listed *Death to the Invader* mural (Mon–Fri 10am–1pm and 3–6pm, Sun 10am–6pm; free). Alternatively, head for the Museo Claudio Arrau (Claudio Arrau 564, Tue–Fri 8.30am–1.30pm and 3–7 pm, Sat 10am–1pm and 4–7.30pm, Sun 10am–2pm; free) dedicated to the famous classical pianist born in Chillán.

The **Mercado de Chillán** (Chillán's market), on Calle Maipón between Isabel Riquelme and 5 de Abril, is the largest and most vibrant in Chile. Here you can find handicrafts from all over the country, as well as the locally made clothing that makes up the typical *huaso* (Chilean cowboy) dress: from the felt (for winter) or straw (for summer) flat-rimmed hats, and small dress ponchos in finely woven, bright colors, to the leather boots and carved wooden stirrups. The market is open every day, but is at its best on Saturdays.

Termas de Chillán

The western-facing slopes of the **Volcán Chillán**, 80km (50 miles) from Chillán, provide some of the finest open-slope skiing in the Andes from June through October. **Termas de Chillán**, named for its famous thermal springs, is the base for the ski resort (www.termaschillan.cl). The resort, at 1,650 meters (5,413ft) above sea level, has nine chairlifts and 28 pistes, covering a total of more than 35km (23 miles). An accomplished skier can stay on the slopes from morning to late afternoon and, as there is so much variety, need never cover the same trail twice. A series of pistes from the summit down to the wooded region around the hotel area connect to produce a 13km (8-mile) run, also the longest in South America.

After a hard day on the slopes, there is no better way to ease tired muscles than to plunge into one of the four outdoor thermal swimming pools in the Parque de Aguas. Both the Gran Hotel Termas de Chillán and nearby Hotel Los Nevados de Chillán (www.nevadosdechillan.

The Termas de Chillán ski resort provides some of the continent's best skiing and snowboarding.

Black-necked swan.

Fruit-laden Lands

With its warm, Californian climate, the Central Valley provides ideal conditions for fruit-farming, one of Chile's most important industries.

In springtime as you drive along the Pan-American Highway south from Santiago, fields of flaming orchards perfume the air and make a brilliant display. You'll see the dark, hot pink blossom of peaches and nectarines, the lighter, rose-colored cherry trees, and the white-flowering almond, apple, apricot, or plum trees and, along the road, the huge cooling and packing plants at which the fruit is prepared for export to markets around the world.

Bounded by the Andes mountains and the Pacific Ocean, and, in the north, the Atacama Desert, Chile is unusually free of the pests with which other countries' fruit-farming industries have to battle, and this is an asset of which it takes great care through strict phytosanitary controls at its borders.

Chile's fruit exports have grown rapidly, helped by its free trade agreements with most of the

Blueberries, a key Chilean export.

world's major economies (including the United States and the European Union) and reached US$2 billion in 2015, up from US$1.4 billion a decade earlier. And that is only fresh fruit; more fruit still is exported frozen and canned or in the form of juice.

Table grapes account for nearly a tenth of fresh fruit exports. Like other fruit, they take advantage of the high prices available in Europe and the United States during the northern hemisphere winter, particularly if – as in the case of the grapes grown around Copiapó in the north – they reach the supermarket shelves in time for Christmas. Increasingly, however, exporters are also targeting Asian markets, particularly China with which Chile has had a free trade agreement since 2006. Its cherries, in particular, which arrive just in time for the Chinese New Year, have established an important niche in this vast market. Farther south in the Central Valley, berries – principally raspberries and blueberries – are the main crop. Often grown by small producers or through co-operatives, they have brought new prosperity to once poor rural areas and, because of the damage dust does to these delicate fruits, have provided a powerful new incentive for paving country roads.

Fruit farming has also meant new job opportunities for women as *temporeras* or pickers employed during the harvest season. Some women even make a long season of it, starting with the early grape harvest in the north of the country and gradually moving south with the ripening crops.

It is hard work and the hours are long but conditions have improved. Protective clothing and proper rest periods are now more common, as are childcare facilities, while a change in regulation has allowed *temporeras* access to social security benefits.

International competition

But, although Chile is the southern hemisphere's largest fruit exporter, competition is on the increase. In recent years, Chile's blueberry production has risen rapidly in response to high international demand but Argentina has followed suit, causing a sharp drop in prices. Similarly, Peru's fruit exports have grown rapidly and, although led by tropical fruits which Chile does not grow – principally mangoes and bananas – they include grapes and other key Chilean exports such as avocados and citrus fruits. It has been suggested that the two countries should, in fact, team up to supply the vast Chinese market, but this has yet to happen.

com) have spas, while more modest hotels and guest cabins can be found in **Las Trancas** or **Recinto**, a few kilometers down the valley.

Many visitors also make the trip in the summer to hike to the geyser-like fuming springs of the thermal waters and bathe in the medicinal muds nearby. A trip in the chairlift reveals stupendous views of the towering volcanic crater and accompanying eternal snows of the Nevada de Chillán mountain range. Guided walking tours and horseback riding excursions are also available.

The road back from the Gran Hotel Termas is lined with lush forest vegetation resembling that found in the Lake District farther south. Huge old oaks join firs, pines, and the delicate, native *ñirre* trees set among giant ferns and red *copihues* – the fleshy, trumpet-shaped national flower that hangs from climbing vines.

Two kilometers (1 mile) from the hotel you can visit an enormous natural cavern, the **Cueva de los Pincheira**. This was used as a hideaway by the Pincheira brothers and their followers – a group of royalist highway robbers who ransacked the area during the struggle for independence. The colossal **Piedras Comadres**, spectacular rock walls that drop straight down from their forest-covered heights, can be seen from the road.

Before the town of **Los Angeles** ❼, 80km (50 miles) south of Chillán, the **Salto del Laja** waterfall can be viewed from the bridge that crosses the River Laja. The falls crash down some 15 to 20 meters (50 to 65ft) from two wide arches into deep, enormous pools, to be swiftly conducted into the narrow river canyon further down. The area has numerous hotels, campgrounds, and restaurants, some with swimming pools and other recreational facilities.

Concepción

The country's second-largest city (even though, including the adjoining port of Talcahuano, it has only a population of around 214,000), **Concepción** ❽ is located some 86km (53 miles) off the Pan-American Highway. It lies at the mouth of the **River Biobío**, the natural boundary between southern

TIP

Visitors can go down the "Devil's Draught" coal mine, near Lota, in which Chile's best-known novel of mining life, *Sub Terra* by Baldomera Lillo, is set.

Salto del Laja waterfall.

and central Chile, and is an important center for the country's forestry industry. Founded by conquistador Pedro de Valdivia in 1550, Concepción was the site occupied by the Real Audiencia, the political, military, and administrative center of the Spanish colony from 1565 to 1573. The location of the city was changed a number of times due to repeated earthquake devastation, particularly in the mid-18th century, and attacks from the Mapuches. Its present location was settled in 1764.

Repeated reconstruction following the natural disasters, combined with economic growth, have made Concepción a modern city with little remaining of its past glory, and many visitors would rather pass on through it.

The city's pride is the **Universidad de Concepción** campus, with its open amphitheater and central green dominated by the university's watchtower. Nearby are the marble-fronted walls of the courthouse, and the train station, above which is a mural depicting the history of the city. The **Casa del Arte** (Pinoteca; Chacabuco cnr. Paicaví s/n; Tue–Fri 10am–6pm, Sat 11am–5pm,

The Universidad de Concepción campus.

Sun 11am–2pm; free), on the corner of Lamas and Larenas, houses an extensive collection of national paintings.

In **Talcahuano**, the battleship *Huáscar* can be visited. Captured from the Peruvian fleet during the War of the Pacific in 1879, it has been held as a trophy of the victory that added the country's northernmost provinces and their rich mineral deposits to the national territory. Worth a visit in nearby **Lota** is the park created by the Cousiño family, the original owner of the area's now mostly disused coal mines.

The Devil's Draught

One of these, the **Chiflón del Diablo** (Devil's Draught; Avenida El Parque 21; daily 9.30am–6pm), is open to visitors as part of a tourist circuit created to help revive the formerly mining-dependent community. Visitors are lowered 40 meters (131ft) down a shaft and guided through its tunnels as ex-miners relate anecdotes about the grueling life at the coal face. Other attractions include the town's museum and the Central Hidroeléctrica Chivilingo, Chile's oldest power plant. Accommodations can

be found in Lota at a number of basic, but clean and friendly, hotels.

The Viña Macul vineyard (www.cousinomacul.com) is still owned and run by the Cousiño family, who built the Palacio Cousiño in Santiago. They also founded Chile's first forestry industry in the Colcura Valley, near Lota, in 1881, to supply beams for use in their mines. Dark pine forests, a faster-growing crop than the native hardwood forests, run south along the road to Curanilahue, which is lined with log-laden trucks. The cellulose plant for paper manufacturing in the beach resort of **Arauco** has contributed to the economic development of the zone. This industry is probably primarily responsible for the paving of the road south, which was taken by the Spanish conquerors as they explored the area between the coast and the Nahuelbuta mountain range.

Ruta de los Conquistadores

Following this so-called Ruta de los Conquistadores, one arrives in **Cañete** ❾. This town has a frontier flavor that announces the beginnings of the Mapuche lands. It was here that the Mapuche *toqui* or warrior chief Lautaro surprised conquistador Pedro de Valdivia and put a dramatic end to his life (see page 73). Cañete's **Museo Mapuche** (www.museomapuchecanete.cl; Tue–Fri 9.30am–5.30pm, Sat 11am–5.30pm, Sun 1–5.30pm; free) displays a large range of native peoples' culture and a traditional Mapuche *ruca* (dwelling house) can be seen behind the museum.

Lodgings are available on the nearby **Lago Lanalhue** where there are a number of hotels and cabins as well as camping facilities. The summer months are ideal for activities such as windsurfing and fishing, and the lake is also used for swimming and nautical sports.

There are also hotels and cheaper lodgings in the quaint neighboring town of **Contulmo**, which was settled by Prussians in 1868. The **Grollmus** house, a large wooden dwelling built in 1923, and mill have 23 varieties of *copihue*, which bloom between March and April, and the remains of a small hydroelectric generator that used to supply the town with its lighting.

A 19th-century ship at Talcahuano City.

Lago Villarrica and Volcán
Villarrica.

THE LAKE DISTRICT

Snow-capped mountains reflected in looking-glass lakes, quaint wooden hamlets steeped in healthy mountain air, fishing ports, and old rural traditions – the Lake District is Chile's wonderland.

The Lake District exercises a near-mythic fascination on Chileans. The south symbolizes everything healthy, unspoiled, and pure in Chile and its people. City folks, particularly in Santiago, look kindly on southerners as their own better selves and foreign visitors will be made to feel very much at home in the Lake District, where European influences of all kinds, including immigration, have long been welcomed. An early pioneer and champion of southern settlement and development, Vicente Pérez Rosales (see page 218), exemplified this Eurocentrism when he announced in 1854 that "the word 'foreigner' has been eliminated in Chile. It is an immoral word and should disappear from the dictionary." Pérez Rosales was not thinking of Peruvians or Brazilians or other mestizo nations – he meant the Germans, Austrians, Swiss, and Italians whose communities are still common in the south.

Unfriendly encounters

However, native Mapuche roots are still not far from the surface of southern Chile's collective memory. The south, where most of the country's rural indigenous population lives, was not fully dominated by the European-descended settlers until the second half of the 19th century. For example, the first European colony was

Church in Puerto Octay.

established at what is now the lakeside resort center of Villarrica, and was besieged by Mapuches in a 1598 uprising, collapsing without survivors in 1602. It was not re-established until a military mission arrived in 1882, nearly three centuries later.

In the interim, an uneasy state of semi-war prevailed. Early in the 1600s, the River Biobío (which reaches the sea at what is now the port of Concepción) was established as the frontier between the Spanish colony and native lands, but the truce was violated

Main Attractions
Parque Nacional Conguillío
Volcán Villarrica
Pucón
Termas Geométricas
Feria Fluvial de Valdivia
Lago Llanquihue
Parque Nacional Vicente Pérez Rosales
Saltos del Petrohué
Volcán Osorno
Frutillar

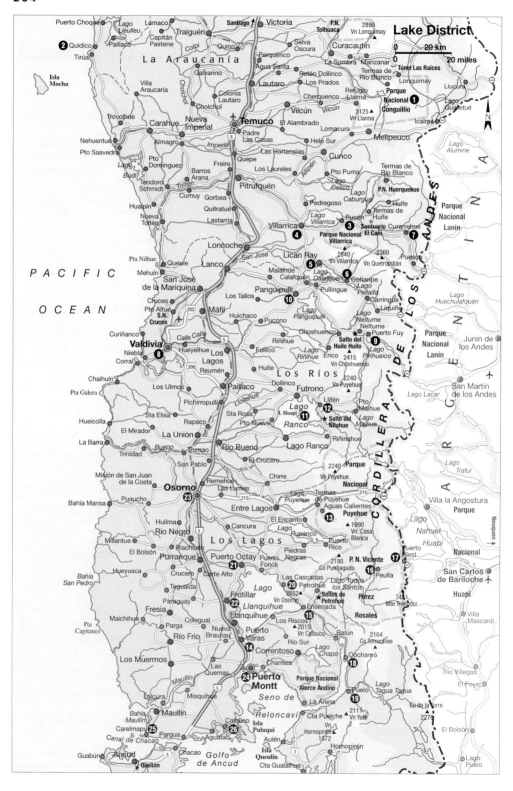

annually in raids from one side or the other. Spanish mercenaries fought to capture Mapuches and sell them into slavery, while the Mapuches raided to plunder cattle and other goods or to punish the invaders. Regular peace conferences between the two sides usually ended in great celebrations of feasting and drinking and vows of friendship – which would invariably last only a few months before the next outbreak of hostilities.

Finally, commerce pacified the situation. A regular trade in cattle, woven goods, knives, arms, and liquor developed, although violent outbursts between Mapuches and European soldiers, brigands, and shady dealers of all sorts continued to occur regularly. Naturally, the mestizo population grew steadily with the constant contact, and colonial garrison commanders preferred them as soldiers since they knew the area well and were notoriously impervious to hardship.

These hostilities meant that the Lake District was, until relatively recently, unexplored territory for those of European descent. Lago Colico, near Pucón, was the last of the big lakes to be discovered by Europeans, making its first appearance on maps in the early years of the 20th century. The great Lago Llanquihue near Puerto Montt was first sighted by Pedro de Valdivia in 1552, but Mapuche raids put it effectively out of bounds to Europeans until new waves of settlers began to arrive three centuries later.

Life in the outback

Chile's south is a more recently tamed version of the North American Wild West, and, in more remote areas, life revolves around horses, farm work, and social events, lubricated with large quantities of wine or *chicha* made from fermented apples. Country families tend to live off seasonal sales of milk, or a cash crop, or tourists, spending long months consuming the stores of grain they harvested themselves, while the men look for paying jobs in the larger towns and cities.

The rural areas are connected by an extensive network of local buses, which transport schoolchildren, farmers, and country residents returning

FACT

The *copihue*, Chile's national flower, grows in forests from Valparaíso to as far south as Osorno. A climbing evergreen, its bell-shape flowers – beloved by humming birds – are usually red, although there is also a white variety.

Farmstead overlooked by Volcán Osorno.

Farming employs many families in the Lake District.

Lago Llanquihue.

from the larger towns with provisions. The buses are slow due to the terrain and the constant stops at every lane or farmhouse, but they are very cheap and reach many remote settlements. The first and sometimes only bus tends to leave before dawn, so it is always prudent to inquire about schedules the day before traveling. As the terrain is ideal for backpacking and hiking, Chilean youth swarm southward in the summertime, many of them spending long hours on the highway awaiting motorists or truckers who will give them a lift. Most have the barest minimum of funds and camp wherever possible.

Gateway to the Lake District

The Lake District is generally considered to begin at the Toltén River, which flows off Lago Villarrica, but this is more a result of the area's fame as a resort region than strict topographic considerations. The characteristic combination of volcanoes and lakes actually begins farther north, around the area of Parque Nacional

Conguillío, northeast of Temuco, which is located 677km (421 miles) south of Santiago. This region is home to several volcanoes, including **Lonquimay** (2,890 meters/9,480ft), which entered into full eruption in 1988 and blanketed the area with dangerous volcanic dust; and **Llaima** (3,125 meters/10,249ft), which erupted in 1994. Lonquimay means "without a head" in the Mapuche tongue, referring to the volcano's flat top.

This is also Mapuche territory – the Mapuches' ancestors used the accessible mountain passes and gathered pine nuts from the ancient *araucaria*, or monkey puzzle tree, which is endemic to the southern Andes. There are male and female *araucaria* trees – biologists can determine their sex by examining their bark. These rare coniferous trees, which take 500 years to mature fully and can live for more than 1,000 years, were endangered by logging activities until President Aylwin's government responded to environmental campaigners and prohibited their destruction in March 1990.

Temuco

Temuco, founded in 1881, following an important treaty between the new republic and the Mapuches, is now a rapidly growing industrial town, and a good base from which to explore the northern Lake District. Its **Museo Regional de la Araucanía** (www.museoregionalaraucania.cl; Tue–Fri 9.30am–5.30pm, Sat 11am–5pm, Sun 11am–2pm; free) provides information on the native people and their history. The **Museo Nacional Ferroviario Pablo Neruda** (Apr–Sept Tue–Fri 9am–6pm, Sat–Sun 10am–5pm; Oct–Mar Tue–Fri 9am–6pm, Sat–Sun 10am–6pm), named after Chile's Nobel poet who spent his childhood in Temuco and whose father was a rail worker, attractively sets out the history of the railroad in Chile.

Mapuches from the surrounding countryside come to Temuco to sell their wares; the central market, although rather touristy, is a good place to buy local handicrafts and to try traditional dishes. The **Cerro Ñielol** hill and forest park, where the national *copihue* flower grows in abundance, offers the best view of the city.

From Temuco, it is worth making a trip to Cholchol, 29km (18 miles) northwest of the city, a typical Mapuche village where you can see *rucas*, the Mapuches' traditional thatched dwellings.

Lago Gualletué – source of the Biobío

The town of **Lonquimay** and the land surrounding it lie to the east of the Andean cordillera, despite the general rule that the highest peaks mark the territorial boundaries between Chile and Argentina. However, **Lago Gualletué** southeast of Lonquimay provides the headwaters of the important **Biobío River**, which then runs north for nearly 100km (60 miles) before turning westward toward the Pacific Ocean at Concepción. As this river was long considered the border dividing Spanish lands from unconquered Mapuche territory, Chile claimed the hydrographic basin.

The main road to Lonquimay passes through the **Túnel Las Raíces**. This was originally a railroad tunnel, built in the 1930s as part of a plan (subsequently abandoned) to connect the Atlantic and Pacific oceans by rail. The tunnel is passable in all weathers (though large icicles form in winter).

On the road to the tunnel from Curacautín there are several thermal baths, as well as the beautiful 50-meter (16ft) Princess Waterfall and two huge volcanic rocks, Piedra Cortada and Piedra Santa, which were considered sacred by the indigenous population.

Parque Nacional Conguillío

Parque Nacional Conguillío ❶ can be reached from Curacautín in the north or Melipeuco in the south. Both routes skirt the snow-covered **Volcán Llaima**, and lead through virgin forests of *araucaria* and other Chilean species such as *coigüe* and *raulí*, as well as oak and cypress. Twelve hundred year-old *araucaria* trees can be seen

Backpacker hangout, Pucón.

in Parque Nacional Conguillío (www. parquenacionalconguillio.cl), which was set up in 1950

Three tiny lakes in the park (Verde, Captrén, and Arco Iris) were formed by lava flows that blocked several rivers. The lakes are just a few decades old, and the trees that once grew on their beds can still be seen below the water. Volcán Llaima now has a small, modern ski resort on its slopes, at Los Paraguas.

The main campground is on the shore of the largest lake, Lago Conguillío, with several log cabins in a stunning location in an *araucaria* forest. In summer a small café operates by the lake. December is the best time to visit, before the Chilean summer vacation crowds arrive in January and February.

To the north of Curacautín is another national park, **Parque Nacional Tolhuaca**, with camping facilities on the shores of the lovely Laguna Malleco. A few kilometers before the park entrance, there are some hot springs, the Termas de Tolhuaca (www. termasdetolhuaca.cl), with a small hostel.

On the coast, west of Conguillío, is **Lago Lleulleu** (in the Mapuche language, a repeated word has extra importance). Aside from the tiny community at **Puerto Choque**, the only civilization nearby is at **Quidico** ❷ on the ocean, which is popular in the summer for its excellent seafood and windswept beach. The end of the main road is just past **Tirúa** where Mapuche chiefs once charged a toll for land traffic between Concepción and Valdivia. According to legend, the bishop of Concepción was kidnapped and held here in 1778, only escaping when a rival chief won his freedom in a game of chance.

Pucón

Next to the beaches at Viña del Mar and Reñaca, the area around Villarrica and Pucón is the most popular holiday resort in Chile. The two towns are the main urban centers on the end of **Lago Villarrica**, which is dominated by the active **Volcán Villarrica** (2,840 meters/9,320ft), just an hour's detour from the north–south Pan-American Highway. **Pucón** ❸ could be called the "Viña of the South" for its success in attracting summer tourists. It is enormously popular among the Chilean middle classes, who are rapidly buying up the summer condominiums along the beach. Many flock to the area in the summer months, sunbathe on the beach, take part in noisy water sports on Lago Villarrica by day, and crowd the casino in the Gran Hotel Pucón (www.pucon.com) by night.

Though it has become very commercial, Pucón provides all the services a tourist could want, including an excellent variety of restaurants, bars, and discotheques, and is extremely popular with backpackers.

The town is also a key center for adventure tourists, and by far the most popular activity is the one-day hike to the lava-filled crater of Volcán Villarrica (see page 108). An increasing variety of water sports, including

Lago Villarrica.

rafting and kayaking are also practiced on the Trancura River. Though the service offered by adventure travel agencies varies, most provide high-quality imported equipment and qualified guides trained to ensure international safety standards.

Skiing is available in winter on the slopes of Volcán Villarrica. More relaxing activities include horseback riding, fishing, and visits to nearby hot springs and national parks.

The area around Pucón has also pioneered environmental tourism projects. **Santuario El Cañi** (www.santuariocani.cl), east of Pucón, is one of Chile's first private natural reserves. Its ancient *araucaria* forest growing on an extinct volcano became a reserve in 1992 with funding from Ancient Forests International and has been developed as a center for environmental education and scientific research. Though it requires a steep three-hour hike, reaching the summit rewards the climber with spectacular views of all the area's volcanoes on a clear day. Visits are best organized through the École hostel (www.ecole.cl) in Pucón.

Villarrica

Numerous Mapuche communities are tucked away in the hills surrounding **Villarrica ❹**, and each summer a Mapuche cultural festival is held in the town. This includes a nightly demonstration of religious rituals. Some unusual craft work can be found among the stands, but most of the work has long been copied by artisans in Santiago and elsewhere.

One of the town's main streets is named after General Emil Koerner, the German military scientist who was hired in the late 19th century by President Balmaceda to reorganize the Chilean armed forces (he used the area for training). Koerner then betrayed Balmaceda to side with an 1891 insurrection fomented by local oligarchs (see page 42). The oligarchs won, President Balmaceda committed suicide, and Koerner proceeded to reshape the army along Prussian lines, a model that remains largely in force today. His prestige led to a surge of pro-German sentiment, which helped to stimulate a second wave of German immigrants,

Sign outside the Cervecería Kunstmann in Valdivia.

Local farmer, Pucón.

FRONTIER TRADITIONS

Rural traditions persist in many frontier towns of southern Chile. Men can often be seen wearing flat-brimmed felt hats, and they are quick to invite visitors to drink a sweet wine that goes down with treacherous ease. On special occasions, a host family will kill a sheep or goat by plunging a knife into the neck and catching the blood in a pan filled with *cilantro* (coriander), where it is congealed with lemon juice to produce *ñache*, which is considered a great delicacy and pre-feast appetizer.

Grains are the traditional farm commodity, though the uncertainty of the weather makes farming risky. Potatoes are easily grown, but transportation costs wipe out any chance of profit, so farmers usually consume them or use them as animal feed. Hops and sugar beet are also grown. Pasture is abundant, and many families earn a few pesos selling milk to the big dairy plants.

To fortify themselves for heavy farm work, the men breakfast on *chupilca*, white wine poured over toasted wheat, or *mudai*, a mushy, carbohydrate-rich juice made from cooked grains. Visitors should avoid giving offense by always accepting anything offered, even if they cannot bring themselves to sample it. When you've had enough, just leave the plate or glass untouched before you.

There are numerous lakeside towns and villages either side of the border between Chile and Argentina.

Kunstmann brewery, Valdivia.

most of whom headed for the newly available lands in the south.

Parque Nacional Huerquehue

Just a short drive from Pucón to the north and northeast are lakes Caburgua and Colico, and, in the mountains of **Parque Nacional Huerquehue**, lakes Tinquilco, Toro, and Verde. Rare outcroppings of "flywing" rock crystal usually observed only in the coastal mountain range 100km (60 miles) to the west give some of Lago Caburgua's beaches white sand rather than the usual black sand that comes from the volcanic rock elsewhere in Chile's Lake District. The lake is surrounded by densely forested hills, some areas of which can be explored on defined paths. Its waters flow underground, producing the springs at **Ojos de Caburgua**, a popular picnic spot. Access to the Huerquehue Park lakes is a serious 5km (3-mile) climb but a small bus company, Buses Caburgua, operates a minibus service that leaves Pucón four times a day and takes visitors right to the park entrance.

Puma live farther up in the mountains; these animals are rarely seen, but come closer to human civilization in winter when food is scarce. Pumas do not generally attack humans unless threatened, but still need to be considered dangerous animals. An 80km (50-mile) route from Caburgua's north shore through the Blanco River Valley can be hiked in about four days, ending up in the outpost of **Reigolil** (where a bus descends to Curarrehue four times a day). A traverse from **Volcán Quetrupillán** to the village of Puesco through *araucaria* forests has increasingly replaced the circuit around Volcán Villarrica as the most popular hiking route in Parque Nacional Villarrica. Local tour agencies leave hikers at the beginning of the trek, and there are public bus services back to Pucón.

South of Villarrica, a half-hour's trip on a paved highway leads to the rapidly expanding resort of **Lican Ray ⑤** on Lago Calafquén. Wood furniture-making is an important economic activity in this area, and there are dozens of workshops, particularly on

the road from Villarrica to Lican Ray. Farther along the lake is **Coñaripe** ⑥, which retains the atmosphere of pre-boom Lican Ray. Regular buses do go this far, but Coñaripe is the end of the line before the rugged unpaved circuit around the lake, and the "back way" into Panguipulli.

Thermal baths proliferate across the area due to the constant activity in the volcanic belt that runs along the cordillera. Some, such as the **Termas de Menetué** (www.menetue.com/) or **Termas de Huife** (www.termashuife.com) farther east of Pucón are upscale commercial operations with eating and lodging facilities and bathing fixtures. Others, including the tiny **Termas de Ancamil**, just before Curarrehue, 45km (28 miles) east of Pucón, are rustic, family-run affairs where one simply descends into the cave with a candle and bathes, while the **Termas Geométricas** (www.termasgeometricas. cl), some 16km (10 miles) east of Coñaripe, have architecturally interesting wooden walkways joining the different pools.

Curarrehue

The town of **Curarrehue** ⑦ is a typical southern frontier center, where families often have relatives on the Argentine side and travel across the border to take advantage of work opportunities. The Chile–Argentina border in the south is lightly guarded, as the mountain passes are essentially uncontrollable. During the Pinochet dictatorship, many of these frontier towns smuggled people in and out who either could not move around legally or were in serious trouble for political reasons. Cattle-smuggling into Chile from Argentina causes occasional outbreaks of foot-and-mouth disease, which cannot be controlled in Argentina's vast ranches but has been basically eradicated in Chile.

Valdivia

Valdivia ⑧ is the best example of the urban face of Chile's south:

sophisticated and festive, rainy and verdant, with a palpable German influence in architecture, cuisine, and culture. Although usually treated as part of the Lake District, Valdivia is located at the crossroads of two rivers and is just a few kilometers from the sea, separated from the lakes by the coastal mountain range. The approaches to the city are marshy breeding grounds for unusual waterfowl. Named for the first conquistador to enter Chile from Peru, Pedro de Valdivia, the city was founded in the mid-1500s but had a difficult time of it for the first 100 years. It was taken over by a Dutch pirate in 1600 and, being on the Mapuche side of the Biobío River dividing line between Crown and Mapuche territory, had to await the building of fortifications in the mid-1600s to achieve a measure of security. The **Museo Histórico y Antropológico Mauricio van de Maele** (http://museosaustral.cl; Mar–Dec Tue–Sun 10am–1pm and 2–6pm, Jan–Feb daily 10am–8pm), on Teja Island in the middle of Valdivia, is housed in an old settler's mansion and includes

FACT

Valdivia is home to one of Chile's oldest and largest independent breweries, the Cervecería Kunstmann. Its beer garden and restaurant on the road to Niebla is a favorite tourist attraction, although rather pricey.

Fresh fish at the Feria Fluvial in Valdivia.

TIP

Part of the road from Villarrica to San Martín de los Andes in Argentina, a distance of 205km (127 miles), is in poor shape but the views are incomparable.

Mapuche artifacts and period furnishings – providing an excellent insight into the prosperous lifestyles of the 19th-century German immigrants (see page 218).

In 1960, Valdivia was the epicenter of the world's largest recorded earthquake, followed by a tidal wave whose effects can still be seen. Most of the old buildings were destroyed, but some European-style buildings remain by the waterfront. The **Museo de Arte Contemporáneo** (Tue–Sun 10am–6pm), also on Teja Island, is built on the ruins of the old Andwandter brewery. It has no permanent collection but holds exhibitions of contemporary Chilean artists.

Valdivia has a popular week-long summer festival in February in which musical shows are staged on bandstands along the river bank, boats parade down the river, and firework shows are presented on the last afternoon and night. There is also a film festival.

The city's long riverside walks are full of visitors throughout the season, as are the nearby beaches. The Parque

Saval on Isla Teja has a riverside beach, and the nearby Botanical Garden, with many native species, is worth a visit.

A highly recommended stop is the **Feria Fluvial**, a lively fish market on the quay from which all the river cruises depart. Fat sea lions come right up into the market, but be careful: they have been known to attack passers-by.

Corral and Niebla

Though swimming is possible in the rivers, most bathers head for the port villages of **Corral** and **Niebla**. Colonial-era fortresses are preserved at the latter site, which independence hero Lord Thomas Cochrane, a dashing Scots navy commander in the service of the Chilean rebels, took from the Spanish against heavy odds in 1820. For a bit of exercise, visitors can row from Corral to the tiny island of **Mancera**, Valdivia's military headquarters during the 18th century, to see its small church and convent.

River trips from Valdivia north to the Santuario de la Naturaleza Río Cruces pass through the habitat of black-necked swans to the confluence of three rivers. A few years ago, this sanctuary was the subject of a major environmental controversy when, following the start of operations at a nearby wood-pulp plant, the swans, a relatively rare South American species, started to die and many more migrated. Effluent from the plant was blamed for the disappearance of the waterweed on which the swans feed. The company was forced to reduce the plant's output, prior to building a duct out to sea, and the swan population now appears to have recovered. Many boats make a stop at the indigenous Huilliche village of Punucapa.

Seven Lakes detour

The largely underdeveloped **Seven Lakes** district is among the least visited by vacationers due to a peculiar topographical layout and poor access. The district is named after seven lakes

Niebla Museum, part of the Valdivian fort system.

that all share the same river basin and include the large lakes Calafquén, Panguipulli, and Riñihue, the smaller lakes Pellaifa, Neltume, and Pirihueico, and Lago Lacar in Argentina. The lakes are generally bordered by heavily wooded cliffs with steep descents; roads are potholed and slippery at the best of times, with difficult climbs and narrow turns through the mountains, which are often impassable in winter. Low-suspension vehicles will fare worst. However, the landscapes are spectacular, and local residents will guide visitors to even more extraordinary spots. These lakes are good for fishing and exploring, but not so good for bathing as beaches are few and far between.

The circuit around Lago Calafquén is dominated by the seemingly changing position of Volcán Villarrica to the north. Finally, **Volcán Choshuenco** (2,415 meters/7,923ft) appears to the south. Recent lava flows can be observed from the highway shortly after leaving Lican Ray. From Coñaripe an alternative route leads to the small **Lago Pellaifa** after

a ferocious climb at **Los Añiques**. The way down leads through an agricultural valley to the Mapuche village of **Liquiñe**.

From there, it is possible to drive to **Lago Neltume** and **Puerto Fuy** ❾ on the finger-shaped **Lago Pirihueico**, which can be crossed in two hours on a ferry boat that connects to an international road to San Martín de los Andes in Argentina.

Panguipulli ❿ (Town of Roses) was formerly the train station that received logs dispatched from the interior via steamboats plying the lake of the same name. The construction of roads later superseded the lake transportation system. The town is brilliantly decorated with rose bushes. As Panguipulli is located on the flat central plain rather than in the mountains, it tends to be hotter than other lake towns, and its beaches are somewhat less impressive.

On clear days, you should be able to make out Volcán Choshuenco, located some 50km (30 miles) to the southeast. The volcano itself can be climbed by motor vehicle up to the

FACT

The Santuario de la Naturaleza Río Cruces, just north of Valdivia, is home to an astounding variety of river birds and plant life. The area was submerged under water in the earthquake of 1960.

Lakeside view at dusk.

FACT

The Termas Puyehue Hotel, located within Parque Nacional Puyehue, is one of Chile's most traditional spa resorts, offering both thermal and mud baths. See www.puyehue.cl for more information.

refuge after a trying, 80km (50-mile) drive along the lake. To the east, about halfway to Puerto Fuy, is the **Salto del Huilo Huilo**, the highest and one of the most impressive waterfalls in Chile, which crashes down a deep vine-covered gorge into the River Fuy. Nearby is the entrance to the Huilo Huilo Reserve, a private park with spectacular scenery and two luxury hotels. Note that it is impossible to continue the circuit around Lago Riñihue out of season (and frequently in season as well) due to a severe, 7km (4-mile) climb with terrible road conditions just after the tiny lakefront community of Enco. An approach can be made from the town of Los Lagos on the Pan-American Highway, passing through the town of Riñihue.

Lago Ranco

The enormous **Lago Ranco** ⓫ and the smaller adjacent **Lago Maihue** have developed considerably as tourist centers in recent years. However, out of season they are very quiet. On the northern shore of Lago Ranco,

the resort of **Futrono** is accessible by turning off the Pan-American Highway at Reumén. For foot travelers, buses to Futrono leave regularly from Valdivia and **Río Bueno** all year round. Guided adventure tourism in the surrounding hills is still little developed, though Futrono has a network of rural tourism.

Many of the communities surrounding the lake originated as fishermen's hostels; a couple are now successful lodges serving upscale clients. The town of **Lago Ranco** itself is full of cheap tourist guesthouses. The pebble beach and a hill behind the town give fine panoramic views. Boats can be rented when available.

The most beautiful and heavily settled part of the lake lies directly east along an unpaved road to the **Riñinahue** peninsula and the Calcurrupe River near **Llifén** ⓬, where the paving starts again. The road from Lago Ranco to Llifén is dotted with colonies of new summer vacation homes and crosses **Salto del Nilahue**, a double waterfall with a tremendous, roaring flow, especially in early summer. From the bridge over the River Nilahue, a tertiary road leads to the lower end of Lago Maihue and the hamlet of **Carrán**, named for the Carrán volcano which just appeared in 1957 and last erupted in 1979.

The 810-hectare (2,000-acre) **Isla Huapi** in the middle of Lago Ranco is an indigenous colony with some 40 Mapuche and Huilliche families. Huilliches were the original inhabitants, but Mapuches from Argentina colonized the island. There are ferry services to the island from Frutono and Lago Ranco.

Lago Ranco can be completely circled crossing the bridge over the Calcurrupe River, which replaced the old vehicle raft. A sturdy high-clearance vehicle is recommended for the unpaved stretches. The Caunahue River Canyon just north of Llifén has a dramatic view.

Parque Nacional Puyehue.

Lago Puyehue

Lago Puyehue is known to many travelers since it lies along the main route to Argentina from southern Chile. In wintertime, when heavy snow covers the Andes mountains, bus and lorry traffic from Santiago sometimes has to detour nearly 1,000km (600 miles) south to this pass, which is much lower and usually remains open throughout the year. The road has excellent views of the lake from gently rolling hills, then climbs to 1,300 meters (4,300ft) through **Parque Nacional Puyehue** on the way to the famous resort of San Carlos de Bariloche on the Argentine side. The main town on the Chilean side is **Entre Lagos** (Between the Lakes) on the western tip of Lago Puyehue, a former railroad center now heavily dependent on tourism.

A detour toward Volcán Casa Blanca (1,990 meters/6,529ft) leads to the open-air hot springs at **Aguas Calientes ⑬**. The park headquarters here make a good starting point for excursions. The road leads past several small lakes, through lush virgin forest, including an unusual temperate rainforest, and ends at a ski resort on the slopes of the volcano, which can be climbed more easily than Volcán Villarrica farther north. Another topographic oddity is the existence of deciduous trees (beech) at the volcano's tree line. At the top the views are very impressive even for this region, as the volcanoes Osorno, Puntiagudo, and Puyehue can all be seen in a semicircle.

The area around nearby **Lago Rupanco** tends to be exclusive and upscale, without the ready facilities for camping and day trips that abound around all the other lakes. Foreigners enjoy it for its extraordinary, mountain-ringed setting and superb fishing. The approach from Entre Lagos leads to a tiny settlement at **Puerto Chalupa**, which has a lovely beach. From the south, the road from **Puerto Octay** is a 25km (15-mile) drive, with no public transportation service. The beautiful campgrounds along the south shore of the lake are also virtually inaccessible without a vehicle.

Lago Llanquihue

Lago Llanquihue is the granddaddy of all the Chilean lakes. It is South America's fourth-largest, covering some 877 sq km (339 sq miles) and nearly 50km (30 miles) across from Puerto Octay to Puerto Varas on the south shore. The lake has an oceanic feel, with breakers that churn higher in winds or rough weather and mini-climates in its interior that keep boaters and fishermen alert; except for the narrow strip of land between Puerto Varas and Puerto Montt, the lake would be part of the ocean. The enormous national park at the eastern end of Lago Llanquihue, stretching all the way to the Argentine frontier, bears the name of **Vicente Pérez Rosales**, the promoter of foreign immigration to the region (see page 218). It was Chile's first, established in 1926.

Lago Llanquihue is one of the most visited sites in all of Chile, and tours of

FACT

As you walk through the woods of southern Chile, you'll probably see a brown bird with a rust-colored breast hopping through the undergrowth; it will be a *chucao*, named for its distinctive call.

Farmland near Parque Nacional Puyehue.

TIP

If you find Chile's southern seas too cold for swimming, try the lakes where the water is appreciably warmer.

Volcán Villarrica.

the district often start in Puerto Montt and then work back toward the north. **Puerto Varas**  is the main lakeside resort town. The beaches (the name of one, Niklitscheck, reflects a later immigration of Slavs, especially in the far south) run for several kilometers with rows of shops and excellent restaurants, and plenty of nightlife. The views from Puerto Varas across to Volcán Osorno (2,652 meters/8,701ft) and Volcán Puntiagudo (Sharp-Pointed), 2,190 meters (7,185ft), are breathtaking, and summer activities abound, making it a fun place to hang out. The ease of transportation and the plentiful accommodations to suit all budgets and tastes mean that all kinds of travelers gather at night to stroll the beach walks and rub shoulders.

Peak season is February; the views are just as fine in January, but the maddening *tábanos* are thickest then – irritating horseflies attracted to dark clothes and shiny objects, which love to buzz around your head in the sunshine. They don't come out in overcast weather, and since their life cycle is only a month, they disappear in early February. But before that they can easily ruin a day out.

Going east from Puerto Varas the road curves and dips, providing countless views of the lake from every imaginable angle. Winds tend to whip across even on bright, cloudless days, so the air is likely to remain cool and tempt the unwary to overdo exposure to the sun. The notorious deterioration of the ozone layer, which becomes progressively worse as one moves closer to Antarctica, contributes to the potency of the sun's rays.

Numerous *hosterías* by the lakeside provide lodging and full meals, but they can be pricey. On a clear day, residents will come down from their rural domiciles and gather in lakefront soccer fields to watch a match in the strong breeze with the sparkling water in the background. **Volcán Calbuco** (2,015 meters/6,611ft) is quite close on the right. This volcano's top was blown off in an 1893 eruption, leaving a jagged cone. About halfway to Ensenada is the **Río Pescado** (Fish River), which, not surprisingly, is famous for its good fishing.

AN ACTIVE LANDSCAPE

Chile has over 2,000 volcanoes, located mostly in the Andes Mountains, of which over 500 are considered geologically active and around 60 have erupted in the last 500 years. The entire country forms part of the Pacific "Rim of Fire" which stretches along the western coasts of North and South America, west to New Zealand and the western Pacific islands and up through Japan and the Kamchatka Peninsula.

Chile's volcanoes are doubly dangerous because of their eternal snows, which melt into rapid, devastating mudslides upon full eruption. The lava itself advances much more slowly but burns away everything in its path. These lava "runs" can be observed at the Villarrica and Osorno volcanoes, and you can climb the Villarrica volcano for a peek down at the magma quite near the surface. Although some of the active volcanoes are considered semi-dormant, a strong eruption can always set off a chain reaction of volcanic activity, as happened in the 1960 earthquake.

The lakes are of glacial origin, their basins carved out by advancing ice, then filled by the melting ice as the glaciers receded. There is also evidence of tectonic influence, with earthquakes causing some lake basins to sink further while newly formed volcanoes sometimes shift the course of rivers as they rise up between them.

Saltos del Petrohué

From **Ensenada** ⑮ most visitors head up the 16km (10-mile) spur to Petrohué, stopping to see the unusual **Saltos del Petrohué**. These are a series of oddly twisting water chutes formed by a crystallized black volcanic rock that is particularly resistant to erosion. Volcán Puntiagudo's odd shape is also due to this erosion resistance: its central core is composed of the same crystallized rock which remains unaffected while the surrounding material erodes away. The water of the Petrohué River is bright green due to the presence of algae, a phenomenon repeated in **Lago Todos los Santos** (All Saints Lake), which begins at the town of Petrohué.

From the falls to the lake the road is cut by several river beds, which will rise suddenly on a warm day with melt from Volcán Osorno. Eruptions from the volcano centuries ago diverted the River Petrohué's flow from Lago Llanquihue south to Lago Todos los Santos; signs of the earlier lava flows can be observed along with strange vegetation and insect life not found even a few kilometers away. **Petrohué** itself is nothing but a lodge, a lakeside campground (the fishing is said to be great), and a forest service outpost, but a large modern catamaran leaves from the dock for day trips on the lake. In the height of summer this area is plagued by two types of biting fly – the *colihuacho* and the *petro* (Petrohué is a Mapuche word meaning Place of Petros). The only relief from these pests is to shelter in the deep shade of the forests.

Small glaciers atop Volcán Tronador, (Thunder Mountain; 3,451 meters/11,322ft), can be observed en route, and Volcán Osorno is even more imposing from the Lago Todos los Santos side than from Lago Llanquihue. The lake itself is narrow, with forested cliffs rising sharply on all sides. Lunch at touristic **Peulla** ⑯ at the other end is expensive and not particularly appetizing. The famous **Cascadas Los Novios** (Bridal Falls) may be only a trickle if rain has been scarce, and the hamlet can be surprisingly hot but the hiking excursions into the mountains from Peulla are excellent. It's possible to continue the same day to San Carlos de Bariloche in Argentina by taking the road to **Puerto Blest** ⑰, from where you pick up another boat.

Estuario de Reloncaví

A turn-off from the road from Ensenada to Petrohué leads to the **Estuario de Reloncaví** (Reloncaví Estuary), which connects with the Seno de Reloncaví (Reloncaví Sound). Fishing here is not what it used to be after years of commercial exploitation, but there are still plenty of unexplored inlets. This area and the region farther south are sometimes called "continental Chiloé" for the similarity in culture with Isla de Chiloé (see page 223). As the road winds down the glaciated Petrohué River Valley onto the east shore of the Reloncaví, the characteristic Chilote tiles begin to appear on many of the buildings. These are made from water-resistant *alerce*, sequoia-related trees that

TIP

In the peak summer season, leave plenty of time for crossing the Chacao Channel to Chiloé: there can be a long queue for the Pargua-Chacao ferry.

Volcán Osorno and the Saltos del Petrohué.

German Settlers

During the 19th century, millions of people fled famine and hardship in Europe and came to the Lake District in search of a better life.

German immigration to Valdivia occurred in two periods: a minor influx in the first half of the 19th century and the more important wave between roughly 1885 and 1910. The immigrants played an important role in commerce and industry, using technical knowledge brought from the old country. Some cultivated their new lands, although climatic conditions were not ideal. Others arrived as ironsmiths, carpenters, tanners, brewers, watchmakers, locksmiths, and tailors.

Chile in 1850 was just emerging from three decades of political anarchy and economic stagnation, and distant provinces like Valdivia were left largely to their own devices.

By 1900, a traveler claimed that upon entering Valdivia, he could not believe he was still in Chile. Many of the tradesmen had converted their shops

An exhibit at the Kunstmann brewery, showing how German settlers made beer.

into factories. Valdivia became Chile's prime industrial center, with breweries, distilleries, shipbuilding, flour mills, tanneries, 100 lumber mills and, in 1913, the country's first foundry. Furniture-making was stimulated by the immense availability of beautiful native woods.

The wealth of the Germans of Valdivia was legendary in Chile until their luck changed, starting with the imposition of a heavy liquor tax in 1902 at the behest of Central Valley vintners. Unfavorable trade conditions wiped out much of the leather market. A great fire laid waste to the city in 1909, while the local merchant class was superseded by mine and estate owners from farther north, closer to the byzantine politics of the capital.

Puerto Montt and Osorno

Beginning in the mid-19th century, the region around Lago Llanquihue was also heavily settled by German immigrants, who disembarked at what is now the Seno de Reloncaví. Vicente Pérez Rosales, the indefatigable promoter of colonization in southern Chile, organized a solemn ceremony to establish Puerto Montt formally with a group of the recent arrivals, none of whom understood a word of Spanish. According to an account of the ritual, led by a Catholic priest, the Protestant settlers interrupted at what seemed to them an appropriate pause with a rousing chorus of *Hier Liegt vor Deiner Majestad* (Here Before Your Majesty). Despite the idiomatic complications, Pérez Rosales's project was a success in the long run.

Osorno is well known as having been settled by Germans. However, despite the many German street names, the immigrants never actually numbered more than 10 percent of the total population of the region.

Chileans were also drawn to these new lands, generally uneducated and destitute people hoping to make a new start. The foreigners quickly established themselves as the dominant class, employing the mestizo citizens and directing economic development.

Chile's largest remaining concentration of Huilliches (southern Mapuches) is to be found in communities scattered between Osorno and the coast, around towns like Puaucho and San Juan de la Costa. Although educational and healthcare facilities have improved in recent years, this is still one of Chile's worst pockets of rural poverty. Huilliches can be seen trading their cash crops in the market in Osorno, which is a drab city compared to more prosperous and sophisticated Valdivia.

live for hundreds of years and can resist forest fires. The wood is so valuable that *alerce* stumps are sometimes harvested and split for sale.

From Ralún, at the mouth of the Petrohué, a bridge crosses the river to **Cochamó** ⓘ farther south, a fishing town which has views of **Volcán Yate** (2,111 meters/6,926ft), and **Puelo** ⓘ. These towns are reminiscent of the isolated communities along the Carretera Austral highway, which winds through the largely uninhabited archipelago region in the far south for close to 1,000km (600 miles).

The area from Ensenada north along Lago Llanquihue was covered in an eruption some 150 years ago and nicely illustrates how plant life gradually returns after destruction by a lava flow; the borders of deciduous forest are abruptly marked on either side.

Three kilometers (2 miles) from Ensenada is the road to **La Burbuja** (The Bubble) refuge on the slopes of Volcán Osorno, well worth the 19km (12-mile) climb. In clear weather, the sunset seen from the top is memorable, and the local refuge/ski center has overnight facilities. The road eases down to the town of **Las Cascadas** ⓘ (The Waterfalls), but there is no public transportation for this 20km (12-mile) stretch. Hitchhiking is easier in the afternoon, but never a sure thing. The road has more than the necessary twists and turns – locals explain that the original track was paid for by the kilometer, and their relatives ensured it was as long as possible.

Las Cascadas is the base for an attractive 4km (2.5-mile) hike into the hills, but it's easy to get lost, so it is advisable to hire a guide from the town.

Volcán Osorno

Volcán Osorno, a perfect, snow-covered cone, dominates the view from the road. Skilled mountaineers can climb to the crater in about six hours, but quickly shifting clouds and hidden crevasses can be deadly even for the expert. Plentiful stories of

people being lost there are intended to discourage freelance exploring. It is worth visiting one of the various farms set back up in the hills a few hundred meters, on the pretext of buying homemade cheese or marmalade – you should be able to get a wide vista of the lake and volcano together, and will understand why the original settlers went to the trouble of making these densely overgrown lands habitable.

Some settlers employed Chilotes, mestizo fishermen from Isla de Chiloé farther south, to help with the backbreaking labor, sometimes abusing their trust to trick them out of fair wages. One whispered story even suggests the imported workers were often "lost" in the thick jungle in order to avoid paying them anything. Settlers dragged logs or their farm produce down to a dock to be picked up by the steamboat from Puerto Varas, sometimes going along to the town for provisions. But the frequent lake squalls could lead to financial disaster: in order to avoid capsizing, passengers would have to dump their

Pampering at the Termas Puyehue resort.

Estuario Reloncaví from the air.

recently bought goods overboard, package by package.

The only surviving pier from the epoch is at **Puerto Fonck** on the road that connects Las Cascadas with the road to Osorno. The long stretches of beach from Las Cascadas toward Puerto Klocker and Puerto Fonck are deserted. European settlers did not feel secure in the area until the Mapuche people were finally defeated in the late 1800s.

Puerto Octay and Frutillar

The idea of Lago Llanquihue as a vacation spot occurred as early as 1912 to a government functionary, Interior Minister Luis Izquierdo, who built a summer mansion on the Centinela peninsula next to Puerto Octay with a group of his friends. The house remains in use today as the Hotel Centinela. Nearby, on the northern lakeshore, **Puerto Octay** ㉑ is a popular resort town, and a bit less crowded than the southern side of the lake. The road along the lake heading south toward Frutillar has more spectacular views.

On the western shore of the lake, the tidy little town of **Frutillar** ㉒ has a famous classical music festival in the summer. It is actually two towns joined together: Lower Frutillar is 4km (2.5 miles) down a steep incline from Upper Frutillar. There are more houses up above, many of which offer summer lodgings at reasonable rates. Fixed-rate taxis will ferry you up and down if the walk is too tiring. Frutillar and other towns in the area are known for their pretty shingled churches, which often appear in tourist brochures with the lake sparkling in the background.

Osorno

Of all the southern cities, **Osorno** ㉓ is the least interesting, partly due to the strange lack of street life. A business day in Osorno feels like a Sunday, and Sunday feels like a day of national mourning. The town was abandoned after the great Mapuche uprising of 1598, its inhabitants fleeing to establish protected outposts on the ocean inlets just north of Isla de Chiloé. Osorno was not refounded until 200 years later, and it is still more of a market center for country residents than an urban entity. The cattle auction is perhaps its most impressive attraction.

City highlights include the modern cathedral on the Plaza de Armas, and the **Museo Histórico** (Mon–Fri 9.30am–5pm, Sat 2–6pm; free), with displays on Osorno's history and the German arrival. Osorno's wooden houses have sharply angled roofs to handle the rain and snow, and when the storm clouds begin to threaten, the place has the air of a city in Quebec or northern New England. The 18th-century **Fuerte Reina Luisa** fort is derelict – the one at Río Bueno, 30km (19 miles) north, is better preserved. It has a good view of the river, also known as El Gran Río, which carries off the water of four lakes (Maihue, Ranco, Puyehue, and Rupanco) – making it the second-largest in Chile.

The pier at Frutillar.

Puerto Montt

Around 110km (68 miles) farther south is the bustling, windy city of **Puerto Montt ㉔**. Connected by rail to the rest of Chile in 1912, it became the contact point for the rest of the south. It remains so to the present day, despite the loss of its railroad line. It is an important fishing center; seafood at the harbor of Angelmó is famous. The port was completely destroyed in the earthquake of 1960. Boats leave from here for the long, slow trip down through the southern archipelago. (Puerto Chacabuco requires 22 hours, Puerto Natales three days.) The port is protected from the strong winds by **Isla Tenglo**.

From the hills above the city there are fine views of the entire Seno de Reloncaví. Local boat trips can be arranged in Puerto Montt. From Chamiza, to the east of the town, it is possible to get close to **Volcán Calbuco** on the southern side of Lago Llanquihue. German settlers built an interesting Lutheran church in Chamiza next to two giant *saav* trees. **Parque Nacional Alerce Andino** has good facilities, and Lago Chapo is off the usual tourist beat. A peaceful rural site located near Puerto Montt threw the archeological world into a frenzy, pushing back the possible date of human arrival in the Americas by thousands of years. During the 1970s, scientists discovered that the area around the Chinchihuapi Creek, known as **Monte Verde**, held human remains dating from 12,500 years ago. In 1998 more remains were found at the site, which suggest possible human occupation 33,000 years ago.

Southwest of Puerto Montt are the port of **Maullín** and **Carelmapu ㉕** one of the oldest settlements, dating from the Spaniards' flight after their defeat by the Mapuches around 1600. On its rough beaches, the original wild strawberries from which commercial strawberries were developed still grow, as in many other remote places in the south of Chile. An alternative route is the road that follows the bay southwest from Puerto Montt to Calbuco. This offers distinctive views of the volcanoes toward the north. **Calbuco ㉖**, like Carelmapu, predates Puerto Montt by some 250 years.

Salmon farm off Chiloé.

SALMON CLEAN-UP

Over the past 20 years, southern Chile has seen the development of a new export industry – salmon farming – and the country now rivals Norway on world markets. The salmon industry's development has increased the number of jobs in a region where employment was previously scarce and explains the rapid growth of Puerto Montt, with its vast salmon processing plants, as well as Puerto Varas, where most of the industry's executives prefer to live.

But the environment suffered. The once-pristine lakes and sheltered sea bays have been polluted with salmon feed, antibiotics, and organic waste. An outbreak of ISA (infectious salmon anemia), a highly contagious salmon virus disease, which began in 2007, however, forced the industry to rethink its practices. As well as reducing the density of seawater cages – as many as a million fish can be fattened in one bay – producers are increasingly starting to use on-land plants, rather than lakes, for hatching and breeding – partly because of environmental pressures, but also because the contamination the industry itself has caused now poses a risk to the health of juvenile fish.

Regulation on where new farms can be located and the distance between them has also been tightened. Partly as a result, the industry is now expanding south into the Aysén and, even, Magallanes Regions, away from the Lake District and Chiloé where its development began.

Palafitos (houses on stilts), Castro.

ISLA DE CHILOÉ

This large, rainswept island is a culturally distinctive
area with its own music, dance, and craft traditions,
and a wealth of spellbinding myths and legends.

For a moment you think you've
misheard, that someone has simply pronounced the word "Chile"
and for some peculiar reason your
ears have given it an extra "o." To some
extent Chiloé is Chile in miniature,
a peculiar time capsule that contains
some of Chile's best and harshest
traditions, shaping them into song,
dance, crafts, and a mythology that
has become one of the main strands of
the country's national identity. Much
of "Chilean" folk music and dance was
born in Chiloé's gentle summer fogs
and wet winters.

December, January, and February
are the better months for a visit to
Chiloé, because the warmer summer weather makes it easier to travel
within the main island and across to
some of the smaller islands. In recent
years, Chiloé has become something
of a standard pilgrimage for the young
and the not-so-young, so you may
meet more people from Santiago than
from the islands.

Chiloé's flood myth

A Mapuche legend tells the story of
what may have been the formation of
Chiloé as witnessed by the Mapuche
and Chono peoples long before the
Spanish reached the continent. It tells
how the twin serpents Cai Cai and
Tren Tren do battle. Cai Cai, the evil
one, who has risen in rage from the sea

and flooded the earth, assaults Tren
Tren's rocky fortress in the mountain
peaks, while the people try in vain to
awaken the friendly serpent from a
deep sleep.

Meanwhile Cai Cai has almost
reached Tren Tren's cave, swimming
on the turbulent waters. Cai Cai's
friends, the thunder, fire, and wind,
help her by piling up clouds to bring
rain, thunder and lightning.

Pleas and weeping don't wake Tren
Tren. Only the laughter of a little girl,
dancing with her reflection in the

Main Attractions

Dalcahue Sunday Market
Mirador Cerro Huaihuén
Caulín
Catedral de Castro
Museo de Arte Moderno
Parque Nacional Chiloé

Dalcahue, Isla Grande de Chiloé.

sleeping serpent's eye, arouses her, and she responds with a giggle so insulting that Cai Cai and her stormy friends fall down the hill.

Cai Cai charges again, all the more furious, shattering the earth and sowing the sea with islands. She makes the water climb ever higher, and almost submerges the mountain where her enemy lives, but Tren Tren arches her back, and with the strength of the 12 guanacos in her stomach, she pushes the cave ceiling upward, so that the mountain grows toward the sky. Cai Cai and her friends keep bringing more water and Tren Tren keeps pushing her cave roof higher until the mountain reaches above the clouds, close to the sun, where the evil serpent cannot reach it. Cai Cai and her servants fall from the peak into the abyss, where they lie stunned for thousands of years.

The waters gradually recede, and the people are able to return to their lands, untroubled by either of the giant serpents, who continue sleeping. However, sometimes, it is said, Cai Cai has nightmares, and an island appears in the ocean or the earth trembles a little. The legend may tell the story of an ancient earthquake which was accompanied by tidal waves and flooding, but it is also remarkably similar to scientific accounts of how the peculiar attributes of the area came about.

Birth of an archipelago

The scientists explain that over thousands of years, two giant tectonic plates forming part of the earth's crust clashed, producing the volcanoes characteristic of mainland Chile: Hornopirén, Huequi, Michimahuida, and Corcovado. During the Ice Age, glaciers bore down upon the Central Valley region, carving a gap through the coastal mountains and pushing the valley farther and farther below sea level.

When the glaciers began to melt at the end of the Ice Age, the ocean poured through the openings located at the north and south ends of what is now the main island of Chiloé, to create the interior sea that divides Chiloé from the mainland, turning what was previously the coastal mountain range

A young Chilote in Castro, one of Chile's oldest towns.

into the series of islands that form the archipelago of Chiloé. Toward the center of Isla Grande de Chiloé, where the lakes of Huillinco and Cucao cut partially through the island's mountain range, the land drops to sea level, and many islanders fear that Chiloé may one day be cut in two.

Chiloé's **Isla Grande** (main island) is the second-largest island in Latin America, after Tierra del Fuego. Like a great ship moored off the Chilean coast it seems to float, surrounded by several smaller constellations of islands called the Chauques, Quenac, Quehui, Chaulinec, and Desertores. Some of these islands are so close to each other they are joined at low tide. The low mountains along the west coast of the main island are nevertheless high enough to stop the damp winds blowing off the Pacific, creating a slightly drier microclimate along the interior sea, where virtually all the settlements are located.

The interior sea, generally calm – at least as seen from the shore – can be difficult to navigate, especially for the many Chilotes who still rely on small rowboats or launches. As the tides roar in through the tiny channel of **Chacao** in the north (crossed by the mainland ferry), they eventually meet and clash with the tides pouring through the channel to the island's south, creating huge whirlpools and waves that have been identified as a potentially rich source of tidal-generated electricity. In Cucao, on the Pacific coast, the difference between high and low tides is 2.5 meters (8ft), while in Quemchi it is 7 meters (23ft), because of the shallowness of much of the interior sea. These powerful tides leave shellfish and fish, a major source of food for the islanders, trapped on the beaches and in sea pools.

The making of the Chilotes

The first known inhabitants of the islands of Chiloé were the Chonos, a tough, seafaring people who have gone down in history for the creation of the *dalca*, a small, canoe-like boat built by binding several rough-hewn planks together. For centuries, the Chonos guided the Spanish and other adventurers through the intricate channels

The Pargua–Chacao car ferry.

and fjords which honeycomb Chile's southern shores. They spoke a different language from the Mapuches or Huilliches (southern Mapuche), who began to invade the islands.

These invasions forced the Chonos to migrate farther and farther south. In the 1700s, the Jesuits pushed the Chonos and the Caucahues, a separate native group who had not been integrated into the Mapuche tribe, into small reserves on Isla Cailín, south of Quellón, and later the Chaulinec Islands, where they eventually mixed with the other inhabitants. The Jesuit mission on Isla Cailín was the southernmost chapel in the Christian Empire.

When Alfonso de Camargo became the first European to see Chiloé in 1540, the archipelago's inhabitants were a mixture of Chono and Mapuche living scattered along the coast, which was at once their main highway, source of food, and the cradle for a wealth of legends and oral histories which are the backbone of Chilote culture to this day. The homes in which they lived were straw *rucas*,

Chiloé National Park.

clustered near beaches and woods in groups of up to 400 people and known as *cabís*, led by *caciques* or chiefs. Using wooden tools, they farmed potatoes and corn in fields protected by fences which were woven using basket techniques, and they reaped the rich harvest of shellfish along the shores.

Serfdom and rebellion

Thirteen years later Francisco de Ulloa's expedition formally "discovered" the islands, and 14 years after that, Martín Ruiz de Gamboa officially took possession of them, calling them Nueva Galicia. On February 12, 1567, he founded the city of Santiago de Castro and for the next 200 years the Spaniards divided up the available land – and the people living on it – in what became known as the *encomienda* system, a kind of serfdom. The idea was that the native peoples worked for free in order to "pay tribute" to the king of Spain. This native labor system was used in the mining of gold in Cucao, the weaving of woolen cloth and the logging of *alerce*, a tough, fine wood native to Chile (which is today

in danger of extinction). In the early years, the products of Chiloé brought considerable wealth to the Spaniards who had taken possession of the land, but desperate poverty to its people.

In 1598, when the Mapuche communities of Carelmapu and Calbuco on the mainland rebelled against the Spanish invaders, the survivors retreated to Chiloé, where they established towns in 1602. The people of Chiloé twice joined forces with "pirates," destroying Castro with Baltazar de Cordes in 1600 and attacking Carelmapu and later Valdivia, across the channel, with Enrique Brouwer in 1643. In the centuries that followed, the Spanish and the Mapuche-Chonos of Chiloé lived in virtual isolation and extreme poverty, with occasional visits from Spanish ships sent from Lima, Peru, sometimes as many as three years apart. Despite this neglect, Chiloé became a royalist stronghold during the wars of independence in the early 19th century. The governor of Chile fled to Chiloé, and despairingly offered the island to Britain. The offer was declined, and

Chiloé surrendered to the mainland republic in 1826.

Over the centuries the two races, Spanish and Mapuche-Chono, fused, preserving much of the native languages and customs. The Chilotes all wore the same clothes and suffered the same hardships, creating a sense of social equality unusual in the Spanish Empire. Settlement continued along the coast until the early 1900s, when lands were given to German, English, French, and Spanish "colonists," and the building of a railway in 1912 between Ancud and Castro finally opened internal communication between Chiloé's two main cities.

A distinct culture

Today the Chilotes continue to be a proud, independent people, clearly distinguishable from their fellow Chileans, with their own dialect mixing influences from 16th-century Spanish with many indigenous words, and a rich tradition of music and dance beloved throughout Chile. The tragic poverty of the early colonization, which forced many

FACT

The island of Chiloé was once covered in impenetrable woods, which have gradually been cleared to make way for agriculture.

Guarding the clam catch, Ancud.

men to take seasonal work on the sheep farms of the Magallanes area and even in Argentina, has now given way to greater prosperity, born of tourism and the introduction of salmon farming.

The one great weakness of the Chilotes is the game of *truco*, which is played with the Spanish 40-card deck. *Truco*, which roughly translated means "trickery," is an extraordinary gambling game divided into two parts, the *envío* and the *truco* itself. The cards are half the game; the other half is the skill and imagination of the players who bluff and jest, using rhyming couplets laden with double meanings. Today, you are as likely to see a lively game of *truco* on a ship at Punta Arenas as in a Chilote bar. And the Chilotes who've gambled away a season's earnings on the sheep ranches and are unable to return home are legendary. This forced migration of working men has also given rise to the image of the Chilote family as a virtual matriarchy of distant, sometimes almost mythical men, and strong women raising their

The wooden interior of the Iglesia San Francisco in Castro.

children, their livestock and tending their crops, keeping the island alive.

A land of chapels

It was during the 200-year period when the Spanish were barred from the Mapuche lands in mainland Chile that the Jesuits began the evangelizing activities which left an enduring mark on the islands' legends and villages. Some of the most strikingly beautiful characteristics of Chilote architecture are the wooden chapels built during the Jesuits' stay, many of which survive to this day. Between 2000 and 2001, Unesco's World Heritage Committee declared 16 of these chapels sites of universal value on the grounds that they represent the only Latin American example of a rare form of ecclesiastical wooden architecture.

The chapels, which often stood completely alone on the coast unaccompanied by human habitation, were built as part of the Jesuits' "Circulating Mission." This consisted of a boat manned by two missionaries who started their annual rounds from

Castro with religious ornaments and three portable altars, complete with a "Holy Christ" to be carried during ceremonies by the *caciques* (chiefs), a "Holy Heart" to be carried by children, a "Saint John" to be carried by bachelors, a "Saint Isidore" for married men, "Our Lady of Suffering (Dolores)" for single women, and "Saint Notburga" for married women.

To this day, a *fiscal*, a sort of native priest, has the custody of chapel keys, and in August people from nearby islands gather on Isla Caguache to celebrate their religion with ceremonies similar to those initiated by the Jesuits and modified by later Roman Catholic missions. The chapel of Vilupulli, near Chonchi, continues to stand alone, with no human settlement around it, exactly as the chapels did in the 1700s. These chapels are an interesting example of the Chilotes' outstanding ability to absorb foreign cultures without losing their own identity. Their design is strongly influenced by German architecture of the period, because several of the Jesuits were from Bavaria.

The *tejuelas* or wooden shingles commonly used to roof buildings throughout southern Chile, and which are one of the most striking characteristics of homes in Chiloé, were also a German idea, brought by the colonists who originally settled in Llanquihue and Puerto Montt on the mainland. The visible part of the *tejuela* is approximately a third of the total length, as they overlap so well that these buildings are extremely resistant to the heavy rains of the region. Before the *tejuelas* were introduced, Chilote homes usually had roofs of straw, similar to those of the Mapuches' *rucas*, and also extremely resistant to rain.

A tradition of handicrafts

For centuries, the women of Chiloé have spent the harsh winters producing clothing and household items. Different parts of the islands are associated with different crafts. The small town of **Chonchi** (south of Castro) is known for its woven wool products, especially blankets and ponchos, as well as *licor de oro*, a liqueur made

FACT

The Sunday morning market in Dalcahue is one of best places to buy local crafts, and just beside it, there are restaurants with lovely views over the harbor.

Preparing curanto, Quellón.

with saffron. **Quellón**  is famous for its ponchos, which are resistant to rain because the wool used for making them is raw and full of natural oils. On **Isla Lingue**, across from Achao, baskets are woven from local fibers, although some have fallen into disuse owing to the difficulty of working with them. Many of the islands' legends have been woven into decorative objects from all areas of Chiloé.

On Sunday mornings, there is a traditional market by the dock in **Dalcahue** ❷, where hundreds of craftspeople from all over the archipelago still gather to sell their wares. They also prepare traditional Chilote meals, particularly the *curanto*, a concoction prepared over a fire built in a hole scooped out of the earth, containing a variety of shellfish and meat and served with *milcao*, a traditional flatbread made with grated potatoes. The traditional woven fences of the Mapuche-Chonos can still be seen separating livestock from planted areas in some parts of the islands, and the *birloche* or *trineo*, a sled-like vehicle towed by oxen,

Potato harvesting on Teuquelín Island.

continues to be used on several of the smaller islands.

Keep your eye out in markets and fairs for the *almudes*, wooden boxes of a fixed size, still used to display a seller's wares. The *almud* is also a unit of measurement, and the boxes have the peculiarity of measuring one *almud* on one end and half an *almud* on the other. Their origin is Spanish. Stone mills introduced by the Jesuits can be seen in several Chilote museums, and they are still in use in some areas between Castro and Dalcahue. In February, wooden *chicha* (cider) presses are still very much in evidence, pressing the sweet juices out of apples piled in traditional baskets. Hanging in the windows of many houses you'll see woolen socks or ponchos, or other handmade items for sale. If you're lucky you may also get a glimpse of a Chilote loom, which is horizontal and nailed to the floor. It is still used by the artisans, who must kneel to work it.

For Chilote sweaters, the women shear the sheep, clean and wash the wool by hand, dye it with colors

TO BRIDGE OR NOT TO BRIDGE

In 2012, President Sebastián Piñera revived old plans for the construction of a controversial bridge, which would link Chiloé Island to mainland Chile. Although the idea was first mooted in the mid-1970s, it only began to be seriously considered in the early 2000s, when then President Ricardo Lagos proposed construction of a suspension bridge – the so-called Bicentennial Bridge in reference to Chile's celebration of the 200th anniversary of its independence in 2010 – across the Chacao Channel. Stretching 2.6km (1.6 miles), the bridge would be the longest of its type in South America. Even though the bridge would reduce the crossing to a matter of minutes (compared to at least half an hour on the current ferry service), not all residents of Chiloé are keen on the idea. Many locals have voiced concerns over the cost of the tolls: although subsidized by the government, the bridge would be built and operated by a private company. Other residents are wary of the impact the bridge could potentially have on their traditional way of life. The overall opinion of many Chilotes is that the money would be better off spent elsewhere, such as on public infrastructure within the archipelago, or, for example, better local health services, which wouldreduce their need to cross to the mainland.

prepared from local herbs, and spin it using a simple spindle which twirls on the floor.

Holding on to the past

Chiloé is in many ways as mysterious, as long-suffering, and as contradictory as it has been for most of its history. Modern fish-processing plants and salmon farming have provided more employment. At the same time, pollution and overfishing of coastal waters are now problems.

Other Chilotes have tried to eke out a living from fishing, with mixed results, and developmental agencies have created programs for improving Chilote agriculture, marketing and handicraft techniques. Even as modern factory ships sail under foreign flags, just outside Chile's 322km (200-mile) limit, the Chilotes themselves continue to live – and die – by traditional rowboats and small motor launches. Chilote culture itself – the music, poetry, and stories – is increasingly packaged for a burgeoning tourist industry, a process which tends to create and preserve caricatures devoid of their original meaning. Like similar attempts in other parts of the world, this has harmed as well as helped the local economy.

Chilote cultural activity is on view during the Festival Costumbrista, held in the second or third week of February in Castro and other towns, and during local summer events.

Ancud and Castro

Ancud and Castro, the main island's two cities, provide good bases for exploring the archipelago. Until 1982, **Ancud ❸**, which has a population of over 40,000, was the capital of Chiloé. The city was an international port until the beginning of the 20th century, and it retains a peculiar mixture of traditional Chilote buildings, docks, and plazas combined with more modern signs and structures.

Ancud's central plaza is flanked by the **cathedral**, government buildings, and the **Museo Regional de Ancud** (www.museoancud.cl; Jan–Feb Tue–Fri 10am–5.30pm, Sat–Sun 10.15am–3.30pm, Mar–Dec Tue–Fri 10am–5.30pm, Sat–Sun 10.15am–1.30pm;

Castro food store.

TIP

If you visit Curaco de Vélez, take a look at the stone mills which are still installed on the Los Molinos brook.

free), which contains exhibits about Chilote culture and mythology.

If you have a vehicle, you can enjoy a lovely drive along the **Costanera** (coast road), with a view of the Gulf of Quetalmahue. Lining the shore are the older, often impressive houses of Ancud's wealthier citizens.

The **Mirador Cerro Huaihuén** (a lookout point) affords breathtaking views of the city and across the Chacao Channel toward the mainland. By following the Costanera, then Bellavista and San Antonio northward, you'll quickly reach **Fuerte San Antonio**, which was built in 1770. On January 19, 1826, it became the last Spanish garrison to surrender to the wave of independence which had swept South America. Ancud then became the focus for colonizing expeditions aimed at southern Chile, including one that settled possession of the Strait of Magellan in 1843. In the late 19th century, Ancud boomed with the whale and wood industries, and newly arrived settlers from Europe, primarily of German origin. However, when the railway extended to Puerto Montt in

1912, Ancud lost its importance, and in 1982 the trade and shipping center Castro became the capital of Chiloé.

Near the waterfront, craftspeople set up stalls selling mostly woolen goods. At the covered fruit and vegetable market on Calle Pedro Montt, look out for the blue, black, and red varieties of potato that are native to Chiloé (see page 86).

An interesting side trip from Ancud is a visit to the oyster beds at **Caulín**. To get there you must travel back along the highway toward the ferry's arrival point at Chacao, and then turn left toward Caulín at Km 24, where you can enjoy fresh oysters at reasonable prices, before spending an afternoon on the beach or heading back to Ancud.

If you drive south from Ancud and then west, you'll find good fishing at the *refugio* (refuge) at **Puerto Anguay**, as well as several good places to picnic. Along the way, look out for the **Butalcura River Valley**, with great patches of dead trees in the water where the 1960 earthquake caused the earth to collapse.

Castro

Castro ❹ has a population of about 42,000, and is located about 90km (56 miles) to the south of Ancud. Although it is technically one of Chile's oldest cities, having been founded in 1567, Castro suffered so many attacks and privations that there are few signs of its antiquity within the city itself. On parts of the waterfront are *palafitos*, Chiloé's distinctive wooden homes on stilts.

It's best to see Castro on foot, strolling from the **Plaza de Armas** with its painted **cathedral** shoreward to enjoy the market area with its lively crafts fair, then back up the hill toward the **mirador** (lookout) with its statue of the Virgin and its bird's-eye view of the city's cemetery, piled high with conventional gravestones and small structures resembling houses that shelter the city's dead.

Palafitos, traditional wooden houses on stilts.

Castro's **Museo Regional** (Jan–Feb Mon–Sat 9.30am–6.30pm, Sun 10.30am–1pm; Mar–Dec Mon–Fri 9.30am–1pm and 3–6pm, Sat 9.30am–1pm; voluntary contribution), is a good introduction to the archipelago's history and is packed with wooden fishing and farming implements.

The plaza is also the focal point for the Festival Costumbrista, a celebration of Chilote customs, food, and crafts, which takes place in February. The **Museo de Arte Moderno** (www.mamchiloe.cl; open during exhibitions only 10am–5pm, until 6pm in summer) has an excellent collection of contemporary Chilean work. Set on a hill just outside the town, it also provides a spectacular view of the interior sea and of the snow-capped mountains across on the mainland. The building, constructed of Chiloé's traditional wood, has won architectural prizes.

Exploring the islands

From Castro you can travel up the shore of Chiloé's interior sea to visit **Dalcahue**, **Llaullao**, and, on **Isla Quinchao** (accessible by ferry), the small towns of **Curaco de Vélez** – famous for its oyster beds – and **Achao** ❺. Achao's 18th-century church of **Santa María** is built entirely of cypress and *alerce*. Farther along the island highway is Chiloé's largest church, **Quinchao**, which was built in the 18th century and refashioned according to neoclassical ideas at the end of the 19th century. While driving around the area, keep an eye out for the traditional woven fences.

Chonchi ❻, about half an hour south of Castro, is a small town built on such a steep incline that it is also known as the "Ciudad de los Tres Pisos" (Three-story City). Local handicrafts abound, and cardboard signs advertise the famous *licor de oro*. Near Chonchi it's possible to catch a ferry to **Isla Lemuy** ❼ or head farther south to **Queilen** ❽. **Parque Nacional Chiloé** can be reached by traveling across the island toward **Cucao**, one of only two towns on the Pacific side of Isla de Chiloé. It's a good place to hike or camp, with a long and wave-pounded beach.

Quellón waterfront at dusk.

Chilote Magic

Chiloé is a magical place. Gods and goddesses, ghost ships, and the lost city of the Caesars are as much a part of the archipelago as the people themselves.

Expressed in music, dance, and popular beliefs, the *Trauco*, the *Pincoya*, the *Caleuche*, and other mythical creatures haunt the forests and fields of Chiloé. Alongside them are the *brujos* or wizards, their human counterparts.

Undoubtedly, many of the mythical characters of Chiloé also serve a social purpose: the *Trauco*, for example, is a creature that is able to seduce young women by hypnotizing them with his magical gaze. Accepting the existence of the *Trauco* provides an explanation for teenage pregnancies, and the mythical creature has even been used to cover up incest. Today, when so much of Chiloé's maritime wealth is threatened by over-exploitation, these people-sized gods also serve as symbols of an ecological balance that was achieved by Chiloé's earlier peoples.

Camahueto statue in Caulín, Chiloé Island.

Seducer of virgins

As you walk through the forests of Chiloé, keep an eye out for the *Trauco*. No taller than a meter, this deformed, man-like creature may make his home in the fork of a tree or a small cave. He wears clothes made of vegetable fibers and always carries a staff which he knocks on the ground and against trees. His legs end in stumps, and just one look from him can kill the beholder or leave him or her mute or stupid, or with a twisted neck or a hump.

Yet, in spite of his limited physical charms, the *Trauco* enjoys considerable success with young women, whom he seduces with the hypnotic effect of his blazing eyes. To defend yourself from the *Trauco*, throw a handful of sand at him. While he's busy counting the grains, make your escape.

Another creature, the blond and beautiful *Pincoya*, slips out of the surf at sunrise and dances on the shore. When her face is turned toward the ocean, it means that abundant shellfish will soon cover the beach. If she looks inland, this means she has taken the fish elsewhere, to where there is more need for them. If you fish or extract shellfish too long from one site, she gets angry and abandons it, leaving the place barren. Legend has it that the *Pincoya* will sometimes rescue drowning sailors and leave them on the beach.

It is difficult to imagine any seagoing culture without its ghost ship, and Chiloé is no exception. The *Caleuche*, with its unlikely cargo of tragic guests caught in an eternal party, sends haunting strains of accordion music across the waves and recovers the bodies of those who have died at sea. Its crew are *brujos*, Chilote wizards with enormous powers, and it travels in a constant cloud produced by the boat itself, always at night. If caught looking at the *Caleuche*, your mouth will suddenly become twisted, your head crooked, or you'll suddenly die.

A magical city

No traveler ever sets eyes on the lost city of the Caesars, even when walking through it. A thick mist always hides it from sight, and the rivers carry approaching boats away. The lost city, with its gold- and silver-paved streets and its ability to make all who go there lose their memory, will appear only once, at the end of the world, to prove its existence to non-believers.

The city, with its enormous riches and infinite pleasures, where no one is born or dies, inspired centuries of expeditions by explorers, beginning in 1528. That was when 14 men led by Captain Francisco César, member of an advance group in

Sebastian Cabot's party, ventured into the southern jungles for two months. Upon returning, they told tales of fabulous treasures, which may have belonged to the Inca Empire. The next expedition to search for the lost city started out from Castro on October 6, 1620, led by Juan Tao. This and following trips were led primarily by the Spanish and their descendants, and included the Jesuit priests José García, Juan Vicuña, and Juan Francisco Menéndez. Both the Spanish Council of the Indies and the Real Audiencia (Royal Audience) in Santiago officially authorized the search for the mystery city.

The brotherhood of warlocks

The *brujería* is a secret brotherhood of male witches organized into an underground network of councils, which meets in cleverly disguised caves, the biggest of which is in Quicaví. The members arrive disguised as birds or wearing the luminous *macuñ*, which gives them the power of flight. The *macuñ* is made of skin taken from the breast of a virgin's corpse and its light is fueled by oil taken from the bodies of dead Christians.

The apprenticeship to become a *brujo* begins at an early age, and consists of a series of increasingly cruel trials. One of the more bearable is a shower in a mountain waterfall, a ritual that is repeated for 40 nights, to cleanse away all trace of baptism. To prove that he is not weakened by sentiment, the apprentice must murder his best friend. Finally, he should dig up the corpse of a recently buried virgin and remove the skin from the breast.

Other trials include races, leaps from cliffs at night, corporal metamorphosis into animals or birds, wearing a lizard bound to the forehead (to transmit wisdom), and spending nights sleeping on a tomb in the cemetery. *Brujos* have the power to make people sleepy, to open doors, to cause illness, hair loss, or deep cuts, and to throw *llancazos* (similar to the evil eye), or to conjure up bad spells cast at a distance.

Guarding the brujos

The *invunche* guards the *brujos'* cave and is the product of a long and painful process: to obtain an *invunche* the wizards steal a first-born son from his parents, within the first nine days after his birth. If he has been baptized they use black magic to annul it; then they break and twist his right leg, until it rides up the back. At three months old they split his tongue and rub his skin daily with a special infusion. In the early months the *invunche* lives on milk from a black cat and later on human flesh obtained from cemeteries.

The origins of this macabre myth may be based in historical fact: the writer Narciso García Barría, considered an authority on Chiloé, relates the *invunche*'s deformities to the Inca culture. They often preferred men with some physical disability to be the guards of their temples.

Women's participation in the *brujería* is usually as a *voladora* (flying woman), for whom many of the secret practices of the brotherhood are forbidden knowledge. The *voladora* often transforms herself into a bird and serves as a messenger for the *brujos*.

The *camahueto* is a huge one- or two-horned cow-like creature that is born from the earth with such force that it leaves a small crater behind it. This creature's horns are essential to the magic of the *machi*, the *brujos'* herb doctor, who uses them to make powders which are believed to impart tremendous strength to anyone who takes them.

According to Narciso García Barría, the origins of the *brujos* may lie in an underground organization of native resistance to the Spaniards, a thesis which is supported by native Chilotes' eager participation in the attacks led by the corsairs.

In Chiloé, as in other cultures with communities of witches, the *brujería* is also the major source of a wealth of information on native herbs and medicines which are still commonly used on the island.

Mapuche witch doctor.

Farmers on horseback.

AISÉN

The gateway to Chile's far south, this beautiful Patagonian region of lakes, forests, and glaciers, still has a certain wilderness quality, despite the construction of the Carretera Austral road.

Aisén is the hispanicized version, local folklore has it, of an English name for the area: "ice end" – the region of glaciers. English, Germans, Swedes, Spaniards, Argentines, and Chileans all did their bit to explore and sparsely colonize this spectacularly beautiful and particularly inhospitable region of fjords, glaciers and, in parts, dense forest. The early settlers at the beginning of the 20th century cleared the land they needed by burning down the woods, and several times the fires got out of control and ravaged great areas. Now, the gray, petrified remains of huge trees stick up into the sky – from the air, it looks as if a giant box of matches has been scattered over the ground.

Inhospitable frontier

The first inhabitants were the Tehuelches and the Alacalufes. The Tehuelches were nomads who lived by hunting guanacos, *ñandúes* (rheas), pumas, and *huemules* (South Andean deer), and the Alacalufes navigated the coastal channels in their light canoes. The Spanish invaders sent down a couple of expeditions in the mid-1550s to explore, to make sure that English marauders were not establishing a presence there, and – incidentally – to convert the natives to Christianity; no one bothered to try to find out how many of them there

were. The Spanish were more interested, in fact, in the legendary "city of the Caesars", said to be hidden in the forests, with fabulous treasures of gold and jewels.

The southern coastline was not properly mapped until 1831, when Charles Darwin and Captain Robert Fitzroy navigated the area in their famous voyage on the *Beagle,* and the region's interior remained unknown for most of the 19th century.

The Chilean government only began to pay attention to Aisén when

Main Attractions

Carretera Austral
Futaleufú River
Parque Pumalín
Parque Nacional San Rafael
Chile Chico
Baker River
Caleta Tortel

Puerto Aisén.

border disputes began to arise with Argentina in the late 19th century. The first attempts to settle these lands were unsuccessful. Between 1859 and 1896 four colonies were founded, two of them at Melinka and Río Álvarez, as simple trading posts for collecting and distributing seal and otter skins, and cypress wood from the area.

At the beginning of the 20th century, the first settlers made their way across the frontier at Balmaceda from Argentina. By 1907 there were thought to be 197 permanent colonizers, with their families, plus another 500-odd employees of the English-owned sheep-farming companies which had begun to exploit the region. The pioneers were naturally a hardy bunch. One government official in the 1920s tried to describe their indomitable spirit: "No incompetent or coward or milksop gives up his home and his fatherland to settle lands uncultivated before in Patagonia, isolated in these solitudes, far from the principles of all authority and justice, suffering hunger often and battling constantly against nature."

Hospitality, he noted, was one of the most developed virtues of the people of the region. "Dismount, unsaddle," the most common greeting to the stranger, was understood as an invitation to eat and stay the night. The guest's best way to repay such hospitality was "to present the most complete account possible of all events, human and divine, in the rest of the world," since other means of receiving news were non-existent.

Carretera Austral

Today, the population of Aisén is just over 90,000, but many aspects of life there have not changed very dramatically from the way they were 50 years ago. The kinds of facilities that urban-dwellers take for granted – doctors, clinics, schools – are still scarce in the remoter parts of this isolated region. In recent years, salmon farming has increased in importance, providing a new source of jobs. Power companies are also eyeing the hydroelectric potential of the region's rivers and, in 2011, the controversial five-dam HidroAysén project on the Baker and Pascua rivers near the town of Cochrane received its environmental go-ahead but had yet to obtain authorization to build its even more controversial power line to Puerto Montt. After numerous legal tussles, the project was suspended in 2014.

Overland access to the area is via the **Carretera Austral Longitudinal** (to give it its official title). This is a mostly unpaved road, which runs the length of the region from Puerto Montt to Cochrane, (880km/547 miles) and on to Villa O'Higgins.

Roads already existed from Puyuhuapi to Chaitén, between Puerto Aisén, Coyhaique, and Balmaceda, and to Puerto Ibáñez, Chile Chico, and Cochrane. But the Carretera, which began to be built in 1976, has for the first time linked the whole region with a single north–south route to which a network of east–west roads has been added. At various points the "road" becomes a ferry from one side of a river to the other.

For the inhabitants of Aisén, the road has meant a real link-up with the rest of the country and has also become a major tourist attraction, opening up some of the most beautiful scenery on earth. The Chilean tourist office, Sernatur, distributes brochures with a description of the route, and the main stops along the way. It also has a map giving details of facilities such as lodgings, telephones, and first-aid and police posts. Information and organization are important – this is not really a suitable area to wander through without your own means of transportation or a tour, unless you have all the time in the world.

Coyhaique

The most central point for exploring Aisén is the region's largest town and capital, **Coyhaique ❶**. It has a population of just over 53,000, and, while pleasant enough, travelers generally use it merely as a jumping-off point for trips to remoter parts. Coyhaique

TIP

Punctures are a frequent occurrence on the stony Carretera Austral, so it's wise to carry more than one spare wheel.

Boats moored in Puerto Cisnes.

FACT

A 1937 colonization law, which allowed only cleared land to be claimed, was responsible for many of Aisén's forest fires.

can be reached by plane from Santiago or Puerto Montt, or by following the Carretera Austral south, but there are sections of the road which have no bus services. Another popular route is by ferry from Puerto Montt to Puerto Chacabuco and then on by bus.

Once in Coyhaique, take a stroll along Calle Prat. That's where most of the travel agents are found. You can book a tour here, or go by public transportation to most parts of the south. A new **Museo Regional de la Patagonia** (currently under construction), with a fine collection of photographs depicting the region's history, is scheduled to open in 2017.

Fish – mainly rainbow trout – are plentiful in all of Aisén's rivers and lakes. Boats for lake expeditions can be organized from Coyhaique, either for the day or for a few days' stay in one of the area's fishing lodges. Skiing is available, too, in winter, at **El Fraile**, 30km (19 miles) southeast of Coyhaique, and 1,000 meters (3,281ft) above sea level.

Also near Coyhaique are the **Reserva Nacional Coyhaique**, with

a 9km (5.5-mile) circuit that can be covered by car, and the **Reserva Nacional Río Simpson**, with the lovely Cascada de la Virgen waterfall just a 1km (0.5-mile) walk from the information center.

Traveling north from Coyhaique, the road runs through bright green woods of *mañío* and *coigüe*. A side road takes you to **Puerto Cisnes ❷**, a remarkably well-established little settlement whose mayoress for years was a formidable Italian lady who ruled the place with a very firm hand. She was a friend and admirer, initially of General Carlos Ibáñez del Campo, and then of General Pinochet (whose horoscope she used to tell). With the ear of both presidents she managed to get facilities in her village that many locals grumble would be better located farther up the main road, at Puyuhuapi.

On the main road just past the junction with Puerto Cisnes on the way to Puyuhuapi is Piedra El Gato, a massive boulder which had to be partly blasted away to build the road. Continuing north to Puyuhuapi, the road

Termas de Puyuhuapi.

passes **Parque Nacional Queulat**, one of the supposed locations for the legendary city of the Caesars. Fishing, camping, and hiking are possible amid lakes and glaciers.

Puyuhuapi to Chaitén

Puyuhuapi ❸ is located near Lago Risopatrón and has thermal springs, a luxury hotel, a garage, and a carpet factory, which turns out sturdy hand-made woolen rugs. The settlement was started by four Sudeten Germans who emigrated from Czechoslovakia at the time of the Nazi invasion, and made their way to this remote spot on the other side of the world, which they are said to have read about in a Baedeker guide.

From **La Junta** ❹, the junction of the Palena and Rosselot rivers, it is possible for experienced sailors to navigate the Palena River to the wide beaches at its estuary, at **Puerto Raul Marín Balmaceda** ❺, a six-hour journey. Beyond La Junta the road leads to Chaitén, 150km (93 miles) to the north. There are some interesting sights along the way, such as the magnificent Cavi hanging glacier, which requires a short detour and a hike.

From Villa Santa Lucía, a road off to the east leads to Lago Yelcho and the estuary of the Futaleufú River, famous for its white-water rafting. Further along the road that follows this river is the village of **Futaleufú** ❻, almost on the border with Argentina, and the **Reserva Nacional Futaleufú**. With basic camping facilities by the river, this reserve is one of the main areas for the protection of the *huemul* (*Andean deer*).

From Lago Yelcho, another road south leads to the village of **Palena** ❼. On the way is El Malito, the starting point of the **Andes Patagónicos Río Palena Heritage Route**, a circular 54km (34-mile) trail, suitable for horseback riding or walking, that passes through ancient forests, along rivers and around fish-rich lakes.

Chaitén and around

Chaitén ❽ was largely destroyed in May 2008 when the nearby Volcán Chaitén erupted after lying dormant for over 9,000 years. All the town's 4,000 inhabitants were successfully evacuated but the town was buried in ash and houses were carried away on the vast mudslide that followed. There were plans to to rebuild the town at a safer location, farther north along the coast, but the inhabitants preferred the original location where they have slowly rebuilt it.

Located just north of Chaitén is **Parque Pumalín**, one of the world's largest private parks. It was established in 2005 by Douglas Tompkins, the North American conservation businessman who founded the Esprit clothing chain, in a bid to protect Chile's indigenous forest. Restaurant and camping facilities are available at Caleta Gonzalo.

Some 25km (16 miles) south of Chaitén, via the village of Amarillo, are the **Termas El Amarillo** ❾ thermal springs, where you can take a warm dip.

Aisén is a popular destination for fly fishing enthusiasts.

North from Chaitén, the road continues via two ferry crossings to **Hornopirén** . This is the northern starting point of the Carretera Austral and 6km (3.7 miles) to the northeast, is the access (on foot only) to the **Parque Nacional Hornopirén**. At the heart of the Park is Lake General Pinto Concha, surrounded by ancient *alerce* trees. The National Forestry Service (CONAF) has a station in the park and basic camping facilities are available.

Parque Nacional Laguna San Rafael

Aisén's most popular attraction is without doubt **Parque Nacional Laguna San Rafael** ⓫, with its magnificent glacier. The sight provoked awe and gloom in Charles Darwin when he visited it in 1831. He described the place as "sad solitudes, where death more than life seems to rule supreme." He must have seen the glacier on one of the many days of low cloud. When the sun is shining, it is an awesome spectacle, with light glinting off the aquamarine ice

San Rafael glacier.

and the landscape alive with black-necked swans and distinctive furry beavers. Passengers are taken by rowboat or motor launch to the very base of the glacier where it meets the sea. Icebergs float by so close you can reach out with your hand and touch them. The climax of any visit is to have a whisky on the rocks, using pieces of ice chipped straight from the glacier.

The glacier can also be visited without going via Coyhaique. Several of the ferry companies in Puerto Montt run services to Chacabuco which detour via Laguna San Rafael. For those who wish to travel in comfort, cruisers such as the *Skorpios* also operate five-day trips from Puerto Montt.

Traveling south

The route south from Coyhaique to Cochrane can be done in a day through hilly country, and then past the beautiful Lago General Carrera. At **Villa Cerro Castillo** ⓬, near Puerto Ibáñez, 100km (60 miles) from Coyhaique, are two famous Stone Age paintings, of which there are several in the area. Off to the west is the **Reserva Nacional Cerro Castillo**, a largely undiscovered area of glistening glaciers, lakes and native woodland considered to rival the beauty of Torres del Paine. A detour goes to **Bahía Murta** ⓭, and from there a horse or boat ride, takes you to **Puerto Sánchez**, a former mining village of some 100 people, where you can see the wave-sculpted "chapel of marble" and the underground caves of the Panichine Islands.

A ferry to the other side of the lake takes you to **Chile Chico** ⓮, one of the region's earliest settlements. The area here enjoys a dry, warm microclimate, which gives the people who live here the opportunity to cultivate a much wider range of fruit and vegetables than in the rest of the region. The place has a quiet, rustic charm that can be quite beguiling. Many travelers who had planned to pass straight through to Argentina find themselves staying for several days in Chile Chico, enjoying the sunshine and taking the occasional dip in the icy waters of the lake.

A six-day boat ride down the **Baker River**, from **Puerto Bertrand** ⓯ to **Caleta Tortel** ⓰, offers thrills and spills. With a population of only a few hundred, Caleta Tortel, on the delta of the Baker River, is a unique town. The houses are built on stilts and, instead of roads, are connected only by wooden walkways made from the local cypress wood.

The River Cisnes is another favorite trip. All of these excursions can be organized from Coyhaique. From Puerto Bertrand, it is a short drive to the entrance of the **Parque Nacional Patagonia**, being developed by Conservación Patagónica (www.conservacionpatagonica.org), a land trust chaired by Kristine Tompkins, wife of the late environmentalist Douglas Tompkins. The Park, which will stretch from Lake General Carrera in the north to Lake Cochrane in the south, and from the Argentine border on the east to the Baker River on the west, is designed to fill a strategic gap between the existing government-protected Jeinimeni and Tamango National Reserves.

CRUISING CHILE'S SOUTHERN SEAS

Beyond the Lake District, Chile breaks up into a mass of islands. Boats can take you to the most beautiful, unspoiled parts that roads cannot reach.

Boats reign supreme in southern Chile's inhospitable but stunningly beautiful fjord region. They are the life-support system of the area's isolated fishing villages during the harsh winters, and in summer they ply a bustling tourist trade. The main attraction is the majestic San Rafael glacier, two days by boat out of Puerto Montt. This spectacular ice wall is the destination of the luxury Skorpios cruise boats, as well as several more modest services.

Another popular trip takes passengers from Puerto Montt down to Puerto Natales, gateway to the beautiful Parque Nacional Torres del Paine. Tourist cabins are modest, but the views and the atmosphere on board more than compensate. Puerto Montt is the starting point for any journey into the fjords, including Chiloé Archipelago. But if you suffer from seasickness, beware. The narrow inland waterways are glassily calm, but the Gulf of Corcovado or, farther south, the Gulf of Penas, can test even the best sailor.

Several services run from Punta Arenas to the southern tip of Tierra del Fuego. One of the best – and most expensive – is the luxurious three- or four-day *Australis* cruise (www.australis.com) between Punta Arenas and Ushuaia.

There are also many enjoyable boat trips in the Lake District. One of the best starts from Petrohué on Lago Todos los Santos and ends 12 stunning hours later in San Carlos de Bariloche in Argentina. (See page 300, for details of tour operators.)

The blue icebergs that glisten in the fjords of Chilean Patagonia are a beautiful sight, but also a reminder of the shrinking of its glaciers.

Visitors disembark from a dinghy in the De Agostini Sound, named after Alberto María De Agostini, an Italian missionary and explorer.

Each spring, several thousand Magellanic penguins return to their breeding grounds on the Otway Sound.

Sightings of sea mammals, such as seals and sea lions, are a highlight of a cruise through the Chilean fjords.

WILDLIFE OF THE FJORDS

Sea mammals such as seals and sea lions are a common sight in southern Chile's remote fjords. In the most remote areas, you may also be lucky enough to see a blue whale – which migrates to the fjords in summer in search of krill – or an orca, often referred to as killer whale but actually a member of the dolphin family.

A sure companion for any boat trip south of Puerto Montt is the *tonina*, or Chilean dolphin. These fast-moving, playful animals usually swim in small groups and delight in chasing a boat, darting from side to side.

Closer to the shore, there are also plenty of Magellanic penguins and, occasionally, a gentoo penguin with its characteristic orange-red bill. In summer, black-necked swans, South America's largest waterfowl, also grace the area's fjords and bays. The steep sides of the fjords are covered with many native trees, including a type of cypress, and ferns – some of them almost tree-size. The dense vegetation is also home to an enormous variety of birds, including a colorful red-headed woodpecker and a tiny hummingbird.

A Skorpios cruise ship stops at a waterfall in the Quitralco Fjord, Aisén, on its way to the famous San Rafael Glacier.

A trip on the Laguna San Rafael provides an unmissable opportunity to see the 30,000-year-old glacier and experience the surreal atmosphere of the laguna.

Pelicans are the constant companions of Chile's fishermen, picking up any scraps they leave behind.

MAGALLANES

A harsh, inhospitable territory in Chilean
Patagonia, formed by bleak plains, fierce winds,
and wilderness areas of extraordinary beauty
crowned by the rocky peaks of Torres del Paine.

Santiago

Stretching toward the windswept southern tip of South America, the province of Magallanes exists quite apart from the rest of Chile. The hardy people who live here consider themselves first as Magallánicos, second as Chileans – hardly surprising, considering that they cannot reach Santiago by road without crossing the border into neighboring Argentina. In order to come and go from this stormy corner of the world, you have either to travel for days by bus across the endless stretches of Argentine Patagonia, to fly direct, or to take a lengthy, rocky cruise through the icy southern seas.

The terrain of Magallanes is formidably harsh. The region is split between impenetrable mountain ranges and bleak Patagonian plains. Yet these harsh physical conditions have helped form a distinct local character. "The sheer difficulty of living here brings people together," wrote Francisco Coloane, the most famous chronicler of Magellanic life. "It creates a human solidarity and sense of honor that people from the rest of Chile don't always share."

Growing in isolation

History has conspired with the tyranny of distance to keep Magallanes apart from centralized rule in Chile. The region was first developed by foreign sheep companies – mostly

British-owned – which had interests on both the Argentine and Chilean sides of the border. Magallanes soon had more in common with Argentine Patagonia than the distant world of Santiago. English was spoken more often than Spanish – followed by a chorus of Croat, Russian, and Italian, as workers arrived from all parts of the globe.

This cosmopolitan tradition can still be felt in the towns and old *estancias* (farm estates) of Magallanes, where the surnames are as

Main Attractions

Palacio Braun-Menéndez
Cementerio Municipal
Pingüineros
Puerto Natales
Cueva del Milodón
Parque Nacional Torres del
Paine
Grey Glacier

Tree bent by the Patagonian wind.

likely to be MacMillan or Covacevic as anything of Spanish origin. The isolation of the south also developed its own political traditions: like the remote mining towns of the north, Magallanes has a long history of left-wing activism. Some of the bitterest strikes in Chilean history occurred in the province, and it was from Magallanes that the socialist leader Salvador Allende was first elected to Congress. Regional independence still marks its politics today, fed by a resentful belief that central government ignores the far south.

What today lures most travelers to this far end of the globe is the province's unspoiled wilderness. Much of Magallanes is made up of a jigsaw of tiny islands and channels without any permanent habitation or regular passenger services. These are the tips of underwater mountains – the continuation of the Andes range that has sunk into the icy sea – and they can only be glimpsed on rare boat journeys or from the air. Down toward the battered coastline of the Strait of Magellan are colonies of penguins, crystal lakes, trees gnarled by the ever-present Patagonian wind, and some of the most spectacular mountain scenery anywhere in South America.

European exploration and occupation

Magallanes takes its name from the Portuguese explorer Ferdinand Magellan who, while working for the Spanish Crown, became the first European to set eyes upon its shores in 1520. A gale blew his fragile sailing ships through what is now the Strait of Magellan toward the ocean he baptized the Pacific. On the way, a landing party stopped off near modern-day Punta Arenas, to find a beached whale and 200 corpses raised on stilts. Shuddering at the gruesome sight, the navigator hurried toward the west.

Further Spanish contact with the area was hardly more encouraging. A group of 300 conquistadors under Pedro de Gamboa tried to set up a settlement on the straits, but the savage winter drove them all to starvation. A lone survivor who had lived among the local people was found three years

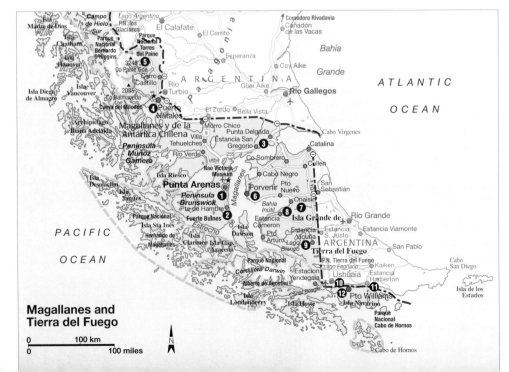

Magallanes and Tierra del Fuego

later by the English pirate Thomas Cavendish. For the next 250 years the region was visited by explorers, cartographers, and naturalists, but few saw any reason to linger. Only in the 1830s did the Chilean government, spurred on by a wave of optimism and economic expansion, cast possessive glances toward the remote south. Prompting action was the occupation of the Falkland Islands by Britain in 1833 and the lengthy explorations made in the region by the British naturalist Charles Darwin on the *Beagle*.

In 1843, President Manuel Bulnes claimed the land around the Strait of Magellan, Tierra del Fuego, and southern Patagonia. A boatload of 21 motley soldiers was sent to found Fuerte Bulnes on the straits, but the location proved so inhospitable that the outpost was abandoned; Punta Arenas was founded in its place five years later. This new settlement grew slowly into a town, with raids by native peoples and a bloody mutiny punctuating its early days. But Chile was forced to abandon its claim to much of Patagonia: Argentina took advantage of Chile's preoccupation with Peru and the north to take the lion's share of the south, leaving Magallanes with the border it has today.

Punta Arenas

Today **Punta Arenas** ❶ is a city of some 123,000 people, the hub of Magallanes and the first port of call for most foreign travelers. Facing out across the straits, it has an almost Dickensian flavor, full of rusting corrugated iron buildings and grandiose mansions from the late 19th century. The class divisions of old are still echoed in the streets: here you can find elegant, if run-down, parlors where apéritifs are sipped with an aristocratic flourish. Sitting adjacent are seedy bars full of sailors, naval recruits, and a ubiquitous collection of weary old men – usually wearing woolen caps and tightly buttoned overcoats, huddled over their glasses

of pisco and whisky, taking refuge from the biting wind.

Weather dominates the city's mood. Despite its latitude, Punta Arenas never experiences the extremes of cold found in equally remote places in the Northern Hemisphere. Nevertheless, the skies bring few comforts. Even in summer, when the sun shines for up to 20 hours a day and temperatures are moderate, the wind and rain can often make Punta Arenas seem a gloomy frontier town. But when the sun breaks through the billowing clouds, its cool air is bracing and a stroll through the quiet streets can be pleasant as well as fascinating.

Memories of a golden age

Scattered around Punta Arenas are opulent monuments to a golden age when it was one of the busiest ports on earth. Its history is in many ways that of the whole far south. A series of unexpected events in the mid-19th century helped lift the town out of obscurity. The industrial age in Europe and North America was creating a boom in sea trade. The Panama

FACT

Alcohol, introduced by whale-hunters during the 19th century, contributed to the disappearance of native communities in Magallanes.

Punta Arenas.

FACT

The hard water of Punta
Arenas produces some
of Chile's best beer.

Canal had not yet been thought of.
Sea clippers and the new steam-
ships making their journeys around
the world – carrying anything from
European machinery to Texan petroleum and Australian wheat – all had
to stop at Punta Arenas, the town at
the end of the world.

The boom soon made Punta Arenas the logical center for Patagonian
sheep farming. In 1877, an English
trader brought a flock of stock from
the Falkland Islands to Elizabeth
Island in the Magellan Straits. The
experiment was a success, and soon
other entrepreneurs were following
suit. A Machiavellian Spaniard named
José Menéndez and the Russian-born
immigrant Mauricio Braun became
leading figures: starting off as rivals,
they were soon linked by marriage to
form a Patagonian dynasty that would
dominate the south for decades.

Farm administrators were brought in
from Scotland, England, Australia, and
New Zealand, making Magallanes, as
writer Bruce Chatwin noted in his classic *In Patagonia*, look like an outpost of
the British Empire. But the *peones*, farm

*Monument to Fernando
de Magallanes, Punta
Arenas.*

hands who worked the land in generally dismal conditions, almost all came
from Chile's own Chiloé.

Punta Arenas's golden age ended
abruptly when the Panama Canal was
opened and boats no longer needed to
travel round Cabo de Hornos (Cape
Horn). Magallanes continued to be a
profitable sheep region until toward
the Great Depression, when a long
decline began. Competition from
Australia, New Zealand, and Canada
squeezed Chile and Argentina from
the major world markets. Many of
the English managers left for their
homeland as land reform carved up
the largest estancias of the south. Even
Don José Menéndez decided to move
to Buenos Aires. This downward economic spiral was only halted with the
discovery of petroleum and natural
gas in 1945. Oil companies stepped up
exploration in the straits over the following decades, and Magallanes again
prospered. Workers looking for high
wages flocked from the north, while
fishing also boomed, and Punta Arenas became a duty-free port. During
this period, Magallanes achieved one

of the highest per capita incomes in Chile, before starting to stagnate again as the oil wells dried up.

Around Plaza Muñoz Gamero

The modern center of Punta Arenas is, as it always has been, the **Plaza Muñoz Gamero Ⓐ**. Surrounded by trees and neat gardens, the plaza is dominated by a bronze statue of Magellan, looking proudly over the heroic figures of various local Mapuches, who were idealized by a sculptor after they had been largely wiped out by marauding European settlers, keen to ensure that no native would interfere with the profitable grazing of sheep. These days children pose for photographs while touching the feet of one of the Mapuche figures for luck.

Flanking the plaza are three box-like buildings – the **Hotel Cabo de Hornos** (www.hotelcabodehornos.com), the **cathedral Ⓑ**, and the grandiose **Palacio Braun-Menéndez Ⓒ**, located opposite the Cabo de Hornos on Calle H. de Magallanes.

Built by the Patagonian pioneer, Don Mauricio Braun, in 1905, it is rightly referred to by locals as "*El Palacio*" (The Palace). The mansion was designed by a French architect to outstrip the finest houses of Santiago. Marble was imported from Italy, wood from Belgium, wallpaper from France, and furniture from England.

Upon entering the mansion, visitors pass through the airy hall with classical frescos painted on its ceiling. Everything in the adjoining rooms is done on a grand scale: the main bedroom contains a massive Louis XV four-poster bed, while the games room has a gigantic billiard table and furniture in Art Nouveau style. The salon – the most important room in the house – is crowded with gilded tables and chairs under a glittering crystal chandelier and stern portraits of long-dead family members. The walls of the dining room are covered with pressed Italian leather, while

the *escritorio* (office) still contains the mahogany desk from which the fate of the south was directed.

The rest of the house's ground floor has been converted into the **Museo Regional de Magallanes** (Oct–Apr Wed–Mon 10.30am–5pm; May–Sept Wed–Mon 10.30am–2pm; free), with exhibits from the time of the foundation of Punta Arenas to the 1920s. The mansion was shared by the Brauns and Menéndezes after constant intermarriage linked the clans. But as land reform took its toll on their estancias and profits, the families handed over the building to the government. It became a national monument in 1974.

The old port

Some of the oldest streets in Punta Arenas stretch down from Calle H. de Magallanes to the straits. A walk along Calle Roca takes you to the old port area, with its range of seedy flophouses, cafés, and bars. Many of the old houses made of tin and corrugated iron seem to be on the point of collapse, but these vestiges of the

TIP

A raft from Río Verde, just north of Punta Arenas, takes vehicles and pedestrians over to Isla Riesco.

Punta Arenas at night.

FACT

The *centolla*, a bright orange king crab, is one of the great delicacies of the south; they look huge and vicious but are actually rather timid creatures.

late 19th century give a glimpse of the bustling days of the past.

Museo Regional Salesiano

Another walk out along Calle Bories leads to the fascinating **Museo Regional Salesiano** (www.salesianos.cl; Tue–Sun 10am–12.30pm, 3–5.30pm), one of the most unusual museums in South America. The Salesians are a religious order that once tried to "save" the native peoples of the region by creating missionary refuges, only to find that European illnesses like influenza killed them as surely as the white settlers' bullets. The museum's disordered exhibits provide a fascinating insight into the lives of several groups of people whose way of life and very existence has been largely destroyed.

A room full of pre-Hispanic artifacts gives a good introduction to the four tribal groups that once lived in Magallanes. Inhabiting the barren plains east of the Andes were the fierce Tehuelches (or Aónikenk) peoples. Their impressive stature and enormous moccasins are traditionally believed to have inspired Ferdinand

Fishing boats in dock.

Magellan to exclaim "Ha! Patagón!" (big foot), giving Patagonia its name.

The travel writer Bruce Chatwin has offered a more plausible explanation, suggesting that the name came from an early 16th-century romantic story where a monster called the Grand Patagon appears. Magellan was likely to have been familiar with the tale, where the man-like creature roars like a bull, just as Magellan noted that the Tehuelches did.

Canoeing around the rough islands of the southeastern Pacific were the maritime nomad tribe the Alacalufes (Kawéskar), who hunted sea lions and dived for shellfish. Today the last survivors of this race live in the remote fishing village of Puerto Edén. The Onas (Selk'nam) hunted guanacos on the northern plains of Tierra del Fuego, while the Yaghanes (Yamanas) navigated the icy forested islands south of the Beagle Channel. The Onas were wiped out in the early 20th century, and only a handful of mixed-blood Yaghanes are still alive.

Keep an eye out in the museum for a piece of skin and some 10,000-year-old droppings from the giant ground sloth found in the Cueva del Milodón (Milodón Cave) near Puerto Natales (see page 254).

The **Nao Victoria Museum** (http://naovictoria.cl) just off Ruta 9, 7.5km north of Punta Arenas, houses full-size replicas of historical vessels associated with the region and explorers such as Magellan, Darwin, and Shackleton. It took the owner 11 years to reconstruct the Nao *Victoria* on which Magellan circumnavigated the world.

Cementerio Municipal

Farther out along Calle Bories is the **Cementerio Municipal** (daily 7.30–8pm), comparable in splendor only to the famous Recoleta necropolis in Buenos Aires. Settlers from every part of the world are buried here, as well as the victims of the many shipwrecks that occurred on this savage coast. Just off the opposite side of the road, a small shop sells Punta Arenas artisan chocolate. It's tucked away in a side street, but the friendly local people will be happy to point you in the right direction.

Penguin colonies

An hour's drive from Punta Arenas are the famous *pingüineros* (penguin colonies) on the Otway Sound. Hundreds of these comical-looking creatures live in burrows dug into the sandy shoreline. It is possible that this was where the Italian Antonio Pigafetta, a member of Magellan's crew in 1520, recorded the first European sighting of the penguin.

The species seen here is the *Spheniscus magellanicus*, named for the straits on which it lives rather than the explorer himself. It is known as the jackass penguin on account of the odd braying sound it makes. Try to visit the *pingüineros* in a small group, since large numbers of people send the penguins scurrying away on their flippers, which they use as front legs to run on all fours. The penguins spend most of April to August at sea, heading north

to warmer climates before returning from September through March to their breeding grounds here.

Some 54km (34 miles) south of Punta Arenas along the inky Strait of Magellan is the reconstructed **Fuerte Bulnes** ❷ fortress on the site of the original 1843 settlement. The highway passes the skeleton of the wrecked ship *Lonsdale* on the outskirts of town, and some classic Patagonian scenery, but the fort itself has a disappointing Disneyland look. On the way back most tours stop at **Punta Hambre**, where the unfortunate Pedro de Gamboa tried to set up his settlement 300 years ago (see page 248).

Estancia San Gregorio

Along the highway 120km (74 miles) north of Punta Arenas is the first sheep farm of the south, **Estancia San Gregorio** ❸, a National Historic Monument. Built in 1878, it was taken over by José Menéndez four years later and extended to 90,000 hectares (222,400 acres).

San Gregorio (www.sangregorio.cl) remains the classic example of the

TIP

The road north from Puerto Natales crosses the border into Argentina to the popular El Calafate tourist center on Lago Argentino.

Magellanic penguins.

many estancias that, in the 19th century, were like small, self-contained towns. The company's own launch, the *Amadeo*, lies rusting by the shore at the estancia's entrance, where the captain decided to leave it after 50 years of service. Two railroad lines ran to the estancia. In the grounds are large wooden shearing sheds, still with old faded stock awards hanging there.

After decades of grinding oppression, the *peones* became drunk on freedom. In scenes reminiscent of the French Revolution, they camped out in the mansion, put the bust of Don José in the outhouse and went through the family cellar. Prize sheep munched freely at the garden before finally being slaughtered for mutton soup. The estancia was returned to private hands after the brutal 1973 military coup. Farther along the road toward Argentina is **Fell's Cave** (tel: 061-207 051), where some of the oldest prehistoric human remains in the Americas have been found. It can only be visited with the help of scientists at the Instituto de la Patagonia in Punta Arenas.

The Mylodon Cave, near Puerto Natales.

Puerto Natales

Puerto Natales ❹, 242km (150 miles) northwest of Punta Arenas, is set prettily on the shores of the Ultima Esperanza Sound. Hotels abound, and surprisingly, in view of Puerto Natales's small size, there are plenty of places to eat, drink, and even to dance. This is the place that the inhabitants of Punta Arenas come to when they want a change of scene.

The waterfront, where black-necked swans bob on the cold waves, is a lovely place to walk, while the climb up the **Cerro Dorotea** hill gives fine views of the whole Ultima Esperanza area. Just outside town there is an old meat-packing plant bought by the British after World War I, now a luxury hotel (Singular Patagonia). In its heyday, thousands of sheep were slaughtered here weekly for the dinner tables of Europe, and many of the steam-driven engines used then are still lying about. One sits in the main plaza.

The meatworks ensured that Puerto Natales would be a leftist town. A riot began here in 1919 when Chilote

THE GIANT SLOTH HUNT

In 1896, German-born landowner Herman Eberhard found a strange 1.2-meter (4ft) -long stretch of hairy skin on the floor of a cave. The following year, part of the skull of a huge mammal, a claw, and a large human thighbone were found. Before long, a scientist in Argentina had announced that the skin was from a Mylodon Listai (named after himself), a giant prehistoric ground sloth endemic to the South American continent. The bones of several mylodons had been found during the 19th century, but Listai asserted that this piece of skin was so fresh, the beast had only recently died – and a living example could not be far away.

"Positive sightings" of huge hairy beasts became the norm in the region. Excitement was sufficient in Britain for the *Daily Express* newspaper to finance a scientific expedition to search for a living mylodon. Despite hearing many ghostly tales, they found no live example (although expedition leader Hesketh Prichard's book *Through the Heart of Patagonia* became an inspiration for Arthur Conan Doyle's *Lost World* tale). Meanwhile, a team of archeologists dug away in the cave, but they found little more than huge amounts of sloth dung. Radio carbon-dating has since shown that the skin is about 10,000 years old but was perfectly preserved in the dark, damp cave.

workers killed an English assistant manager, lynched three policemen, and looted the stores. But before long the government sent in the army, and 28 ringleaders were taken away, among them some Maximilianist Russians who were blamed as foreign agitators.

Puerto Natales is the gateway to some of the most spectacular sights in Magallanes. Most easily reached is the **Balmaceda Glacier** to the northwest. Boatloads of tourists leave most mornings to see this aquamarine river of ice that inches its way down from the Andes to the sea. Gigantic ice blocks crash regularly from the glacier, sending shock waves across to the boat, while powerful winds whistle through the narrow channel. Most boats pull up at a small jetty, and passengers can safely walk along paths near the side of the glacier. On the way, the jagged Torres del Paine mountain peaks can be seen on the horizon, while the channel shore is lined with waterfalls. Groups of seals and sea lions sit on rocky outcrops, while porpoises, steamer ducks, and black-necked swans can be spotted in the icy waters.

Cueva del Milodón

A quite different day trip can be made to the enormous **Cueva del Milodón** (Mylodon Cave), focus of a scientific furore nearly a century ago and a key element in Bruce Chatwin's classic travel book *In Patagonia*.

Today, the Cueva del Milodón is a popular picnic spot outside Puerto Natales. A life-size model of the mylodon, rearing back on its hind legs, has been placed at the cave mouth, but nothing else remains to suggest its past. A piece of the mylodon's skin and its dung can be seen in the Museo Regional Salesiano in Punta Arenas (see page 249). The cave is a good starting point for the 45km (28-mile) Mylodon Heritage Route leading to the southern entrance of Torres del Paine National Park. In February, it is also used as a venue for the annual Patagonia Film Festival.

From Puerto Natales, the road north continues to **Cerro Castillo** on the border with Argentina and, from there, to **El Calafate**, the gateway to Argentina's **Los Glaciares National Park**. Inexpensive bus services run regularly from Puerto Natales to El Calafate (around a five-hour trip) in summer and the main hotels offer minivan services. Rental cars are also allowed to cross the border, but, unless you plan to return to Chile, beware of a hefty drop-off charge.

Parque Nacional Torres del Paine

By far the most impressive sight in the Chilean south is **Parque Nacional Torres del Paine** ❺ (pronounced pie-nee). Lying at the far south of the Andes mountain chain, it became a nature reserve in 1959 but only reached its present size in the early 1970s (Unesco made it a Biosphere Reserve in 1978). The uninhabited park is crowded with glaciers, lakes, and gnarled Magellanic trees, and provides some of the most magnificent walking in the world. The dramatic

Puerto Natales.

Guanaco, Torres del Paine National Park.

Lake Pehoé.

mountain formations are a sight that few people will forget, while the park itself is full of animals, including guanacos, flamingos, *ñandúes* (ostrich-like creatures), and condors.

Every morning in summer and several times a week at other times of the year, vans and buses make the three-hour drive from Puerto Natales to the park along a rough dirt road. The trail winds through mountain passes before descending to the foot of the Andes, providing the first view of the **Cuernos del Paine** (Paine Horns), twisted pillars of gray granite, dusted with snow and rising from the flat Patagonian plains into a sky usually full of billowing clouds.

Like everywhere else this far south, weather in the park can be unpredictable, to say the least. The best times to visit are December to March, but even then clear skies are rare and can disappear within minutes. The famous Torres (Towers) del Paine are even more spectacular than the Cuernos, but often difficult to see because of cloud cover. The one thing that never seems to change is the gusting Patagonian wind that drives from the plains to the west.

All visitors to the park must sign on at the administration building, where the wardens (*guardaparques*) will give advice on the condition of the trails. In the past, large areas of the Park have been ravaged by fires, started accidently by visitors, and it is essential to keep to the trails, and only camp and use cooking equipment in the permitted areas.

The classic views of the park can be easily reached by road and on day-trips operating from Puerto Natales. If you want to stay in the park, advance booking is essential. There are several hotels, all of which are expensive. A luxury hotel, the **Hotel Salto Chico** (www.explora.com) is beautifully designed and set on the shore of one of the lakes. It runs some of the best guided tours around the park but is very pricey.

Roaming in the wilderness

Several day trips, as well as more ambitious walks, can be made from these bases. The park has more than 250km

(155 miles) of walking tracks, including the classic seven-day circuit and the four-day "W" route. Along the way are *refugios* or shelters, often-primitive wood-and-corrugated-iron edifices that barely keep out the wind and rain; good sleeping bags, and cooking gear, are essential. If you plan to do the seven-day circuit or the "W" route, you should bring a tent as well, since the *refugios* can get full.

This hike starts at the administration building at the southern end of **Lago Pehoé** and gives ever-changing views of the Cuernos. The walking can be strenuous – the longest stretch in one day is 30km (19 miles). Many people make two- or three-day walks rather than the full circuit. A good compromise is to walk to the first *refugio* next to Lago Grey, camp overnight, take a day-trip to **Grey Glacier** and then walk back to the administration center the next day.

Those who make the effort are rewarded with superb views of snow-covered peaks, turquoise lakes, and lush valleys. The walking trails are lined with flowers, sometimes crossing wide pasture and at other times hugging mountainsides or passing through verdant forests. The Grey and Dickson glaciers, when discovered in the wild, are somehow more impressive than others more easily reached.

Most routes in the park allow walkers to see plenty of animals, most commonly guanacos: unlike in other parts of South America, they appear unafraid of people and can be easily photographed from up close. Condors cruise between mountain peaks, hares and foxes dash about in the scrub, and swans and flamingos can be seen on many of the lakes.

Although the weather can turn from fair to foul and back again within minutes, the memories of this national park will last well after your clothes have dried out. Many people who go for a few days stay for a week: the liberating sensation of being in one of the most remote and untouched wilderness areas on earth is worth savoring for as long as possible.

Parque Nacional Bernardo O'Higgins

The map of Magallanes shows hundreds of scattered islands stretching to the Pacific. Very few are visited, and fewer still are inhabited. A large area of the south has been incorporated into **Parque Nacional Bernardo O'Higgins** and into forestry reserves. There is little chance of visiting these wilderness areas without hiring your own boat in Punta Arenas or Puerto Natales.

For most travelers, the way of seeing these islands is to take the pricey week-long *Skorpios* cruise from Puerto Natales or to travel on the Navimag passenger boats between Puerto Natales and Puerto Montt (see page 293, for details). This three-day journey goes through the Estrecho Smith and Estrecho Estebán. It is not particularly comfortable unless you hire a cabin, which increases the price significantly, but some travelers are captivated by the romance of a sea voyage and the chance to watch the remote islands drift by.

FACT

New oil and gas exploration under private concession contracts is giving the Magallanes economy a boost.

Hikers on a trail at the Torres del Paine National Park.

THE PICK OF THE NATIONAL PARKS

With most of the population concentrated around Santiago and Concepción, the rest of Chile has some beautiful wilderness areas to explore.

Almost one-fifth of Chile is protected to varying degrees in national parks and reserves. The national park service, CONAF, administers 36 national parks, 49 national reserves, two marine parks and 16 natural monuments. The first national park in Chile, Vicente Pérez Rosales (see page 215), in the southern Lake District, was founded in 1926. Entrance fees contribute to maintenance and conservation work.

Chile's long, narrow geography means that its national parks are very varied. Not many people want to trek in the hot, dry desert north – the main attractions of parks like Lauca and Volcán Isluga are the wildlife and the superb scenery. These parks are best tackled in a four-wheel-drive vehicle, preferably with a driver who knows the area well. Farther south, coastal parks like the popular Pan de Azúcar give protection to sea life and are popular for camping.

Many national parks such as Nahuelbuta, Alerce Andino, and Conguillío have been created to protect Chile's native forest. Unfortunately, the popularity of Parque Nacional Conguillío, in the northern Lake District, has brought with it serious erosion.

In the far south, parks like Laguna San Rafael and Bernardo O'Higgins protect Chile's southern lakes and glaciers, while prime trekking territory is found in the magnificent Parque Nacional Torres del Paine in Magallanes.

Finally, the archeological monuments of Easter Island are protected by Parque Nacional Rapa Nui. For more information, contact CONAF's central office, at Av. Bulnes 285, Santiago; tel: 02-663 0000; www.conaf.cl.

Hiking or horse riding are the only ways to explore the Torres del Paine National Park near Puerto Natales in southern Chile's Magallenes Region.

The Petrohué river in Parque Nacional Vicente Pérez Rosales is popular with white-water rafters.

The copihue, Chile's national flower, grows on a tree ivy in the Central Valley and farther south; it is mostly red, but there is also a white variety.

The grey fox, an imported species, is a more common site in the Torres del Paine National Park than the native red fox.

THE PLEASURE OF PAINE

Parque Nacional Torres del Paine, 112km (70 miles) north of Puerto Natales in Magallanes, covers a wilderness area of 181,400 hectares (450,000 acres). Created in 1959, the park achieved World Biosphere Reserve status from Unesco in 1978, and is today one of Chile's best-known and most beautiful tourist attractions.

The park's crowning glories are the spectacular Torres (towers) and Cuernos (horns, pictured above), stark granite peaks that form part of the Paine Massif. The range continues into Argentina's Parque Nacional Los Glaciares, with the Fitzroy Range, attracting climbers from all over the world.

Parque Nacional Torres del Paine is a haven for the *ñandú* (rhea) and the guanaco, which European settlers slaughtered to near-extinction to make room for sheep but has since recovered. Used to visitors, they aren't unduly bothered by cars and it's usually possible to get quite close to take pictures. You might also see flamingos, condors and, if you're really lucky, a puma.

Most people visit in January and February but the best month is December. As well as greater solitude, it is the time when the wildflowers are in best bloom.

The ñandú or rhea is a large, flightless bird similar to an ostrich that can run surprisingly fast and, when doing, so spreads its wings to act as sails.

The active Volcán Llaima, which rumbles quite regularly, crowns the devastatingly popular Parque Nacional Conguillío in the northern Lake District.

The Pan de Azúcar National Park in northern Chile includes the island of the same name, home to Peruvian Pelicans and an important breeding place for Humboldt penguins.

POLO·NORTE
16.112 Kms.

NUEVA YORK
10.778 Kms.

TOKYO
19.556 Kms.

SANTIAGO
2.555 Kms.

RIO DE JANEIRO
3.978 Kms.

ESTOCOLMO
17.223 Kms.

BERLIN
16.112 Kms.

LONDRES
15.223 Kms.

LAUTARO
1.991 Kms.

VALPARAISO
2.744 Kms.

TIERRA DEL FUEGO

The land at the southernmost tip of South America
is the bleakest, stormiest part of the continent,
yet it exerts a constant fascination for travelers
who want to visit the last stop before Antarctica.

Main Attractions
Bahía Inútil
Onaisin
Lago Blanco
Estancia Harberton
Isla Navarino
Museo Martín Gusinde

L ashed by wind and wild seas at the southern tip of South America, Tierra del Fuego exerts a perverse fascination. Despite – or because of – its desolate image, few who travel to the far south of Chile can resist paying a visit to the literal end of the earth, the last fragment of land before the treacherous, forbidding territory of Antarctica.

The archipelago's name, which means "land of fire," came from the explorer Ferdinand Magellan, who in 1520 saw smoke rising from campfires on its shores (Magellan originally called it "land of smoke," but the Spanish King Charles I thought "land of fire" might be more poetic). It took the navigator no less than 38 days to force a passage through the strait that now bears his name. Fear of returning through these waters drove Magellan's men ever westward after their captain's death in the Philippines, eventually making the few survivors of the expedition the first to circumnavigate the globe.

For centuries afterward, Tierra del Fuego was dreaded by sailors for its frequent storms and freezing rains. Rounding Cape Horn between the Atlantic and Pacific oceans became a nautical vision of hell, as can be seen in the works of Herman Melville, Samuel Taylor Coleridge, Jules Verne, and Edgar Allen Poe. Today Tierra del Fuego maintains its sense of being a

Klondike-style frontier. Despite the grisly past, the people of its remote, windswept towns have a rawness and surprising warmth toward strangers. And, most importantly for many travelers, the islands of Tierra del Fuego contain some of the last great wilderness areas on earth.

Darwin among the savages

The British naturalist Charles Darwin added a new dimension to the image when he visited Tierra del Fuego on the *Beagle* in the 1830s. He pronounced

Sea lions and cormorants.

FACT

Beavers, brought from Canada, have become a pest on Tierra del Fuego, damming rivers and destroying woods.

Cape Horn Island.

the native people, who had been living in the far south for tens of thousands of years, to be the lowest on the human evolutionary scale.

"I never saw such miserable creatures," Darwin wrote in his classic, *Voyage of the Beagle*, "stunted in their growth, their hideous faces bedaubed with white paint and quite naked… Their red skins filthy and greasy, their voices discordant, their gesticulation violent and without any dignity. Viewing such men, one can hardly make oneself believe that they are fellow creatures placed in the same world… What a scale of improvements is comprehended between the faculties of a Fuegian savage and a Sir Isaac Newton!"

Darwin's verdict was to be shared by the first settlers of Tierra del Fuego. By the end of the 19th century the Fuegian indigenous people would be exterminated in one of the most extraordinary cases of genocide in history (see page 264).

A fitful invasion

Although a constant stream of explorers and later whalers followed Magellan's path, European settlement of Tierra del Fuego was generally slow in coming. The Spanish had constant plans to outwit the English and Dutch pirates by setting up a naval base on the island, but the dismal conditions prevented settlement. It was not until the 1840s that Chile and Argentina both laid claim to the area, and several decades later before anybody could be convinced actually to live there. A border was drawn up; some missionaries made tentative landings; and in the 1880s the first miners arrived in search of gold.

While there were some clashes between these fortune-seekers and the indigenous peoples, the real problems between newcomers and natives did not begin until entrepreneurs realized that the Northern Plains were possibly the best sheep country in South America. On the Chilean side of the border, the first *estancia* or ranch was set up in 1893 by the Sociedad Explotadora de Tierra del Fuego, with the Russian-born Don Mauricio Braun as director general. He named it Josefina after his wife and appointed a New Zealand-born sheep farmer as manager.

The elimination of indigenous people allowed sheep farming to reach new heights. Some of the largest farms ever built were opened up on Tierra del Fuego and became enormously profitable for the mostly British-owned companies. As in the rest of Patagonia, immigrants drifted in from around the world, including a large number of exiles and eccentrics. Chilean Tierra del Fuego received an unusual number of arrivals from what was then Yugoslavia.

In modern times, the discovery of oil gave the island's economy a temporary boost. But the population remains thin. Argentina has more successfully settled its part of Tierra del Fuego by making Ushuaia a duty-free zone and holiday resort, while the Chilean section remains a sleepy and undeveloped part of the country where little seems to have changed since the late 19th century.

Exploring the "large island"

The term "Tierra del Fuego" properly includes the whole archipelago at the southern tip of South America, although the Isla Grande de Tierra del Fuego is the largest island and is usually the one referred to. It is divided between Chile (70 percent) and Argentina (30 percent), with its northern and western sections a treeless Patagonian plain and the southeastern part a lush, mountainous land full of forests and peat bogs. The Chilean section is physically the less dramatic of the two, and travelers to the island crossing over from Punta Arenas will normally want to visit both sides.

Thanks to relatively warm ocean currents, the island's weather is not as harsh as parts of Norway and Canada, which lie at an equivalent latitude in the Northern Hemisphere. Even so, it lives up to its stormy reputation. A recommended time to visit is during the summer months, from November to March, when daylight lasts for up to 20 hours and the sun is relatively warm. The weather shifts erratically from cloudless sky to drizzle and spectacular rainbows, or a deluge and back again within minutes, with the only constant being a gusty wind. It is worthwhile preparing for a range of weather conditions to pass by every day.

FACT

Porvenir started out as a police post during the 1880s gold rush. Today, pink flamingos and black-necked swans swim along the waterfront.

Exploring the Agostini Fjord.

The Lost Tribes

The appropriation of their lands during the 19th century led to the persecution and demise of southern Chile's indigenous peoples.

In the mid-19th century, Tierra del Fuego was home to four native groups. The most numerous were the Onas, or Selk'nam, a nomadic race that hunted guanacos over the open plains with bows and arrows. The Haush people occupied the eastern tip of the Isla Grande, living in huts made of branches and skins. Roaming the southern islands with bark canoes and dressed in seal hides were the Yaghans. The men hunted otters with spears and Yaghan women would sometimes dive into the icy waters to pluck *centollas* (king crabs) from the ocean floor. Finally, living in the fjords of southern Chile, were the Alacalufes.

Christian missionary Thomas Bridges compiled a dictionary of the Yaghan language that shows how they ordered their harsh world with metaphors. Bruce Chatwin lists a few phrases in his book, *In Patagonia*: "mussels out of season" was a synonym for shriveled

Yamana woman near Cape Horn.

skin and old age; "jackass penguin" meant lazy; "sleet" was the same word as "fish scales."

Traditionally roaming the pampas to hunt guanaco, the Onas naturally found sheep an easy and satisfying prey. For the farm owners, stealing their property was the ultimate crime and they killed the Onas in retribution. But the Onas could not accept that the fences across their traditional lands were meant as boundaries, and continued to hunt the "white guanaco." The estancia owners hired gunmen to protect their lands and the gruesome rumor soon began to circulate that they were paid one pound sterling bounty for each Ona they shot dead (ears were supposedly demanded as proof).

The missions

Salesian missionaries argued that the native peoples could only be saved if they were transferred en masse to nearby Isla Dawson, and the estancia owners agreed to this method of removing the "pest."

Official records show that most of the people in the Dawson mission died of European diseases to which they had no immunity, but the folk memory persists of active resistance, battles, and massacres. Old-timers still tell of such gruesome characters as the Scotsman Alex McLennan, nicknamed the "Red Pig" for his face made ruddy by constant boozing. He is said to have lured families into traps by offering food, only to have his men open fire from their position in hiding. The Englishman Sam Hyslop, who boasted of gunning down 80 Onas, was finally caught by a group of Onas and flung to his death from a cliff.

Argentines were well schooled in eradicating indigenous peoples and hunts went on unrestricted on that side of the border, but the Chilean population had moments of conscience-stricken doubt. The ugly rumors, coupled with the fact that mostly women and children were being brought back from raids, caused a public outcry.

The Chilean police found a mass grave and were going to prosecute the estancia owners. But by this stage some native people were fighting back – a handful of white deaths (a total of seven in ten years) were registered and few people raised their voices against clearing the island any longer. In the Isla Dawson mission, epidemic followed epidemic and by 1925 the last Ona had died.

The Museo Martín Gusinde in Puerto Williams (see page 267) documents the history of the indigenous peoples of Tierra del Fuego, while the Museo Yamana in Ushuaia, Argentina, has interesting displays depicting the way of life of the Yaghan or Yamana people.

Porvenir

Travelers coming from Chile usually cross the dark Strait of Magellan from Punta Arenas on the ferry that sails daily except Monday usually at 9am, although this can vary widely depending on the weather (tel: 061-728 100). Prior booking is required for vehicles. As tradition suggests, the crossing is usually a rough one, but the water is also on occasion as smooth as glass. The optimistically named port of **Porvenir** ❻ (Future) is the landing point on Tierra del Fuego, heralded by a cluster of battered fishing boats on shore and a sign that gives the distances to every point in Chile. Arica, Chile's northernmost town, is 5,300km (3,250 miles) away.

Descendants of Yugoslavs still make up the bulk of Porvenir's 4,700 inhabitants, few of whom seem to take to the streets. At weekends, it is like a ghost town. The buildings are corrugated-iron constructions mostly dating from before World War I. A wooden church steeple dominates the skyline, adding to the haunting impression. The **Museo Provincial Fernando Cordero Rusque** (Mon–Thu 8am–5.30pm, Fri 9am–4pm, Sat–Sun 10.30am–1.30pm and 3–5pm) is connected to the municipal buildings on the main plaza, with historical photographs and a Fuegian mummy discovered in the nearby countryside. A waterfront stroll brings you to a lookout on the south side of Bahía Porvenir.

Onaisin

Most travelers spend one night at the most in Porvenir before heading for the open countryside. A dirt highway runs along the barren slopes of **Bahía Inútil** (Useless Bay) for 90km (56 miles) to **Onaisin** ❼, the original home of the Caleta Josefina estancia. Keep an eye out for the **Cementerio de los Gigantes**, (Cemetery of the Giants), a set of huge, regularly shaped stones scattered in the pampas. Just a couple of minutes farther south is the historic **Cementerio Inglés** (English Cemetery), where the British-born estancia workers were buried. In this windswept, forsaken spot are the graves of the few whites who fell to the arrows of native peoples at the end of the 19th century.

Ushuaia, Argentina – the world's southernmost city.

FACT

Some estancias have
been converted into
fishing lodges in an
attempt to develop a
new tourist trade.

Along the bay 50km (31 miles) farther south is **Estancia Cameron** ❽ (http://estanciacameronlodge.com), founded in 1904. Nestled in a picturesque gully by the choppy gray sea and still with its original wooden buildings, the estancia was revived as an active sheep farm a few years ago by a Santiago-based investment group and is a good base for exploring the area on foot or on a horseback. Travelers with their own vehicles can continue along the road into the more remote, mountainous and rainy area of the island, taking their own fuel, food, and camping gear, although lodging is available on some of the estancias. **Lago Blanco**, surrounded by Fuegian peaks, is considered the most beautiful in the far south of Chile. The highway then leads south to **Vicuña** ❾. A large part of this area, including forests of *lenga* (southern beech) and vast peat bogs, was donated to the New York-based Wildlife Conservation Society by the Goldman Sachs investment bank to form the Karukinka reserve (http://karukinka.cl). It is working to control the beaver population; with no natural enemies, this imported species has multiplied rapidly, doing

Puerto Williams.

extensive damage by damming and diverting waterways. Basic accommodations are available in two different sectors of the reserve and activities include trekking, birding, and fly-fishing. A 34km (21-mile) trail links the uplands with coastal areas home to seabirds, penguins, and elephant seals.

From Vicuña the road returns north along the frontier. A road from Vicuña to Bahía Yendegaia, 140km (87 miles) south on the Beagle Channel, is slowly being built.

Most travelers who come this far south will want to continue into the Argentine side of Tierra del Fuego. The easiest way is to head directly from Porvenir to the frontier at **San Sebastián**, then continue onward to **Río Grande**. This rough-and-ready oil town on the island's east coast is little more than a place to pass the night before continuing south.

Ushuaia

On the southern coast of the Argentinian part of Tierra del Fuego, squeezed between dramatic mountain peaks and the blue Beagle Channel, is the island's largest and most attractively placed town, **Ushuaia** ❿. Its setting is majestic, with the wicked-looking granite peak of Mount Olivia dominating the skyline. Despite the often-bitter weather, this is a popular resort town and base. Its energy and faith in progress sets it apart from other towns of the south, with new buildings being flung up everywhere amongst mud and twisted trees.

Boat trips on the Beagle Channel pass islands crowded with sea lions and penguins, or scattered with the rotting remains of shipwrecked boats. And just outside of Ushuaia is **Parque Nacional Tierra del Fuego**, also in Argentina, which preserves the sense of being at the end of the world: paths wind over spongy moss oozing cold water, past tough shrubs, thorny bushes, and trees that have grown bent 45 degrees with the prevailing wind.

A pleasant drive eastward along the Beagle Channel leads to **Estancia**

Harberton , the first farm on the Argentine side of Tierra del Fuego set up by the missionary the Reverend Thomas Bridges in 1886. On a narrow peninsula surrounded by green meadows of bright flowers, the estancia is worth visiting as much for its serene beauty as its history. Across the water are three obscure islands over which Chile and Argentina nearly went to war in 1978, until Pope John Paul II intervened and drew up a settlement.

Puerto Williams

While Ushuaia is the southernmost town of its size in the world, the title of southernmost permanent human settlement outside of Antarctica goes to Chile's **Puerto Williams** ⑫ on Isla Navarino. Established in 1953 as a naval base, it can be reached by plane or ferry from Punta Arenas. The setting is, once again, magnificent.

Isla Navarino was home to the native Yaghan people and was first visited by the *Beagle* on its maiden journey. The captain, Robert Fitzroy, took four young Yaghans back to England for education, and returned with them on the famous journey with Charles Darwin. The friendliest Yaghan was named Jimmy Button by the crew. He had learned some of the manners of an English gent, but on his return to Tierra del Fuego he quickly returned to his former Yaghan lifestyle. Fitzroy had hoped that Button would be a force for "civilizing" the Yaghan people but the reverse proved true: two decades after his return, Button commanded attacks on the first European settlements in the area and bled the slaughter of several missionaries on Isla Picton and Isla Navarino.

Today, there are no full-blooded Yaghans, though a few mestizos live near Puerto Williams in a settlement called **Ukika**. The splendidly renovated **Museo Martín Gusinde** (www. museomartingusinde.cl; Nov–Mar Tue–Fri 9.30am–1pm and 3–6pm, Sat–Sun 2.30–6.30pm, Apr–Oct Tue–Fri 9.30am–1.30pm and 2.30–5.30pm, Sat 2.30–6.30pm; free) in the naval township, which is considered one of the best in the south, focuses on the history and demise of the Yaghans culture and also has some exhibits about European settlement and missionaries in the area.

TIP

Some of the smaller cruise ships sailing around Cape Horn allow passengers to disembark on this southernmost tip of Tierra de Fuego where it is possible to visit one of the lighthouses and the large sculpture - the silhouette of an albatross - erected in the memory of all the sailors who have died trying to "round the Horn."

Trekking the Dientes de Navarino, Isla Navarino.

Easter Island moai.

EASTER ISLAND

Chile's Polynesian possession, nearly 4,000km (2,400 miles) west of the mainland, is one of the world's most intriguing islands, dominated by more than 600 giant stone statues of unknown origin.

Main Attractions

Ahu Tahai
Ahu Vinapu
Rano Kau
Orongo
Rano Raraku
Ahu Te Pito Kura

One of the island's imposing moai.

The first inhabitants of Easter Island called their home Te Pito o Te Henua – the Navel of the World. Gazing down from one of the island's three volcanic crater rims, it is easy to see why. This tiny volcanic island, only 164 sq km (63 sq miles) in area, is almost lost in the endless blue of the Pacific Ocean. The nearest Polynesian island, Pitcairn, is 2,000km (1,240 miles) to the west; the coast of South America is some 3,800km (2,360 miles) to the east. The island has a maximum length of 24km (15 miles) and width of 12km (8 miles). Volcanic in origin, it has several dead craters dotted over its sparsely covered surface, one of which now contains a freshwater lake. The terrain on the treeless volcanic slopes is fairly grassy, but most of the island is covered in rugged lava fields. Dotted around the coast are hundreds of caves, which were once used as refuges (in times of war) or secret burial places.

Until 30 years ago, Easter Island was visited only once a year by a Chilean warship bringing supplies. But even though few people before the 1960s could make a personal visit, Easter Island has gripped the world's imagination for centuries. One baffling image made it famous: littering the island are hundreds of giant, tight-lipped basalt statues, unique in the whole of Oceania. The tiny island and its mysterious statues have presented us with one of the most fascinating archeological riddles of all time.

How did an early seafaring people find this remote speck in the Pacific Ocean? Where did they come from? How did they transport their enormous statues, carved from a quarry in the side of a volcano, to the coast and erect them on giant stone altars? And above all – *why* did they do so?

Today, regular flights from Santiago have broken the island's isolation. People visiting Chile have the chance to see this legendary site, marvel at the remains of an enigmatic Pacific culture, and make up their own minds on the origin of the statues.

Polynesian or American?

The long-standing assumption that the first Easter Islanders were Polynesians was thrown into doubt in 1947 when the Norwegian explorer Thor Heyerdahl sailed a balsa raft, *Kon-Tiki*, from Peru to Tahiti. The highly publicized journey showed that it was theoretically possible for a pre-Inca South American culture to have colonized the Pacific.

Heyerdahl went on to spend a year digging on Easter Island, and concluded in his best-selling book *Aku-Aku* that the first islanders actually came from the Peruvian coast, fleeing the destruction of the ancient South American empire of Tiahuanaco around Lake Titicaca in Bolivia. According to this theory, the seafarers brought with them a number of American plants that are still found on the island (including the sweet potato and totora reeds), as well as their sun-worshipping religion and famous skills as stonemasons. Heyerdahl argued that

they were eventually joined by a group of Polynesian settlers. The two groups lived in harmony until an eventual war finally destroyed the islanders of South American origin.

Most archeologists now discount the bulk of Heyerdahl's findings, although his groundwork is still valuable and makes stimulating reading. Nor do his theories seem so outlandish compared to an extraordinary rash of more recent claims. Crackpot visionaries have announced that the Easter Islanders were descendants of ancient Egyptians, interplanetary travelers, red-haired North Africans, or even survivors of the lost continent of Atlantis.

The Long Ears and the Short Ears

The absence of historical records on the island has fueled speculation. Almost all of the original islanders were wiped out by slave raids during the 19th century, so that by the time serious archeological work began in the 1980s the old culture was virtually dead.

TIP

Whether you're using a digital or film camera, make sure you bring extra film or batteries. Photo opportunities on the island are endless, but supplies are limited and the shops are often closed.

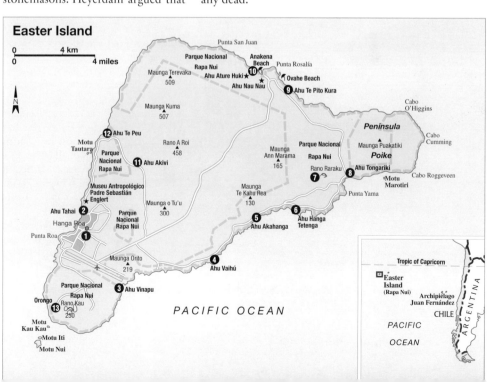

Easter Island

0 _____ 4 km
0 _____ 4 miles

N

Punta San Juan

Parque Nacional Rapa Nui

Anakena Beach
Punta Rosalía

Maunga Terevaka ▲ 509
Ahu Ature Huki ★ ⑩
Ovahe Beach

Ahu Nau Nau
⑨ Ahu Te Pito Kura

Maunga Kuma ▲ 507

Cabo O'Higgins

⑫ Ahu Te Peu

Motu Tautara

Rano A Roi ▲ 458

Península

Cabo Cumming

Parque Nacional Rapa Nui
⑪ Ahu Akivi

Maunga Ann Marama ▲ 165

Parque Nacional Rapa Nui

Maunga Puakatiki ▲ **Poike**

Rano Raraku ⑦
⑧ Ahu Tongariki

Cabo Roggeveen

Museu Antropológico Padre Sebastián ★ Englert

Maunga o Tu'u ▲ 300

Maunga Te Kahu Rea ▲ 130

●Motu Marotiri

Punta Yama

Ahu Tahai ②

Parque Nacional Rapa Nui

⑤
Ahu Akahanga

⑥
Ahu Hanga Tetenga

Hanga Roa ①

Punta Roa

Maunga Orito ▲ 219

④ Ahu Vaihú

Tropic of Capricorn

□ **Easter Island** (Rapa Nui)

Archipiélago Juan Fernández

Parque Nacional Rapa Nui
Orongo
Rano Kau ▲ 250
⑬ ③ Ahu Vinapu

Motu Kau Kau°
°Motu Iti
Motu Nui

PACIFIC OCEAN

CHILE

PACIFIC OCEAN

ARGENTINA

"Easter Island is the loneliest inhabited place in the world. The nearest solid land the inhabitants can see is in the firmament, the moon and the planets. They have to travel farther than any other people to see that there really is land still closer."

Thor Heyerdahl

According to those few surviving inhabitants who were first interviewed in the late 19th century, Easter Island was discovered by King Hotu Matua – a name meaning "prolific father" in Polynesian – who arrived on Anakena beach on the island's northern coast from a scorched land to the east. Tradition holds that 57 generations of kings succeeded Hotu Matua until the 1680s, during which time another set of ancestors arrived under a chief called Tuu-ko-ihu.

The legend goes that the two groups were divided between so-called "Long-Ears," who carved the *moai*, and the newcoming "Short Ears," who were kept in an inferior class and helped in manual labor. Eventually the Short Ears rebelled and slaughtered all of the Long Ears bar one. Unfortunately, so many different versions of this story soon cropped up – mostly completely contradictory – that they only added confusion to research. Most investigators are now finding it safer to believe that none of the versions is authentic.

Orthodox opinion now holds that Easter Island was first populated before AD 500 by Polynesians coming from the Marquesas Islands, remaining in isolation until the arrival of Europeans. The bizarre culture was developed by the islanders themselves, who lived in a fairly egalitarian society dominated by small independent warring tribes. According to this view, 1,200 years of total isolation allowed the creation of a new language, of the famous statues that still preside over the island, and of the only writing system known in all Polynesia and the Americas – the *rongo rongo* script. This conclusion is far from watertight, and most visitors to Easter Island will want to decide the truth for themselves.

The first European contact

The first European to stumble across this speck in the Pacific Ocean was the Dutch Admiral Jacob Roggeveen. He and his crew landed and spent a day ashore on Easter Sunday, 1722 – and christened the island for the occasion. Roggeveen's logbook tells how the party anchored off the mysterious island at dusk to be greeted by fair-skinned Polynesians, similar to those

Restoring a moai to its original position.

in Tahiti and Hawaii. Some had darker skins, the Dutchman wrote, while others were "quite white" like Europeans, with reddish hair.

Roggeveen records with awe that the *moai* were still standing, many up to 9 meters (30ft) tall, and with great cylinders on their heads. The inhabitants of the island, he wrote, "kindle fires in front of certain remarkably tall figures they set up; and, thereafter squatting on their heels with heads bowed down, they bring the palms of their hands together and alternately raise and lower them." The islanders kept up the ritual until dawn, when they praised the sunrise. Many of the worshippers wore long wooden plugs in their ear lobes, lengthening them to their shoulders – a practice found in much of Polynesia and also among nobles of Peru, whom the conquistadors called *orejones* or "Long Ears."

The islanders lived in long, low huts of reed that looked strangely like boat hulls turned upward, the remains of which can still be seen. Their lands were neatly cultivated, Roggeveen noted, and "whole tracts of woodland" were visible in the distance. Examining the *moai* closely, the Dutchmen decided that they were not of stone but were modeled from a strange clay stuffed with small stones. With that curious decision, the crew rowed back to their ships and weighed anchor.

After less than 24 hours on shore, they had decided that the islanders were friendly but expert thieves, pinching a few hats and tablecloths. A misunderstanding led to one Easter Islander being shot on board their boat, followed by another dozen being gunned down on shore, giving islanders an ominous taste of what European contact would bring.

The Spaniards, English, and French

The island was left in peace for another 50 years before the arrival of a Spanish captain named Don Felipe González. In typical colonial Spanish fashion, he marched with two priests and a squadron of soldiers to a high point on the east coast, planted the cross and claimed the island for his king. The men of the island, he noted

FACT

Easter Island was given the name *Rapa Nui* (Great Rapa) by Tahitian sailors in the early 1860s, as it reminded them of an island called Rapa near their home. That island is now known as Rapa Iti, or Small Rapa.

The almost treeless landscape of the island.

later, were naked except for feather headdresses, while women wore short cloaks around their breasts and hips. Don Felipe also observed with some interest that the islanders looked nothing like the indigenous peoples of South America, then recorded how he taught some to recite in Spanish, "Ave Maria, long live Charles III, king of Spain," before disappearing over the horizon.

Next came the renowned English navigator Captain James Cook, landing in 1774 after a journey through the Society Islands, Tonga, and New Zealand. Cook had no doubt that the islanders were of Polynesian descent, although they seemed to be few in number and living in a miserable state. Little land was in cultivation. Meanwhile, dozens of the stone statues had been overturned, Cook found, and those that remained were no longer worshipped but used as burial sites. The scurvy-ridden Englishmen were forced to leave with nothing but a few baskets of sweet potatoes – although even then they were cheated, since islanders had weighed down the baskets with stones and laid only a few potatoes over the very top.

What had happened since the days of the Dutchmen's visit? Modern evidence confirms that serious environmental degradation was already well under way on Easter Island by the time of the Dutch visit in 1722: pollen samples show that the island was heavily forested when man first arrived in AD 500, yet there were no trees left by the beginning of the 19th century. Most writers now believe that the population of Easter Island had simply outgrown its resources. The food supply began to fail, the island's forests were felled, and the soil began to erode. Without wood for canoes to escape the island, the tribes turned on one another in destructive wars: the giant statues were toppled and broken, while cannibalism became common. The resulting ruin is seen by many today as a taste in miniature of the Earth's own future, as the human race consumes the planet's limited resources with increasing voracity.

Kai kai strings competetion.

The slave traders arrive

Easter Island's internal destruction pales into insignificance compared with the devastation finally wreaked by contact with the outside world during the 19th century. Whalers and slave traders put the island on their itineraries, bringing a series of tragedies to this hitherto isolated outpost.

The most dramatic blow was the Peruvian slave raid of 1862. Early on Christmas Eve, strangers rowed ashore with brightly colored clothes and presents that enticed the islanders out to greet them. On a given signal, the slave hunters attacked, tying up those who surrendered and shooting any who resisted. One thousand islanders were kidnapped, including the king and most of the learned men, to be taken to work on the guano islands off the coast of Peru – but not before the slavers celebrated Christmas on board with rum and salt pork.

Brutal conditions at the guano mine, starvation, and epidemics had killed off 900 islanders before the bishop of Tahiti was finally able to intervene on their behalf. Of the remaining hundred who set sail for their homeland, 85 died en route from smallpox. The handful who returned brought the plague with them: by the 1870s only 110 men, women, and children were alive on Easter Island.

Following this devastation came the first missionary to the island, Eugène Eyraud. Unsurprisingly, he met a hostile reception and was forced to flee – only to return two years later with reinforcements. Many of the islanders were converted to Christianity, however superficially, over the next few years.

Chile takes over

Spain may have claimed Easter Island for itself in 1770, but the Crown hardly bothered to maintain its claim. No other expeditions were sent to the island and, with the collapse of Spanish control of Latin America in the early 1800s, the way was left open for another colonial power to walk in and take over.

As part of its 19th century burst of expansionism, Chile annexed Easter Island in 1888. The republic wanted to

Moai at Ranu Raraku.

show off its powerful naval force and show itself the equal of major European powers by grabbing a piece of South Pacific territory. Apart from the perceived prestige of such an acquisition, Chile saw the island as having valuable agricultural potential, and a gateway to Asian trade.

Few Chileans showed much interest in colonizing this new jewel in the nation's crown. The government found itself handing over control of the island to sheep-grazing companies – first a Chilean concern run by a Valparaíso businessman, then in the early 1900s to the British company Williamson Balfour. The Liverpool-based company used the Compañía Explotadora de la Isla de Pascua (CEDIP), leased from the Chilean government, to manage the island, and made handsome profits until their license was revoked in 1953. Islanders recall the company's rule as a time of dismal subjugation. They were effectively restricted to living in Hanga Roa, the island's only town, so that the rest of the island would be free for sheep to roam. Generally they were forced to

Moai lined up along the coast.

work for little or no wages. It was during this period that immigrants interbred with the remaining few Easter Islanders, leaving little trace of the original inhabitants. Three-quarters of the population in the 1930s was of mixed descent, with everyone from North Americans to Germans and Tahitians living in Hanga Roa. Many years later, when news arrived that Thor Heyerdahl had floated a raft from Peru to Tahiti, several islanders made boats to stage their own escape. Some succeeded, and guards were posted to stop the exodus.

After 1953, the island's government was given to another authoritarian hand: the Chilean navy. The islanders suffered the same humiliations as in the days of the sheep company: the inability to vote, their local language suppressed, and having to endure the navy's arbitrary and often absurd decisions.

The biggest change came in 1967, when the completion of the airport finally allowed flights from Tahiti and Santiago. The sudden possibility of large-scale tourism helped

THE PURPOSE OF THE MOAI

Each of the brooding *moai* was carved from the island's soft volcanic rock to the same general pattern. There are estimated to be close to 1,000 on the island: all with the distinctive heavy foreheads, pointed chins and (in all but a couple of cases) elongated ears. The hand position is typical of Polynesian carving, but the form of the figures is clearly unique. Their average height is around 6 meters (20ft). Most are male, but some are women with breasts and vulvas. While archeologists originally thought they were carved eyeless, the *moai*, in fact, had eyes: the whites were made of coral and the pupils from the glistening black obsidian that can be found on the island.

Archeologists generally agree that the *moai* were figures of deceased chiefs or gods. (A key piece of information recorded by George Foster on Captain Cook's 1774 visit was that the *moai* were often named after these dead heroes.) The eyes of the *moai* are believed to have transmitted *mana* or power to the living family chief, signifying prosperity in peacetime and success in war. At one point there were as many as 15 *moai* set up on any particular *ahu*, or platform. From this viewpoint, it is not difficult to imagine what effect a fully constructed *ahu* must have had on its family – as well as the utter devastation of morale when it was pulled down.

focus international attention on the island, and the Chilean government was forced to make some improvements. During the 1970s and 1980s, better water supplies, electricity, a hospital, and a school were installed. The most astonishing change to the island was the extension of its airport as an emergency landing site for the US space shuttle. Opened in 1988, the airstrip has completed the Easter Islanders' transition from the Stone Age to the Space Age. However, the increase in tourism on the island has had some detrimental effects. The garbage left by the approximately 90,000 tourists who visit the island each year has to be sent to the mainland for recycling which is prohibitively expensive. Proposals to impose a cap on visitor numbers have not yet been implemented, but a US$60 entrance fee for the Parque Nacional Rapa Nui has been introduced to raise funds for the preservation of the island's unique environment.

Downtown Hanga Roa

Almost all visitors now arrive at the airport, on one of the daily LAN flights, and are greeted by their first glimpse of Easter Island's famous *moai* (statues). Rather small affairs compared to others on the island, the airport *moai* still provide a taste of the mysteries to come.

About 15 minutes' walk from the airstrip is the tiny township where Easter Island's 5,000 people almost all live, **Hanga Roa ❶**. Built around a few wide roads, with thick, heavy palm trees hanging at regular intervals, the village looks like a classic South Pacific hideaway. The pace of life is relaxed, and a speed limit of 20kmph (12mph) is imposed on the town.

There are a handful of large hotels on Easter Island, but many visitors prefer to stay in one of the small *residenciales* scattered about Hanga Roa. Reservations are not necessary – the owners crowd around the airport gates after every arrival offering their

prices. There are also small restaurants, bars, and several discotheques. Don't miss the Hanga Roa Crafts Market where you can buy a variety of items made by local and Polynesian artisans. At a nearby Santa Cruz Parish church a mass featuring local vestments and hymns in the Rapa Nui language is celebrated every Sunday at 9am.

Tourism is Easter Island's biggest industry, and many of Hanga Roa's inhabitants now make a living from selling woodcarvings to travelers, endlessly repeating the same basic forms. The best-known piece is also the ugliest: the *moai kavakava* or "statue of ribs." This human figure with a huge nose, ears, and starved physique, is said to have been first carved by King Tuu-ko-ihu. Apparently, the king was sleeping at the foot of a cliff when he awoke to find two ghosts staring down at him. He ran home and immediately carved their image, and islanders have followed the pattern ever since.

While one or two archeological sites can be reached on foot, the best way to explore the island is on an

Local craftsman carving a moai kavakava.

organized tour or by jeep (the island has several car rental outlets). Motorbikes can be hired by the hardy (anyone who doesn't mind bouncing over volcanic rock for several hours), as can horses (although these are often in poor shape), and bicycles.

Most hotel or *residencial* owners will provide information about island tours. Some of these tours are great value for money, with university-trained guides who will explain the orthodox history as well as discussing some of the wackier theories. The most important *ahus*, or *moai* platforms, can be covered in one day, and the rest in another day's tour. Certainly, if you want to visit all the sites on foot, you'd better bring a tent. Whichever mode of transportation you choose, take plenty of sunblock, especially in summer, a good sun hat, and a large supply of water – the tropical sun on Easter Island is notoriously fierce, yet the sea breeze can make the temperature seem deceptively cool. Mosquitoes can also be a problem so take some insect repellent.

Painting event at the annual Tapati festival.

In search of moai and ahus

One short stroll from Hanga Roa allows a pleasant introduction to what Easter Island has to offer. Starting from the small fishing port, follow the coast road north, away from the shops. On the outskirts of the village, a cemetery appears. The missionary presence has ensured that the population is at least nominally Catholic, and one of the less well-known pleasures of Easter Island is visiting a Mass service on Sunday and listening to the singing.

Just past the cemetery stands one of the most photographed archeological sites, **Ahu Tahai ❷**. Here, five statues stand in a row on their *ahu* with their backs to the sea. Like other *ahu moai*, they were knocked down, probably some time during the 18th century. The archeologist William Mulloy restored them to their rightful position in the 1960s; his grave is only meters from the site. You can also see the remains of ancient boat-shaped houses. This is a favorite spot at sunset, when the *moai* are silhouetted against a scarlet sky.

Just north of Ahu Tahai is the small **Museo Antropológico Padre Sebastián Englert** (www.museorapanui. cl; Tue–Fri 9.30am–5.30pm, Sat–Sun 9.30am–12.30pm; free). Exhibits include the *rongo rongo* tablets, *moai kavakava* figures, and some wonderful late 19th- and early 20th-century photographs of Easter Island's earlier inhabitants.

Having had a taste of the most accessible *moai*, your appetite will be whetted for a day tour of the island. By heading east from Hanga Roa you can follow the general chronology of the island and gain an insight into how archeologists and historians have pieced together their theories on where the Easter Islanders came from, as well as how, why, and when they carved their statues. In the process, you will probably see enough *moai* in one day to last a lifetime.

Vinapu ahus

From the airport, follow the airstrip southeast and then turn right past an oil depot to reach **Ahu Vinapu ❸** – probably the most important site in

establishing the chronology of Easter Island. There are two *ahus* here, both of which once supported *moai* before they were toppled and broken – *moai* parts are scattered all around the site. The most famous *ahu* – known as Vinapu No. 1 – contains a wall of perfectly carved and fitted stone blocks that is strikingly similar to the walls at Tiahuanaco near Lake Titicaca, Bolivia, and some of the Inca walls around Cuzco. Not surprisingly, it is a key element in Thor Heyerdahl's argument that the Easter Islanders themselves originally came from South America. Vinapu No. 2 is a much rougher version of the same model *ahu*.

Heyerdahl's Norwegian expedition used Carbon 14 dating of fire remains and other materials near here to divide the island's prehistory into the Early Period (AD 400–1100), Middle Period (1100–1680), and Late Period (1680–1868). It appears that some *ahus* – including Vinapu No. 2 – were constructed in the Early Period, in the earliest centuries of human colonization, although their exact purpose is a matter of conjecture. The erection of

Foundations of a hare paenga boat-shaped house at Ahu Tahai.

Fallen moai on the south coast of Easter Island.

FACT

According to the Chilean government, Easter Island is at the limit of the number of visitors it can sustainably receive. However, a proposal to establish an annual cap on visitor numbers has been controversial.

the majority of *ahus* and *moai* belongs to the Middle Period; while the Late Period belongs to the bloody cannibal wars that probably resulted in the end of *moai* production and the destruction of the statues and their *ahus*.

Heyerdahl found that the finely worked *ahu* of Vinapu No. 1 actually predated the cruder No. 2, supporting his argument that the first inhabitants of the island were skilled South American carvers. But later archeologists have reinterpreted the Norwegian expedition's findings to show that No. 2 came first. It is now generally believed that the masonry skills of the islanders improved over many generations, and that Vinapu No. 1 is the climax of their own achievement, independent of developments in Bolivia or Peru.

The south coast

Continuing along the southern coast of the island brings you to the most striking examples of the Late Period's *moai*-toppling wars.

Ahu Vaihú ④ is probably the most extraordinary sight along this

Ahu Tongariki.

stretch. Eight large statues have been pulled in a row from their *ahu*, looking rather forlorn with their noses in the dirt and top-knots scattered. One of the *moai* has been completely shattered. Farther along, **Ahu Akahanga ⑤** has four similarly humiliated statues, with another bunch scattered from a second *ahu* across a nearby estuary. The remains of a village have been found on the hill slopes opposite – the foundations of several boat-shaped houses can be seen, as well as some round houses. Another site, **Ahu Hanga Tetenga ⑥**, has been almost completely devastated and its two *moai* shattered.

The moai mine

From here, a dirt road runs inland toward the huge volcanic crater of **Rano Raraku ⑦**. This so-called **Road of the Moai** is littered with more and more fallen giants before reaching the most impressive site on the island.

By far the most famous of the *moai* are the 70 standing sentinels embedded up to their shoulders in grass on the south slope of the volcanic crater.

They lead the way to the quarry or "nursery" cut into the side of the impressive crater rim. This was where the *moai* were cut from volcanic tufa. Some 400 figures have been left there in all stages of completion, paying mute testimony to the unknown disaster that stopped all work dead in its tracks.

A trail leads straight up from the car park to the largest *moai* ever built – a 21-meter (69ft) monolith. Leading off to the right, the trail comes to two other huge statues still part of the rock, while 20 or so more stand on the inside of the crater.

Many obscure differences have been found in the *moai* of Rano Raraku. Some have unusual carvings on their flanks or backs. One figure displays a rough three-mast sailing ship on its chest. A line hangs from its bow to a round figure that may be an anchor or turtle caught on a fishing line. With a little imagination, the boat has been explained as either a European ship or a large totora-reed vessel.

Also found buried at Rano Raraku by the Norwegian expedition was the unique kneeling statue, now found on the right slope of the crater, which looks like no other *moai*. Somewhat less than 4 meters (13ft) high, it has a rounded head and face, as well as a beard and short ears.

Two kilometers (1 mile) east of Rano Raraku on the coastal road is **Ahu Tongariki** ❽ where 15 *moai* stand side-by-side on the longest *ahu* ever built. They were re-erected and restored after being felled by a tsunami in 1960 and gaze inland across a large ceremonial area.

Carving from the rock

The remains in the quarry give very clear evidence on how the *moai* were originally modeled from the rock. Trenches were cut for the easy access of carvers, who chipped away until only the spine was left down the *moai*'s back. Eventually, the spine was severed and the statue was lowered by ropes to a temporary upright position on the slopes below, where it was finished off. The sheer fact that these giant figures were cut from vertical as well as horizontal rock-faces testifies to the skill

A wooden Christ figure, one of many impressive carvings in the Iglesia Hanga Roa.

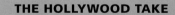

Jason Scott Lee in the film 'Rapa Nui.'

THE HOLLYWOOD TAKE

Walking around the outskirts of Hanga Roa, you may encounter some unusual *moai* bearing a striking resemblance to some of the ancient megaliths found in Latin America. According to National Park staff, these *moai* were produced by the fertile imaginations of a Hollywood film crew, who designed them as props for the film *Rapa Nui*, which was shot on Easter Island in 1993.

Produced by Kevin Costner and starring Jason Scott-Lee, the film is a story of forbidden love in a time of war. It is set during the period of conflict between the Long Ears and the Short Ears, but also draws on stories related to the Bird Man cult (see page 285). Easter Islanders, many of who worked as extras on the film, still remember its controversial shooting. Fans of the film argue that it brought money and new fame to the island; while critics maintain that it is a travesty of their customs and that a number of authentic monuments were damaged during the shooting.

Archeologists and historians were also irritated by what they denounced as the film's gross inaccuracies. As well as its loose interpretation of the island's complex history, they complained, for example, that the scanty costumes designed for the Native islanders owed more to Maori traditions than those of Easter Island.

Dwarfed by a giant.

*Stone rongo rongo
tablets from Polynesia.*

of the workers, while the number of broken statues on the slopes reveal the work's danger. The tools used to carve the *moai* were small basalt picks called *toki* – thousands of them have been found at the quarry.

Thor Heyerdahl's Norwegian expedition decided to find out how long it might take to carve a *moai* by commissioning a team of islanders to work on a statue at Rano Raraku. The incident is recounted in Heyerdahl's *Aku-Aku*: the then mayor of the island brought a family team to work non-stop for three days before giving up with fingers twisted from the work. But they had begun to make an impression, and the experience suggested that it would take a skilled team between 12 and 15 months to carve a *moai* about 4 meters (13ft) high, using two teams constantly in shifts. But how did the islanders move the other *moai* to different parts of the island?

Making the statues walk

Following the coast road on to the north of the island gives you an idea of the enormous scale of the problem. Here is located **Ahu Te Pito Kura** ❾ – at 9.8 meters (32ft), it is the largest *moai* ever successfully erected. The name means "navel of light," and the rock from which it was hewn is said to have been brought by King Hotu Matua himself.

Heyerdahl was able to convince some 180 merry dinner guests to pull a 4 meter (13ft) -long *moai* across a field with ropes made from tree bark, showing that it was easier to move the statues than had first been expected. In *Aku-Aku* he suggested that a much larger statue could be pulled using more people and wooden rollers. Others suggested that small rocks could be used like marbles to move the statues. But these theories still seem unconvincing when faced with the size of Ahu Te Pito Kura and the ruggedness of the volcanic terrain around Rano Raraku.

The archeologist William Mulloy came up with a theory that has won widespread support. First a huge forked sled (made from the large trees that tests have shown once covered the island) would be attached to the front

THE RONGO RONGO SCRIPT

As if enigmatic megaliths and intriguing legends were not enough, there is yet another Easter Island mystery that may never be solved: the strange inscriptions known as *rongo rongo* writing. Found on small wooden boards, this script contains 120 different figures based on "bird man" or human forms and is read alternatively from left to right then right to left. When outsiders first glimpsed the boards in 1865, none of the surviving islanders knew how to read them, the priests who understood them having perished after the Peruvian slave raids. Attempts by Russian and German experts to decipher the strange script have so far borne little fruit.

Furthermore, few scholars agree on where the writing first came from. Guesses range from the Indus Valley of Pakistan to the Andes mountain range. But other archeologists have begun to doubt whether *rongo rongo* is in fact prehistoric at all: since no similar pictographs are carved in stone elsewhere on the island, it is possible that the script is an emulation of European writing. *Rongo rongo* may have developed from observation of the Spanish treaty of annexation in 1770, possibly fixing chants into some concrete form – only to be forgotten as the island priests died in droves after they were forced to work on Peru's guano islands.

of each statue, tied into place over the protruding belly and stuck beneath the chin. This sled protected the statue from the ground and allowed it to be moved by leverage using a bipod. The statue's own weight could then be used to help move it along in a repetitive series of upward and forward movements. While hardly foolproof (and there are numerous broken *moai* around the island), the method is at least possible. Curiously, the theory of short jerking movements recalls the islanders' own belief that the *moai* "walked" to their *ahu*.

An experiment in ancient engineering

One more baffling mystery remains: once the statues had been moved by this painstaking method, how did the islanders then erect them – along with top-knots – onto their stone altars?

When the Norwegian expedition arrived in the mid-1950s, not one *moai* was at its post on an *ahu*. All lay where they had fallen centuries before, and nobody had even attempted to move them. Heyerdahl resolved to

raise a *moai* using only the materials that would have been available to the original islanders. The lone statue now standing at **Ahu Ature Huki** on **Anakena Beach** ❿ was the result of the experiment that put the first *moai* upright since they were toppled.

Having dragged the *moai* to the *ahu*, Heyerdahl's team carefully worked a series of long poles underneath the statue's stomach. Three or four men heaved at the end of each pole as another man, lying on his belly, slipped small stones underneath the giant's face. Slowly the statue began to rise from the ground, supported on this mattress of tightly packed pebbles. It took a dozen men working for nine days to get the statue on a 45-degree angle. Another nine days and it was almost upright. Finally, it slid with the guidance of ropes to a standing position. Raising a *moai* with a top-knot would have been done in the same fashion, Thor Heyerdahl argued, strapping the stone "hat" to the statue's head with ropes and poles.

Since that date many other *moai* have been restored to their *ahus*, as can

Anakena Beach.

be seen today. But it is still astounding to consider raising a statue on Ahu Te Pito Kura – with its top-knot it would have been a massive 11.5 meters (38ft) tall. William Mulloy estimated that it would have taken 30 men one year to carve this *moai*, 90 men two months to move it 6km (4 miles) from the quarry to the *ahu* and 90 men three months to erect it. Yet this pales in comparison with the 21-meter (69ft) monolith still being cut in the quarry when work was abandoned.

These theories of how the *moai* were moved and raised also suggest why carving suddenly ceased at the Rano Raraku quarry: the Easter Island workers simply ran out of trees. Eighteenth-century explorers had reported the island's lack of lumber. It seems likely that work was abandoned when there was no wood left to take the statues from their nursery to the coast.

Golden beaches

Only 100 meters (330ft) away on the headland at Anakena is **Ahu Nau Nau** and seven more *moai*. Having viewed statues all day, it probably comes as a welcome relief to find that these last *moai* stand above the white sands of Anakena Beach. This was the legendary landing place of Hotu Matua, the founder of the island. Many of the caves nearby are said to have been his refuge while waiting for a boat-shaped house to be built nearby.

But if you are in the mood for a swim after a hard day of *moai*-spotting, one small bay is even more appealing than the wider expanses of Anakena: nestled beneath a cliff of volcanic rock, **Ovahe Beach** must be one of the most beautiful on earth. Its sands are pure and golden, a match for any South Pacific paradise, and the water is so clear that you can count your toe hairs while swimming but beware of the strong undercurrents.

From here you also have a view of the **Poike peninsula**. This area has a major place in local legend. When the "Short Ears" tired of working for their "Long Ear" rulers and rebelled, the Long Ears were said to have gathered on this peninsula behind the Poike trench. Filled with branches and tree trunks, the ditch was intended as

Stone sentinels at Anakena beach.

a fiery defense rampart. But a traitor who was married to a Short Ear woman alerted the Short Ears, who slipped into the peninsula and surrounded the Long Ears, driving them into their own flaming ditch – where all but the traitor died.

Interestingly, while this had been considered a fable by most researchers, the Norwegian expedition found thick layers of charcoal and ash here. They were able to show that a great fire had occurred in the trench some 350 years before, suggesting that there may be some truth in the islanders' tales.

From here, the road through the center of the island leads past the old sheep estancia back to Hanga Roa. From the town you can make another excursion along the island's northern roads to sites like **Ahu Akivi** ⓫ and **Ahu Te Peu** ⓬. These are interesting enough sites, but they offer few surprises to those who know the rest of the island.

Center of the mysterious "bird man" cult

A quite different excursion from Hanga Roa can be made directly south to the volcanic crater of **Rano Kau**. Instead of *moai*, its interest centers on a bizarre "bird man" ritual that flourished here among the original inhabitants. It is also without doubt the most visually spectacular spot on Easter Island.

A road and path run steeply upward from Hanga Roa through typical scrubby terrain. Without warning, the enormous crater of Rano Kau appears below. It's not hard to see why Heyerdahl described it as a "giant witch's cauldron." Filled with black water and floating green fields of totora reeds, its steep, 200-meter (656ft) -high wall is gently eroded on the seaward side to include a view of the Pacific. The ruined ceremonial village of **Orongo** ⓭ is perched atop this breathtaking location, with the volcano on one side and sheer cliffs on the other, dropping some 400 meters (1,300ft)

down to the crashing sea. Scattered in the briny void are three tiny, craggy islands – Motu Kau Kau, Motu Iti, and Motu Nui.

Orongo is now restored and part of a specially created national reserve. The entrance ticket (available to purchase at the ranger's office) is valid for five days and covers entry to Rano Raraku and other heritage sites across the island. The ancient village contains a range of 53 oval buildings, constructed in the 16th century, with their floors cut into the side of the slope. Walls were made from overlapping slabs of stone, with other large slabs meeting horizontally to make an arch. The entrances are small tunnels big enough for only one person to enter at a time. But the main attraction is a string of 150 "bird man" carvings on rocks on the edge of the cliffs: a man's body is drawn with a bird's head, often holding an egg in one hand.

Archeologists know a considerable amount about the "bird man" cult as its ritual was performed up until 1862, and survivors were able to describe it in detail to later investigators. The

FACT

A variety of small sweet pineapple grows on Easter Island; look for the plantations along the road from Hanga Roa to Anakena Beach.

Archaeological site with petroglyph of birdman.

strange ceremony is linked to the supreme deity Makemake, who is said to have created the earth, sun, moon, and stars. Makemake rewarded good and punished evil, and for centuries was considered responsible for bringing the only visitors to the island from the outside world: an annual migration of sooty tern birds.

Begun in the warring period of the 18th century, the "bird man" cult may have been an esoteric attempt to direct tribal competition toward a peaceful course. It may also have symbolized a wish to escape from the increasing horror of confinement on the island.

The quest for the first egg

The basis of the "bird man" cult was finding the first egg of spring laid by the sacred *Manu Tara* bird, or sooty tern. The chief of each tribe on the island sent one chosen servant to Moto Nui, the largest of the islets below Orongo. Swimming across the dangerous waters, the unfortunate servants or *hopus* each spent about a month looking for the first egg while islanders gathered on the Orongo cliffs making

offerings and prayers to Makemake. When the egg had been found, the successful *hopu* plunged into the swirling waters (with the egg apparently strapped to his forehead), swam to the mainland and climbed back up the cliffs to present the prize to his master.

The successful master would then be named the "bird man" for that year, an important status position. Strangely, the advantages which this office conferred are far from clear. The chief would have his head, eyebrows, and eyelashes shaved, then his head painted red and black. His standing in the community would be increased, but for the whole of the following year he would remain in seclusion in a special house, presumably having gained the favor of Makemake.

A final verdict?

After visiting all the major sites and immersing oneself in the mystery of Easter Island, few visitors can resist making some sort of decision for themselves on the most debated question of all: did the first islanders travel from Polynesia or were they South

Making traditional reed boats.

American refugees as Thor Heyerdahl suggests, escaping in fleets of reed boats from the collapse of a magnificent Andean empire?

It is fair to say that modern archeological opinion weighs heavily against Heyerdahl's dramatic interpretation. Peter Bellwood in his work *Man's Conquest of the Pacific* provides a fairly balanced summary of the latest research, arguing that while nobody can prove Heyerdahl 100 percent wrong, the chances of him being right are quite remote.

Firstly, the language of Easter Island – which is believed to have been spoken since before AD 500 – is completely Polynesian. Secondly, the skeletons found on the island are Polynesian – although they are all from the Late Period. Thirdly, there is no evidence that any portable artifacts dug up on the island came from South America, while many items are certainly Polynesian in style. Finally, the posture of the *moai* can be found in the art of Polynesia as well as in Tiahuanaco-style carving from South America, and may be a common inheritance from past millennia.

But there are some points on which Heyerdahl apparently has a case. The sweet potato and totora reed are South American plants and may have been introduced at a late date, and the stone house designs found on the island recall those of Peru. However, the most surprising piece of evidence for anyone who has visited Peru and Bolivia must be the close-fitting stonework of Ahu Vinapu No. 1, so strikingly reminiscent of Tiahuanaco and Inca work. Its date is set at around AD 600, within the classical period of Tiahuanaco culture.

Yet of the 300-plus *ahus* on the island, this is the only piece of stonework that is reminiscent of a uniquely South American culture. So while a case for major South American migration cannot be made, it is not impossible that at some point in the remote past people from Tiahuanaco visited Easter Island.

The orthodox view of Easter Island's past can be summed up simply: Polynesian seafarers arrived between AD 400 and 500, slowly increasing in numbers and building their statues. As the centuries passed, the island's environment could no longer sustain them. They fought among themselves, destroyed their own achievement and left the rest of the world to puzzle over the ruins.

To some this may seem a little dull without the grand arrival of Incas or survivors of an unknown Atlantis carrying on their lost civilization. But, to quote Bellwood: "Is it not even more exciting that a group of isolated Polynesians could have evolved such a magnificent prehistoric record by using their own ideas, brawn, and procreative ability rather than someone else's? Too many anthropologists in the past have held the view that all good things come from a very few areas, and that most of these areas were inhabited by Caucasoids… The peoples of Oceania deserve the credit for their achievements, not the peoples of some imaginary Mediterranean colonial enterprise."

Banana race at the Tapati festival.

TRAVEL TIPS

CHILE
& EASTER ISLAND

TRANSPORTATION

A – Z

LANGUAGE

TRANSPORTATION

GETTING THERE AND GETTING AROUND

GETTING THERE

By Air

Except for some flights from neighboring countries, almost all international flights arrive at Santiago's modern Arturo Merino Benítez (AMB; www.nuevopudahuel. cl) airport which will be extended and will count with a new terminal by 2020. On entry, passengers from the Australia, Mexico, and Albania, which charge Chileans for tourist visas, are liable to a so-called "reciprocity tax." This can be paid by credit card as well as in cash. The amount is subject to change but, as of April 2016, was: Australia, US$95; Mexico, US$23; Albania, US$30.

Arriving passengers are advised to declare all food products on the

Regions of Chile

Chile is divided into the following **15** administrative regions. The capital of each region is given in brackets.
I Tarapacá (Iquique)
II Antofagasta (Antofagasta)
III Atacama (Copiapó)
IV Coquimbo (La Serena)
V Valparaíso (Valparaíso)
VI O'Higgins (Rancagua)
VII Maule (Talca)
VIII Biobío (Concepción)
IX Araucanía (Temuco)
X Los Lagos (Puerto Montt)
XI Aisén (Coyhaique)
XII Magallanes y Antártica Chilena
(Punta Arenas)
XIII Santiago (Santiago)
XIV Los Ríos (Valdivia)
XV Arica and Parinacota (Arica)

form provided for this purpose on the plane. The strict checks carried out by the Agricultural Inspection Service (SAG), which include sniffer dogs, are designed to preserve Chile's freedom from agricultural pests and undeclared items, even if not specifically mentioned on the list of forbidden products (principally dairy products, meat, fruit, vegetables, and plants) may be confiscated and a US$200 fine imposed. Products that have been declared, even if considered inadmissible, are not liable to the fine, although they will still be confiscated.

AMB charges international passengers a departure tax of US$30, but this is almost always included in the original price of the ticket.

From the US and Canada

It is possible to fly directly to Santiago from the US, with American Airlines (www.aa.com), Delta Air Lines (www.delta.com), or United (www.united.com), and from Canada with Air Canada (www.aircanada.com). Chile's excellent airline, LAN (www.lan. com), also has several flights nightly from major US cities.

From Europe

LAN operates flights to/from Madrid, while European airlines serving Chile include Air France-KLM (www.air france.com; www.klm.com), Iberia (www.iberia.com), and Swiss Airlines (www.swiss.com). In the case of Iberia, some flights are operated by LAN. Other European airlines, including British Airways, have connections via Buenos Aires or São Paulo.

In the UK, tickets can also be obtained through specialist travel

agencies such as Journey Latin America (tel: 020-3432 3949; www.journeylatinamerica.co.uk), Cox & Kings (020-3733 1163; www. coxandkings.co.uk), and Western and Oriental Travel Limited (tel: 020-3131 7641; www.westernoriental. com).

From Australasia

The most direct route from Australia or New Zealand is on the LAN and Qantas Airway flights from Sydney with a stopover in Auckland.

From Latin America

A number of South American airlines, including Aerolíneas Argentinas (www.aerolineas. com), Avianca (www.avianca.com), GOL (www.voegol.com), and TAM (www.tamairlines.com), fly to Chile. From Santiago, there are regular LAN flights to most major Latin American destinations, and the airline also has a service to Tahiti via Easter Island.

LAN offers Visit South America Pass that allows holders to purchase one-way tickets to 65 destinations in South America at preferential rates. This must be acquired at least 14 days prior to departure date and is available only to residents outside South America (except Brazil) who travel to the region with LAN or another member of the oneworld (www.oneworld.com) alliance.

By Rail

Two previous rail connections from Bolivia to Arica and Antofagasta no longer operate, and there are currently no international rail links to Chile.

TRANSPORTATION

A road trip requires preparation, but is a wonderful way to see the country.

By Sea

Except as part of cruises, there are no boat services to Chile from other countries. It is, however, possible to cross from Bariloche in Argentina to southern Chile's Lake District by a combination of road and lake ferries (see page 293).

By Bus

There are a number of bus services from Argentina of which the most frequent are from Mendoza to Santiago and, in the south, from Bariloche to Osorno. The overland journey from Buenos Aires to Santiago via Mendoza takes about 24 hours. The crossing from Peru goes from Tacna to Arica in the far north of Chile. From Bolivia, buses take the road from La Paz to Arica and from Oruro to Calama.

By Road

The main border passes from Argentina to Chile are Los Libertadores in central Chile, Paso Jama in the north, and Cardenal Samoré in the south. However, there are also many more, some of which are not paved and are often closed in winter including the crossing in Patagonia from El Calafate to Puerto Natales. The main road from Peru runs from Tacna to Arica while the main roads from Bolivia are from La Paz to Arica and from Oruro to Iquique, via Colchane.

GETTING AROUND

Despite its length, Chile is an easy country to explore. Santiago is its transportation hub and has frequent flights to all other major cities and some towns and, filling a previous gap, there are an increasing number of flights between provincial cities.

Excellent overnight bus services run up and down the Pan-American Highway, the country's north–south backbone, and there are also direct services from Santiago to other major cities including a virtual shuttle service to Valparaíso and Viña del Mar. The train service that once played a key role in transportation to the south has fallen into increasing disrepair and now only reaches down to Chillán (and even in that case is prone to cancellations and delays).

The more difficult part of Chile to explore is the fjord region to the south of Puerto Montt where the only road, the Carretera Austral, is unpaved and does not reach Punta Arenas, which can only be reached by road through Argentina. However, ferries and small planes serve this area.

To and from the Airport

Arturo Merino Benítez International Airport (tel: 02-690 1752) is 26km (16 miles) west of central Santiago.

Porters are available to assist you with your luggage. A respectable tip for this service would be about US$1.

If you're traveling by taxi, use one of the official services that have desks just inside the arrivals exit. Plenty of other taxis moonlight at the airport, and it is possible to negotiate a cheaper price than the official service (approximately US$30), but, for the unwary, these services also have a few tricks up their sleeve. Alternatively, you can use the regular airport shuttle service (www.turbus.cl), which will take you to the city, or the bus to the subway (www.centropuerto.cl).

The major car rental firms all have offices in the airport terminal. These include Avis, Budget, and Hertz, all with desks in the arrivals hall.

Orientation in Santiago

Santiago is a sprawling city, but the city center is relatively small and easy to explore. "El centro" is roughly triangular-shaped, bounded on one side by the enormous Avenida del Libertador General Bernardo O'Higgins, more conveniently known as the Alameda, on another side by the muddy Río Mapocho, and on the third by the North–South Highway.

In the center is the Plaza de Armas, a city square common to most Spanish-founded cities in South America. Another typical feature is the grid pattern of city streets, which couldn't be simpler for your orientation – although keep in mind that the street names change on either side of the plaza.

Between the plaza and the Alameda is where the traditional

hive of business activity can be found, with wall-to-wall office blocks, shops, hotels, and cinemas. Two main streets, Paseo Huérfanos and Paseo Ahumada, have been turned into pedestrian precincts to accommodate the crowds, but are still almost always highly congested. The Alameda continues eastwards into Avenida Providencia and the suburb of the same name, and, as Avenida Apoquindo, on into the Las Condes district.

Santiago's city center, especially between the Plaza de Armas and the Alameda, is incredibly hectic and congested during the working week – you'll find yourself tiring very quickly. The most pleasant time to stroll around is in January and February, when the city empties for the summer holidays, although it gets hot at this time, so don't plan to do too much.

By Air

Chile's national airline, LAN, has offices in most large towns and on Easter Island, but attends telephone inquiries or bookings only through its national number (tel: 0800-026 0728). It also has a reliable internet

booking service (www.lan.com), with tickets for collection at the airport.

Another small national carrier, **Sky Airline**, (tel: 600-600 2828; www.skyairline.cl) operates to most destinations.

In Aisén, two local companies cover routes within the region: **Aerotaxis del Sur**, Puerto Montt, tel: 065-9583 8374, www.aerotaxis delsur.cl.

Don Carlos, Coyhaique, tel: 067-231 981.

Cielo Mar Austral, a tour operator in Puerto Montt (tel: 065-226 3654; www.cielomaraustral.cl) sells tickets for two other small airlines that fly from Puerto Montt to Chaitén.

In Magallanes, the airline **Aerovías Dap** (http://dapairline. com)connects Punta Arenas to destinations on Isla Grande de Tierra del Fuego and in Argentine Patagonia. They have office in Punta Arenas (tel: 061-261 6100).

To the Juan Fernández Islands

Three airlines offer flights to Isla Robinson Crusoe:
ATA, Av. Larraín 7941, Santiago, tel: 02-275 0363, www.aerolineasata.cl.
Lassa, Av. Larraín 7941, Santiago, tel: 02-2273 43353

Illegal Products

It is illegal to transport any type of seafood on buses. The officials of SAG (the Agricultural Inspection Service) conduct rigorous searches at all international borders and several regional borders and, depending on the area of the country, may confiscate fresh fruit, vegetables, and dairy products. SAG checkpoints are clearly marked on road maps.

Aerocardal, Diego Barros Ortiz 2065, tel: 02-2377 7444, www.aero cardal.com.

To Easter Island

LAN has at least five weekly flights to Easter Island (more in summer). Early booking may yield one of the (scarce) cheaper tickets, expect to pay around US$550 return. The flight takes just over five hours.

By Bus

Chilean bus companies provide comfortable conditions for long-distance travel. The vehicles are well maintained, clean (except for the restrooms), and comfortable. They always depart on schedule, and smoking is prohibited.

The routes are well served, so you rarely need to book more than a few hours in advance, and the cost is low. For long trips, you have the luxurious option of traveling on a *bus cama* (sleeper bus), with first-class seating arrangements – reclining seats with lots of legroom. These buses are very comfortable and include meals, color TV, stereo headphones, and hostess service.

Make sure that you do not lose your token for any baggage placed under the bus.

Santiago Bus Stations

There are four main bus terminals in Santiago managing nearly all international and domestic traffic:
Terminal Santiago, Av. B. O'Higgins 3850, tel: 02-376 1750, www.terminaldebusessantiago.cl.
Terminal San Borja (formerly known as Terminal Norte), Borja 184, tel: 02-776 0645.
Terminal Los Héroes, Tucapel Jiménez 21, tel: 02-2420 0099.
Terminal Alameda (Tur-Bus), Av. B. O'Higgins 3750, tel: 02-270 7425.

This can be confusing, and it is important to make sure you

Transportation in Santiago

Subway: Santiago's metro (www.metrosantiago.cl) is comfortable and efficient. There are five lines (and two under construction): confusingly they are numbered 1 to 5 but without a Line 3. Line 1 runs east–west beneath Av. B. O'Higgins and on through Providencia up into Las Condes while the other three link residential suburbs in the south and north of the city to this line. The 4A express line links lines 2 and 4. Buy tickets at the various stations – currently US$1.04 per ticket – or, preferably, buy the rechargeable Bip! smart card.

Buses: The Transantiago bus system uses smaller buses on short "feeder" routes that connect with "trunk" routes along major arteries, served by larger articulated buses and the metro. Fares are paid using only the Bip! card which can be purchased at metro stations. One fare, currently around US$1.04, covers up to two connections (only one of which can be to the subway), within a two-hour period. Maps are available at subway stations or at www.transantiago.cl (in Spanish). Watch out for pickpockets.

Taxis: Taxis are black with yellow roofs. They each display on the windshield their minimum fare and the rate per 200 meters/ yds, and must also carry a license certificate. All taxis have meters that should be turned on when you enter the car, although some drivers conveniently forget. While most city taxi drivers are trustworthy, it is best to avoid those waiting outside major hotels, who often try to overcharge tourists. Women on their own at night are best advised to call a radio taxi rather than to flag one down in the street. Reliable services include Andes Pacifico (tel: 02-2912 6000; www.andes pacifico.cl) and Neverías (tel: 02-207 0709; www.neverias.cl).

Colectivos: These are simply taxis that take up to four passengers for a flat rate on a fixed route. *Colectivos* are even cheaper than taxis, but the routes they take are limited. The price is usually around US$1, and the routes are similar to those of the buses. *Colectivos* are readily available, and particularly useful, at the metro terminal stations.

understand from which terminal a bus will leave. Buses to Valparaíso and Viña del Mar are best caught outside the Pajaritos station of the metro (Av. General Bonilla 5600), where they leave approximately every 15 minutes. Most international bus companies depart from the Terminal Santiago. However, buses for Mendoza in Argentina depart from the Terminal San Borja. There are also *colectivos* (communal taxis) to Mendoza, departing from the Terminal Santiago.

Two main bus companies cover most domestic destinations. **Tur-Bus** (tel: 600-660 6600; www.turbus.cl) has offices at the Universidad de Chile and Tobalaba metro stations and other locations around the city. **Pullman Bus** (tel: 600-320 3200; www.pullman.cl) has offices in the Universidad de Chile, Pedro de Valdivia, Los Leones, Tobalaba, and Escuela Militar metro stations. Again, check which station your bus will depart from. For bus schedules and more details go to www.horariodebuses.cl.

By Rail

Sadly, rail travel in Chile is a shadow of its past glories. The remaining services cover only destinations between Santiago and Chillán in the south. There are no services to the north or to the coast. All trains leave from Santiago's Estación Central.

Train timetables can be obtained and bookings made online (www.efe.

cl), by calling 02-2585 5050 (Mon–Sat 7.30am–9.30pm), or in person at Estación Central, (Av. B. O'Higgins 3170) or at the railway office in the Universidad de Chile metro station (tel: 600-585 5000). EFE also runs several tourist trains (check their website for details).

By Boat

From the Lake District south, boats become important and, particularly in Aisén, provide vital support for the local inhabitants as well as glorious trips for visitors.

Lake District

The Lake District offers dozens of spectacular boating options. The trip from Petrohué to Puella across Lago Todos Los Santos is the first leg of the "Journey of the Seven Lakes," a magnificent route to Bariloche in Argentina.

The Southern Channels

A number of *transbordadores* (ferries) cross from Chiloé to Chaitén and Puerto Chacabuco in Aisén, and other ferries cross the region's fjords where these interrupt the Carretera Austral.

Navimag, operates a regular roll-on ship from Puerto Montt to Puerto Chacabuco, calling in at the San Rafael glacier, as well as a service from Puerto Montt to San Rafael and back. Tickets can be bought from their website (www.navimag.cl) or their offices in, Puerto Montt (Angelmó 1735; tel: 02-2869 9900), Puerto Chacabuco (Terminal

de Transbordadores; tel: 067-235 1111), Coyhaique (Eusebio Lillo 91; tel: 067-223 3306), and Puerto Natales (Av. de España 1455; tel: 02-2869 9903).

Skorpios (www.skorpios.cl) operates weekly cruises from Puerto Montt to San Rafael from September to May. Santiago: Augusto Leguía Norte 118, Las Condes, tel: 02-2477 1900.

Magallanes

Navimag also operates a weekly service from Puerto Montt to Puerto Natales, while Skorpios offers weekly cruises from Puerto Natales to the Southern Ice Fields.

By Road

Car hire in Chile is relatively expensive, especially in the provinces. However, in some places, it is well worth the cost, particularly if you share expenses with other travelers. For example, in the Lake District and the Central Valley, having one's own transportation opens up many more opportunities.

Car drivers should make sure they have the original registration document of their vehicle. There are plenty of modern service stations on the tourist routes, and fuel is about US$1.06/liter, but varies significantly in line with international oil prices.

Santiago has a number of new high-speed roads with an electronic toll system. These can be used without the windscreen-mounted bleeper but a daily pass, available at most service stations and at main entry points to the city, should be acquired either before or shortly after using the highway.

Hertz has one of the largest car rental networks, with branch offices in most major cities. It has offices at Andrés Bello 1469, Providencia (tel: 02-2360 8617) and at Arturo Merino Benítez Airport (tel: 02-2360 8714) in Santiago; www.hertz.cl. Other major companies are **Budget** (tel: 02-2795 3900; www.budget.cl) and **Avis** (tel: 02-2795 3900; www.avis.cl). The Automóvil Club de Chile also rents cars and has offices throughout Chile (tel: 600-464 4040; www.automovilclub.cl).

Car hire rates start at around US$80. Some companies offer weekly rates with unlimited mileage. It's worth shopping around. A substantial deposit or credit-card voucher may also be required.

See Maps (page 298) for where to purchase detailed road maps if you're planning to drive in Chile.

International Airlines

The main international airlines flying to Chile are:

Aerolíneas Argentinas
Tel: 800-610 200
www.aerolineas.com

American Airlines
Tel: 02-2601 9272
www.aa.com

Aeromexico
Tel: 02-2390 1000
www.aeromexico.com

Air Canada
Tel: 02-800 400 142
www.aircanada.com

Air France-KLM
Tel: 02-2580 9696
www.airfrance.com; www.klm.com

Avianca
Tel: 02-2270 6613
www.avianca.com

Copa
Tel: 02-200 2100

www.copaair.com

Delta Airlines
Tel: 02-800 202 020
www.delta.com

Gol
Tel: 188-800 420 090
www.voegol.com

Iberia
Tel: 02-2870 1000
www.iberia.com

Quantas
Tel: 02-2601 8889
www.taca.com

SKY
Tel: 600-600 2828
www.skyairline.cl

UNITED
Tel: 123-0020 5425
www.united.com

TAM Airlines
Tel: 02-2862 6500
www.tamairlines.com

A – Z

A HANDY SUMMARY
OF PRACTICAL INFORMATION

A

Accommodations

Take Chilean hotel star ratings with a pinch of salt. In Santiago, they're generally reliable but in the rest of the country, they can be a bit haphazard. However, standards are mostly high and improving all the time. As a general guide, three-star and up is almost always comfortable and clean. A double room in a three-star hotel in Santiago is likely to cost upwards of US$100 a night.

Like other Latin American countries, Chile's main cities can seem noisy to overseas visitors, particularly in summer when windows are open and pavement cafés stay in full swing until late into the night. It can, therefore, be worth asking for a "quiet" room when booking a hotel.

Boutique hotels are fashionable in Santiago and other tourist spots including, particularly, Valparaíso. Lodges, many geared to the fly-fishing market, are increasingly common in the south of Chile.

The busy seasons are the summer months (December–March) and the week around the Independence Day holiday, on September 18. During these periods, it's essential to book ahead, particularly in the Torres del Paine National Park, where there's a serious shortage of hotel accommodations, and at other popular tourist spots.

There's not much difference between hosterías and hotels, but residenciales are more basic affairs, with none of the hotel frills – usually no meals apart from breakfast and, possibly, shared bathrooms. At an hospedaje, you'll get a room in a private house, but standards vary a lot (they are particularly good value for money in the Lake District and Chiloé). Ultimately, the best guide as to what sort of stay you'll have at an hospedaje is the friendliness of the owner, so it is worth having a chat with him or her before making your choice.

Addresses

Most Chilean towns and cities are built as a grid of parallel streets, making it easy to find your way around. Street numbers – odd on one side, even on the other – progress steadily, with 100 to a block. The only complication is that the numbers can be divided when a street is crossed by a main road, starting with 1 on one side and 01 on the other. The letters s/n stand for sin número and are used where there is no street number in the address, usually in smaller towns.

Admission Charges

Admission charges in Chile are rarely expensive and there are mostly reductions for students and senior citizens. In some museums, admission is free on Sundays.

B

Budgeting for Your Trip

In recent years, Chile has become one of the more expensive countries in Latin America after Brazil. Public transportation is still very cheap by European standards, and restaurant prices are moderate but hotels, in particular, have become far more expensive measured in dollars or euros. Average prices in Santiago are:

A beer or a glass of house wine: US$2.70
A main course at a budget, a moderate and an expensive restaurant: US$6, US$12, US$18
A cheap, a moderate, and a deluxe hotel: US$25, US$80, US$180
A taxi journey to or from the airport: US$30
A single bus/subway ticket: US$1.04.

C

Children

Chileans make a great fuss of children and they are made welcome everywhere, except in expensive restaurants where they will be frowned on even at lunchtime. Menus don't usually include children's meals but efforts will be made to accommodate them. Admission for children is free or reduced-price in museums.

Between December and March is a good time to visit Chiloé.

Climate

When to Visit

As a general rule, Chile's climate makes a steady transition from the extreme arid heat of the desert north to the bitterly cold and wet conditions of the far south. Most of the country can be visited at any time of the year, except Aisén, Magallanes, and Tierra de Fuego. In the far north, the so-called "Bolivian winter" in January or February can bring torrential rain, but usually only lasts for a few days.

The North

Rainfall is virtually non-existent in the Atacama Desert. Typical desert conditions prevail all year round, with searingly hot days and chilly nights. High winds shift the desert sands and make northern highways more dangerous for motoring. The northern skies are generally very clear, although on the far northern coast, at Arica, there is higher humidity and frequent cloud cover. Temperatures here are less extreme, from 15°C (59°F) to 22°C (72°F). At the same latitudes, towards the Bolivian border, snow often covers the high mountain passes.

Central Valley

The area, known as the transitional zone, between Copiapó and Illapel, only receives light winter rainfall, and agriculture is therefore dependent on artificial irrigation.

Immediately south, the lush central region continues through to Concepción with higher inland temperatures and ever-increasing rainfall from north to south. The climate is idyllically Mediterranean, mild and temperate, the warmest months being November to February, when the temperatures can reach 34°C (93°F). July and August are the coolest months, with temperatures as low as 10°C (50°F) during the day. Nights are rather cool, even in summer.

The best months in Santiago are between October and April, when the days are nearly always fine – although December and January can be uncomfortably hot in the congested city center.

The summer heat is more tolerable on the coast at the famous seaside resorts, with fresh cooling breezes. The weather is excellent for skiing during the winter months at the resorts of Portillo, El Colorado, La Parva, and Valle Nevado, east of Santiago.

Lake District

As far south as Puerto Montt, the Lake District has a temperate climate, although heavy rain falls throughout much of the year. The temperature is cooler than in the central region, and icy winds originate from the lakes and mountains. Winter brings snow to the chalet-style resorts in the higher regions of Petrohué, Puella, and Lago Todos Los Santos, and some Andean highways between Chile and Argentina can become snowbound or otherwise impassable due to fog and storms.

Chiloé

The islands of Chiloé are cold and foggy for most of the year, but for about 60 days, usually between December and March, when the sun shines, the countryside is especially picturesque. Chiloé is a particularly rainy place, especially along its western, Pacific coast.

Aisén

South of Puerto Montt, the region of Aisén has a steppe climate, with fairly low temperatures all year round. Abundant snow falls from early autumn to late spring, so the best months to visit are November to March. Summer brings beautifully crisp, clear days to the region, although cold winds and torrential rainstorms can also occur unpredictably. Worth noting is the agreeable microclimate found around the village of Chile Chico, which is suitable for growing fine fruit and vegetables.

Magallanes

In this region of glaciers and wilderness, snow covers the land in winter (except along the coastline), while rain is frequent in summer, and freezing winds of up to 80kph (50mph) are common in spring. The climate and scenery have been likened to those of Norway. It is best to visit the far south in December, January, or February, when the sun is higher in the sky and the summer average temperature climbs to 11°C (52°F).

Easter Island

This isolated Pacific Island has a semi-tropical climate throughout the year, with a particularly fierce sun that is not to be underestimated. July and August are the coolest months for wandering among the *moai*.

What to Wear

Most middle-class Latin Americans spend a great deal of their income on their appearance. Travelers aren't

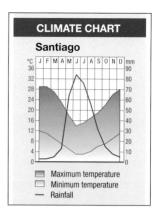

CLIMATE CHART

Santiago

- Maximum temperature
- Minimum temperature
- — Rainfall

expected to appear as immaculately groomed as residents; however, it's sensible, especially in Santiago, to take a little extra care. You might receive better service in some establishments if you dress more formally, or if your casual wear is fairly smart. If in doubt about the dress requirements, err on the formal side. Chileans are naturally conservative dressers.

If you are traveling extensively through Chile, take clothing that is most useful for all extremes of climate. Remember that southern Chile is as cold as the northern deserts are hot, so take warm socks, gloves, headgear, and a windproof and waterproof jacket. The ozone layer is particularly thin in the southern regions, so bring sunglasses, sunscreen, and headgear. Thermal underwear will come in handy if you're heading for southern regions such as the Torres del Paine National Park, Punta Arenas, or Tierra del Fuego. Travelers often prefer to buy their woolen sweaters or ponchos from *artesanías* in Santiago or en route, since they are very reasonably priced and of high quality.

If you're trying to cut down on shoe luggage, take some solid walking shoes that won't look too out of place in a casual restaurant. Synthetic fabrics won't crush in your suitcase, but these don't breathe as well in the hot weather. It's a good idea to use your hotel's laundering service, as cleaners tend to be less reliable and just as expensive.

Crime and Safety

Visitors to Chile, especially its larger cities, should watch out for their belongings but need not worry about their personal safety as, although theft is quite common, the rate of violent crime is one of the lowest in Latin America. In other words, just take basic precautions: watch out for pickpockets in crowded places and don't hang bags on the back of your chair in restaurants. It is also better to avoid out-of-the-way areas at night.

Customs Regulations

During your flight you will fill out a customs declaration form and supply identity details on your tourist card. The allowed quota of duty-free goods extends to 400 cigarettes, 50 cigars, 2.5 liters of liquor, and all items for personal use.

It is prohibited to import meat products, flowers, fruit, vegetables, and seeds unless one has a relevant certificate issued by the Department of Agriculture in the country of origin. Most overseas visitors with "nothing to declare" find no delays in passing through customs. Chilean wine and finely crafted stones such as lapis lazuli are popular souvenirs.

D

Disabled Travelers

Although progress is slowly being made, Chile can be difficult for disabled visitors, especially outside Santiago. Most large hotels present no problems but not all public buildings have access facilities. New buses in Santiago have pavement-level access but, in other places and on intercity services, the steps are high (although help will usually be provided) and not all stations on the Metro, the city's subway, have access facilities. Before booking an air ticket, check the airline's policy; there have been unfortunate cases in which disabled passengers have not been

Chile's national flag: the lone star.

allowed to board on grounds of lack of mobility or self-sufficiency.

E

Earthquakes

Chile is earthquake territory, and tremors, sometimes quite strong, are fairly frequent. Rule number one – don't panic! Modern buildings are earthquake-resistant – although that implies elasticity, and high floors can "swing" uncomfortably – and older buildings have already proved their capacity for survival.

In buildings: take cover under door-frames or sturdy furniture such as tables, and try to keep as far away as possible from windows or glass doors; on no account use elevators. In built-up areas: do not walk out in the street because of the danger of falling rubble, and keep clear of trees and electric cables. On country roads avoid bridges or any elevated sections of highway. If on the coast, beware of the risk of a tsunami and be ready to move to higher ground if necessary.

Embassies and Consulates

In Santiago

Argentina
Miraflores 285
Tel: 02-582 2500.
Australia
Isidora Goyenechea 3621, Piso 13
Tel: 02-550 3500.
Bolivia (Consulate only)
Av. Santa María 2796
Tel: 02-232 8180.
Brazil
Alonso Ovalle 1665
Tel: 02-876 3400.
Canada
Nueva Tajamar 481, Torre Norte,
Piso 12

Emergencies

For any emergency services, call the following numbers:
Ambulance Service: 131
Fire Brigade: 132
Police: 133/134
Police Information: 139
Tourist Card Extension: Passport Office, San Antonio 580, Santiago, tel: 600-626 4222. Hours: Mon–Fri 8.30am–2pm.

Tel: 02-652 3800.
New Zealand
Isidora Goyenechea 3000, Piso 12,
Tel: 02-616 3000.
Peru
Av. Andrés Bello 1751
Tel: 02-339 2601.
South Africa
Av. 11 de Septiembre 2353, Piso 17
Tel: 02-820 0300.
UK
Av. El Bosque Norte 0125, Piso 3
Tel: 02-370 4100.
US
Av. Andrés Bello 2800
Tel: 02-330 3000.

Chilean Embassies Abroad

Australia
10 Culgoa Circuit O'Malley ACT 2606,
Canberra
Tel: 612-628 62430.
Canada
50 O'Connor Street, Suite 1413,
Ottawa, Ontario
Tel: 613-235 4402.
New Zealand
The Pencarrow House 1, Willeston
Street, Wellington
Tel: 4-471 6270.
UK
37–41 Old Queen Street, London
SW1H 9JA
Tel: 020-7222 2361.
US
1732 Massachusetts Avenue, N.W.,
Washington, D.C. 20036
Tel: 202-785 1746.

Etiquette

Chileans have a warm but clearly defined way of greeting. Men and women meeting, or women greeting women, will kiss one another once on the cheek. Men greeting men will always shake hands. When dealing with officials, you'll find the response more agreeable if you say *buenos días* (good day), and wait for the reply before you continue speaking. Chileans are not as unpunctual as other Latin Americans, but are still likely to be half an hour late for social

appointments. When invited to a Chilean home, never arrive early; it's far better to be late.

G

Gay and Lesbian Travelers

In recent years attitudes to homosexuality, particularly among young people, have changed dramatically in Chile. However older men, particularly in the countryside, can be homophobic. There are an increasing number of gay and gay-friendly bars, restaurants, and discotheques in Santiago, especially in the Bellavista area. The following organizations advocate for LGBTIQ+ rights in Chile:
Movimiento de Integración y Liberación Homosexual
Coquimbo 1410, Santiago, tel: 02-2671 4855, www.movilh.org
Movimiento Unificado de Minorias Sexuales
Santa Monica 2317, Santiago, tel: 02-2671 4568, www.mums.cl

H

Health and Medical Care

Chile is one of the safest countries in South America as regards health concerns. There is no malaria or yellow fever, the tap water is chlorinated, and the general standard of hygiene is high. The country is fortunate in producing an abundance of fresh fruit and vegetables in its Central Valley region, while meat products are also plentiful, thus ensuring quality foods for most people.

Precautions
Most travelers go without vaccinations. Some people have hepatitis and typhoid shots, although the possibility of encountering these diseases is very remote. The tap water in Santiago is safe to drink, although sensitive systems should use bottled mineral water and avoid the adjustment period.
Sudden changes in diet and lifestyle often cause temporary **bowel**

Electricity

220 volts/50Hz is the standard current throughout the country. Chile uses the round two-pin plug. Travelers from the UK and the US will need to bring an adaptor.

disorders, which are rarely anything to worry about and just a typical part of travel. The best remedy is to eat very little and drink plenty of liquid in small sips for a day or so. Tea without milk or flat lemonade are ideal. Symptoms should improve within 48 hours. If the problem lasts longer than a few days, antibiotics or a visit to the doctor may be necessary.
Do not collect and eat shellfish from beaches unless you are very sure there is not an algae bloom – known in Spanish as *marea roja* – in the area as this can cause very serious illness.
When camping, particularly in central and southern Chile, keep food in sealed containers and be otherwise careful not to attract rodents; some country mice carry a hantavirus that causes a flu-like illness, which is occasionally fatal.

Hot and Cold
The only other problems come from Chile's extreme climate and geography. In the Atacama Desert and on Easter Island, the heat can cause serious **exhaustion** and **sunburn**. Don't overestimate your skin's resistance. Bring sufficient water, sunscreen, a hat, and preferably sunglasses, too. Even thus prepared, the sun and heat can be trying to the mildest of temperaments. Take things slowly and don't expect to achieve as much as usual.
In the far south, from Puerto Montt to Tierra del Fuego, the bitter cold in mountain areas and at all altitudes in winter can cause **hypothermia** to those who are unprotected: symptoms include exhaustion, numbness, slurred speech, and shivering. High winds are notorious in Patagonia, often carrying icy rain and sleet, so bring protective clothing to cover your head and body. Again, it's best to move more slowly, staying aware of your energy level. Mountain climbers should take the usual precautions.

Altitude
Though not as severe as the altitudes of Bolivia or Peru, some popular sightseeing spots in the north, and some Andean passes between Chile and Argentina, are high enough to cause slight **altitude sickness** in some people. The symptoms can become noticeable from around 900 meters (3,000ft), and include shortness of breath, headache, weakness, and mild nausea. Aspirin is one of the best remedies for mild altitude sickness. In rare cases, severe altitude sickness is indicated by dizziness and intensity of

the other symptoms. The immediate treatment for this condition is to move to a lower altitude.

Medical Treatment
The Chilean national health service is generally of a reasonable standard. Hospitals have outpatient departments, which will treat visitors' accidents and emergencies, but are likely to be much busier than private clinics. Ask your embassy or hotel to recommend doctors who speak English.
Pharmacies in Chile are usually well stocked with the latest medical supplies, and many products are available without a prescription. Many pharmacies remain open until midnight, and some operate round the clock. Ask your hotel for a list of addresses. There are also increasingly popular homeopathic outlets in most cities.

Clinics in Santiago
For a private clinic contact:
Clínica Las Condes, Estoril 450, tel: 02-210 4000, www.clc.cl.
Clínica Santa María, Av. Santa María 0500, tel: 02-913 0000, www.clinica santamaria.cl.
Clínica Alemana, Av. Manquehue Nte. 1499, tel: 02-210 1111, https://portal.alemana.cl.

I

Insurance

All travelers should invest in comprehensive travel insurance, which is available through travel agents. Check that this will cover the cost of your return flight if you're flown home in an emergency, as well as covering stolen or damaged valuables.

Internet

Internet access is ubiquitous and cheap in Chile. In Santiago free Wi-Fi is available in hotels, cafés, libraries, and neighborhoods such as *barrio República*, as well as areas near the university. The main shopping malls and some cinema complexes also have facilities while subway stations and the airport have all clearly marked hotspots.

L

Lost Property

Although Santiago's subway and airports have lost property offices, the chances are that, if you've left something behind, you've lost it. It's worth marking objects like cameras with your name and a telephone number so an honest finder can call you, but don't bother with the police station, except in small towns.

M

Maps

Maps are available at the Santiago office of Sernatur, the national tourist board, which is located at Providencia 1550.

The *Plano del Gran Santiago* (city map), which can be purchased at most newsstands, shows the city center and inner suburbs, and metro lines. Outside Santiago, Sernatur branch offices can supply free city maps.

Addresses in Santiago can be found on www.mapcity.com, a free website, from which maps can also be printed.

The *Gran Mapa Caminero de Chile* is the most practical map of Chile – also available at newsstands.

Excellent road maps are available from the Automóvil Club de Chile, Av. Andrés Bello 1863, Santiago, tel: 600-464 4040.

Turistel is the name of a series of Chilean guidebooks (in Spanish) that contain maps, details of accommodations ranging from campsites to hotels, and other tourist information. Available at COPEC gas stations.

Gas stations sell road maps.

Topographical maps are sold by the Instituto Geográfico Militar in Santiago (sales office: Nueva Santa Isabel 1640, tel: 02-410 9300).

Media

Radio

There are many AM and FM radio stations currently broadcasting in the country. The radio stations play mostly rock and pop music. As you would expect, the popular stations, such as Pudahuel (90.5), concentrate on Spanish-speaking singers and groups, while their upmarket competitors offer a more international variety. Only three stations – radios Beethoven (96.5), Universidad de Chile (102.5), and Universidad de Santiago (94.5) – regularly broadcast classical music. For news bulletins, try either the popular Cooperativa (93.3), a stalwart that goes back to the dictatorship days when it dared say things that other stations didn't, or Radio Bío-Bío (99.7).

If you're out in the country, and you understand a bit of Spanish, listen to the local radio stations. In remote areas, people use them to keep in touch, and you'll get an interesting insight into local life.

Television

Chile has dozens of television channels, two of which transmit only news: CNN Chile and Canal 24 Horas. TVN (Televisión Nacional) is state-owned while two, Canal 13 and Mega, belong to local business groups and the fourth, Chilevisión, is owned by Time Warner. The programming is relatively similar, although Mega targets lower income groups.

Print

Chile has seven main national newspapers, as well as around 50 provincial dailies. One of the most widely read is the conservative morning daily *El Mercurio*, which first appeared in 1827. Every Friday it publishes a supplement called *Wikén* (weekend), which provides information about events in Santiago.

Other newspapers include *La Tercera* as well as two business newspapers, *El Diario Financiero* and *Estrategia*. An afternoon paper, *La Segunda*, circulates in Santiago and a free morning newspaper is distributed on the city's subway.

Magazines include a weekly *Qué Pasa* and biweekly *Ercilla*, while *Newsweek* and *Time* are readily available in Spanish and English. In central Santiago's Paseo Ahumada, newsstands offer a wide variety of slightly out-of-date international newspapers.

Money

Money can be exchanged in hotels, exchange bureaux *(casas de cambio)*, and banks. The rate varies little between establishments, although it might not be quite as good at hotels. Banks are open to the public Monday through Friday 9am–2pm. If you have a credit card, cash can be withdrawn from ubiquitous automatic cash machines, which also take most bank cash cards.

Casas de Cambio

If you don't have a credit card, exchange bureaux are probably the best choice. They are usually found within travel agencies and are open Mon–Fri 9am–2pm. In Santiago, exchange offices and banks are located mostly in the central business district and Providencia, but there

are also exchange offices in the main shopping malls. Money can be sent to major banks from other parts of the world with minimum delays.

US dollars are the most easily exchanged unit of currency throughout Chile. In Santiago, it's possible to exchange pounds sterling, Australian dollars, yen, and other currencies at banks, but elsewhere you'll need US dollars cash.

O

Opening Hours

Banks are open to the public Monday through Friday 9am–2pm. Exchange bureaux are open Monday through Friday 9am–2pm, except in the main shopping malls, where they open until 9pm and at weekends.

Government offices and other businesses are usually open to the public 9am–1pm and 2–6pm.

Most **shops** in Santiago are open Monday to Friday 10am–8pm. Major shopping centers, such as Parque Arauco and Alto Las Condes, are open throughout the week, including Sundays, until 10pm.

P

Postal Services

The Chilean postal service is more reliable than that of most South American countries. Mail sent by air *(por aéreo)* takes around seven days to the US and UK or 10 days to Australia. Sea mail takes about 10

Public Holidays

January 1 New Year's Day
Easter Good Friday, Easter Sunday
May 1 Labor Day
May 21 Commemoration of Iquique sea battle; opening of Congress
June Monday closest to St Peter and St Paul
July 16 Day of the Virgin of Carmen (Chile's patron saint)
August 15 Ascension of the Virgin
September 18 Independence Day
September 19 Army Day with parade
October 10 Encuentro de dos Mundos
November 1 All Saints' Day
December 8 Immaculate Conception
December 25 Christmas Day

TRANSPORTATION

Cheap hostels are a good option for student travelers and backpackers.

weeks. There is a daily airmail service to Europe with connections to the UK.

The general delivery service, or poste restante *(Lista de Correos)*, is located in the Correo Central (central post office) on the Plaza de Armas, in Santiago. The system is fairly well organized, although they will hold your mail no longer than 30 days before returning to sender. Opening times vary, but most post offices are open Monday to Friday, 9am to 7pm and on Saturday morning. No offices are open on Sunday.

R

Religious Services

Mass is celebrated at least once a day, and several times on Sunday, in most Catholic churches. In Santiago, a number of Protestant churches also hold services in English. These include the Santiago Community Church, Av. Holanda 151, tel: 02-232 1113, www.santiagochurch. org (Sunday 10.30am), and the San Marcos Presbyterian Church, Padre Hurtado Central 599, tel: 02-224 5893 (Sunday 9.30am).

S

Shopping

As in most other Latin American countries, shopping malls are common in Chile. With department stores as their anchor, along with multiplex cinemas and food courts, they're much like malls in the United States and are where the vast majority of better-off Chileans do their shopping. Similarly, supermarkets have gradually replaced corner grocery shops, most petrol stations now have convenience stores, and strip malls – typically with a

bank branch, a pharmacy, and a drycleaners, as well as other small shops – abound.

The range of both domestic and imported products is wide and you'll be almost certain to find anything you forgot to pack.

Fair trading is a concept that is only just beginning to gain ground in Chile but Artesanías de Chile, a foundation, with two outlets in the city, does ensure that its artisans get a proper price for their work.

Sales tax (VAT) is 19 percent and is already included in the displayed price. Under Chilean consumer law, shops must sell at the price on display so insist on your rights if it doesn't match what you're being charged.

What to Buy

Chile's rich geology provides a wide diversity of minerals for handicrafts. Most outstanding are lapis lazuli (which is found only in Chile and Afghanistan), silver, bronze, and wrought copper.

Other popular souvenirs include: Traditional pottery from different regions.

The colorful attire of the *huaso* (Chilean cowboy) from the Central Valley, some of which can be bought in local *talabarterías* (saddlers' shops).

Leather goods, boots, and handbags, available in the main street stores and malls of Santiago.

The beautifully worked silver jewelry of the Mapuches.

Chilean wine and pisco, the local grape liquor.

What Not to Buy

Street vendors offer a wide variety of pirated products, ranging from books and DVDs to imitation Louis Vuitton handbags. This is a thriving industry and the standard of many products is high and their prices attractive. However, buying from these vendors

is, in theory, an offense – although charges are rarely pressed – and is a violation of intellectual property rights for which the US has put Chile on an international blacklist.

Student Travelers

Holders of an International Student Identity Card or International Youth Travel Card are entitled to reduced entrance fees at most museums and discounts at some restaurants, movie theaters, discotheques, bookshops, and tourist agencies. Cut-price airline tickets and more information can be obtained at the Student Flight Center, Hernando de Aguirre 201, Of. 401, Santiago, tel: 02-411 2000.

T

Tax

VAT (19 percent), known as IVA in Spanish, is already incorporated into prices displayed in shops but not always in hotel rates where foreigners are exempt. Airport tax is almost always included in the ticket price, except for an entry tax levied on visitors from some specific countries (see page 290). If traveling by car on Chile's main highways, make sure you have enough cash for tolls (mostly around US$1–6 each) and note that credit cards are not accepted.

Telecommunications

International Calls

Calls overseas can be made direct from public telephones and from call centers. You must prefix the code of the carrier you want to handle your call: there are over 30, but the largest – although not necessarily the cheapest – are Entel (its code is 123) and Movistar (188). It is possible to call collect (reverse the charges), and the quality of the lines is excellent. Off-peak rates apply after 8pm on weekdays, after 2pm on Saturday, and all day on Sunday. The international dialing code for Chile is +56.

Time Zone

From April to October, Chile is four hours behind GMT. From end October through March, daylight saving time is in operation and the country is three hours behind GMT during this period.

A – Z

LANGUAGE

Tour agencies abound in popular destinations like Pucón.

Main area codes:
Ancud 65
Antofagasta 55
Arica 58
Calama 55
Castro 65
Chillán 42
Concepción 41
Copiapó 52
Coquimbo 51
Coyhaique 67
Curicó 75
Easter Island 32
Iqueque 57
La Serena 51
Osorno 64
Puerto Montt 65
Puerto Natales 61
Puerto Varas 65
Puerto Williams 61
Punta Arenas 61
Rancagua 72
San Antonio 35
Santiago 2
Talca 71
Temuco 45
Valdivia 63
Valparaiso 32
Viña del Mar 32
International dialing codes:
Australia +61
Canada +1
Ireland +353
New Zealand +64
South Africa +27
UK +44
US +1

Tipping

In restaurants, service is not generally included and a 10 percent tip is usual. Taxi drivers do not expect to be tipped, but it's usual not to ask for small change.

Toilets

Public washrooms (*baños*) are a rarity in Chile, but bars and cafés will usually let you use their facilities. In bus and train stations the washrooms are manned by an attendant who provides you with toilet paper for a small fee.

Tour Operators and Travel Agents

Chile's main travel agents are all based in Santiago and include:
Cocha
El Bosque Norte 0430
Tel: 02-464 1300
www.cocha.com
One of the best options for booking international flights. Cocha also has several other offices in Santiago as well as in Viña del Mar and Concepción and in most Ripley department stores around the country.
La Casa Roja
Agustinas 2113
Tel: 02-695 0600
www.lacasaroja.cl
This hostel has an excellent travel agency geared to backpackers.
Latitud 90
Av. Kennedy 7268
Tel: 02-241 1900
www.latitud90.com
Well-organized tours, with English-speaking guides, but significantly more expensive than other options.
Turismo Mostrando Chile
Antonio Varas 175, Of. 1205
Tel: 02-235 0624
www.turismomostrandochile.cl
This agency specializes in tours within Chile, but also offers some to neighboring countries.

In Santiago, you could be blinded by the choice of tour services, but they offer basically the same tours, including a city tour starting from your hotel. The cost is around US$60. Night tours include a view from the top of Cerro San Cristóbal and a restaurant meal with floorshow for around US$100. There are various day excursions to Viña del Mar and Valparaíso, visiting the lush Chilean vineyards en route, which include lunch at an elegant restaurant for around US$160. The Turistik (www.turistik.cl) tourism company also operates a hop-on hop-off service on red double-decker buses for which a ticket costs around US$33.

The Sernatur Tourist Office will give you a long list; some tour operators and travel agencies have offices in the main hotels.

You'll also find a whole range of tour operators in San Pedro de Atacama, most of which also offer very similar itineraries and services.
Cosmo Andino Expediciones
Calle Caracoles cnr. Tocopilla
Tel: 055-285 1069
www.cosmoandino.cl
Expediciones Corvatsch
Tocopilla 406
Tel: 055-285 1087
www.corvatschchile.cl

Famous for its beaches, La Serena is also a center for visits to the Tololo, Gemini South, Las Campanas, and La Silla astronomical observatories and the Elqui Valley, renowned for its pisco (a grape-based liquor) and the birthplace of the famous poet Gabriela Mistral.
Ecoturismo La Serena
Andres Bello 937
Tel: 09-7615 2371
www.ecoturismolaserena.cl
Intimahina Travel
Arturo Prat 220
Tel: 051-222 4350
www.itravel.cl

Pucón is a resort town that comes alive during the holiday season. In summer, the tour operators run groups to the various *termas* (thermal springs), or to participate in adventure sports like white-water rafting and volcano climbing.
Expediciones École
General Urrutia 592
Tel: 045-244 1675
www.ecole.cl
Politur
O'Higgins 635
Tel: 045-244 1373
www.politur.com

Puerto Natales is the starting point for excursions to Parque Nacional Torres del Paine and also farther north to the town of El Calafate in Argentina. From Puerto Natales, regular boat trips also operate to the Balmaceda and Serrano glaciers.
Big Foot Expediciones
Bories 206
Tel: 061-241 4611
www.bigfootpatagonia.com
Erratic Rock
Baquedano 719
Tel: 061-410 355
www.erraticrock.com

Tourist Information

The headquarters of the Sernatur Tourist Office is located at Av. Providencia 1550, Santiago (tel: 02-731 8310), between the Manuel Montt and Pedro de Valdivia metro stations. The office opens Mon–Fri 9am–6pm, Sat 9am–2pm. There is also a Sernatur information desk in the baggage reclaim area of the Santiago airport (open daily 8.30am–8pm) and, in other cities and towns around the country:

Ancud: Libertad 665
Tel: 065-262 2800
Antofagasta: Prat 384, Piso 1
Tel: 055-245 1820
Arica: San Marcos 101
Tel: 058-225 2054
Chillán: 18 de Septiembre 455
Tel: 042 222 3272
Concepción: Aníbal Pinto 460
Tel: 041-274 1337
Copiapó: Los Carrera 691
Tel: 052-221 2838
Coyhaique: Bulnes 35
Tel: 067-224 0290
Easter Island:
Policarpo Toro s/n
Tel: 032-210 0255
Iquique: Anibal Pinto 436
Tel: 057-241 9241
Osorno: Bdo. O'Higgins 667, Edificio Gobernación, Piso 1
Tel: 02-2731 8627
Puerto Montt: Antonio Varas 415, Piso 2
Tel: 065-222 3016
Puerto Natales: Pedro Montt 19
Tel: 061-241 2125
Punta Arenas: Lautaro Navarro 999
Tel: 061-248 790
Rancagua: Germán Riesco 277, Of. 11 & 12
Tel: 072-230 413
San Pedro de Atacama: Tocopilla 360
Tel: 055-851 420
La Serena: Matta 461, Of. 108
Tel: 051-225 138
Talca: 1 Oriente 1150, Piso 1

Tel: 071-222 6940
Temuco: Claro Solar cnr. Manuel Bulnes
Tel: 045-312 857
Valdivia: Prat s/n
Tel: 063-223 9060
Valparaíso: Plaza Sotomayor 233, Piso 1
Tel: 032-223 6264
Viña Del Mar: 8 Norte 580, Edificio Nogaleda
Tel: 032-269 0082

Useful Websites

Basic tourist information in English can be found on Sernatur's website (www.sernatur.cl), but it is not always up to date. A number of other websites also provide useful information for visitors to Chile in English, including:
www.gochile.cl
www.turismochile.com
http://chile.travel/
http://www.allsantiago.com/
http://santiagochile.com/

Visas and Passports

All foreigners require a valid identity document. While residents of neighboring countries can use their identity card in Chile, all other foreigners require passports, and most can stay in Chile for up to 90 days. All foreigners wishing to work in Chile need visas.

A tourist card is issued to all foreigners on arrival. Visitors from some countries are charged an entry fee (Australia, US$95; Mexico, US$23). The tourist card contains your identification data and is generally valid for 90 days. It is renewable for a further 90 days, though if you wish to stay longer than six months, it's simplest to take a short trip to an adjoining country and you will be

Metric measurements are used to calculate distances and weights.

issued with a new tourist card on your return. Renewal applications must be submitted personally at the Passport Office (San Antonio 580, Santiago, tel: 600-486 3000), open Monday through Friday 8.30am–2pm. The card must be surrendered when leaving the country. Don't lose it.

What to Bring

Chile is probably the most materially modern country in South America, with exhaustive shopping potential in Santiago, so if you forget to pack something, you'll probably be able to purchase it there.

Note that foreign books, including travel guidebooks in English, can be surprisingly expensive so it is better to purchase these in your home country. Clothing for all weathers is necessary if you plan to tour the whole country. Take a first-aid kit for travel to remote areas.

Good camping and hiking equipment is available, but the range is limited and prices are high.

A pocket knife or Swiss Army knife might come in handy, since fruit should be peeled, or at least washed, before eating.

Take your driver's license if you plan to hire a road vehicle.

Other useful items: a small sewing kit, a water container for walking trips, sunglasses, aspirin (often desirable in areas of high altitude), swimming costume, and protective clothing for sports and boat trips.

Women Travelers

Providing women travelers take sensible precautions, they are as safe in Chile as in most European countries. Chilean men often stare, whistle and can make vulgar remarks, but it hardly ever goes beyond that, and stranger rape is extremely rare. The metro, Santiago's underground rail system, is safe at all hours, as are the buses, as long as you don't go off the beaten track. However, late at night, it is sensible to call a radio taxi, rather than flagging one down on the street. In remote country areas, where male alcoholism is a serious problem, a little extra care is also advisable.

Chile is generally a safe place for solo women travelers.

LANGUAGE

UNDERSTANDING THE LANGUAGE

Of the many versions of Latin American Spanish in South America, the Chilean version is one of the hardest to understand. Chileans neglect to pronounce some consonants clearly, if at all. Television newsreaders are the only exception.

So Chile is not the ideal place to learn Spanish. (Best value for classes, as well as best for understanding, is probably Quito, Ecuador, if you are considering further travel in South America.) At any rate, it is much better to know a little Spanish when you arrive. English is spoken at major hotels and by quite a few Chileans, but don't count on it with taxi drivers, waiters, or porters.

Language schools, apart from advertised private tuition, include the Chilean-British Institute and the Chilean-North American Cultural Institute. The main private language schools offer tailor-made individual courses, but these tend to be expensive. Most reputable language schools ask for at least US$1,300 a week for full-day courses.

It may not always be essential for foreign speakers to have the correct form of address, i.e. formal or informal, or even the correct masculine or feminine conjugations, as long as you can make yourself understood. Many travelers learn Spanish to the present-tense stage and manage very well on this alone. However, in order to be well received in Chile, there are a few things worth remembering. Upon meeting someone, whether they be a taxi driver or a long-lost uncle, you should always use the greeting, *Buenos días* (Good morning) or *Buenas tardes* (Good afternoon/evening). It is then appropriate to wait for the response before continuing your conversation. A woman is addressed as *Señora*, a girl or young woman as *Señorita* (unless she's wearing a wedding ring), and a man as *Señor*.

BASIC COMMUNICATION

Yes *Sí*
No *No*
Thank you *Gracias*
You're welcome *No hay de que/ Por nada*

Greetings

Hello! *¡Hola!*
Hello (Good day) *Buenos días*
Good afternoon/night *Buenas tardes/noches*
Goodbye *Ciao/¡Adios!*
My name is... *Me llamo...*
What is your name? (formal) *¿Cómo se llama usted?*
Mr/Miss/Mrs *Señor/Señorita/ Señora*
Pleased to meet you *¡Encantado!*
I am English/American/

Canadian/Irish/Scottish/ Australian *Soy inglés(a)/ norteamericano(a)/canadiense/ irlandés(a)/escocés(a)/ australiano(a)*
Do you speak English? (formal) *¿Habla inglés?*
How are you? (formal/informal) *¿Cómo está?/¿Qué tal?*
Fine, thanks *Muy bien, gracias*
See you later *Hasta luego*
Take care (informal) *¡Cuídate!*

Alright/Okay/That's fine *Está bien*
Please *Por favor*
Excuse me (to get attention) *¡Permiso!/¡Por favor!*
Excuse me (to get through a crowd) *¡Permiso!*
Excuse me (sorry) *Perdóneme, Discúlpeme*
Wait a minute! *¡Un momento!*
Please help me (formal) *Por favor, ayúdeme*
Certainly *¡Claro!/¡Claro que sí!/¡Por cierto!*
Can I help you? (formal) *¿Puedo ayudarle?*
Can you show me...? *¿Puede mostrarme...?*
I need... *Necesito....*
I'm lost *Estoy perdido(a)*
I'm sorry *Lo siento*
I don't know *No sé*
I don't understand *No entiendo*
Do you speak English/French/ German? (formal) *¿Habla inglés/ francés/alemán?*
Could you speak more slowly, please? *¿Puede hablar más despacio, por favor?*
Could you repeat that, please? *¿Puede repetirlo, por favor?*
slowly *Despacio/Lentamente*
here *Aquí, Acá*
there *Allí, Allá, Ahí*
What? *¿Qué?/¿Cómo?*
When? *¿Cuándo?*
Why? *¿Por qué?*
Where? *¿Dónde?*
Who? *¿Quién(es)?*
How? *¿Cómo?*
Which? *¿Cuál?*
How much/how many? *¿Cuánto?/¿Cuántos?*
Do you have...? *¿Hay...?*
How long? *¿Cuánto tiempo?*
Big, bigger *Grande, más grande*
Small, smaller *Pequeño, más pequeño/chico, más chico*

I want.../I would like.../I need... *Quiero.../Quisiera.../Necesito...* **Where is the lavatory (men's/women's)?** *¿Dónde se encuentra el baño (de hombres/de mujeres)?* **Which way is it to ...?** *¿Cómo se va a ...?*

TELEPHONE CALLS

The area code *El código de área* **Where can I buy/Do you sell telephone cards?** *¿Dónde puedo comprar tarjetas telefónicas?/¿Se venden aquí tarjetas telefónicas?* **May I use your phone to make a local call?** *¿Puedo usar su teléfono para hacer una llamada local?* **Of course you may** *¡Por supuesto que sí!/¡Como no!/¡Claro!* **Hello (on the phone)** *¡Aló!* **May I speak to...?** *¿Puedo hablar con... (name), por favor?* **Sorry, he/she isn't in** *Lo siento, no se encuentra* **Can he/she call you back?** *¿Puede devolver la llamada?* **Yes, he/she can reach me at...** *Sí, él/ella puede llamarme a...* **I'll try again later** *Voy a intentar más tarde* **Can I leave a message?** *¿Puedo dejar un mensaje?* **Please tell him/her I called** *Por favor avísele que llamé* **Hold on** *Un momento, por favor* **Can you speak up, please?** *¿Puede hablar más fuerte, por favor?*

IN THE HOTEL

Do you have a vacant room? *¿Tiene una habitación disponible?* **I have a reservation** *Tengo una reservación* **I'd like...** *Quisiera...* **a single/double (with double bed)/a room with twin beds** *una habitación single/una habitación matrimonial/una habitación doble*

Months

January *enero*
February *febrero*
March *marzo*
April *abril*
May *mayo*
June *junio*
July *julio*
August *agosto*
September *septiembre*
October *octubre*
November *noviembre*
December *diciembre*

Safe to swim.

for one night/two nights *por una noche/dos noches* **on the ground floor/first floor/top floor/with sea view** *en el primer piso/en el segundo piso/en el último piso/con vista al mar* **Does the room have a private bathroom or shared bathroom?** *¿Tiene la habitación baño privado o baño compartido?* **Does it have hot water?** *¿Tiene agua caliente?* **Could you show me another room, please?** *¿Puede mostrarme otra habitación, por favor?* **Is it a quiet room?** *¿Es una habitación tranquila?* **What time do you close (lock) the doors?** *¿A qué hora se cierran las puertas?* **I would like to change rooms** *Quisiera cambiar de habitación* **This room is too noisy/hot/cold/small** *Esta habitación es demasiado ruidosa/calorosa/fría/pequeña* **How much is it?** *¿Cuánto cuesta?* **Does the price include tax/breakfast/meals/drinks?** *¿El precio incluye el impuesto/ desayuno/ comidas/bebidas?* **Do you accept credit cards/travelers' checks/dollars?** *¿Se aceptan tarjetas de crédito/ cheques de viajeros/dólares?* **What time is breakfast/lunch/dinner?** *¿A qué hora se sirve el desayuno/el almuerzo/la cena?* **Please wake me at...** *Favor despertarme a...* **Come in!** *¡Pase!/¡Adelante!* **I'd like to pay the bill now, please** *Quisiera cancelar la cuenta ahora, por favor*

Useful Words

bath *el baño*
dining room *el comedor*
elevator/lift *el ascensor*
key *la llave*
push/pull *empuje/tire*

safety deposit box *la caja de seguridad*
soap *el jabón*
shampoo *el champú*
shower *la ducha*
toilet paper *el papel higiénico*
towel *la toalla*

DRINKS

What would you like to drink? *¿Qué quiere tomar?* **coffee...** *un café...* **with milk** *cortado* **milky coffee** *café con leche* **strong** *fuerte* **small/large** *pequeño/grande* **with sugar** *con azúcar* **tea...** *té...* **with lemon/milk** *con limón/cortado* **herbal tea** *té de hierbas/agüita* **hot chocolate** *chocolate caliente* **fresh orange juice** *jugo de naranja natural* **orangeade** *naranjada* **soft drink** *bebida/refresco* **mineral water still/carbonated** *agua mineral sin gas/con gas* **with/without ice** *con/sin hielo* **cover charge** *precio del cubierto* **minimum consumption** *consumo mínimo* **beer hall/pub** *pub* **discotheque** *disco/discoteca* **nightclub** *club nocturno* **a bottle/half a bottle** *una botella/ media botella* **a glass of red/white/rosé wine** *una copa de vino tinto/blanco/rosado* **beer** *una cerveza* **Is service included?** *¿Incluye el servicio?* **I need a receipt, please** *Necesito un recibo, por favor* **Keep the change** *Está bien, gracias* **Cheers!** *¡Salud!* **ice cream** *helado* **sandwich** *sandwich* **savory turnover (filled with meat, cheese etc.)** *empanada*

TRANSPORTATION

A – Z

LANGUAGE

IN A RESTAURANT

I'd like to book a table *Quisiera reservar una mesa, por favor*
Do you have a table for...? *¿Tiene una mesa para...?*
I have a reservation *Tengo una reservación*
breakfast/lunch/dinner *desayuno/almuerzo/cena*
I'm a vegetarian *Soy vegetariano(a)*
Is there a vegetarian dish? *¿Hay un plato vegetariano?*
May we have the menu? *¿Puede traernos la carta/el menú?*
wine list *la carta de vinos*
What would you recommend? *¿Qué recomendaría?*
homemade *casero(a)*
fixed-price menu *menú fijo*
special of the day *plato del día/sugerencia del chef*
The meal was very good *La comida fue muy buena*
waiter *garzón/mozo*

MENU DECODER

Entrada (First Course)

sopa/crema **soup/cream soup**
sopa de ajo **garlic soup**
sopa de cebolla **onion soup**
ensalada... **salad...**
mixta **mixed**
ensalada de palta con tomate **avocado and tomato salad**
pan de ajo **garlic bread**

Plato Principal/de Fondo (Main Course)

crudo **raw**
vuelta y vuelta **rare**
término medio **medium rare**
tres cuartos **medium**
bien cocido(a) **well done**

La Carne (Meat)

a las brasas/a la parrilla **charcoal grilled**
a la plancha **grilled**
ahumado(a) **smoked**
albóndigas **meatballs**
asado(a) **roasted**
cerdo/chancho **pork**
chorizo **Spanish-style sausage**
chuleta **chop**
conejo **rabbit**
cordero **lamb**
costillas **ribs**
apanado(a) **breaded**
frito(a) **fried/battered**
guisado(a) **stewed**

hamburguesa **hamburger**
hígado de res **beef liver**
jamón **ham**
lomito **tenderloin**
milanesa **breaded and fried thin cut of meat**
pernil **leg of pork**
riñones **kidneys**
salchichas/vienesas **sausages or hot dogs**
ternera **veal**

Ave (Fowl)

alas **wings**
chicharrón de pollo **chicken cut up in small pieces and deep fried**
pato **duck**
pavo **turkey**
pechuga **breast**
pollo **chicken**
truto **thigh**
truto chico **leg**

Pescado/Mariscos (Fish/Shellfish)

almejas **clams**
anchoa **anchovy**
atún **tuna**
bacalao **cod**
calamares **squid**
camarones **shrimp**
centolla **king crab**
cholgas **mussels**
congrio **kingclip**
corvina **sea bass**
jaiba **crab**
langosta **lobster**
lenguado **sole or flounder**
mero **grouper**
ostiones **scallops**
ostras **oysters**
pulpo **octopus**
salmón **salmon**
sardinas **sardines**
trucha **trout**

Verduras (Vegetables)

ajo **garlic**
alcachofa **artichoke**
arvejas **peas**
berenjena **eggplant (aubergine)**
betarraga **beets/beetroot**
brócoli **broccoli**
camote **sweet potato**
cebolla **onion**
champiñones **mushrooms**
choclo **corn on the cob**
coliflor **cauliflower**
espárrago **asparagus**
espinaca **spinach**
lechuga **lettuce**
pepino **cucumber**
pimentón **(bell) pepper**
porotos verdes **green beans**
puerro/porrón **leek**

repollo **cabbage**
zanahorias **carrots**
zapallito italiano **zucchini (courgette)**
zapallo **pumpkin or yellow squash**

Frutas (Fruit)

cereza **cherry**
ciruela **plum**
dátil **date**
durazno **peach**
frambuesa **raspberry**
frutilla **strawberry**
guayaba **guava**
higo/breva **fig**
limón **lemon**
mandarina **mandarin**
manzana **apple**

Conversion Tables

Length

Inches/Centimeters
1/2.54
2/5.08
3/7.62
6/15.24
9/22.86
Feet/Centimeters
1/30.48
2/60.96
3/91.44
6/182.88
9/274.32
12/365.76

Weight

Pounds/Kilograms
1/0.45
2/0.90
3/1.36
4/1.81
5/2.27
6/2.72
7/3.18
8/3.63
9/4.08
10/4.53
20/9.07
50/22.68
100/45.36

Volume

US Pints/Liters
1/0.47
2/0.95
3/1.42
4/1.89
US Gallons/Liters
1/3.78
2/7.57
3/11.36
5/18.93
10/37.85
20/75.71
50/189.27

TRANSPORTATION

Arturo Merino Benítez Airport, Santiago.

melón **melon**
mora **blackberry**
naranja **orange**
palta **avocado**
papaya **mountain papaya/carica**
pera **pear**
piña **pineapple**
plátano **banana**
pomelo **grapefruit**
sandía **watermelon**
uvas **grapes**

Miscellaneous

arroz **rice**
azúcar **sugar**
empanada **savory turnover**
huevos (revueltos/fritos/a la copa)
eggs (scrambled/fried/boiled)
mantequilla **butter**
mermelada **jam**
mostaza **mustard**
pan **bread**
pan integral **wholewheat bread**
pan tostado **toast**
pimienta negra **black pepper**
queso **cheese**
sal **salt**
salsa de tomate/ketchup **ketchup**
salsa picante **hot sauce**
tallarines **spaghetti**
tocino **bacon**
tortilla **omelet**

TOURIST ATTRACTIONS

aguas termales **hot springs**
artesanía **handicrafts**
campamento **camp**
capilla **chapel**
castillo/fuerte **fort**
catedral **cathedral**
cerro **hill**

comunidad indígena **indigenous community**
convento **convent**
cumbre **(mountain) peak**
galería **gallery**
iglesia **church**
isla **island**
jardín botánico **botanical garden**
lago **lake**
laguna **lagoon**
mar **sea**
mercado **market**
mirador **viewpoint**
montaña **mountain**
monumento **monument**
Océano Pacífico **Pacific Ocean**
oficina de turismo **tourist information office**
parque **park**
parque infantil **playground**
piscina **swimming pool**
playa **beach**
plaza **town square**
postal **postcard**
puente **bridge**
quebrada **gorge**
río **river**
ruinas **ruins**
sanctuario **sanctuary**
teleférico **cable car**
torre **tower**
zona colonial **colonial zone**
zoológico **zoo**

TRAVELING

airline *línea aérea*
airport *aeropuerto*
arrivals/departures *llegadas/salidas*
bus stop *parada (de bus)*
bus terminal *terminal de buses*
bus *bus/micro*
car *auto*
car rental *arriendo de autos*

connection *conexión*
dock for small boats/large boats
embarcadero/muelle
ferry *transbordador*
first class/second class *primera clase/segunda clase, clase turista*
flight *vuelo*
luggage, bag(s) *equipaje, maleta(s)*
next stop please (for buses) *La próxima parada, por favor*
one-way ticket *pasaje de ida*
platform *el andén*
round trip/return ticket *pasaje de ida y vuelta*
sailboat *velero*
ship *barco*
subway *Metro*
taxi *taxi*
yacht *yate*

ADDRESSES/ DIRECTIONS

a la derecha **on the right**
a la izquierda **on the left**
al lado de **beside**
alrededor de **around**
arriba/abajo **above/below**
avenida (Av.) **avenue**
calle **street**
cerca de **near**
cruce **crossroad(s)**
cruce con **at the junction of (two streets)**
debajo de **under**
delante de **in front of**
derecho **straight ahead**
detrás de **behind**
doble hacia la izquierda/la derecha
turn to the left/right
edificio (Edif.) **high-rise building**
en **in, on, at**
en frente de/frente de/frente a **in front of**

A – Z

LANGUAGE

Colors

light/dark claro/oscuro
red rojo
yellow amarillo
blue azul
brown café/marrón
black negro
white blanco
beige beige
green verde
wine burdeo
gray gris
orange color naranjo
pink rosado
purple púrpuro
silver plateado
gold dorado

en la parte de atrás **in the rear area (as behind a building)**
encima de **on top of**
entre **between**
esquina (Esq.) **corner**
penthouse/primer piso/segundo piso/entrepiso/subterráneo
penthouse/ground floor/second floor/mezzanine/basement
residencial (Res.) **small pension**
torre **tower**
una cuadra **a block**

AIRPORT OR TRAVEL AGENCY

customs and immigration aduana e inmigración
travel/tour agency agencia de viajes/de turismo
ticket pasaje/boleto
I would like to purchase a ticket for... Quisiera comprar un pasaje/boleto para...
When is the next/last flight/departure for...? ¿Cuándo es el próximo/último vuelo para...?
What time does the plane/bus/boat/ferry leave/return? ¿A qué hora sale/regresa el avión/el bus/la lancha/el transbordador?
What time do I have to be at the airport? ¿A qué hora tengo que estar en el aeropuerto?
Is the tax included? ¿Está incluido el impuesto?
What is included in the price? ¿Qué está incluido en el precio?
departure tax? ¿el impuesto de aeropuerto?
I would like a seat in first class/business class/tourist class Quisiera un asiento en primera clase/ejecutivo/clase turista
lost luggage office oficina de reclamos de equipaje
on time a tiempo

late atrasado
I need to change my ticket Necesito cambiar mi pasaje
How long is the flight? ¿Cuánto dura el vuelo?
Is this seat taken? ¿Está ocupado este asiento?
Which is the stop closest to ...? ¿Cuál es la parada más cerca a ...?
Could you please advise me when we reach/the stop for ...? ¿Por favor, puede avisarme cuando llegamos a/a la parada para ...?
Is this the stop for ...? ¿Es ésta la parada para ...?

DRIVING

Where can I rent a car? ¿Dónde puedo arrendar un auto?
Is mileage included? ¿Está incluido el kilometraje?
comprehensive insurance seguro completo
spare tire/jack/emergency triangle rueda de repuesto/ gato/triángulo de emergencia
Where is the registration document? ¿Dónde se encuentra(n) el padrón/los documentos del auto?
Does the car have an alarm? ¿El auto tiene alarma?
a road map/a city map un mapa carretero/plano de la ciudad
How do I get to ...? ¿Cómo se llega a ...?
Turn right/left Doble a la derecha/izquierda
at the next corner/street en la próxima esquina/calle
Go straight ahead Siga derecho
You are on the wrong road Está en el camino equivocado
Please show me where am I on the map Por favor, indíqueme dónde estoy en el mapa
Where is...? ¿Dónde se encuentra...?
Where is the nearest...? ¿Dónde se encuentra el/la ... más cercano(a)?
How long does it take to get there? ¿Cuánto tiempo se requiere para llegar?
driver's license licencia de conducir
service station/gasoline station estación de servicio/bomba de bencina
My car won't start Mi auto no parte
My car is overheating Mi auto se está recalentando
My car has broken down Mi auto está en pana
tow truck una grúa
Where can I find a car repair shop? ¿Dónde se encuentra un taller mecánico?
Can you check the...? ¿Puede revisar/chequear...?

There's something wrong with the... Hay un problema con...
oil/water/air/brake fluid/light bulb aceite/agua/aire/líquido de frenos/ampolleta
trunk/hood/door/window maleta/capó/puerta/ventana

ROAD SIGNS

autopista **freeway**
bajada/subida peligrosa **dangerous downgrade/incline**
calle ciega **dead-end street**
calle de un sentido **one-way street**
carretera **highway, road**
cede el paso **yield/give way**
conserve su derecha **keep to the right**
cruce **crossroads**
cruce de ferrocarril (sin señal) **railway crossing (without signal)**
despacio **slow**
doble vía **two lanes**
enciende luces en el túnel **turn on lights in the tunnel**
entrada prohibida **entrance prohibited**
estacionamiento **parking**
hundimiento **sunken road**
no estacionar/prohibido estacionarse aquí **no parking**
no gire en U **no U-turn**
no hay paso/vía cerrado **road blocked**
no hay salida **no exit**
no pare **no stopping here**
no toque la bocina **no horn honking**
¡ojo! **watch out!**
pare **stop**
paso de ganado **cattle crossing**
paso de peatones **pedestrian crossing**
peaje **toll booth**
peligro **danger**
pendiente fuerte/curva fuerte **steep hill/sharp curve**
rotonda **traffic circle (roundabout)**
salida **exit**
semáforo **traffic light**
trabajos en la vía **roadworks**
una sola pista **single lane**

EMERGENCIES

Help! ¡Socorro!/¡Auxilio!
Stop! ¡Pare!
Watch out! ¡Cuidado!/¡Ojo!
I've had an accident He tenido un accidente
Call a doctor Llame a un médico
Call an ambulance Llame una ambulancia
Call the... Llame a...
...police la policía/los carabineros
...the fire brigade los bomberos
This is an emergency, where is there a telephone, please?

Es una emergencia. ¿Dónde hay un teléfono, por favor?
Where is the nearest hospital? ¿Dónde se encuentra el hospital más cercano?
I want to report a robbery Quisiera denunciar un robo
Thank you very much for your help Muchísimas gracias por su ayuda

HEALTH

shift-duty pharmacy farmacia de turno
hospital/clinic hospital/clínica
I need a doctor/dentist Necesito un médico/dentista (odontólogo)
I don't feel well Me siento mal
I am sick Estoy enfermo(a)
It hurts here Duele aquí
I have a headache/stomach ache/ cramps Tengo un dolor de cabeza/de estómago/retorcijones
I feel dizzy Me siento mareado(a)
Do you have (something for)…? ¿Tiene (algo para)…?
a cold/flu resfrío/gripe
diarrhea diarrea
constipation estreñimiento
fever fiebre
aspirin aspirina
heartburn ácidez
insect/mosquito bites picadas de insectos/zancudos

Numbers

1 uno	**100** cien
2 dos	**101** ciento uno
3 tres	**200** doscientos
4 cuatro	**300** trescientos
5 cinco	**400** cuatrocientos
6 seis	**500** quinientos
7 siete	**600** seiscientos
8 ocho	**700** setecientos
9 nueve	**800** ochocientos
10 diez	**900** novecientos
11 once	**1,000** mil
12 doce	**2,000** dos mil
13 trece	**10,000** diez mil
14 catorce	**100,000** cien mil
15 quince	**1,000,000** un millón
16 dieciséis	**2,000,000** dos millones
17 diecisiete	**first** primer(o)/a
18 dieciocho	**second** segund(o)/a
19 diecinueve	**third** tercer(o)/a
20 veinte	**fourth** cuart(o)/a
21 veintiuno	**NOTE**
25 veinticinco	In Spanish, in numbers, commas
30 treinta	are used where decimal points are
40 cuarenta	used in English and vice versa. For
50 cincuenta	example:
60 sesenta	**English/Spanish**
70 setenta	$19.30/$19,30
80 ochenta	1,000 m/1.000 m
90 noventa	9.5 %/9,5 %

SHOPPING

antique shop antigüedades
bakery panadería
bank banco
barber shop/hairdresser peluquería
beauty shop peluquería, salón de belleza
bookstore librería
butcher's carnicería
currency exchange bureau casa de cambio
delicatessen delicatessen
department store tienda por departamentos
florist florería
gift shop (tienda de) regalos
greengrocer's verdulería
hardware store ferretería
shopping center centro comercial, mall
jewelry shop joyería
laundry lavandería
library biblioteca
liquor store botellería
market mercado
newsstand kiosco
pastry shop pastelería
post office oficina de correos
shoe repair shop/shoe store zapatería
small grocery store almacén
small shop tienda
stationer's papelería/librería
supermarket supermercado

toy store juguetería
What time do you open/close? ¿A qué hora abren/cierran?
open/closed abierto/cerrado
I'd like… Quisiera…
I'm just looking Estoy sólo mirando, gracias
How much does it cost? ¿Cuánto cuesta?
It doesn't fit No queda bien
Do you have it in another color? ¿Tiene en otro color?
Do you have it in another size? ¿Tiene en otra talla? (clothing), tamaño (objects)
smaller/larger más pequeño/ más grande
It's too expensive Es demasiado caro
Do you have something less expensive? ¿Tiene algo más económico?
Where do I pay for it? ¿Dónde está la caja?
Anything else? ¿Quiere algo más?
a little more/less un poco más/ menos
That's enough/no more Está bien/ no más

DAYS AND DATES

morning la mañana
afternoon la tarde
late afternoon, dusk el atardecer
evening la noche
early morning la madrugada
sunrise el amanecer
sunset la puesta del sol
last night anoche
yesterday ayer
today hoy
tomorrow mañana
the day after tomorrow pasado mañana
now ahora
early temprano
late tarde
a minute un minuto
an hour una hora
half an hour media hora
a day un día
a week una semana
a month un mes
a year un año
weekday día laboral/hábil
weekend fin de semana
public holiday día feriado

Days of the Week

Monday lunes
Tuesday martes
Wednesday miércoles
Thursday jueves
Friday viernes
Saturday sábado
Sunday domingo

TRANSPORTATION

A - Z

LANGUAGE

FURTHER READING

TRAVEL IN CHILE

Aku-Aku – The Secret of Easter Island by Thor Heyerdahl. In this sequel to *The Kon-Tiki Expedition*, Heyerdahl examines the history of the Easter Island statues.

Cape Horn and Other Stories from the End of the World by Francisco Coloane. One of many books from this author about the wonders and struggles of life in Patagonia.

How to Survive in the Chilean Jungle by John Brennan and Alvaro Taboada. A humorous but very useful dictionary of Chilean slang and sayings.

In Patagonia by Bruce Chatwin. A classic and vivid account of the author's journey to the "uttermost part of the earth" in the 1970s.

The Old Patagonian Express by Paul Theroux. Theroux's account of his train journey down the length of South America is a travel classic.

Santiago's Children: What I Learned about Life at an Orphanage in Chile by Steve Reifenberg. A moving and insightful account of a young American's experience of working in an orphanage in a poor area of Santiago in the early 1980s.

Tierra del Fuego by Rae Natalie Prosser Goodall. Written by the biologist wife of the great-grandson of Thomas Bridges who set up Estancia Harberton, the first farm on the Argentine side of Tierra del Fuego.

Travels in a Thin Country: Journey Through Chile by Sara Wheeler. An entertaining and insightful account of Wheeler's six-month journey from the top to the bottom of Chile.

FICTION

Isabel Allende: All Isabel Allende's novels were written after she left Chile in the wake of the 1973 military coup, but *House of the Spirits* is set in Chile, tracing four generations of the Trueba family through the country's social and political upheavals, while *Inés of My Soul* is the fictional memoir of Inés Suárez, the first Spanish woman to live in Chile in the 1500s. In *My Invented Country: A Memoir*, Allende reflects fondly but clear-sightedly on the idiosyncrasies of her home country.

Burning Patience by Antonio Skármeta. The book that inspired the film *Il Postino* weaves a story around Pablo Neruda's life and death after the military coup.

By Night in Chile by Roberto Bolaño. One of the easiest of Bolaño's novel to read, this is a satire about Chilean literature and writers.

Chile: A Traveler's Literary Companion Edited by Katherine Silver.

Robinson Crusoe by Daniel Defoe. Classic novel based on Alexander Selkirk's time on the Juan Fernández islands.

Curfew by José Donoso. A harrowing depiction of life in Santiago during the Pinochet era.

Send Us Your Thoughts

We do our best to ensure the information in our books is as accurate and up-to-date as possible. The books are updated on a regular basis using local contacts, who painstakingly add, amend and correct as required. However, some details (such as telephone numbers and opening times) are liable to change, and we are ultimately reliant on our readers to put us in the picture.

We welcome your feedback, especially your experience of using the book "on the road". Maybe we recommended a hotel that you liked (or another that you didn't), or you came across a great bar or new attraction we missed.

We will acknowledge all contri-butions, and we'll offer an Insight Guide to the best letters received.

Please write to us at:
   Insight Guides
   PO Box 7910
   London SE1 1WE
Or email us at:
   hello@insightguides.com

POLITICS AND HISTORY

Allende's Chile by Edward Boorstein.

Chile – The Legacy of Hispanic Capitalism by Brian Loveman.

Pinochet in Piccadilly: Britain and Chile's Hidden History by Andy Beckett.

Pinochet: The Politics of Torture by Hugh O'Shaughnessy.

THE NEW SONG MOVEMENT

Victor, An Unfinished Song by Joan Jara. An account of the heroic folk musician's life and music written by his wife.

A nation of Enemies by Pamela Constable and Arturo Valenzuela. A 17-year dictatorship seen through eyes of the interviewed Chileans.

FOOD AND WINE

The Chilean Kitchen: Authentic, Homestyle Foods, Regional Wines, and Culinary Traditions of Chile by Ruth Van Waerebeek-Gonzalez.

Chilean Wine: The Heritage by Rodrigo Alvarado.

POETRY

My Life with Pablo Neruda by Matilde Urrutia.

Pablo Neruda – Selected Poems translated by Andrew Kerrigan.

A Translation of Alonso de Ercilla's La Araucana by Louis Carrera. English translation of the 16th-century epic poem.

OTHER INSIGHT GUIDES

Among nearly 200 companion books to this one are several guides highlighting destinations in this region, including *Insight Guides* to *South America*, *Argentina*, *Brazil*, *Peru*, and *Ecuador & the Galápagos*.

CREDITS

Insight Guide Credits

Distribution
UK, Ireland and Europe
Apa Publications (UK) Ltd;
sales@insightguides.com
United States and Canada
Ingram Publisher Services;
ips@ingramcontent.com
Australia and New Zealand
Woodslane; info@woodslane.com.au
Southeast Asia
Apa Publications (SN) Pte;
singaporeoffice@insightguides.com
Hong Kong, Taiwan and China
Apa Publications (HK) Ltd;
hongkongoffice@insightguides.com
Worldwide
Apa Publications (UK) Ltd;
sales@insightguides.com
Special Sales, Content Licensing and CoPublishing
Insight Guides can be purchased in bulk quantities at discounted prices. We can create special editions, personalised jackets and corporate imprints tailored to your needs.
sales@insightguides.com
www.insightguides.biz

Printed in China by CTPS

All Rights Reserved
© 2016 Apa Digital (CH) AG and Apa Publications (UK) Ltd

First Edition 1991
Seventh Edition 2017

Every effort has been made to provide accurate information in this publication, but changes are inevitable. The publisher cannot be responsible for any resulting loss, inconvenience or injury. We would appreciate it if readers would call our attention to any errors or outdated information. We also welcome your suggestions; please contact us at:
hello@insightguides.com
www.insightguides.com

Editors: Rachel Lawrence & Tom Fleming
Author: Ruth Bradley
Head of Production: Rebeka Davies
Update Production: AM Services
Picture Editor: Tom Smyth
Cartography: original cartography Polyglott Kartographie, updated by Carte

Contributors

This new edition was commissioned and edited by Rachel Lawrence and Tom Fleming, and builds on previous versions written by Tim Frasca, Lake Sagaris, Patricio Lanfranco, Imogen Mark, Malcolm Coad and Rebecca Gorman.

Ruth Bradley, a British journalist who lives and works in Santiago de Chile, and a regular contributor to Insight Guides, thoroughly updated the entire book, expanded the fascinating chapter on modern

history and added a new section on Parque Qinta Normal in Santiago.

Other contributors whose work is retained from previous editions include Mike Gonzalez, Jane Letham, Mark Thurber, Shannon Shieland and Jan Fairley.

The principal photographer was Abe Nowitz, ably assisted by his father Richard, but many other talented photographers contributed their work, including Eduardo Gil, Helen Hughes and Daniel Bruhin.

About Insight Guides

Insight Guides have more than 45 years' experience of publishing high-quality, visual travel guides. We produce 400 full-colour titles, in both print and digital form, covering more than 200 destinations across the globe, in a variety of formats to meet your different needs.

Insight Guides are written by local authors who use their on-the-ground experience to provide the

very latest information; their local expertise is evident in the extensive historical and cultural background features. All the reviews in **Insight Guides** are independent; we strive to maintain an impartial view. Our reviews are carefully selected to guide you to the best places to eat, go out and shop, so you can be confident that when we say a place is special, we really mean it.

Legend

City maps

	Freeway/Highway/Motorway
	Divided Highway
	Main Roads
	Minor Roads
	Pedestrian Roads
	Steps
	Footpath
	Railway
	Funicular Railway
	Cable Car
	Tunnel
	City Wall
	Important Building
	Built Up Area
	Other Land
	Transport Hub
	Park
	Pedestrian Area
	Bus Station
	Tourist Information
	Main Post Office
	Cathedral/Church
	Mosque
	Synagogue
	Statue/Monument
	Beach
	Airport

Regional maps

	Freeway/Highway/Motorway (with junction)
	Freeway/Highway/Motorway (under construction)
	Divided Highway
	Main Road
	Secondary Road
	Minor Road
	Track
	Footpath
	International Boundary
	State/Province Boundary
	National Park/Reserve
	Marine Park
	Ferry Route
	Marshland/Swamp
	Glacier / Salt Lake
	Airport/Airfield
	Ancient Site
	Border Control
	Cable Car
	Castle/Castle Ruins
	Cave
	Chateau/Stately Home
	Church/Church Ruins
	Crater
	Lighthouse
	Mountain Peak
	Place of Interest
	Viewpoint

INDEX

Main references are in bold type